An Islandwide Struggle for Freedom

An Essential Guide for Reading

GRAHAM T. NESSLER

An Islandwide Struggle for Freedom

Revolution, Emancipation, and
Reenslavement in Hispaniola, 1789–1809

The University of North Carolina Press *Chapel Hill*

This book is published with the assistance of the Authors Fund of the University of North Carolina Press.

Set in Arno by Westchester Publishing Services

The paper in this book meets the guidelines for permanence
and durability of the Committee on Production Guidelines for
Book Longevity of the Council on Library Resources.

The University of North Carolina Press has been a member of the
Green Press Initiative since 2003.

Cover illustrations: Map of Hispaniola from 1796 by Nicolas Ponce in *Recueil de vues des lieux principaux de la colonie francoise de Saint-Domingue* (Paris, 1971); and General Hédouville speaking with a black officer (possibly Toussaint Louverture), both courtesy of the John Carter Brown Library at Brown University.

Library of Congress Cataloging-in-Publication Data
Names: Nessler, Graham T., author.
Title: An islandwide struggle for freedom : revolution, emancipation, and
    reenslavement in Hispaniola, 1789-1809 / Graham T. Nessler.
Description: Chapel Hill : The University of North Carolina Press, [2016] |
    Includes bibliographical references and index.
Identifiers: LCCN 2015047523| ISBN 9781469626864 (pbk : alk. paper) |
    ISBN 9781469626871 (ebook)
Subjects: LCSH: Slavery—Hispaniola—History. | Slaves—Emancipation—Hispaniola. |
    Slaves—Hispaniola—Social conditions. | Slavery—Law and legislation—Hispaniola—
    History. | Hispaniola—History—18th century. | Hispaniola—History—19th century. |
    Haiti—History—Revolution, 1791-1804. | Dominican Republic—History—To 1844.
Classification: LCC HT1081 .N47 2016 | DDC 326/.809729309034—dc23
    LC record available at http://lccn.loc.gov/2015047523

Portions of this book previously appeared as "Arrancar el árbol de la libertad:
Una interpretación de la era de Toussaint Louverture en Santo Domingo, 1801–1802,"
from *Estudios Sociales* 40, no. 151 (2012): 11–31, used by permission; " 'They always
knew her to be free': Emancipation and Re-Enslavement in French Santo Domingo,
1804–1809," *Slavery & Abolition: A Journal of Slave and Post-Slave Studies*, 2012,
Taylor & Francis Ltd., www.tandfonline.com, reprinted by permission of the publisher;
" 'The Shame of the Nation': The Force of Re-Enslavement and the Law of 'Slavery'
under the Regime of Jean-Louis Ferrand in Santo Domingo, 1804–1809," *New West
Indian Guide* 86, nos. 1–2 (2012): 5–28.

To my mother and father

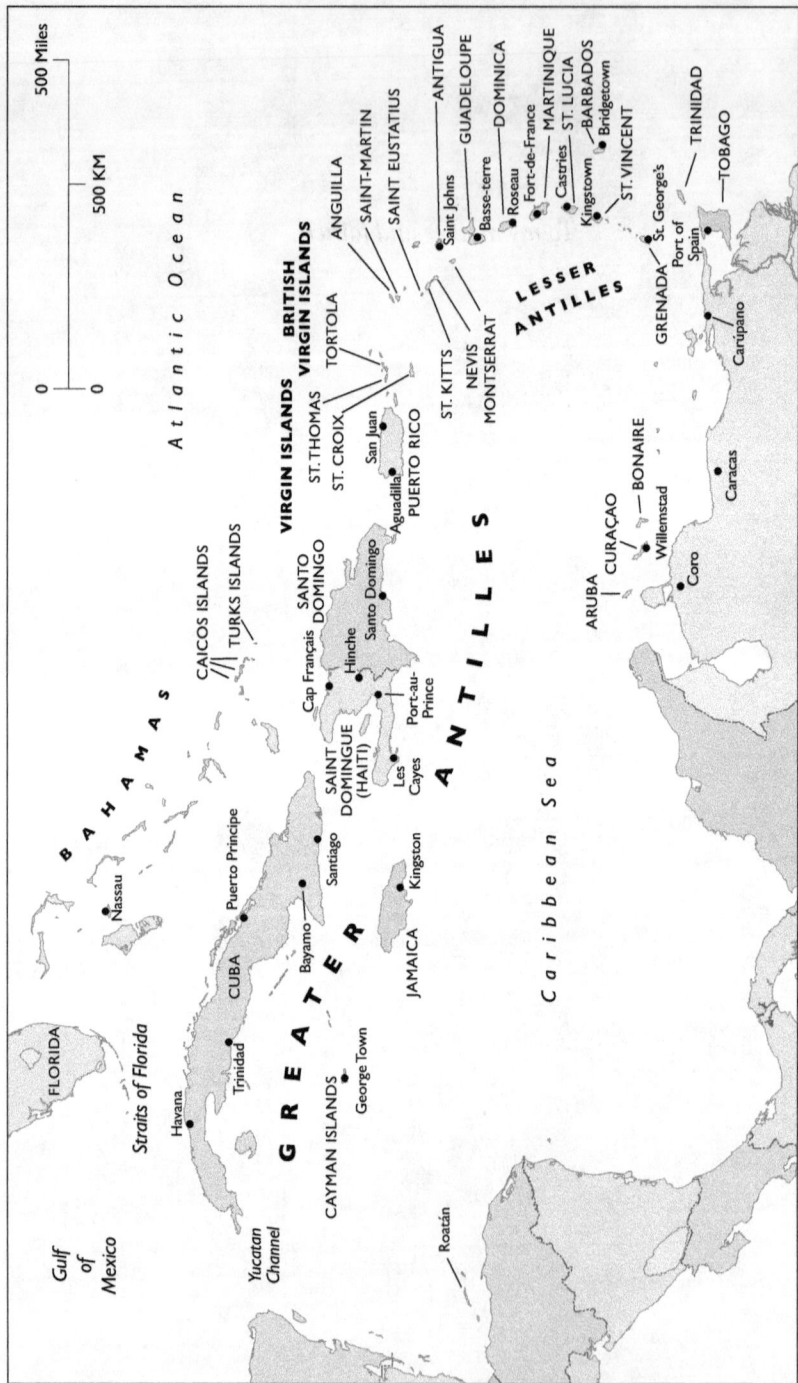

MAP 1. Greater and Lesser Antilles, 1789. Adapted by permission of Indiana University Press from a map with the same caption in Geggus and Gaspar, *A Turbulent Time*.

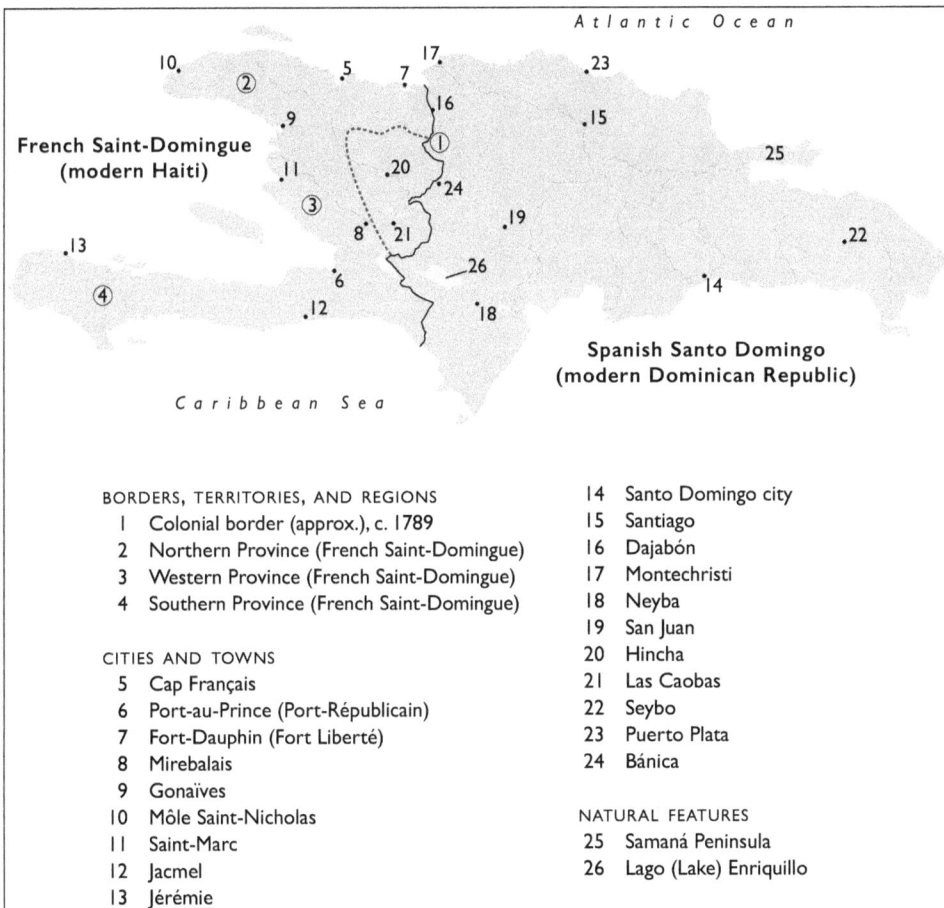

Atlantic Ocean

French Saint-Domingue
(modern Haiti)

Spanish Santo Domingo
(modern Dominican Republic)

Caribbean Sea

BORDERS, TERRITORIES, AND REGIONS
1   Colonial border (approx.), c. 1789
2   Northern Province (French Saint-Domingue)
3   Western Province (French Saint-Domingue)
4   Southern Province (French Saint-Domingue)

CITIES AND TOWNS
5   Cap Français
6   Port-au-Prince (Port-Républicain)
7   Fort-Dauphin (Fort Liberté)
8   Mirebalais
9   Gonaïves
10 Môle Saint-Nicholas
11 Saint-Marc
12 Jacmel
13 Jérémie

14 Santo Domingo city
15 Santiago
16 Dajabón
17 Montechristi
18 Neyba
19 San Juan
20 Hincha
21 Las Caobas
22 Seybo
23 Puerto Plata
24 Bánica

NATURAL FEATURES
25 Samaná Peninsula
26 Lago (Lake) Enriquillo

MAP 2. Hispaniola: Key Points of Interest. The solid line indicates the modern political border between Haiti and the Dominican Republic. The dotted line represents where the colonial border of 1789 diverged from the modern border.

Contents

Maps and Figures

Acknowledgments

Many individuals and institutions gave generously of their time, resources, and moral support to help enable this project's completion. Though I am pleased to use this space to thank many of them, it would be impossible to list here all those individuals who have positively influenced this study in some way. What follows is thus by necessity condensed, and I regret any omissions. Any errors or faults contained in the following work are solely mine.

I first thank my colleagues whose insightful feedback proved integral in shaping this project. Legal scholars Sam Erman and Malick Ghachem offered thoughtful assistance on legal and other aspects of this book, while the careful analysis of fellow Caribbean and Latin American scholars Julia Gaffield, Anne Eller, Francisco Moscoso, Ada Ferrer, John Garrigus, Dominique Rogers, and Sigfrido Vázquez Cienfuegos also proved invaluable. I am also grateful to Lindsey Gish, a specialist on African history, and Marlyse Baptista, a linguist, for their much-appreciated aid and moral support. I also thank my mentors Richard Turits, Rebecca Scott, Paulina Alberto, Laurent Dubois, Jean Hébrard, Ghachem, and Baptista for their advice and encouragement.

As with any project of this scope, a number of institutions and their dedicated staff played key roles at critical junctures in the book's evolution. The research that forms the basis for this book was enabled with the generous funding of the French government's Chateaubriand Fellowship and the Social Science Research Council. The staff of all of the archives and libraries mentioned in the bibliography were generous and efficient allies in the research for this study. I also thank the organizers of conferences at which I presented scholarship deriving from this project, such as the University of Michigan Law School, the Centre International de Recherches des Esclavages of the Centre National de la Recherche Scientifique (CIRESC-CNRS) in France, and the Dominican Studies Institute (DSI) based in New York City. Ramona Hernández, the director of the DSI, is a driving force behind the growing field of Dominican studies in the United States and has been a kind and helpful colleague. Martha Jones and other organizers and fellow members of the Law in Slavery and Freedom Project at the University of Michigan also provided critical fora for scholarly exchange, and several offered useful suggestions on aspects of this book. In addition, a Foreign Language and Area Studies fellowship enabled me to undertake an intensive course in Haitian Kreyòl (Creole) in the summer of 2006 at Florida International University. This course benefited my project in ways I did not foresee at the time and introduced me to a new community of scholars and activists.

The University of Michigan and Bentley University offered me stimulating and collegial environments in which to pursue this scholarly endeavor. I thank in particular the leadership, affiliated faculty, and staff of the Institute for the Humanities, the Eisenberg Institute, and the History Department at the University of Michigan (particularly Kathleen King, who truly went above and beyond the call of duty). I also wish to acknowledge the assistance of Gesa Kirsch, Cyrus Veeser, Marc Stern, and other Bentley faculty as well as the staff of the Jeanne and Dan Valente Center for Arts and Sciences at Bentley, particularly Janice McMahon.

My colleagues at Florida Atlantic University have also been very supportive. I am grateful for the opportunity that this institution provided me during a transitional phase in my career.

Elaine Maisner, my editor at the University of North Carolina Press, has also been instrumental in the project's completion. I am particularly grateful to the two anonymous expert readers chosen by the Press to review this work. Their comments significantly enhanced the arguments and coverage of this book.

I am also grateful for the assistance of the editors of the journals *Estudios Sociales, New West Indian Guide,* and *Slavery and Abolition.* My articles in these journals (cited in the present work's Bibliography) form parts of chapters 4, 5, and 6, respectively; thanks to the Centro Bonó (Santo Domingo, Dominican Republic), Brill Online, and Taylor & Francis Ltd. for granting me permission to reproduce these articles in modified form. The comments of the editors and of the articles' anonymous reviewers strengthened each piece and are much appreciated.

Writing this book has been as much a personal journey as a professional one. I would be remiss if I did not acknowledge the intangible but crucial contributions of my friends Kenneth Garner, Dagmar Francikova, Lindsey Gish, Erik Huneke, Amy Firestone, and Robert Rodríguez. During this entire journey, my family of birth—Craig Nessler, Susan Terwilliger, Reed Nessler, and Laura Nessler—have continually shown me love and support. I dedicate this book to my parents, who have shaped me into who I am today. (My mother, an editor, also generously copyedited the entire manuscript— thanks, Mom!). Finally, *mèsi anpil* to Natalie Cotton-Nessler and to my cat Mal for their love and patience during the years of writing and editing.

An Islandwide Struggle for Freedom

Introduction

In October 1806, a refugee from Haiti named Rozine *dite* Alzire appeared before a notary in Santo Domingo (modern Dominican Republic) and presented him with a curious document.[1] This document, a notarial act that had been drawn up on 19 August 1803 before another notary in Cap Français (now Cap-Haïtien), the commercial capital of French Saint-Domingue (today Haiti), declared that Rozine's mother, Rosalie *dite* Dufay, had purchased her daughter for the sum of 2,500 colonial pounds "on the Express condition" that Rosalie free Rozine.[2] Why did Rosalie purchase her own daughter in order to free her, even though both had presumably been freed by a law passed in 1794 by the French Republic that had outlawed slavery in all French territories—the first such sweeping emancipation act in the Americas?[3] Why did the daughter then deem it necessary to present this document to a notary three years later on the other side of the island of Hispaniola (shared by Santo Domingo and Saint-Domingue/Haiti)?

Encounters such as these at the notary's office are emblematic of struggles over the lived meaning of freedom during a collection of events that Anglophone and Haitian scholars typically call the Haitian Revolution.[4] The revolutionary processes of 1789–1809 involved slave revolt, foreign war, and political upheaval that engulfed the entire island and the region. They resulted in the overthrow of French colonialism and the destruction of slavery in the French colony of Saint-Domingue, and the temporary abolition of slavery in the neighboring colony of Santo Domingo (which passed from Spanish to French rule and then back to Spain in these two decades). Though the former slaves and free-born persons of African descent who liberated their land from French rule founded the free nation of Haiti in 1804, French aggression on the island was not over, as a reactionary French Napoleonic regime tried to reimpose slavery in Santo Domingo for the next five years. This regime's efforts represent a brutal coda to what was arguably the most radical of the "Atlantic Revolutions" of the eighteenth and nineteenth centuries.

Indeed, in spite of its unprecedented attacks on slavery and institutionalized racism, the Haitian Revolution gave rise to new struggles for freedom against novel (and reconstituted) forms of coercion. For instance, after 1794, many formally freed individuals fled the restrictive regime of emancipation in Saint-Domingue in order to resettle across the border in the east, a land where proslavery authorities still held power. Moreover, after claiming command of Santo Domingo in 1801, a onetime slave and onetime slave owner named Toussaint Louverture reaffirmed the abolition of slavery across all of Hispaniola. Yet he also proceeded to impose a number of harsh restrictions on the mobility of freed individuals in Santo Domingo in an effort to create a profitable plantation system there. He was simultaneously attempting a revitalization of the plantation economy in Saint-Domingue by employing similar tactics.

Scholars of the Haitian Revolution have ably analyzed many such apparent paradoxes, although they have largely left aside Santo Domingo in their analyses.[5] On the eve of the Haitian Revolution in 1789, the land that Columbus had long ago christened *la isla española,* or "the Spanish island" (anglicized as "Hispaniola"), was divided into two distinct colonies: Saint-Domingue, the crown jewel of the French empire that occupied the western third of the island, and Santo Domingo, perhaps the least valued outpost of the Spanish empire. Since the island's partition by Spain and France in the seventeenth century, these two colonies shared a history of contentious diplomacy, profitable trade, slave flight, and other cross-island connections that strongly influenced not only each colony's political and economic development but also the trajectory—and even the fate—of the Haitian Revolution. This book proffers a social, political, intellectual, and legal history of emancipation and reenslavement in Hispaniola from the advent of the French Revolution in 1789 to the expulsion of the French from the island twenty years later. It offers a reinterpretation of the Haitian Revolution as an islandwide struggle over the meaning and boundaries of liberty, citizenship, and racial equality.

Fundamentally, the Haitian Revolution was a transimperial and intercolonial story in which enslaved people, free people "of color," and numerous other parties sought to defend, reconfigure, or dismantle the parameters of empire and slavery.[6] In the Haitian Revolutionary era, Hispaniola was a key arena in intertwined French and Spanish political crises that crushed Napoleon's dreams of reasserting French power in the Americas, proved critical in enabling the United States' westward expansion, helped catalyze the Spanish-American independence wars, and reshaped the geopolitics of the Western world. In examining the far-reaching reverberations of the Haitian Revolution while remaining moored in on-the-ground circumstances in

Hispaniola, this book builds upon scholarship that has fruitfully combined the seemingly quite disparate scales of Atlantic history and microhistory in order to "elucidate historical processes transcontinental in scope," in the words of historian Lara Putnam.[7]

Such a multilayered perspective enables us to see that although many of the catalyzing forces of the Haitian Revolution originated in the Francophone sphere, this revolution did not simply "spill over" from French Saint-Domingue into Spanish Santo Domingo by virtue of geographical proximity. Rather, Santo Domingo's own history—and, paradoxically, its very neglect by the colonial powers and reputation as a backwater—made it a critical theater in what Laurent Dubois has called "a central part of the destruction of slavery in the Americas, and therefore a crucial moment in the history of democracy, one that laid the foundation for the continuing struggles for human rights everywhere."[8] Furthermore, Haiti's founders deliberately invoked the history of the entire island in their greatest symbolic political act. "The adoption of the term 'Hayti' as the name of the country, referring back to an indigenous name for the island at the time of the arrival of Columbus," writes Deborah Jenson, "further suggests that the Haitians imagined the overthrow of French colonial rule in terms of an *island of freedom*, rather than a free *section* of an island."[9]

Yet what follows is a story of great hardship as well as hard-won triumph: slavers trafficked thousands of human beings through Santo Domingo during the revolutionary era; purportedly emancipationist French Republican authorities persecuted "maroons" (formerly enslaved fugitives) along the island's contested colonial boundary using methods that differed little from those of the ancien régime slave catchers; and for every "slave" who won his or her freedom under the slaveholding Napoleonic regime of General Jean-Louis Ferrand in Santo Domingo (1804–09), a thousand more found no respite from servitude (at least until the final abolition of slavery in Santo Domingo in 1822).

A Note on Geography

Before proceeding further, a note on geography is in order. The variety and ambiguity of the terms that referred to the island of Hispaniola and its political subdivisions in the colonial and revolutionary eras often present a vexing problem even for specialists on the island's history. Hispaniola, the second-largest island in the Caribbean, is located at a strategic crossroads of the Caribbean Sea and the Atlantic Ocean. (See map 1.) Hispaniola had been known by several names to its native Taíno population before early European settlers renamed it *la isla española*, as noted in the preceding section. ("Hispaniola" today is not a political term but rather a strictly geographical one, like "North America.") In the 1490s, the Spanish colonizers founded on this island's southeast coast the first European-built capital city in the Americas, Santo Domingo de Guzmán (now the capital of the Dominican Republic); over time, this name (shortened to Santo Domingo in common parlance) came to refer to the entire island. Then, in the seventeenth century, the French colonized the western third of this island that the Spanish had virtually abandoned; the French uncreatively named their colony Saint-Domingue—their translation of Santo Domingo. All this led to a highly confusing situation in which "Santo Domingo" could indicate either the eastern two-thirds of the island, which remained under formal Spanish control, or this Spanish colony's capital city that still bore this name. In order to minimize ambiguity, my usage of the term "Santo Domingo" in this book will refer only to the *colony* of that name, as opposed to the city, unless specifically indicated.[10] I will, moreover, reserve the term "Saint-Domingue" (used in many French primary sources to indicate the entire island) for the French colony in western Hispaniola that became Haiti in 1804.

Both primary and secondary sources on the colonial and revolutionary eras employ a variety of demonyms to refer to the island's inhabitants. For the sake of convenience, familiarity, and precision, I use the modern term "Dominican" to indicate the residents of the colony of Santo Domingo (the term typically employed in Spanish-language primary sources, *español* or "Spaniard," is overly vague).[11] Furthermore, the somewhat awkward term "Dominguan," a rough anglicization of the French *saint-dominguois*, shall refer to residents of Saint-Domingue (as with the preceding example, the term most often used in period sources, *français* or "French," lacks specificity, while "Haitian" only properly came into usage after 1804, when victorious liberation armies rechristened French Saint-Domingue as Haiti, resurrecting an indigenous term for the island).

An "Archive of Liberty"

The forgotten Dominican chapters of the Haitian Revolution reveal not only a new framework for understanding this seminal chapter in modern history but also a multifaceted struggle for freedom that was at once at the heart and at the margins of French Republican emancipation. In July 1795, at the height of the Haitian Revolution, Santo Domingo formally passed from the rule of slaveholding Spain to that of the emancipationist French Republic via the Treaty of Basel. This cession precipitated a political crisis of sovereignty concerning the status of Santo Domingo, since France failed to assert effective military or administrative control over the eastern portion of Hispaniola until Toussaint Louverture's occupation in 1801. This crisis of sovereignty intersected with uncertainty regarding the legal condition (slave versus free) of the approximately 15,000 people who were claimed as slaves there. Did the empirewide general emancipation decree passed by the French National Convention in 1794 extend to this territory?[12]

Would-be masters exploited these legal and political uncertainties in their efforts to keep their "slaves" in servitude. Those held in or vulnerable to enslavement nonetheless skillfully maneuvered within a sedimented and hybrid legal system in which both French and Spanish law influenced governance, the regulation of enslavement and manumission, and the resolution of legal disputes. This book draws upon a rich corpus of correspondence, notarial records, petitions, periodical articles, and many other sources preserved in six Spanish, French, and North American repositories to demonstrate how marginalized individuals in Hispaniola forged their own archive of liberty, even as their efforts to secure their freedom in some cases condoned the continued enslavement of others.

The archives of race, slavery, and emancipation in revolutionary Hispaniola open new windows into the study of slave and postslave societies in the Americas.[13] This book, for instance, interrogates more than one hundred notarial records created by freed persons in French Santo Domingo in order to analyze the strategies that they employed to assure their liberty. Moreover, rich but often fragmentary extant governmental and private correspondence in French, Spanish, and Kreyòl offers insights into slaves' and freed persons' vernacular conceptions of liberty and creative uses of legal tools rooted in the slave societies of both of the island's colonies.[14] In addition, as rare direct traces of ex-slaves' voices in the early modern Atlantic, an assortment of letters by freed military officers allied with Spain during an early phase of the Haitian Revolution has enabled a reassessment of these leaders' heterogeneous political ideologies. Ultimately, the story that I tell, like Malick Ghachem's recent legal history of slavery in French Saint-Domingue, "showcases the imaginative opportunities that exist for disenfranchised persons and their advocates to reconfigure the cards they have been dealt and to arrange them in a hand that comes closer to justice."[15]

This study also seeks, where possible, to elucidate the perspectives of another class of "disenfranchised persons": the women who suffered some of the worst forms of exploitation in slavery and who were then denied the rights of full citizenship and equal remuneration under the new regime of emancipation.[16] Though most of the records that comprise this book's source base were composed by men and exclude or occlude female voices, more than three-quarters of the freed persons who safeguarded their freedom via the notarized freedom acts were women, reflecting the gendered nature of slavery, manumission, and emancipation in Hispaniola. In discussing these and other women's experiences, this study has profited from scholarship that has demonstrated that the intertwined conflicts over the shape of postslave societies in the colonies and over the nature of a new society in France during the revolutionary period were inseparable from questions concerning the rights of women, the structure of the family, and the roles of men and women in society.[17] Though much of this study discusses the decisions of powerful men such as Toussaint Louverture and the male-dominated domains of diplomacy, war, and geopolitics that shaped the revolutionary Atlantic World, I also delve into the effects of these forces on the women and men who sought to survive and thrive in a world of pervasive violence, exploitation, and material insecurity—and how these individuals in turn influenced these forces, especially as concerns slave emancipation.

The legacies of these struggles are still evident in present-day Hispaniola. This book not only represents an important step in placing into greater dialogue the quite distinct historiographies of Haiti and the Dominican Republic but also offers a counterpoint to simplified narratives of Haitian-Dominican antagonism.[18] As this book goes to press, these narratives have unfortunately become exacerbated by a political and legal controversy related to a September 2013 Dominican Constitutional Court decision stripping citizenship from all Dominicans not born to at least one Dominican (citizen) parent since 1929.[19] In foregrounding the importance of the two colonies' shared histories in the Haitian Revolution, this study militates against master narratives of division and essential difference. In the Haitian Revolution, "maroons" from both colonies together defied centralizing Spanish and French colonial governments and forged their own distinct communities, ex-slaves from French Saint-Domingue sought to emulate centuries-old Dominican patterns of peasant smallholding rather than enrich others on plantations, and "French" and "Spanish" men on the island fought side by side for and against a variety of colonial regimes in the two decades prior to 1809. It is hoped that these and other examples will join the efforts of others in highlighting the more positive and nuanced sides of historical Haitian-Dominican relations in the service of building a better future.[20]

At the same time, this study carefully contextualizes the cross-border conflicts that *did* transpire in the revolutionary period, such as the Haitian leader Jean-Jacques Dessalines's 1805 attack on the French revanchist slaveholding regime headquartered in Santo Domingo city and the efforts of both the leaders of this regime and their emancipationist 1790s predecessors to delineate and control "French" and "Spanish" "blacks," which would leave a terrible legacy for the next two centuries of Haitian and Dominican history. In seeking solutions to Hispaniola's and the Caribbean's contemporary problems, such as labor exploitation, racism, and political instability, we must first take account of these issues' genealogies stretching deep into the colonial era.[21] This study takes stock of a critical moment in these genealogies.

As is so often the case today, those dissatisfied with repressive political regimes or a lack of economic opportunities voted with their feet in revolutionary Hispaniola, often traversing a terrestrial border that in the words of Eugenio Matibag "constitutes a rocky interface allowing what has been, since colonial days, a traffic in goods and a flow of people, culture, and language from west to east and back again."[22] This border influenced, but did not define or contain, the trajectory and scope of the Haitian Revolution. The island's seacoasts, moreover, witnessed a mass exodus of thousands to Puerto Rico, Cuba, the United States, and numerous other locations in the revolutionary period. These two diasporas—that from Santo Domingo and the better-known one from Saint-Domingue—constituted important precedents for contemporary Caribbean migration from and within Hispaniola.[23]

The inability to resolve either the question of sovereignty over Santo Domingo or the border issue during the six years following the cession supports a reinterpretation of the Haitian Revolution as a transimperial episode in which the emerging revolutionary nation-state collided with centuries of fragmentation and interdependence in Hispaniola. For instance, the revolutionary and Napoleonic eras in France, and to a lesser degree in the colonies, witnessed a great wave of centralization marked by efforts to codify and rationalize diverse provincial and colonial laws, redraw the map of France (and later the colonies) by replacing the old provinces with more compact *départements* (departments or administrative units), and even re-order time and space by way of the short-lived French Republican calendar and the more enduring metric system. Yet the physical and psychological border between the two colonies in Hispaniola stood in sharp relief with such models of rational centralization and circumscribed metropolitan attempts to refashion the island's political boundaries. More generally, the shifting politics of the border played a significant role in the Haitian Revolution, and these politics in turn grew out of the deep history of the entire island.

While the emancipationist experiment contributed to the foundation of Haiti ten years after the passage of the French universal emancipation law, Santo Domingo followed a different path, hosting a counterrevolutionary Napoleonic regime bent on turning back the clock on emancipation. This regime not only threatened the liberty of thousands of freed persons but also worked to thwart foreign diplomatic recognition of Haiti and warred with the Haitian leader Dessalines. In a very real sense, then, the saga of the Haitian Revolution did not end in 1804 but rather continued until 1809 (if not later), when this Napoleonic regime fell. In proposing such an adjustment of the Haitian Revolution's chronology, I contend that reenslavement was as much a conceptual and analytical problem in this era as emancipation or revolution. Fundamentally, over the twenty-year period detailed in this study, the political, economic, and moral meanings of "slave" were on trial in Hispaniola and in other key parts of the larger Atlantic stage.

Background and Foreground

The eighteenth century was a tale of two colonies in Hispaniola, whose geographic diversity—lush plains, the highest mountains in the Caribbean, and bays suitable for splendid harbors—presented a fitting setting for an economically, ethnically, and linguistically diverse population. While French Saint-Domingue stood at the center of the French Atlantic economy, its neighbor held a somewhat ambiguous status in the Spanish empire as an administrative center, a regional hub for slaving, and a drain on the coffers of New Spain (Mexico) due to the Caribbean colony's poverty.[24]

In the younger of these two colonies, French Saint-Domingue, nearly half a million slaves produced the sugar, coffee, and other cash crops that not only created fabulous wealth for a handful of planters but also underwrote much of the economic and political power of eighteenth-century France. Since its origins in the seventeenth century as a fledgling settlement based on raiding, cattle raising, and tobacco cultivation by French-speaking buccaneers who had found abundant land in the western part of Hispaniola, French Saint-Domingue had been a world marked by both great danger and great opportunity. Tales of the colony's wealth attracted many Frenchmen (and it was usually men) who traveled to this faraway land to seek their fortunes in the hope of returning to France to live in luxury.[25] This wealth was created by these French migrants' unfree or semifree fellow travelers: indentured and enslaved individuals (also disproportionately male) whose labor powered the tobacco, cacao, coffee, indigo, and sugar enterprises that, from modest beginnings in the seventeenth century, came to form the backbone of the world's wealthiest colonial economy by the 1780s.[26]

In the century following Spain's cession of what became French Saint-Domingue via the 1697 Treaty of Rhyswick, a combination of entrepreneurial plantation development, the ever-increasing importation of laborers, access to numerous (though often illicit) trade routes, and the colony's rich and varied terrain (including mountains ideal for coffee cultivation and plains on which sugar thrived) gave rise to an extremely productive plantation system. French Saint-Domingue was, in the words of historian John Garrigus, "one of the most profitable and exploitative systems of plantation slavery in world history" where by the 1760s illness, extreme labor demands, cruel punishments for the smallest infractions, and poor nutrition killed an estimated one-half of newly arrived Africans within eight years.[27]

In an effort to more effectively administer this profitable colony, the French Crown divided it into three provinces: north, west, and south. Each acquired a distinct character in the course of the century of French rule. The richest province, the north, contained the commercial capital of Cap Français, the colony's principal port of trade and the center of French culture in the tropics. The city's littoral boasted many of the most profitable sugar and coffee plantations in the colony; not coincidentally, this area later became the focal point of the great 1791 slave revolt that transformed Saint-Domingue's fortunes. The northern province was also the home of several key figures in the Haitian Revolution, including Toussaint Louverture.[28]

At the other extreme, geographically and economically, lay the south province, which covered most of the peninsula on Saint-Domingue's southern coast. (See map 2.) The south's geographic isolation from the main routes of (legal) French commerce and relative isolation from the rest of Saint-Domingue due to geographical barriers, combined with the province's relative proximity to British Jamaica, the Spanish colonies in Central

America, and the eastern Caribbean, made it a hub of contraband trade in coffee and particularly in indigo. According to John Garrigus, the latter crop proved integral in the rise of a wealthy planter class of *gens de couleur libres* (free persons of color) who would exert enormous influence in the province's revolutionary history. The final province, the west, possessed characteristics of each of the other two: though it contained the political capital and de facto second city, Port-au-Prince, and two plains that enabled lucrative sugar production, it too was fairly isolated from the north. The west thus played second fiddle to the north as the eighteenth century wore on.[29]

Due in large part to its buccaneer roots and the centrality of illegal commerce, French Saint-Domingue always exhibited an independent streak, which would manifest itself particularly acutely in acrimonious disputes concerning militia service in the 1760s and in the efforts of many upwardly mobile colonists on the eve of the Haitian Revolution to loosen or even eliminate the notorious *exclusif*, the mercantilist system of commercial restrictions devised in the seventeenth century that sought to tightly control colonial trade.[30]

Any pretensions toward emulation of the North American revolutionaries of the 1770s, however, were muffled by the perceived imperative to maintain firm control over the massive enslaved labor force. While in 1687 the colony had contained 4,411 whites and 3,358 slaves, by 1750 the 150,000 slaves were more than ten times more numerous than whites, and in 1789 the colony was home to around half a million slaves, who comprised 90 percent of the population.[31] By the time of the storming of the Bastille prison in Paris, the labor of those held in abject servitude in French Saint-Domingue had made that colony the globe's premier sugar and coffee exporter. These slaves' toil produced half of the coffee on world markets and as much sugar as several of the colony's leading competitors combined.[32]

For the Martinican lawyer, scholar, politician, and chronicler Médéric-Louis-Elie Moreau de St Méry, all this meant that a sound understanding of all aspects of French Saint-Domingue, ranging from its fairly short history of French rule to its demography and environment, was essential not only to ensure the colony's continued prosperity but also to improve governance and productivity in the entire Francophone sphere.[33] "The French Part of the island of Saint-Domingue," Moreau wrote in the introduction to his now-canonical *Description* of that colony, "is, of all the French possessions in the New-World, the most important by the wealth that it renders to its Metropole and by the influence that it has over its agriculture and its commerce." This importance also extended to the realm of administration, for the challenges of ruling French Saint-Domingue made it "worthy of observation by all men who engage in the study of governments," and lessons learned there could help to "enlighten government, and to show the real bases of a superior system of public prosperity." Yet studying this French colony in isolation was not sufficient. All of his arguments concerning the importance of French Saint-Domingue would, Moreau insisted, "acquire a still newer force when one notes that possession of the island is shared among two nations, that have had to adopt views particular to each, as concerns their colonies, because they have in their principles of government, and even in their character, considerable differences." Therefore, "an exact portrait of the entirety of the island of Saint-Domingue, should have the double advantage of acquainting [the reader] with the French and Spanish genius, acting at great distances, and of showing the means by which each carried out its designs."[34] Moreau thus realized that in order to understand the origins and trajectory of what would become known as the Haitian Revolution, one must take into account the histories of both parts of the island and comprehend the Spanish/Dominican as well as the French/Dominguan context.

If French Saint-Domingue was Moreau's archetype of the lucrative plantation colony, he recognized that Spanish Santo Domingo had constituted the original on which the archetype was modeled. As "the prototype of all the sugar and slave colonies" in the hemisphere, Santo Domingo was the first site of the "transplantation of ideas from the old world, in the new," and the "first European vestige marked on a vast part of the globe," which for that reason alone "has the right to attract the gazes of the philosophical observer."[35]

Moreau understood that European conquest and colonization in Santo Domingo had involved the transfer of much more than just ideas, though. Following his landing in Hispaniola in 1492, Columbus instituted a short-lived regime that sought to use the labor of the native Taínos to extract the island's precious gold reserves.[36] Despite Columbus's removal from power, the exhaustion of the gold supply, and numerous ineffective measures by Columbus's onetime sponsors, King Ferdinand of Aragon and Queen Isabella of Castile, and their successors to ameliorate the condition of the indigenous population, warfare, overwork, and disease virtually destroyed the Taínos in the first half-century of European presence on the island.[37] This prompted Spanish authorities and colonists to turn to enslaved African labor and to seek new sources of revenue. In 1503 if not before, the first African slaves to reach the Americas landed on the island's shores, while enterprising colonists found in the sugar plantations of the Canary Islands and elsewhere a prototype that might profitably be replicated in the tropical Americas.[38]

By the middle of the sixteenth century, this lucrative and lethal experiment of combining forced African labor with the infrastructure of the plantation had made Spanish Santo Domingo a rich sugar exporter, which by some accounts produced several thousand tons annually. The 20,000 or so slaves who labored in the sugar mills as well as in other agricultural enterprises and in domestic labor by the late 1560s greatly outnumbered the 6,000 Spanish colonists and 500 indigenous survivors. This was the first example of the grossly disproportionate slave-to-free ratio that would characterize the tropical American plantation complex, but it was not destined to endure long. By the end of this century, the confluence of Spanish commercial restrictions, a decisive shift in colonial policy toward New Spain and Peru (which became the centers of the Spanish empire due to their silver wealth and comparatively large sedentary indigenous populations), and the rise of a profitable Brazilian sugar industry doomed the Dominican plantation economy. In one indication of this dramatic reversal, a 1606 colonial census listed only 800 slaves employed in sugar and 9,696 slaves overall among a total population of perhaps 16,000 souls.[39] As discussed earlier in this introduction, nearly two centuries later in 1789, Santo Domingo still contained only 15,000 slaves, who constituted around 15 percent of the total population.

The collapse of the sugar boom led to political and economic shifts that would shape subsequent Dominican (and Haitian) history. In the absence of a prized commodity that would attract the ablest administrators and the most ambitious settlers, metropolitan neglect translated into a situation in which both church and state were among the weakest in Spanish America. These forces greatly frustrated elites but created unexpected opportunities for many of those who had suffered the most under the fleeting plantation regime.

Throughout the countryside in the centuries following the end of the sugar boom, the sugar plantations largely gave way to cattle ranches, tobacco estates, and plots of land worked by peasants (often immigrants or freed people and their descendants), often far from significant direct state control. "The Spanish part of St-Domingue conducts almost no commerce," wrote Moreau in an overstatement typical of elite descriptions of the colony. Partly as a result of its poverty, Santo Domingo "has almost no relation with the metropole [Spain]," while the resources of most colonists were "extremely limited." In Moreau's depiction, Spanish Santo Domingo possessed a very modest agricultural base that included generally unprofitable coffee and indigo estates and just twenty-two sugar plantations of any importance, which employed a mere 600 "blacks." Aside from meat, hides, and limited mahogany production, the only commodity of any quality produced in the colony was tobacco, but even this crop was concentrated in only one area (in the north near the second city of Santiago) and grown mostly for domestic consumption and contraband with neighboring islands.[40] The Dominican framers of a 1784 slave code offered a similar appraisal. In their estimation, aside from tobacco from the Santiago area, sugar was the colony's only valuable export commodity. By their account, only 760 "*negros y pardos*" (black and brown people) labored on the paltry nineteen sugar mills in the colony.[41]

Mountain ranges carved Santo Domingo into distinct regions whose economies all to a greater or lesser degree became linked to that of French Saint-Domingue in the seventeenth and eighteenth centuries. Situated on the Ozama River along the southern coast, Santo Domingo city served as the Spanish colony's political capital, principal port, and cultural center. (See figure 1.) Its hinterland contained most of the territory's few profitable sugar and cacao plantations. These products, however, paled in comparison to the cattle trade in the eighteenth-century Dominican economy. Dominicans frequently traded cattle products (such as meat and hides), among other goods, to the British, French, Dutch, and others in exchange for the manufactured goods (such as textiles, wine, arms, and ceramics) that often came much more cheaply and in higher quality through illegal trade than through the restrictive official channels.[42]

The central institution in the Dominican cattle economy was the *hato*, or ranching estate.[43] As the eighteenth century progressed, the demand for meat to feed the growing slave population and hides for multiple uses (not least of which was to fashion the dreadful whips used to discipline the slaves) in neighboring French Saint-Domingue gave rise to a thriving cross-border trade in cattle products whose impact went far beyond supporting the expansion of the Dominguan plantation complex.[44] According to Roberto Cassá, the role of French colonists as commercial intermediaries between Spain and Santo Domingo meant that Spain "had to tolerate [Santo

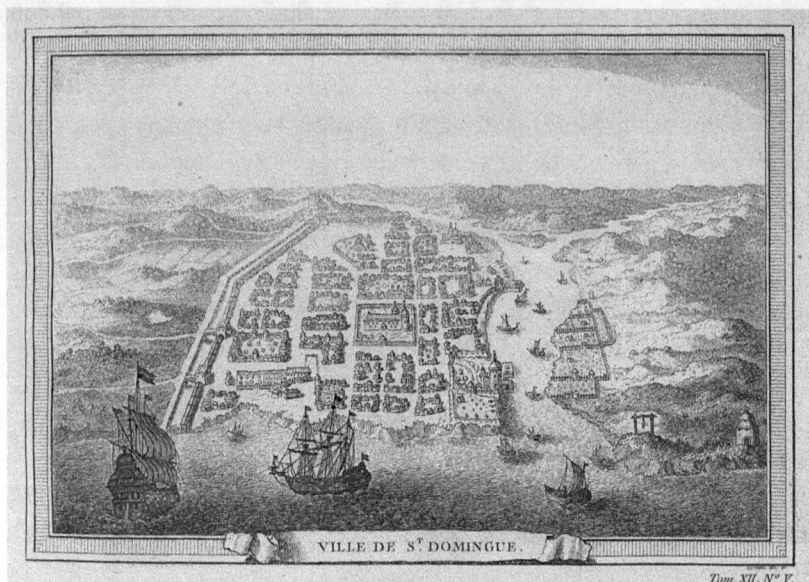

FIGURE 1 "Ville de St. Domingue." A bird's-eye depiction of Santo Domingo city published in 1754. Courtesy of the John Carter Brown Library at Brown University.

Domingo's] becoming an accessory to the prosperity of Saint Domingue as the price of maintaining sovereignty over [Santo Domingo]."[45]

This cattle trade—which was at various points in the eighteenth century illegal, under legal monopoly control, and under a tax-exempt free trade arrangement[46]—connected the key Dominican municipalities of Santiago, Neyba, and Montechristi to the French colony. In addition to its prominence as a tobacco exporter to the neighboring colony, Santiago's location in the fertile Cibao valley—Santo Domingo's breadbasket—enabled its hinterland to boast by far the most *hatos* of any region in the Spanish colony.[47] Moreover, in the words of Cassá, French Saint-Domingue was also the "economic center of gravity" in the valleys of Neyba and San Juan, located near the mountainous colonial border in southwest Santo Domingo. These mountains also harbored maroon communities comprised of escaped slaves from both colonies who would play an important role in the revolution. Other towns near the border, such as Las Caobas and San Miguel in the center-west, were founded in part as a result of the trade in cattle with French Saint-Domingue and revolved around that trade in the eighteenth century, while northern Dominican ports, such as Puerto Plata and Montechristi, welcomed French and Dutch vessels on a regular basis.[48]

The bleak portrait of Santo Domingo as an impoverished backwater offered by Moreau and many others, then, tells only part of the story. Alongside the undeniable poverty and relative metropolitan neglect—which became magnified in the perceptions of many chroniclers due to the Spanish colony's proximity to the rich French Saint-Domingue—one also finds evidence of thriving (though often illegal) trade, substantial immigration, new investments, and even a population boom. We have already seen the centrality of the cattle trade to the Dominican economy; this trade was in fact part of a larger historical trend wherein Santo Domingo and other Spanish Caribbean colonies constituted integral parts of the Caribbean economy in the seventeenth and eighteenth centuries. In this period, not only cattle products but also wood, salt, mules, ginger, and other items from these Spanish lands were vital "inputs" for plantation production in the "sugar islands" under French, British, and Dutch rule.[49]

Furthermore, Santo Domingo's population more than tripled in the eighteenth century. This increase was fueled in part by the immigration of Canary Islanders and of slaves from the neighboring colony. There were also signs of investment and potential economic growth in the Spanish colony in the latter portion of the eighteenth century, such as the establishment of new cotton, cacao, and indigo plantations in the environs of the capital city and a 1763 royal order mandating the construction of a tobacco factory in that city.[50] Fundamentally, rather than existing as an outlier from the early modern Atlantic capitalist world, Santo Domingo was part and parcel of this world. "The 'traditional' rural economy and mode of existence that prevailed in colonial Santo Domingo," Richard Turits writes, "was not a legacy of a precapitalist world, but rather was born, ironically, of modernity. It had no precolonial past and followed rather than preceded the penetration of world market forces."[51]

In spite of these new ventures, Santo Domingo's plantation infrastructure still lagged far behind that of its neighbor and many other Caribbean colonies. Nevertheless, what was a perennial source of frustration for authorities and would-be planters turned out to present new opportunities for many of those held in bondage in the Spanish colony. Weak demand for slave labor and comparatively liberal laws and customary practices regarding manumission enabled many slaves to attain freedom. While many of these slaves' strategies, such as fleeing from their masters and purchasing their freedom, were also present in the "sugar islands," conditions in Santo Domingo facilitated escape from bondage on such a scale that, a full 150 years before the abolition of slavery, a free peasantry comprised substantially of former slaves and their descendants came to constitute the majority of the colony's population. Some free people of African descent in urban areas, moreover, attained prominent positions in institutions such as the church and the military in contravention of racist legal interdictions.[52]

As elsewhere, peasant life in colonial Santo Domingo had its share of hardships, but life in *el monte*, as the sparsely populated Dominican countryside was known, offered a number of advantages over labor on large estates, paid or unpaid: relatively easy access to land for one's own use, the ability to enjoy the fruits of one's own labor in a manner more commensurate with the effort expended, and typically a much less pronounced color line. The rise of the cattle economy and the lesser influence of the landowning elite relative to many other colonies gave rise to a particular system of land usage in which a wide gap existed between legal land ownership and actual land usage.[53] Under this system, Dominican peasants—who were often effectively squatters—enjoyed a remarkable degree of autonomy, raising cattle and growing crops both for markets and for their own consumption.[54]

This situation contrasted sharply with that in French Saint-Domingue, marked as it was by the enslavement of nine-tenths of the population and by a strong plantation- and urban-based elite class. In the Haitian Revolution, the two colonies' histories of resistance to slavery and racial oppression nonetheless intersected to create new political ideologies, legal strategies, and concepts of freedom.

Summary of Chapters

In the late 1780s and early 1790s, a fatal confluence of conflicts destabilized the prized plantation colony of French Saint-Domingue. The calling of the Estates-General, the destruction of the Bastille, and the promulgation of the Declaration of the Rights of Man and the Citizen in France (1788–89) precipitated a decade-long French Revolution that irrevocably altered that nation's political and social structure. When news of these events reached the colonies, it ignited intense speculation on the possible reverberations among colonial authorities, slaves, and everyone in between. The retrospective words of Norbert Thoret, a French tailor who set up shop in Saint-Domingue during the early phases of the French and Haitian Revolutions (and who then returned a decade later), likely reflect the sentiments of many other white French men and women who also survived these events: that the "most prosperous state" and the "perfect tranquility" of prerevolutionary French Saint-Domingue would soon dissolve in the "storms" of "the French Revolution."[55]

Yet French Saint-Domingue prior to these revolutions had been far from tranquil, which owed in part to a fierce struggle between *gens de couleur libres* and recalcitrant whites over the political and civil rights of free persons of African descent. The powerful new discourses of freedom and citizenship emanating from France provided new bases for equal rights claims by activist *gens de couleur libres* from Saint-Domingue and other colonies who had been engaged for years in a campaign to repeal racist laws that gravely undermined the rights of even propertied nonwhites. Those in bondage seized upon this dissent among the free population to carry out a massive revolt in August 1791 that commenced in the rich sugar-producing heartland near Cap Français.

The advent of revolution in French Saint-Domingue and Spanish Santo Domingo is the focus of chapter 1, which situates the early events of the Haitian Revolution within the island's "long" eighteenth century. Long-standing conflicts over the extradition of fugitive slaves, the colonial boundary, maroon communities, and numerous other issues influenced Dominican authorities' responses to racial conflict and slave revolt in Saint-Domingue. In particular, the famed mixed-race leader Vincent Ogé's ill-fated quest for legal reform in Saint-Domingue in 1790–91 emerges with new clarity from the vantage point of Spanish Santo Domingo. After vainly seeking refuge from French colonial forces in Santo Domingo, he and others in his party were returned to Saint-Domingue and executed by French officials in early 1791 due to their perceived threat to the social and racial order. Extant correspondence and reports by Ogé and several French and Spanish authorities reveal that Ogé strategically appealed to the royalist political convictions of his Spanish "hosts" in his efforts to gain asylum in Santo Domingo, while his extradition from the Spanish colony owed partly to racial ideologies and anxieties that had developed in Santo Domingo and partly to long-established patterns of interaction between leaders from both sides of the island.

After a discussion of the effect of such patterns on the Spanish response to the 1791 slave revolt and to the French colonial state's futile attempts to quash it, I discuss the pivotal role of enslaved and freed warriors and their political discourses in the Franco-Spanish-British war for Hispaniola

(1793–95). Rather than dismissing royalist sentiment among slaves and freed people as an aberration or evidence of some type of "false consciousness," I argue that these individuals advanced their own ideas of freedom that contributed to the declarations abolishing slavery in Saint-Domingue issued by the French Republican civil commissioners Léger-Félicité Sonthonax and Étienne Polverel in the summer and fall of 1793. In contextualizing the numerous letters and proclamations created by several freed leaders and those of the civil commissioners within military and political events on the ground, I present a political and intellectual history of the coming of emancipation to Hispaniola.

The French National Convention subsequently ratified the commissioners' general emancipation orders of 1793 and extended them to all French colonies in the landmark emancipation law of 4 February 1794. The resulting surge in military recruitment among the newly freed enabled the embattled French Republic to turn the tide of war. By late summer 1795, the French had not only expelled the Spanish from the parts of Saint-Domingue that the latter had occupied in the war but also won formal control over Spanish Santo Domingo via the Treaty of Basel. Yet as discussed earlier in this introduction, it remained unclear to what extent, if any, this would portend a change in the condition of those still claimed as slaves in the eastern part of the island, especially given the weak French governmental and military presence in Santo Domingo. Chapter 2 argues that this confusion regarding the status of Santo Domingo made it a central proving ground in battles over the scope of a radical political and social experiment that had, in theory, transformed thousands of slaves into citizens virtually overnight.

Shortly after the signing of the Treaty of Basel, the French Republic promulgated a new constitution that consolidated the hard-won legislative gains of the first half of the decade—the abolition of legalized racism (proclaimed in a 4 April 1792 metropolitan law) and that of slavery—in its declaration that the inhabitants of all French realms would henceforth enjoy equal citizenship rights. Nonetheless, efforts to incorporate Santo Domingo into this new legal framework met with mixed results. On the one hand, the attempts of many Dominican emigrants to force those whom they claimed as slaves to accompany them out of the colony prompted some French officials to compose some of the most eloquent defenses of the "natural right" of liberty ever offered in the French and Haitian Revolutionary era. Yet when freed individuals took their rights into their own hands through such means as rising up on Santo Domingo's largest plantation, joining "maroon"

communities, or simply attempting to escape the restrictions on their freedom in Saint-Domingue by migrating to the eastern part of the island, these
same Republican officials' responses often differed little from the actions
that their predecessors had taken under slavery.

Perhaps no French leader better exemplified these tensions between the
old and the new than Toussaint Louverture. The third chapter of this study
treats the role of Santo Domingo in the military history of Hispaniola from
1795 to 1801. This history was in many ways that of the rise of François Dominique Toussaint Louverture, a coachman who had gained his freedom from
slavery in the 1770s.[56] Toussaint's legacy takes on a somewhat different character in light of his experiences in Santo Domingo. After joining the slave
rebels in November 1791, Toussaint enlisted with the Spanish armies two
years later, only to defect to the ranks of the French Republic in the spring
of 1794. In the six years following the conclusion of war with Spain in 1795,
Toussaint outfought and outmaneuvered powerful internal and foreign adversaries to become the supreme leader of the entire island.

As he led thousands of soldiers into battle against the slaveholding British who occupied many parts of the island from 1793 to 1798, Toussaint won
control over numerous strategic Dominican towns that connected once-
prosperous parts of French Saint-Domingue with the Dominican interior,
often via the old cattle-trading routes. After Toussaint negotiated the
surrender of the British and their departure from the island in 1798, he
sought to subdue General André Rigaud, his main rival for control over
Saint-Domingue, and to establish an independent foreign policy while still
professing loyalty to France.

Following the defeat of Rigaud, Toussaint turned his attention to asserting his control over Santo Domingo as the final military stage of his plan to
unite the entire island under his rule. This heightened his rivalry with Napoleon, who had taken power in France in 1799. In order to limit Toussaint's
power, Napoleon unsuccessfully sought to maintain the status quo, wherein
Spanish officials in Santo Domingo still wielded considerable authority in
spite of the cession. The Dominguan general's invasion of Santo Domingo
city in early 1801 in turn owed substantially to his strategic concern with preventing a French or foreign invasion force from disembarking in the vulnerable eastern part of the island.

After ejecting the Spanish governor and installing his own regime in
Santo Domingo, Toussaint embarked on an ambitious program to revive its
economy. Chapter 4, a reexamination of Toussaint's brief reign in Santo

Domingo, details his efforts to establish a viable plantation infrastructure in the former Spanish colony. Several of Toussaint's decrees, along with governmental and personal correspondence and scattered eyewitness accounts, document his twofold strategy to attain this goal: restrictive labor policies tying ex-slaves to the colony's few productive estates and economic incentives and concessions for plantation entrepreneurs, such as reduced taxes on key cash crops like sugar and coffee. In elaborating upon the effects of these policies and Toussaint's mixed record in eliminating enslavement, I present Toussaint as a Dominican as well as a Haitian leader whose vision of a united Hispaniola was as much economic as political.

Partly in response to Toussaint's invasion of Santo Domingo city, Napoleon deployed a huge military expedition to Hispaniola in late 1801 and early 1802. Its main aims were the overthrow of Toussaint and the imposition of Paris's (read: Napoleon's) unequivocal authority. Though the expedition did indeed depose Toussaint, after which Napoleon's agents carted him off to France to die in a remote mountain prison, the invaders failed to retake Saint-Domingue, as the French expeditionary force could not overcome the resistance of thousands who fought desperately to avoid the reimposition of slavery.[57] The expedition's defeat led to the creation of two states: the new nation of Haiti, constructed on the ruins of the old Saint-Domingue, and a renewed colonial regime based in Santo Domingo city led by General Jean-Louis Ferrand, a survivor of the expedition.

The legal order in Santo Domingo under Ferrand rested upon the questionable presumption that Napoleon's government had legally authorized the reestablishment of slavery there. In chapter 5, I assess slavery's dubious legality in Santo Domingo in the Ferrand period and examine some of the ways in which freed people in the colony resisted Ferrand's regime. While Ferrand issued a series of racist orders that sought to disenfranchise all those deemed nonwhite and to enslave those among this group who could not document their freedom, evidence reveals that those claimed as slaves made use of tactics such as compelling authorities to call them as witnesses in disputes over their purported ownership and fleeing to independent Haiti. Some of those targeted by the regime's racial repression also joined the armies of its enemies in the 1808–9 war that resulted in the regime's collapse.

Moreover, a number of freed persons in Ferrand-era Santo Domingo came before French notaries in order to create notarized acts attesting to their free status. These acts are the focus of chapter 6. These freed individuals employed three types of strategies: presenting prior evidence of free status, such as a manumission act; offering monies for self-purchase; and summoning witnesses to vouch for one's condition as a nonslave. Exploiting small openings in the hybrid French-Spanish legal system, these individuals archived their liberty in the creation of these acts.

While chapters 1 through 5 (and the first part of the epilogue) tell a political history of Hispaniola from 1789 to 1809, chapter 6 complements this narrative by offering an on-the-ground "snapshot" of freed persons' strategies based on a rich source base of notarial records. These sources permit fuller development of many of the themes introduced in the earlier chapters such as the malleability of "slave" status across colonial borders, freed persons' manipulation of documentary and legal mechanisms to secure their freedom, and the complexities of slave law across empires during a moment of revolutionary upheaval and attempted reenslavement. Chapter 6, more than any other, offers a glimpse into the archives of race and slavery forged partly out of these struggles and presents a vantage point into the lived reality of the revolutionary and counterrevolutionary projects of the era.

When Rosalie *dite* Dufay, the mother discussed in the opening vignette, purchased her own daughter with the intention of freeing her in August 1803, she sought to protect Rozine from the imminent threat of reenslavement in the wake of the collapse of French Republican emancipation. When Rozine in turn procured a notarized act attesting to her freedom three years later in the eastern part of the island, she too utilized the legal mechanisms of a slave society to stake her own claim to liberty. Santo Domingo turns out to have been integral to the struggles to redefine citizenship rights, the relationship between metropole and colony, and the boundaries of freedom during the Haitian Revolutionary era, and individuals such as Rozine and her mother were at the center of these dynamics.

As a historian and a participant in two revolutions, the chronicler Moreau de St Méry understood that writing history is a profoundly political act. "It is in tracing it, this history [of Hispaniola], that I remind myself, almost on every line, that the historian possesses true authority," Moreau declared, "and that he should cast aside his pen in terror, if he has forgotten, for a single instant, that one day posterity will want to cast judgment on a deed or on an individual, having access to no testimony to invoke but his [the historian's], and that if his judgment fails [his pen], it makes him guilty of irreversible injustices."[58] Moreau was keenly aware of the importance of an integrated and detailed history of the island for the posterity who would surely puzzle over why such monumental events occurred there in the

1790s. Two centuries later, I offer this study as a means by which to promote a more comprehensive understanding of the French and Haitian Revolutions and of the historical roots of contemporary Haitian-Dominican relations. This book also responds to Laurent Dubois's call for scholars to "seek to construct a picture of an integrated space of debate over rights, of universalism, over governance and empire" so that they may "understand the Atlantic as an integrated intellectual space" in which people in Europe, the Americas, and Africa all actively shaped emergent discourses on rights, citizenship, and democracy.[59] The island of Hispaniola in the Haitian Revolutionary era was one such "integrated space," even as it was also a divided terrain.

In his effort to reconstruct a vanishing colonial world through his writing, Moreau knew that the past, present, and future of the island were inextricably connected. What follows is a narrative that ties together the stories of slaves, freed people, and others from both parts of the island so that we may better understand these histories and their role in the making of the modern world.

I Am the King of the Counter-Revolution

Revolution and Emancipation in Hispaniola, 1789–1795

My lord: If something has moved me, to place in your hands the present letter, it is not for any other end than to manifest the truth, and [to] affirm religion. I have directed these Arms for two years now, and it has been two more years since I have undertaken to detain the progresses [of the] one thousand two-hundred criminals that there were, seeking to transform the entire World; and that without flattering myself I dare to say that I am the king of the counter-revolution . . . that I undertook a war, almost without arms, without munitions, without provisions, and in the end without any means.

—Georges Biassou (1793)

With these words, Georges Biassou, "General of the Conquered Part of the North of [Saint-Domingue]," opened a letter that affirmed his passionate defense of the Spanish king and his willingness to "shed [his] last drop of blood" for his sovereign.[1] Biassou was in fact only one of several prominent former slaves who ironically helped to bring about the most radical act of the French Revolution through their seemingly counterrevolutionary discourses and allegiances. Indeed, even as Biassou proclaimed his unswerving commitment to serve the Spanish king, his letter represented a demand for greater political representation on the part of individuals of African descent who had long been subjected to servitude and disfranchisement in Hispaniola.

Why did Biassou depict the Western Hemisphere's greatest slave rebellion as a "war to save my King" and to "liberate such a great King from the tyranny to which he was reduced?"[2] Why did he and many other onetime slaves in the Haitian Revolution fight under the banners of Spanish royalism against a French Republic that came to espouse universal liberty and equal citizenship? Any answer must involve decoupling dyads that pervade modern thought, such as slavery-racism and republicanism-liberty, in favor of an interpretation grounded in the uncertain and highly complex political context of Hispaniola in the 1790s. Both the political discourses that Biassou and other freed military leaders crafted and the militancy of the thousands of slaves who had risen against their masters in French Saint-Domingue in August 1791 were indispensable in forcing the new French Republic to move beyond what Fernando Coronil termed the "provincial universalism" of a polity that professed the Declaration of the Rights of Man for the metropole and slavery for the colonies.[3] The heterogeneous political ideas of those such as Biassou who had helped carry out this insurrection were, moreover, not simply reactionary aberrations from a story of revolution and emancipation. Instead, they represented articulations of distinct concepts of liberty that had emerged in part from the history of the island of Hispaniola.

Less than two years after the August 1791 slave revolt, unforeseen geopolitical and internal events would transform the unsuccessful military campaigns undertaken by French forces aiming to crush this insurgency. In 1793, when France went to war against Spain and Britain, both of the latter powers invaded French Saint-Domingue. In this conflict, all three belligerents attempted to enlist the slaves-in-arms as soldiers and officers in their armies, promising freedom in exchange for military service. In their efforts to win over these insurgents, these powers competed to offer them a superior version of liberty. For their part, Biassou and other rebel leaders who embraced the monarchical Spanish appealed both to slaves' aspirations for freedom and to the royalist sentiments that many appear to have held; indeed, these leaders posited intimate connections between the two. These efforts helped to persuade thousands of bondsmen to take up arms in the service of Spain. In their attempts to defuse the potency of these appeals, key French Republican leaders on the island portrayed both African and European monarchs as enslavers and as implacable enemies of liberty, juxtaposing these monarchs with a Republic whose Declaration of the Rights of Man now extended to all who lived in French territories. This ideological warfare helped to bring about the proclamations of general emancipation in Saint-Domingue that the French civil commissioners Léger-Félicité Sonthonax and Étienne Polverel issued in the latter half of 1793.

These emancipation decrees, along with the sweeping emancipation act proclaimed by the French National Convention in 1794, occupy a central place in the historical literature. This has in turn led to a tendency to privilege the story of Toussaint Louverture, who for nearly a decade claimed the mantle of primary defender of emancipation in Hispaniola, over that of Biassou, who never allied with the French Republic. One prominent scholar has argued that Biassou and other freed leaders who rejected the Republic "ended up on the wrong side of history," as their story "has found little room in the master narrative of the Haitian Revolution."[4] Yet slaves and freed individuals who articulated ideas associated with monarchism contributed in their own way to the discourses of rights and citizenship that were at the center of the French and Haitian Revolutions.

From the start of the French Revolution in 1789 to the cession of Santo Domingo to France in 1795, these emerging liberation discourses intersected with political, economic, and social forces that had developed over the course of Hispaniola's "long" eighteenth century. Patterns of diplomacy between the island's two colonial regimes and the racial history of Spanish Santo Domingo influenced racial conflicts in French Saint-Domingue, particularly the infamous episode that resulted in the execution of Vincent Ogé, a businessman-turned-activist who championed the rights of fellow free persons of African descent. Then, long-standing quarrels and irregularly enforced treaties between the two governments shaped the Spanish regime's response to the 1791 slave revolt across the border. Finally, upon the outbreak of open hostilities between France, Spain, and Britain in 1793, the political discourses of Biassou and other ex-slaves contributed to the emergence of radical new political possibilities in a world that had been largely defined by racial subjugation and the reduction of human beings to units of labor—possibilities epitomized by former slaves' reworkings of the images and ideas of colonialism to create new spaces of liberation and political participation.

Santo Domingo and the Ogé "Revolt"

On 23 February 1791, several men working in the service of the French colonial regime in Saint-Domingue tortured and executed Vincent Ogé and Jean-Baptiste Chavanne. After each victim had taken his final breath, their persecutors placed their heads on pikes as grisly warnings to those who would dare emulate them. In spite of the brute simplicity of this spectacle, it was the culmination of a complex series of events related to the tumult in revolutionary Paris and struggles over the rights of free individuals of African descent in both French Saint-Domingue and the neighboring colony.

Vincent Ogé, a wealthy merchant from the northern Dominguan town of Dondon, was part of the most economically influential "free colored" group in the history of the colonial Americas. Known in local parlance as *gens de couleur libres* (free people of color), this group encompassed a great degree of economic diversity. Among its upper ranks were numerous planters and slaveholders, while others occupied a range of artisan trades or served in colonial military or police forces. Nevertheless, in the wake of the disastrous French defeat in the Seven Years' War in 1763, a confluence of forces produced a racist backlash against this group. The most visible and powerful manifestation of this backlash was a series of laws that ranged from restrictions on interracial dining to prohibitions on nonwhites holding public office. These laws had several interrelated aims: to ensure the political disfranchisement of free persons of African descent; to curb their economic power; to weaken the familial, social, and economic ties that many whites shared with many *gens de couleur libres*; and to limit the latter's numbers by means of taxes and other hindrances to manumission.[5]

While authorities had passed these racist laws in late colonial Saint-Domingue largely in response to perceived nonwhite mobility, in Spanish Santo Domingo the disjuncture between state-sanctioned racism and relative social advancement by those deemed *negro* (black), *pardo* (brown), *mulato* (mixed race), or another nonwhite designation stemmed from a much longer racial history that was shaped by the early rise and fall of the hemisphere's first sugar boom in the sixteenth century. Long before the Haitian Revolution, the decline of the Dominican plantation economy, which in turn led to a relative scarcity of capital and white immigrants, had produced a situation that would set the Spanish colony apart from its neighbor: a free African-descended majority carved out lives in the sparsely populated countryside as ranchers and farmers, while the colony's few productive plantations (along with many smaller enterprises) exploited an unfree labor force that constituted a small fraction, in relative and absolute terms, of that on the French side of the island.[6]

The early collapse of the sugar plantation complex, the relative weakness of the colonial state and the white elite, the success of many slaves in winning their freedom, and numerous other forces forged what Richard Turits terms a "powerful heritage of contradictions" that "combined racial hierarchy and a significant degree of racial integration, racist laws with relatively fluid practices, as well as racial slavery . . . with a deracialization of certain forms of liberty."[7] Over the course of several centuries, a complicated racial order had emerged in Santo Domingo in which many free nonwhites attained important positions in the military, church, government, and other institutions in defiance of laws that barred such individuals from these posts.[8] These developments did not eliminate racism but rather led to a situation in which, according to Silvio Torres-Saillant, the "social distance between blacks and whites shrunk significantly" as substantial numbers of people of African descent became "decolorized in the eyes of the ruling class."[9]

This comparative mobility seduced some foreigners into imagining that Spanish Santo Domingo was a relative bastion of racial equality. The chronicler M. L. E. Moreau de St Méry, for instance, insisted that the numerous discriminatory laws in the Spanish colony, which formally barred "freed people" from most key positions and stipulated other indignities such as a ban on freed women wearing precious metals, were now "in absolute disuse." "Color prejudice," Moreau argued, "so powerful in other nations, where it establishes a barrier between the white and the freed person or his descendants, is almost nonexistent in the Spanish part [of Hispaniola]."[10] In the late 1790s, a veteran French colonial officer named Charles Vincent likewise remarked that many of the most distinguished residents of the Dominican city of Santiago had "a little of that which one calls mixed blood." "Considerably wiser than us, the Spanish never hesitate to admit in all employment, good and talented men who are not of rigorously white origin; they even accord the distinction of *Don* to men of a very pronounced color provided that they possess good manners and wealth," opined Vincent. Vincent cited the specific examples of Manuel Constanza, the "Black Captain of the Company of Blacks of Santiago"; Diego Silverio, a marine entrepreneur; and Carlos de Rosas, who may have been a signatory to the constitution promulgated by Haitian Revolutionary leader Toussaint Louverture in 1801.[11]

Among these foreign observers of Santo Domingo's racial order, those targeted by racial repression in Saint-Domingue possessed a particularly strong incentive to paint the Spanish colony as a foil for the rising tide of racism in the French part of the island. In one extended argument against racist legislation written to the French minister of the navy in 1786, Julien Raimond, a prominent *homme de couleur* (man of color), had contended that the inhabitants of Spanish Santo Domingo did not share the "contempt" that the French whites in Saint-Domingue held toward free people of African descent, who "enjoy in this part of the island [Santo Domingo] the consideration that every honest citizen ought to expect from society."[12]

As a wealthy indigo planter and slaveholder of French and African ancestry from the southern part of Saint-Domingue, Raimond became a leader of the movement aiming for the repeal of the colony's racist laws and the restoration of equal rights for the *gens de couleur libres* in line with the provision in the *Code Noir* (the comprehensive slave code for the French colonies promulgated in 1685) granting ex-slaves "the same rights, privileges and liberties that persons born free enjoy."[13]

An alliance forged between Raimond and Vincent Ogé in Paris in the late 1780s, coterminous with the initial stirrings of what would become known as the French Revolution, gave new impetus to the struggles of the *gens de couleur libres*. Ogé, who had initially traveled to France on business, eventually returned to Saint-Domingue, where he became involved with the efforts of activists such as the militia officer and American Revolutionary War veteran Jean-Baptiste Chavanne to pry open the doors to participation by black and mixed-race men in the colonial assemblies formed by whites in the wake of the upheaval in France. Following an unsuccessful petition by Ogé and Chavanne to the provincial assembly in Cap Français (also known as Le Cap) and to Governor Philibert François Rouxel de Blanchelande demanding inclusion in these assemblies and the enforcement of an ambiguously worded 28 March 1790 French law on voting rights, colonial authorities dispatched troops from Le Cap to suppress what these officials deemed to be an armed uprising. The evidence suggests that Ogé himself did not actually raise an armed rebellion or take on any military leadership role—indeed, he apparently rejected Chavanne's advice to enlist slaves in the "revolt"— but when confronted by a large colonial force in late October 1790, the 300 men allied with Ogé and Chavanne held their ground in a battle and then dispersed before the arrival of a second force.[14]

Following their confrontation with the French colonial troops, Ogé, Chavanne, and their contingent of survivors (who numbered twenty-six according to a 15 July 1791 report by the Council of the Indies, Spain's principal governing body on colonial matters) crossed the border into Santo Domingo in early November 1790. The idea to leave their post in Grande-Rivière, Saint-Domingue, in favor of traveling to the Spanish colony may have come from Chavanne, who had spent the middle months of 1790 in Santo Domingo and had apparently gained temporary asylum there following flight from earlier racial conflict in Saint-Domingue. Chavanne, Ogé, and their men gambled that Spanish authorities, whose continual squabbles with their French counterparts had now become exacerbated by the French Revolution, might once again offer asylum or even military support.[15] The gamble failed, with catastrophic results for these men. Nonetheless, Ogé and his followers made Spanish Santo Domingo a significant theater in their fateful struggle to open the arena of citizenship.

Upon his arrival in the Spanish colony, Ogé wasted little time in offering his version of events to authorities. In a 12 November 1790 letter to several Spanish colonial officials, Ogé presented himself not as a rebel leader but as an "Ambassador" who, along with other "men of color from the French part," had been sent to Santo Domingo to "swear an Oath of Loyalty" as "faithful subjects of the King of Spain as of the King of France." In Ogé's recounting, he and his followers had been wrongfully arrested and detained in Hincha (near the colonial border) after soliciting a "Passport" from the "Commandant of San Rafael." In this letter, Ogé combined his denunciation of the bitter history of racism in French Saint-Domingue with a savvy appeal to the royalist political convictions of his Spanish interlocutors. "The disappointments that men of color have experienced in the French part for two hundred years," Ogé asserted, "[and] the aid and the refuge that they have had in the Spanish part unites them more than ever to your Fatherland."[16]

In presenting his plight as part of a long history of racial conflict and assistance-granting that had transpired across the entire island, Ogé tapped into a century of disputes between the French and Spanish colonial regimes over the extradition of fugitive slaves, the precise definition of the border, French settlements on what Spanish authorities deemed to be Spanish land, and other matters.[17] Particularly vexing to French officials was the fact that Spanish colonial policy had for decades featured enticements to some Saint-Domingue slaves to migrate across the border in spite of Spanish officials' repeated assurances of their resolve to return such escapees. The most notable example was a royal order issued on 21 October 1764 that required the Spanish king's subjects to "consider [some French fugitive] blacks as free, and to attempt to advise them by gentleness to form communities, nonetheless taking the necessary precautions to ensure that these communities do not threaten public tranquility."[18]

Nonetheless, several treaties between the two powers signed in the 1760s and 1770s had repudiated the spirit of this order by stipulating the extradition of fugitives (enslaved and otherwise) from one territory to the other and the punishment (by fines) of those who sheltered slave runaways, even as the very existence of multiple slave extradition agreements implies persistent slave flight between the two sides of the island and spotty enforcement.[19] Although Ogé and his band were, of course, not slaves, the island's deep history of slave flight and contested boundaries clearly played a role in the Ogé affair.

Both Joaquín García, the governor of Santo Domingo, and his French counterpart indeed invoked these treaties in their communications concerning Ogé. On 14 November 1790, the French governor Blanchelande demanded the immediate extradition of the "rebels," currently in the custody of the Spanish authorities, in accordance with "Article VI of the treaty between the courts of France and Spain signed at Aranjuez on 3 June 1777," which had declared that "fleeing from one jurisdiction [on the island] with the intent to take refuge in the other" merited the death penalty. (This article did not specify the legal status—slave or free—of those subject to it.)[20] In offering asylum to Ogé and his partisans, García likewise worried that he would "violate the general treaties of alliance of both nations" on "reciprocal restitutions" of fugitives and on the "demarcations of Limits" between the two colonies that both monarchs had signed. "I would have made myself guilty," García wrote, "if I had lent acquiescence and shelter to this wicked attempt of Ogé ... betraying the obligations of friendship and mutual aid which the treaties of the sovereigns impose on these Governments." Such assistance would, moreover, prove particularly egregious due to Ogé's lack of real political authority in García's eyes. According to García, Ogé and Chavanne had presented themselves as "ambassadors, as if there were already a Mulatto state within the French Part, capable of sending a delegation, full powers, and sovereign elections."[21]

Spanish officials also acted against Ogé due to anxieties that he might incite Santo Domingo's own nonwhite majority to revolt. Such a rebellion had been deemed a threat grave enough to warrant military patrolling in parts of the colony earlier in the century,[22] and the actions of Haitian Revolutionary–era Dominguan political groups comprised of *gens de couleur libres* apparently contributed to uprisings among their counterparts in several Spanish colonies.[23] Moreover, six months before Ogé landed in Santo Domingo, García had asserted that a subordinate in Montechristi had been informed by the French commander in Le Cap of "some malefactors [*malevolos*] who from the City of Paris propose to disembark in the Spanish land [Santo Domingo] and particularly in Montechristi, with the fatal design of disrupting the colony and obtaining perfect equality between the persons of Color and the whites." Among these "malefactors" was Ogé.[24] In late 1790, Ogé now found himself extradited to Saint-Domingue partly as a result of Spanish authorities' perception that they must "avoid sparking the fire of sedition among the many mixed-bloods [*gente de castas*] that there are in the Spanish part." "Although nothing has been discovered against the loyalty of the Spanish Mulattos," the authors of the Council of the Indies report proclaimed, "it was suitable to continue the confidential investigations and detain the Guilty ones."[25]

Notwithstanding such anxieties, Ogé, as a property owner and probable slaveholder, had staked the lives of his men on the hope that these affinities would help convince the right Dominican authorities to enable his men to fight another day.[26] Although some elites in Santo Domingo did indeed speak out against the extradition—a member of the *audiencia* (high appeals court) of Santo Domingo named Pedro Catani notably argued that the French "mulattos" (in Catani's words) could serve as useful allies to the Spanish in the event of an invasion from the French part, while several others took García to task for failing to consult the king and for allegedly contorting the facts of the case to fit his ideas[27]—Ogé and his allies in the end found themselves the victims of a confluence of racial fears, ideological distrust (notwithstanding Ogé's professions of royalism), and political expediency in Santo Domingo. Such forces enabled García and others of like mind to override the objections of those opposing extradition and to oversee the return of Ogé's party to the French in late December 1790.

Back in French Saint-Domingue, authorities moved swiftly to make an example of these men, whom they accused of attempting an armed insurrection against the state. Rather than conducting a public trial in Saint-Domingue or shipping the accused to France to stand trial, the council of Le Cap carried out a secret interrogation of Ogé and Chavanne and then proceeded to publicly torture and execute them, along with a number of their men, in February 1791.[28] (French authorities sentenced some other members of this group to slavery, while many others remained at large.) Norbert Thoret, a Frenchman who claimed to have observed the execution of Ogé and Chavanne as a member of the National Guard, later wrote: "It was the first time that I found myself at such a horrible spectacle; I was so frightened by it that I turned my head to not see anything; but I [still] heard their horrible cries."[29]

It was an ignominious and gruesome way to perish for the two leaders—a self-styled patriot of means and a proud veteran of the American War of Independence—who had dedicated themselves to the struggle for racial equality, at least among the free population. Furthermore, rather than put an end to the tumult in the colony, the cruel deaths of Ogé and Chavanne not only heightened the conflicts between reactionary whites and the *gens de couleur libres* in French Saint-Domingue but also contributed to the pivotal slave uprising in the late summer of 1791.[30]

Though Spanish authorities succeeded in extraditing Ogé and his band, the episode illustrates the intercolonial and transnational nature of the expanding conflict on the island. This would become even more apparent as the 1791 slave revolt unfolded. As he lay dying on the torture rack, Ogé could scarcely have imagined that such a rebellion—and a new global war—would enable not only his dream of the end of institutionalized racism in Saint-Domingue but also the destruction of slavery in the plantation colony where it had most flourished.

"A Global Upheaval"

In September 1791, Governor García wrote to a count named Alange with frightening news. An armed uprising had erupted in the environs of Le Cap in the neighboring colony in which "black slaves, some free mulattos," and even some whites had in García's recounting undertaken a campaign to kill planters, burn the plantations, and ultimately murder "every white man" unfortunate enough to cross the rebels' path. Clearly shocked at the extent of the rebellion and unnerved at its potential implications for his own slave-holding colony, García informed Alange that these "public enemies," by virtue of their superior numbers and zealous determination to wreak havoc in Saint-Domingue, had neutralized almost all French officials' attempts to suppress them. The only individual who had experienced less than complete failure against these rebels, García wrote, was the Marquis de Rouvray, a planter who, at the head of 600 men, had "succeeded in destroying a large number of blacks," but only at the cost of the "dismembering" of many of the counterinsurgents. García further wrote that "in this confederation [of rebels], one finds many blackened whites, which are those who direct the most atrocious deeds, and the most severe crimes."[31] Although García thus appears to have initially credited white leaders with a significant, if not the dominant, role in fomenting this violence, in reality this revolt was the fruit of meticulous planning and execution by a well-organized cadre of slaves.

García did get part of the story right, though: during the night of 22–23 August 1791, just six months after Ogé had been put to death in the northern part of Saint-Domingue, hundreds of forced laborers rose up in this same province, destroyed the plantations on which they had toiled, and killed many of their masters and overseers. Though it had arisen partly as a result of (false) rumors that the French king had granted all slaves three free days a week and decreed other reformist measures, such as the elimination of the hated whip, the revolt soon transformed into a campaign for more capacious aspirations for freedom. The composition of the rebellion nonetheless reflected the stratification of the enslaved population, for the early leaders of this revolt—including Georges Biassou, a black creole (Dominguan-born) slave known as Jean-François Papillon, a coachman named Boukman Dutty, and another slave called Jeannot—were generally relatively privileged slaves who exercised authority over other bonded laborers.[32] These advantages enabled them to organize the rebellion efficiently and to recruit other slaves to their cause.

After receiving word of this uprising, García acted promptly to protect the Spanish portion of the island, deploying several regiments of troops under his most trusted lieutenants to the most sensitive border areas in order to secure the "defense of the border."[33] As the plantations burned around them, French military and political leaders for their part sought assistance from the Spanish in Santo Domingo. On 31 August 1791, the Marquis de Rouvray, the planter who killed many rebel slaves with a force of 600 men, implored an unnamed "Spanish commander" to send him "aid" in his fight against the slave rebels, arguing that the lack of such assistance would contribute to the "end" of both colonies in Hispaniola in three months and the loss of all of Spain's colonies within two years.[34] Other Frenchmen also called on Spanish officials to intervene, invoking accords signed earlier in the eighteenth century, much as they had in the Ogé episode. In a letter to Governor García composed in the immediate aftermath of the 1791 slave revolt, Governor Blanchelande of Saint-Domingue requested financial and military assistance in suppressing the rebellion. Declaring that "the white race, and the class of people of color, and free blacks are united, and it is only slaves that are in open revolt, and that kill their masters, and burn the plantations," Blanchelande invoked Article IX of a recent Franco-Spanish treaty, which had stipulated that "in case of war or of unforeseen attack on one of the two parts of the Island, the nation [that was] not attacked will provide to the other all the assistance possible in men as well as in money." In Blanchelande's eyes, 400,000 to 500,000 "internal enemies" threatened to "decapitate" 60,000 free Dominguans, whose Dominican counterparts might then suffer a similar fate. "After the defeat of the French," Blanchelande wrote, "if [the slave rebels] are able to carry this out, the Spanish could have the same luck."[35] In response to these entreaties, García in a 25 September 1791 letter to the Marquis de Bajamar denied that Article IX applied to the situation, which was in his mind a "domestic dispute" among "many whites and mulattos."[36]

Political developments in Europe also influenced García's thinking. With the coming of the French Revolution, the French state had, according to García, "disrupted the order of its primary Laws," and was now paying the price.[37] While the powerful planters of northern Saint-Domingue found their prosperity and status threatened by the slave rising, the old ruling classes in France also faced the specter of sweeping political and social change. Following on the heels of the fall of the Bastille, the proclamation of the Declaration of the Rights of Man and the Citizen, and the abolition of feudal privileges for the nobility and clergy, the French king Louis XVI was impelled to accept a new constitution on 13 September 1791 that substantially limited royal power by according much authority to the National Assembly.[38] Though France and Spain maintained their uneasy alliance in Europe for the time being, events in revolutionary France and in Europe more broadly would soon transform the course of the slave revolt and contribute to the formation of an unlikely partnership between the Dominican governor and those whom he had denigrated as "public enemies" in his September 1791 missive to Alange.

In the immediate wake of the outbreak of slave revolt, however, García and other Dominican administrators were caught between the wish to suppress a possible threat to their slaveholding territory and the presence of an opportunity to undermine their long-standing rivals on the island. From late 1791 until mid-1793, these authorities became involved in a delicate diplomatic game of trying to minimize the adverse effects of the Saint-Domingue revolt on their own society while often tacitly aiding the rebels. After August 1791, García thus adopted a policy of official neutrality toward the neighboring colony while permitting the provision of assistance to the slaves-in-arms.

In Santo Domingo, Dominguan insurgents accordingly found that they could exchange items taken from ransacked plantations for much-needed arms and food. (The geographical proximity between the focal point of the revolt in the parishes around Le Cap and the border with Santo Domingo facilitated these exchanges.) Though the extent of the Spanish monetary and military aid to slave insurrectionists remains unclear, the French general Pamphile de Lacroix would later write of an "infernal Machiavellianism" in which both parties worked together against a common enemy.[39] Governor Blanchelande and some of his subordinates likewise angrily protested that the material benefits accruing to both the Spanish in Santo Domingo and the insurgent slaves had fueled this trade that these French officials demanded their Spanish counterparts suppress. Many Dominicans "have not ceased to trade with the brigands," wrote one French military officer. These Dominicans continued to "encourage [the slave rebels] in their crime; to give them provisions, arms and munitions; [and] to export the furniture of the burned plantations and the product of the slaves' thefts."[40]

Among the "commodities" offered up by the insurgents to the Spanish for barter were captives. In an undated letter to a Spanish military officer, the rebel leader Jean-François repeated an ancient basis for enslavement in his contention that, "not having the heart to destroy" several captives, "we appeal to your good heart to ask you to take them out of the country." Instead of executing these unfortunates, "we would rather sell [the captives] for the benefit of the king and use the same sums to buy useful things for the army," Jean-François asserted.[41]

These economic and military incentives to trade became complemented by ideological and religious ties. Though the insurgents drew upon both "royalist" and "republican" political ideologies, monarchical and Catholic affinities facilitated the collaborations between the rebels and the Spanish that became formalized in 1793. In spite of the destruction that they wrought on plantations, slave rebels not only allowed most of the northern province's priests to remain in their parishes but also frequently called upon their services, even periodically requesting their assistance in political tasks.[42] As the French Revolution in Europe took on an increasingly antimonarchical and anticlerical character, the Dominguan slaves' sympathy toward Catholicism even led some members of the Dominican clergy to herald these slave warriors as agents of divine retribution against the supposedly godless French regime in Paris.[43] Although evidence detailing the perspectives of slaves, rebel or otherwise, is much sparser, some sources suggest that among the insurgents' motivations was a wish to defend the embattled French king. On 21 April 1792, a former plantation owner named Peyredieu from Grande Ravine, Saint-Domingue, informed the Municipality of Le Cap that during his two months of captivity among the "rebels," he had heard Jean-François state that these insurgents "did not fight for Freedom but to restore the [French] executive power as it was before the new constitution [of 1791]."[44] Furthermore, according to a 6 March 1793 account of battles between

French colonial armies and slave rebels in northern Saint-Domingue, numerous captured insurgents claimed that "they fight for the king, who has promised them general liberty, and that they will die with weapons in their hand." Perhaps due in part to such royalist leanings, "the principal rebel leaders withdraw towards Spain [Santo Domingo]."[45]

Scholars have offered numerous explanations as to why royalist sentiments were apparently widespread among slaves and freed persons in French Saint-Domingue during the early phases of the Haitian Revolution. In addition to the omnipresence of royal symbols and rituals in Saint-Domingue and other French colonies, many slaves well understood that French kings had undercut the power of masters in various ways during the seventeenth and eighteenth centuries through a variety of decrees and laws that proscribed extreme cruelty and stipulated other protective measures, such as the requirement that slaves receive adequate food and clothing. (Many of these provisions were articulated in Louis XIV's *Code Noir* of 1685, which remained the foundation of French slave law in the late eighteenth century.[46]) Moreover, the thousands of Africans who arrived in Saint-Domingue each year (tens of thousands per annum by the 1780s) brought their own ideas of monarchical justice to the colony.[47]

The political ideas held by slave rebels were, of course, not static but rather evolved as the movement pursued its goals of reform of the slave system and then wholesale emancipation. For nearly two years after the outbreak of the August 1791 revolt, the war between the insurgents and the French colonial state remained a bloody stalemate. This owed in part to the fact that even though the insurgency dominated much of the countryside, it held little control over major port cities until the summer of 1793.[48] By 6 December 1791, according to one report, 10,000 to 12,000 slave "rebels" were fighting under assorted chieftains; 2,000 to 3,000 of these answered to Jean-François and Biassou, who were based in Grande-Rivière. The Count of Gaston, this report's author, further argued that the "Mulattos" were the "hidden leaders of the revolt" who "had spread out easily and quickly in traversing the Spanish Lands with their Comrades and their brothers from Mirebalais [Saint-Domingue]."[49] Nonetheless, Jean-François and Biassou were the insurgency's most important leaders.[50] In late 1791, seeking to end the grinding conflict, the former presented a series of conditions for surrender to the Colonial Assembly: freedom for several hundred of the principal insurgents, complete amnesty for all rebels, and prohibition of the whip. French colonial authorities rejected these demands.[51]

In the months following the failed negotiations, the rebellion came to embrace more radical goals, which were articulated in a remarkable July 1792 entreaty to "the general assembly, the national commissioners and the citizens of the French part of Saint Domingue" purportedly signed by Jean-François, Biassou, and a third individual named Belair.[52] This missive denounced the institution of slavery as antithetical to "natural right," fiercely attacked racism, and demanded "general liberty for all men detained in slavery," a blanket amnesty, and "the guarantee of these articles by the Spanish government." In exchange, the authors promised the cessation of armed resistance and the rebels' return to the plantations, where a new wage labor system would commence. The authors also eloquently invoked the "French constitution"; the "declaration of the rights of man"; and "the natural rights [including] liberty, property[,] security and resistance to oppression."[53] Assuming that this letter indeed reflects the motivations and political thinking of at least a portion of the slave rebels,[54] it attests to their creative engagement with the intellectual currents of the revolutionary Atlantic and to their comprehension of the importance of Santo Domingo to the events unfolding in the French colony.

Though the prospects for "general liberty for all men detained in slavery" appeared remote in both parts of the island in the summer of 1792, by that time the slave insurgency had yielded a more limited but still momentous gain: the passage of a law on 4 April 1792 by the French National Assembly that at last granted equal political rights to all free men in Saint-Domingue, regardless of race, in unequivocal terms.[55] The law's framers had designed it largely with the aim of ending the acrimonious struggle between whites and *gens de couleur libres* so that they might put aside their differences to confront a common enemy. Yet anticipating the difficulties that would arise as authorities tried to enforce the new law, the National Assembly deployed a fleet headed by a warship called the *America* to Saint-Domingue that contained 6,000 troops (more than France had sent several decades earlier to assist in the liberation of the Thirteen Colonies), a new governor-general to replace the despised Blanchelande, and three members of a Civil Commission named Léger-Félicité Sonthonax, Étienne Polverel, and Jean-Antoine Ailhaud. The assembly's deputies charged the expedition with two principal tasks: protecting the rights of the "citizens of 4 April" and crushing the slave revolt. The fleet arrived in the harbor of Le Cap on 13 September 1792.[56]

Sonthonax and Polverel (having been abandoned by Ailhaud soon after their arrival on the island) confronted an adversary that was perennially threatened by disunity in spite of its numerical superiority. Leaders such as Jean-François, Biassou, and an obscure but strong-willed and militarily gifted former slave (and onetime slave owner) named François Dominique Toussaint Louverture (who had joined the rebellion in November 1791) competed for authority over the movement.[57] At first, it appeared that Sonthonax and Polverel would prove no more willing than their predecessors to make meaningful concessions that might bring the warfare to a halt. In a 24 September 1792 proclamation to the "Free Men of Saint-Domingue," the civil commissioners had declared that "slavery is necessary to agriculture and to the prosperity of the colonies, and it accords with neither our principles, nor the will of the national assembly and of the king, to affect in this regard the prerogatives of the colonists."[58] Though both men opposed slavery in principle, they initially professed imminent abolition to be incompatible with their mission to defeat the slave uprising and defend the colonial plantation system. (Their hesitance to support immediate abolition placed them in the company of prerevolutionary French abolitionists, most of whom had advocated gradual emancipation.[59]) It would take severe military setbacks to convince them to align "principles" with policy.

Meanwhile, as they played their diplomatic double game regarding the Dominguan slave revolt, Dominican authorities confronted a refugee crisis exacerbated by the proximity and extent of the border, which touched all three provinces of Saint-Domingue and was quite close to the initial locus of the rebellion, as we have seen. On 18 November 1792, García informed one Pedro Acuña that in late October several of García's subordinates had helped to resettle numerous "Free mulattos" from Saint-Domingue who were "requesting asylum in our lands to free themselves from the furor of the Blacks who pursue their lives." "The Blacks traverse the entire frontier [with Santo Domingo] pursuing families of Mulattos, free Blacks, and Whites that they encounter," García wrote. "Neither women, nor young children are pardoned, and people look from the Spanish land with great vigilance and caution." In their efforts to assist these refugees, Spanish authorities resettled near Marmelade (a northern parish in Saint-Domingue on the colonial border) seventy-two "Persons of color of both sexes, fleeing the harshness of the Blacks."[60] Though these polemics clearly reflect the anxieties and fears of Spanish authorities, flight from the neighboring colony does appear to have had significant demographic effects in Santo Domingo. On 25 September 1793, Fernando Portillo y Torres, the archbishop of Santo Domingo, described that colony as "a dominion on Spanish land almost more populated by Frenchmen than by Spaniards." Many of these refugees had, according to Portillo, arrived on "unarmed Boats . . . loaded with Frenchmen, and French women, who flee from the colony [Saint-Domingue]."[61]

Enslaved refugees also made their way to Santo Domingo, prompting some Spanish and French colonial authorities to temporarily close ranks for the sake of stability. In November 1792, Gaspar de Casasola, a Spanish official in the town of Dajabón near the border with Saint-Domingue, promised the acting governor of Saint-Domingue, Donatien Marie Joseph de Rochambeau, that he would return to French officials the nearly one hundred fugitive slaves under his control plus any who fled to Dajabón in the future in order to preserve "the strongest union of the two nations" and to "return to the colony [Saint-Domingue] its former happiness."[62] In a report on military victories against the "brigands" in this border area dated 9 November 1792, Rochambeau asserted that Casasola had exhibited the "happiest dispositions" toward his request for the prompt return of "many blacks who have taken refuge in Laxavon [Dajabón], that I have claimed from the governor by virtue of [several] treaties" signed between the two powers.[63]

The vicissitudes of race, diplomacy, imperial rivalry, the long history of intercolonial contraband and conflict, and ideological tensions thus produced contradictory policies in Santo Domingo with respect to the crisis in Saint-Domingue. The coming of war between France and Spain in Europe in 1793 would dramatically alter this situation and reshape the political geography of the island.

The War for Hispaniola, 1793–1795

On the eve of the August 1791 slave uprising, a piece in a periodical based in Le Cap called *Les Affiches Américaines* had compared French soldiers under the ancien régime to "such perfect slaves," who had been subject to "cruel prejudice." By contrast, under the new order a man of even the humblest background could acquire full citizenship following sixteen years of military service.[64] The motif of slavery was favored by many political thinkers of the era, such as Jean-Paul Marat, whose 1774 treatise, *Chains of Slavery* (republished in 1793), cautioned against the menace of despotism and juxtaposed liberty against the servitude imposed by despotic rulers.[65]

The fall of 1792 witnessed a sea change in both the struggle against real slavery in the colonies and that against metaphorical slavery in mainland France. In September of that year, Sonthonax and Polverel disembarked in

Saint-Domingue; meanwhile, in France, political leaders proclaimed the birth of the French Republic, replacing the National Assembly with a new legislative body called the National Convention. Though the establishment of a constitutional monarchy the previous year had inspired hopes in France that the political turmoil was at an end, fierce conflicts between ideologically diverse political factions over a range of issues—especially the extent of the king's powers under the new arrangement—contributed to an insurrection in Paris on 10 August 1792 that effectively ended the constitutional monarchy.[66]

This tumult in France intersected with the complicated geopolitical chessboard that was European politics in the late eighteenth century. France and Britain, the two superpowers of that century, had traded victories in the Seven Years' War and American Revolutionary War, but a number of other European actors, such as the Dutch, Prussians, and Spanish, also competed for power in shifting alliances that played out in the seemingly incessant wars fought between these nations across the globe. The advent of the French Revolution, however, created dramatic new fault lines for conflict on a continent dominated by monarchs. In 1792, Austria and Prussia went to war against France over a series of issues, including the status of the Austrian Netherlands (now Belgium) and the threat posed by the French Revolution to the Holy Roman Empire (based in Austria) and to monarchy in general. This catalyzed a protracted series of international conflagrations that would end in 1814 with the defeat of Napoleonic France. The manpower needs of France in these wars, combined with emerging ideologies of nationalism, helped create the potent political device of the "citizen-soldier" in Europe and the Caribbean during these decades—a device that would prove integral when this geopolitical conflict intersected with the ongoing slave revolt in Hispaniola.[67]

The geopolitical crisis in Europe, along with events in the Americas, also shattered the old alliance between France and Spain, which had been based on the "family compact" between the Bourbon monarchs who had ruled both lands. In addition to Spanish-American colonial officials' antipathy toward the radical ideas associated with the French Revolution and the long history of intercolonial squabbling in Hispaniola, the failure of France to intervene on Spain's behalf in a dispute between the latter and Britain over territory in the Nootka Sound in the North American Pacific Northwest in 1790 contributed to a major diplomatic and geostrategic defeat for Spain, which in turn weakened relations between the Iberian nation and France.

Then, following the establishment of the French Republic, the Republic's conquest of the Austrian Netherlands in late 1792, and the execution of King Louis XVI on 21 January 1793 following a trial by the National Convention, Spain formally joined an anti-French military coalition that also included Britain, Austria, Holland, Prussia, and several other nations in February 1793.[68]

Once news of the war with France reached Governor García in Santo Domingo in May 1793, the old colonial hand finally abandoned the fiction of official neutrality and mobilized three militia companies of whites and two of *morenos* (dark-skinned individuals) in preparation for an invasion of Saint-Domingue.[69] García and his superiors in Madrid hoped to recapture the western part of the island and to then harness its great wealth; Madrid accordingly ordered Dominican authorities to recruit slave rebels with enticements of freedom and land.[70]

The Spanish military mobilization against France in the Caribbean cannot be fully understood without taking into account the centrality of Cuba as Spain's principal military nerve center in the Caribbean and as an aspiring successor to French Saint-Domingue as the hemisphere's premier plantation colony. Though Santo Domingo city was the oldest seat of European authority in the Americas and still stood as an important regional center of governance, the eastern part of Hispaniola had long played second fiddle militarily to Cuba due to the latter's strategic location. Havana accordingly constituted a staging ground for the deployment of military forces from places such as New Spain to Santo Domingo and Spanish Louisiana during the early 1790s.[71] The résumés of many military leaders in Santo Domingo in the latter part of the eighteenth century had in fact included a stint in Cuba;[72] this was reciprocated during the Franco-Spanish war in the 1790s, when thousands of the "Spanish" men fighting in Hispaniola against the French were Cuban.[73] This, in combination with an influx of refugees of all colors from both parts of Hispaniola, afforded many Cubans a personal view of the Haitian Revolution.

Havana's influence on Santo Domingo became particularly salient within the context of Madrid's relatively lax oversight over the latter, at least before the war with France. During the early years of the Haitian Revolution, García often acted semi-independently of the Crown, as we have seen with his policy of offering aid to the insurgents behind a veneer of official neutrality. Though García was hardly the first Spanish-American official to circumvent royal authority, the marginal status of Santo Domingo in the Spanish empire may have given him a freer rein than his counterparts in New Spain or Peru.[74] In any event, perhaps García's brashest show of autonomy was his decision to experiment with a quasi-formal alliance with the Dominguan insurgents even before learning of the declaration of war with France.

As news of a growing diplomatic crisis with France reached the island, García had proclaimed on 19 April 1793 that he was implementing a policy that would "admit under [the king's] sovereign protection all the [Saint-Domingue] Blacks who have sustained the war against the diabolical maxims of the whites."[75] In a 14 May 1793 letter to Don Pedro de Acuña, García detailed the successes of three emissaries in their overtures to the three principal black "Chiefs": Jean-François, Georges Biassou, and Hyacinthe.[76] "All [of these black leaders] with their soldiers are disposed to follow the royal standards of His Majesty, [and] live under his royal Protection, and [they are] ready to sacrifice their lives in honor of his crown," García told Acuña.[77]

Despite such pronouncements, these and other black leaders carefully weighed their possibilities for freedom and the military balance of power between Spain and France (and later Britain) in their decision making. Ex-slaves such as Biassou who opted to ally with Spain against France made an "informed and pragmatic" decision, in Jane Landers's words, within the context of the unstable political situation on the island and the Spanish king's and other authorities' previous concessions of freedom, land, and remuneration for slaves who had defected to Spain or enlisted in colonial armies in diverse parts of the empire.[78] Some Dominguan slaves' support for the Spanish king may have even been reinforced by their possible knowledge that their counterparts in Santo Domingo often enjoyed much more autonomy from the colonial state and the plantation than they did.[79]

Jean-François, Biassou, Toussaint Louverture, and other rebel leaders who accepted Spain's offer became part of a military unit known as the "Black Auxiliaries of Carlos IV," whom Spanish colonial authorities kept segregated from the "Spanish militias" that had long defended Santo Domingo.[80] Though it would take the destruction of Saint-Domingue's most important city in June 1793 to convince the French to follow suit, the eventual French military manumission policy coupled an offer of liberty for slaves who chose to enlist with an attempt to achieve a greater degree of racial integration within the military in the spirit of the 4 April 1792 law.[81] The new imperial conflict thus transformed thousands of rebel slaves from feared insurgents into coveted targets of military recruitment campaigns. In the words of

Julius Scott, this conflict between the Spanish and the French in Hispaniola and other parts of the Caribbean "involved a struggle for hearts and minds as much as a military contest."[82]

Nonetheless, these new recruits needed weapons. Jean-François and other black officers repeatedly requested and often received arms and provisions from white Spanish officials, though financial stringencies and other considerations resulted in the inconsistent distribution of these items.[83]

Did the military successes of the slave rebels impel colonial authorities to recruit enslaved soldiers, or was such recruitment merely another utilization of a proven, if risky, military strategy that saw the insurgents as pawns in great power politics? European powers had been waging armed struggles against each other on American battlefields for centuries before 1793, and some of these conflicts (perhaps most famously the American Revolution) had involved the arming of slaves.[84] Yet according to David Geggus, the 1793–95 war in the Caribbean marked a significant departure from previous instances in which authorities had armed New World slave populations.[85] While prior official sanction of martial activity among slaves had chiefly involved arming them in a condition of clear subjugation, in 1793 European colonial authorities appealed to slaves who had "effectively already freed themselves."[86]

In addition, the political and ideological terrain was undergoing dramatic changes. "With the greatest ardor they speak in [Le Cap] of granting Freedom to all the Blacks, and expatriating them so that they carry the lighted fuse in one hand and in the other the revolution to this entire new world," García had warned Pedro de Acuña on 13 January 1793. According to García, many partisans of the revolution in France wished to "achieve, or put in motion the treacherous ideas that the first moments of the French Revolution displayed in its seditious Public Papers."[87]

In their war against the French, García and his colleagues struggled to appease two groups with seemingly diametrically opposed interests: the slave warriors and French royalist émigrés, especially planters. On 13 July 1793, an official in the city of Santo Domingo (probably García) explained to a subordinate that the former understood "the arduous undertaking of reconciling the wills of the French whites, with the Blacks our allies upon whom [the whites] yesterday looked with a superiority and scorn that is evident."[88]

In their efforts to "reconcile the wills" of these groups, Spanish officials drew upon one of the oldest and most respected forms of traditional authority: the clergy. As we have seen, Catholic religious authorities were held in high esteem by many of the slave rebels. This common bond between the insurgents and the white royalist French led García, the leader of the hemisphere's oldest Catholic polity, to call upon priests in his attempts to bridge the seemingly insurmountable divide between former slaveholders and those whom they had once held in bondage.[89] García and his peers probably reasoned that this strategy would also serve to counteract the influence of the anticlerical radicals purportedly responsible for destroying the French monarchical regime. Above all, Spanish officials aimed to utilize religion as a form of social cohesion in order to lessen the dangers that arming these former bondsmen might present to the colonial regime. While the use of spiritual influence to buttress political and military authority will not surprise those familiar with Spanish colonialism in the Americas, this would prove to be no ordinary colonial war.

In April 1793, García had entrusted Don José Vázquez, a curate from Dajabón, with the task of effectively recruiting the services of Jean-François. According to a detailed account composed by García, Vázquez departed to meet with Jean-François on the night of 30 April 1793. After traveling to several plantations in search of the elusive leader, the priest finally met Jean-François when the latter presented himself with more than 200 men in tow; the fact that the enigmatic chieftain also arrived with twelve close advisors may not have been lost on this priest. In any event, with much pomp and circumstance on both sides, Jean-François met his interlocutor with "veneration" and pledged his loyalty to the cause of God and King, while Father Vázquez accepted his allegiance and promised that he and his men would be amply rewarded.[90]

Although Catholic doctrine had long provided certain rights for slaves throughout Spanish America, rarely had religious officials interacted with slaves or ex-slaves on terms of equality or near equality.[91] In Santo Domingo in early 1793, Father Vázquez and Jean-François engaged in a complicated ritual that went far beyond a simple story of subordination. Not only did Jean-François keep the priest waiting for several hours and appear (in elegant clothes and on horseback) only after the latter sent an underling out to find him, the black leader also obtained promises of munitions, food, clothing, and high military ranks for himself and his followers. Though Jean-François and his partisans did show a certain amount of deference as well as "love and loyalty" to the priest and his cause, offering to "sacrifice their lives for the Spanish Crown," this was no different from what white Spanish subjects at the time might have pledged in a political crisis.[92] Furthermore, Vázquez played the role of not just a religious leader but also a political ambassador and military advisor. Thus, even as the Spanish sought to reaffirm their power through the figure of the priest, Jean-François in his actions and words created new possibilities for the assertion of political will by those who had toiled in servitude only months or years earlier. Religious and political ideas, personalities, and military circumstances combined in unique ways to empower this leader to negotiate on equal terms with a priest sent to recruit him to defend a colonial regime. Jean-François acceded to these entreaties, but on his own terms and largely for his own ends.

Spanish appeals to traditional authority sometimes also were met with creative responses by black leaders who employed symbols considered subversive by many European colonial authorities. Sometime around February 1793, the black general Hyacinthe had informed Governor García that his French enemies had forced him into retreat. "I have the honor of assuring you," Hyacinthe declared, "that I am a maroon [*cimarrón*] in the woods awaiting your response [to my letter]."[93]

Hyacinthe deployed powerful language to affirm his freedom in a correspondence with a representative of a colonial regime committed to the maintenance of slavery. His French adversaries, meanwhile, in response to the continued militancy of black rebels, military losses to the Spanish, and a devastating civil conflict in Le Cap, soon adopted the most daring tactic of all: complete emancipation.

The Coming of Emancipation to the Island

"The Sword of vengeance is suspended above your heads: a fatal error enchants you: what blind fury animates you, arms you against your protectors, your brothers, against your Friends, against your fatherland?" On 8 August 1793, an anonymous author or authors sympathetic to the French Republic composed a polemical tract addressed to formerly enslaved insurgents from Saint-Domingue who had taken up arms for the Spanish enemy. "Open your eyes, and know your true interests!" this author exhorted these rebels. By renouncing the Spanish "yoke of oppression" and proclaiming loyalty to the French Republic, these wayward souls might achieve a "perfect equality" with all other men, according to this tract. Nonetheless, this newfound liberty and equality would have conditions. Though liberty was an "inherent right of man," these soldiers would enjoy this right only "when you submit to order, when you put yourselves under the protection of the Law, [and] when you make yourselves useful to your Fatherland in the type of work in which it judges you ought to be employed." Failure to do so would risk a perilous descent into an "immoral liberty" that could lead to the ruin of the Republican state itself.[94]

Though this letter underwent a process of translation and transcription by Spanish colonial authorities, it conveys a sense of the intensity of the effort to recruit ex-slaves—and it also hints at the restrictions that French authorities would place on the liberty of the newly freed. Over the summer of 1793, the French Republican civil commissioners Sonthonax and Polverel gradually abandoned their attempts to preserve the slave system by first offering freedom to those who would fight for the French Republic and then taking the unprecedented step of unilaterally decreeing the end of slavery in French Saint-Domingue. Though this outcome was far from certain upon the outbreak of war with Spain, the French ended up having to free the slaves who had built the colony's prosperity in order to save the colony itself.

At the beginning of that fateful summer, the ideological and military conflict with Spain intersected with an internal contest for political power among French Republicans. This struggle pitted Sonthonax and Polverel and their allies (including many *gens de couleur libres* along with some white soldiers and civilians) against hundreds of mostly white sailors and soldiers. Many of the latter had become resentful of the efforts of the commissioners to enforce the 4 April 1792 racial equality law, and many also blamed Sonthonax and Polverel for the widespread disease, acute supply shortages, frequent suspensions of pay, and resultant lack of morale afflicting them, which was worsened by an economic crisis.[95]

These disaffected individuals came to rally around François-Thomas Galbaud du Fort, the colony's new governor-general, who shortly after arriving in Le Cap in early May 1793 commenced a personal and political rivalry with the commissioners. Events escalated into an armed struggle in Le Cap between the two factions that resulted in a fire that destroyed this once-prosperous city as well as the departure of Galbaud, numerous naval officers and enlisted men, and a contingent of refugees for France on 23–25 June. Nonetheless, the threat of the city's capture had convinced the commissioners to offer freedom to all "black warriors who will fight for the republic" via a proclamation issued on 21 June 1793.[96]

This document, limited as it was, contained the seeds of a much more radical transformation. Aside from its promise of manumission in exchange for military service, the proclamation proposed measures to improve the condition of those still in slavery: assurances that masters would not "mistreat [slaves] as before"; that slaves would receive more substantial food rations and have more time for their "own affairs"; and that slaves would have "sure means by which to purchase themselves, in return for a predetermined sum." Perhaps most notably, Sonthonax and Polverel also proposed a scheme of emancipation characterized by "gradually giving freedom to blacks who will offer superior proof of their good conduct and assiduity to labor, and at the same time giving them land in property sufficient for their honest subsistence and that of their families."[97]

In a 10 July 1793 letter to the National Convention composed in defense of their actions during the carnage in Le Cap, which had cost an estimated 3,000 to 10,000 lives,[98] the commissioners lamented the pillage and looting of the city, wherein "brigands of all colors fought over the fruit of their rapine, [and] fired their guns indiscriminately." Amid this disorder, the commissioners found themselves among "several troops of insurgent slaves" who, despite possessing numerous "Spanish cockades," had "abandoned the royal colors to take those of the republic," vowing to "serve the [French] nation against kings." "We explained to them, and they understood very well that it was kings who sold men, that the republic by contrast only wanted free men," proclaimed the commissioners. As for Galbaud's partisans, many had by the commissioners' account fled to Santo Domingo, where they collaborated with about a thousand "traitors" to the Republic to take three key posts in the border area.[99]

Galbaud's version of events offered a starkly different interpretation. In a letter that the former governor composed on 17 July 1793, he presented himself as having engaged in a valiant struggle against the interconnected threats of the "Rebel blacks" and the Spanish enemy. According to Galbaud, attempting to depose the commissioners by military force had been necessary in order to ensure Saint-Domingue's stability and security. With "our borders threatened by the Spanish, no army to oppose them, the impotent pain of seeing the Rebel Slaves Supported by the Spanish, [and] a universal discontent against the Commissioners," Saint-Domingue had in Galbaud's depiction been in an acutely vulnerable position upon his arrival. Declaring that he had been "received in Le Cap as the Savior of The Colony," Galbaud justified appointing his brother César to the post of commander in the northern towns of Fort-Dauphin and Ouanaminthe as a necessary measure to combat the Spanish threat from nearby Dajabón.[100]

In spite of Galbaud's defeat, his warnings concerning the Spanish menace began to appear more prescient in the months following the episode in Le Cap, as the Republicans suffered numerous defeats at the hands of the Spanish and their formerly enslaved allies. The formalization of the alliance between García and Jean-François, Biassou, and Toussaint had garnered some 10,000 men for the Spanish side. With this military assistance, much of the northern part of French Saint-Domingue fell to the Spanish by the end of 1793.[101] Julien Raimond would later write that "eight to ten thousand French blacks under the orders of Jean François, armed for their Liberty at the beginning of the revolution; were attracted by the Spanish government" via the bestowal of "titles and decorations" on rebel leaders and promises of "Liberty for all black soldiers in the name of the King of Spain."[102]

The failure of the commissioners to attract the principal insurgent leaders to the French side impelled them to appeal directly to the insurgent rank and file with inducements that went beyond their 21 June military manumission decree.[103] Chief among these were two orders issued in July and August 1793 that loosened restrictions on manumission. In the first, dated 11 July, the commissioners decreed that a marriage contracted between a free and an enslaved partner would liberate the unfree person as well as the couple's children.[104] The second proclamation stipulated that henceforth a master could free his slave "notwithstanding all opposition and without needing to satisfy the formality of posting and publication that preceded the ratification of liberties, which is and remains abrogated." Though the master still had to appear before his or her municipality and present either a "title of property" or the testimony of three local citizens in order to legalize the manumission, there was no requirement to obtain the approval of higher authorities, contrary to the law in Saint-Domingue since 1711.[105]

The commissioners' evolving policy toward slaves and freed persons, though somewhat haphazard, was shaped by ideas of citizenship rooted in masculine virtue and female subordination. This became particularly evident in the 11 July order, which specifically aimed to liberate the wives of newly freed soldiers. According to Elizabeth Colwill, "Republican marriage and martial fraternity would serve as the twin pillars of the commissioners' vision of racial equality" under their new regime; by this logic, "women would win their freedom by virtue of their relationship to men," rather than by their own merits or actions.[106] Yet women played key roles in the complicated transition to emancipation in these critical years, especially in their resistance first to slavery and then to the forced labor regimes that Sonthonax and Polverel would enact after abolition.[107]

Such resistance, in combination with the limitations of the July and August decrees and the military power of Spain's black allies, contributed to the failure of the commissioners to significantly alter the course of the war with Spain as the summer of 1793 wore on. This led the commissioners to consider more radical measures. In a letter to the National Convention dated 30 July 1793, Sonthonax had argued that the defeat of the "Spanish power" in Hispaniola would represent the first step in the "inauguration of Liberty in the new world." He then called upon the rulers of France to finally couple their rejection of the metaphorical slavery of the ancien régime with the abolition of real slavery in the colonies. "It is now up to you, citizen representatives, to pronounce upon a great matter, which is the state of unfree people in the colony," Sonthonax proclaimed. Elaborating that "the [National] convention is too Just and too fond of humanity, to not proclaim great principles," the politically savvy Jacobin lawyer then delivered the coup de grâce: "The declaration of rights no longer permits [the convention] to tolerate one man being the property of another: Slavers and kings should be treated equally: they must cease their tyranny, and abandon their prey, or they will disappear from the surface of the globe."[108]

The key leaders of the so-called black auxiliaries who remained allied with the Spanish nevertheless had their own ideas of freedom. On 25 August 1793, Biassou issued his own proclamation to all black soldiers serving under the Spanish in the occupied part of Saint-Domingue. Imploring these individuals to continue to reject the "seduction" and "deception" of the French Republican siren song of liberty that was but a "chimera," Biassou portrayed the commissioners as a continuation of the French colonial forces that had fought in vain for two years to "reduce us to the most astonishing servitude." As nothing less than "enemies of the human race," the French Republicans in Biassou's mind not only fought against the cause of liberty but did not possess the right to grant liberty to anyone, as only "our master," the Spanish king, had that right.[109]

Although it is unclear to what extent such royalist-inflected appeals by prominent ex-slaves directly influenced the actions of Sonthonax, the limited efficacy of the French efforts to "fuse the black insurgency with the French [Republican] cause," in Popkin's words, appears to have convinced

Sonthonax that waiting on Paris to act on the question of emancipation was militarily untenable.[110] The fact that many of the ex-slave soldiers and those still in slavery held monarchical loyalties was also well known to Sonthonax and other French leaders; indeed, as we have seen, Sonthonax had already apparently attempted to discredit the institution of monarchy in the eyes of some insurgents by equating it with slavery even before his 30 July appeal to the National Convention. Toussaint Louverture himself, in a 27 August 1793 letter intended as a public statement, doubtless spoke for many other freedmen-in-arms: the "criminality" of the French Republicans, who "put [King Louis XVI] to death like the worst of villains," was reason enough to remain allied with Spain. "As long as God gives us the force and the means," Toussaint declared, "we will acquire another Liberty, different from that which you tyrants [the French commissioners] pretend to impose on us."[111]

The fact that Sonthonax emitted his landmark 29 August 1793 general emancipation decree during an epistolary and ideological battle with Toussaint[112] further suggests that Sonthonax aimed to disarm the potency of the Spanish arguments that merged ex-slaves' embrace of elements of royalist ideologies with their struggles to preserve their freedom. As the month of August drew to a close, Sonthonax came to realize that the only way to convince the black majority that the French Republic indeed "only wanted free men," to quote the 10 July 1793 letter authored by Polverel and him, was to dismantle the slave system itself.

Other forces also conspired to tip the scales in favor of emancipation. The departure of Polverel, who was more cautious on the issue of slavery, to the French colony's western province at the end of July may have left Sonthonax (based in the north) with a freer hand to act. Moreover, in addition to the continuing difficulties of recruiting black troops, black soldiers' apparent refusal to enforce discipline on the plantations that remained in operation convinced Sonthonax that desperate times did indeed call for desperate measures. A final factor was, fittingly enough, a manifestation of the Jacobin ideal of popular democracy: on 24 August, an assembly of 15,000 persons in Le Cap voted for the elimination of slavery in the north of Saint-Domingue.[113] Sonthonax informed Polverel on 10 September that he had received in Le Cap a petition with more than 600 signatures—including those of many "landowners"—urging him to "declare the general liberty of all the slaves in the Northern Province." In this letter, Sonthonax also decried French royalist émigrés and the "Spanish" for enticing "brigands" to fight on their side by appealing to the "liberty that Louis XVII [the son of the executed French king] had accorded them." "If our armies had disadvantages," Sonthonax claimed, "it was because the black soldiers fought with repugnance against their brothers, who had [as] the excuse for their error, the desire to see the black race enjoy the rights of man."[114]

On 29 August 1793, Sonthonax issued a decree composed of thirty-eight articles that formally emancipated all slaves in the northern province of Saint-Domingue. Though Sonthonax advanced legalistic arguments to explain his decision to reverse his previous policy toward slavery, he presented this proclamation as a revolutionary triumph for all those freed by it.[115] In the preamble to this emancipation decree, Sonthonax again condemned both African and European kings as enslavers, asserting that "kings are only happy in a society of slaves: it is they who, on the coasts of Africa, sold you to the whites: it is the tyrants of Europe who would wish to perpetuate this notorious traffic. The REPUBLIC adopts you as its children; kings only aspire to place you in chains or to destroy you." Toward the end of this preamble, Sonthonax eloquently summarized his appeal: "And you, citizens fooled by the notorious royalists; you who, under the flags and the liveries of the cowardly Spaniard, fight blindly against your own interests, against the freedom of your wives and children, finally thus open your eyes to the immense advantages that the Republic offers you. Kings promise you freedom: but do you see that they grant it to their subjects?"[116]

In the key article of this 29 August order, Sonthonax proclaimed that "all the blacks and mixed-bloods, currently in slavery, are declared free to enjoy all the rights associated with the title of French citizen; they will nonetheless be subject to a regime whose details are contained in the following articles."[117] After issuing a series of gradual emancipation orders, Polverel followed Sonthonax and declared the institution of slavery dead in Saint-Domingue's other two provinces, the west and south, on 31 October 1793.

Yet Saint-Domingue was still a colony of France, and Sonthonax knew that the survival of his emancipation decree ultimately depended on Paris's assent. Sonthonax had accordingly supervised the election of a multiracial delegation composed of six men in late September 1793 whom he entrusted with convincing the National Convention to confirm his emancipation order. Though only three of these men escaped the efforts of refugees to detain them during a stopover in the United States, the three who made it to Paris (a French-born plantation owner named Louis Dufay, a mixed-race individual named Jean-Baptiste Mills, and a freed military officer named Jean-Baptiste Belley) outmaneuvered their enemies in the French capital.

Assisted by the impassioned oratory of Dufay, the party succeeded in persuading the National Convention not only to uphold Sonthonax's abolitionist measure but to extend it to the entire French empire by a universal emancipation law of 4 February 1794.[118]

"To Die before Being Slaves"

By the end of the summer of 1793, emancipation had thus triumphed in the northern province of Saint-Domingue, with the rest of the colony and then Paris to soon follow. Yet on the heels of Sonthonax's emancipation decree, another slaveholding power invaded the French part of Hispaniola. Earlier in the 1790s, anxious white planters in French Saint-Domingue had appealed to the British for assistance, responding to the slave insurgency, the alliance between the commissioners and the *gens de couleur libres*, fears of a possible general emancipation decree, and other forces. These overtures became formalized in a capitulation accord signed by British officials and some of these planters in 1793.[119] The coming of war with France that same year led to a five-year British campaign for French Saint-Domingue that commenced with an initial landing on the island in September. This ill-fated campaign, which is discussed in further detail in chapter 3, quickly came to rely on black troops, who were recruited with promises of eventual freedom. This recruitment owed in part to the dreadful loss of life among the forces deployed to this theater by Britain from beyond Hispaniola.[120] Although the British managed to occupy a third of Saint-Domingue in the first eight months of the invasion (including the key posts of Saint-Marc in the west, Jérémie in the south, and Môle Saint-Nicholas in the north), the redcoats' enterprise in Hispaniola was gravely undermined by their reliance on slavery and their maintenance of a strict racial hierarchy among free persons in the areas that they occupied.[121]

Though Governor García and his colleagues in Santo Domingo would likewise refuse to emulate the French example of general emancipation, they undertook their own strategies to combat the possibility that the French commissioners' "ideas and intentions will take their place in the hearts of our black allies," as García put it in an October 1793 letter. Namely, in response to Sonthonax's emancipation act, García promulgated two counter-proclamations.[122] While he directed the first proclamation at the "whites and people of honor"[123] living in Saint-Domingue who might be persuaded to swear allegiance to the Spanish monarch, García composed the other in order to reassure his black troops that the cause of "God, King and State" was just.[124]

In the address to the "people of honor," García offered a simple and stark choice: submit to the will of the Spanish monarch and swear to henceforth "be loyal and obedient Spaniards" in exchange for royal protection and the rewards of the king's "highest equity and benevolence," or face swift military persecution. García promised that "all good French people, without distinction of state or condition," would receive the king's protection should they join the Spanish side. He also vowed that Spanish rule would bring about the "reflourishing" of Saint-Domingue and usher in a new era of "prosperity" and "stability."[125] Though García did not explicitly mention slavery, many of the colonists to whom García addressed his communication would doubtless have equated "prosperity" and "stability" with the restoration of white supremacy and plantation slavery in Saint-Domingue.

While in his first proclamation García spoke of "liberating" Saint-Domingue from the French Republicans, he offered a very different definition of liberty to former slaves. To his black troops, García presented the civil commissioners as having recently "promised in the Parish Church of [Le Cap] in the presence of the Most Holy Sacrament, and with the agreement of the People, that a thousand lives would be lost before permitting the Slaves to attain liberty." García framed the emancipation decree of the previous August, along with other acts of the commissioners, as desperate and insincere maneuvers undertaken by cowards motivated by "insatiable ambition and greed" who "only aspire to . . . despotism."[126] In depicting these men as hypocritical tyrants, García hoped to remind black recruits that only a short time earlier, Sonthonax and Polverel as well as their predecessors had militarily opposed the liberty that they held so dear. "The disposition [of the rebels]," García had stated in a January 1792 letter, "is to die before being slaves."[127]

Though García was hardly a card-carrying abolitionist—he had sought to circumscribe or eliminate some forms of manumission as a colonel in Santo Domingo in the 1780s, and as discussed earlier in this chapter, he never sought to dismantle slavery in his colony[128]—his appeal to former slaves may have been strengthened by the limitations of the new postslave regime instituted by the French commissioners. In his 29 August freedom proclamation, Sonthonax had established a strict labor code that would serve as the basis for "free" labor regimes in the colony for the next eight years. Seeking to generate revenue and procure manpower to fuel the French Republican war effort, Sonthonax set forth a series of instructions that aimed to tie ex-slaves to their plantations or enlist them in Republican armies. "A new order will be reborn," Sonthonax declared, "and the old servitude will vanish. Do not believe nonetheless that the liberty that you will enjoy, is a state of laziness and idleness. . . . Return to your plantations or the location of your former owners, you will receive a salary for your troubles; [and] you will not be subjected anymore to the humiliating punishment that had once been inflicted on you."[129]

In Articles IX–XI of the 29 August proclamation, Sonthonax laid out the crux of his labor code: the "blacks currently attached to the plantations of their former masters, will be required to remain there; they shall be employed in cultivating the land"; currently enlisted black soldiers could opt for plantation labor, but only if they received permission from their commanding officer and found a suitable replacement; and the "formerly enslaved cultivators" must continue to labor on their old plantations for one year, unless a judge of the peace granted them permission to change plantations. Moreover, within two weeks of the issuance of this proclamation, all men who did not own property and were not in the military, working on a plantation, or in domestic service were to be arrested and imprisoned, while women who did not have "known means of existence" and were not engaged in either plantation work or domestic labor were to also be detained. Plantation laborers and domestics also had to remain in their local district unless they received written permission from a municipal authority to depart.[130]

Along with these restrictions came certain limited rights. While Sonthonax followed the old *Code Noir* in granting the *cultivateurs* (plantation laborers) the right to have Sundays to themselves, he surpassed the code in abolishing the whip and in giving these *cultivateurs* two hours per day to cultivate their own grounds. In another departure from the slave regime, these plantation laborers were to receive a salary (drawn from one-quarter of plantation revenue), and children aged ten to fifteen years could only be employed in guarding animals and in gathering and sorting coffee and cotton. Article XIX remarkably declared that the *cultivateurs* were to receive small plots of land that were to be "divided equitably between each family, with respect to the quality of the land and the quantity that should be accorded." This could potentially have served as a basis for the attainment of greater economic independence by former slaves. Precisely for this reason, this article was virtually ignored by successive Republican administrators in Saint-Domingue.[131]

Resistance to this new plantation regime commenced as soon as news of the 29 August proclamation became known. In his letter to Polverel dated 10 September 1793, Sonthonax had complained that "the warriors [entrusted with enforcing the new labor code] have constantly refused to force the cultivators and the laborers to work."[132] What is more, the laborers themselves offered resistance in a variety of forms, such as demanding additional rest days, flight, theft, selling plantation products for their own benefit, and armed insurrection.[133]

Those allied with the Spanish strove to win over some of these discontented individuals by offering their own path to freedom. In a 10 September 1793 letter to García, Biassou's trusted subordinate, Gabriel Belair, outlined a plan that would eventually manumit new military recruits while maintaining a subservient labor force on the plantations of a newly conquered Spanish Saint-Domingue. Arguing that "a force without discipline is a Ship without a rudder," Belair proposed the formation of three "Regiments of Blacks" who would be recruited in all three provinces of Saint-Domingue. Each regiment would contain 2,400 men. Each soldier would "hire himself out," and after a set period of time (approximately twelve years) of "having served His Majesty faithfully," these soldiers "will be owners of their will" and be "recognized as the other vassals of His Catholic Majesty." During these twelve years, these recruits would seemingly occupy a liminal position between slave and free man. Rather than receiving a stipend, each soldier would instead obtain compensation for his services in arms, clothing, and rations from the king, though the greatest reward would come from promoting the "happiness and the glory of this Powerful Monarch."[134]

Belair also outlined a labor regime for the rest of the "blacks" in Saint-Domingue under Spanish rule that shared significant commonalities with the policies of Sonthonax and Polverel. In Belair's proposal, "all the blacks who are still in the conquered parts" of Saint-Domingue would be "obligated to return without delay to their plantations to perform the work that Your Greatness [García]" should deem necessary. Every person, including children, who failed to adhere to this rule would be arrested, detained, and further penalized according to his or her specific infraction. Finally, no exiled plantation owner would be able to return to his or her property or "command his blacks" until the Spanish king authorized this.[135]

Fundamentally, both the French and Spanish labor regimes tried to limit the work options of most ex-slaves to either the plantation or the military (or, in some instances, domestic service) while offering concessions that would entice these individuals to serve one of the belligerent sides. Yet despite these similarities, the decrees of general emancipation became an increasingly effective recruiting tool for the French Republic in the months after August 1793. In Laurent Dubois's words, general emancipation came to represent the "key weapon of war" that helped to reverse the fortunes of the Republic in the Caribbean.[136] French recruitment efforts among the newly freed may have been bolstered by the fact that both the Spanish and the British not only preserved slavery in the areas that they conquered but also found eager allies in many planters who had a vested interest in maintaining slavery. (Notwithstanding, as discussed in chapter 4, Toussaint Louverture would later invite exiled planters back to French Saint-Domingue in his efforts to revive the colony's war-ravaged plantation economy.)

Sonthonax also skillfully exploited bitter memories of the Ogé affair to win support. In a letter to Pedro Acuña dated 25 September 1793, the archbishop Fernando Portillo y Torres accused Sonthonax of distorting recent history to suit his own agenda. "You will note, Your Excellency," wrote the archbishop, "the care of Sonthonax in reminding the Mulattos who compose his forces, and the Blacks of ours whom he has managed to conquer, of the wretched extradition of Ogé, blaming even more the Spanish who did it, than the Murderers who took his life, for he knows well that this is to rub salt in the wound, that the former [the Mulattos] have not been able to forget."[137]

Incessant disputes among the "black auxiliaries" further undermined the Spanish cause. In the spring of 1794, Toussaint Louverture, who had loyally commanded troops under the Spanish flag since 1793, turned on Jean-François and Biassou and proclaimed his allegiance to the French Republic. While the precise reasons for Toussaint's *volte-face* remain unclear, the decision likely resulted from a confluence of the emancipation decrees of 1793–94, Toussaint's personal enmity with both Jean-François and Biassou, and the worsening military situation of the Spanish on the island, among other forces.[138] The defection of Toussaint—who commanded 4,000 men and the talented military leaders Jean-Jacques Dessalines, Moïse, and Henry Christophe—struck a fatal blow to the Spanish campaign for Saint-Domingue.[139] With Toussaint came control over perhaps half of the land that the Spanish had conquered north of the Artibonite River, and by the

FIGURE 2 "Vue de la baye du Fort-Dauphin. Isle St. Domingue" ("View of the Bay of Fort-Dauphin"), 1791. Courtesy of the John Carter Brown Library at Brown University.

end of 1794 Toussaint had captured Jean-François's stronghold of Grande-Rivière as well as a number of Dominican towns such as San Rafael and San Miguel.[140] With these losses, Spanish Santo Domingo found itself vulnerable to invasion from French Saint-Domingue, which forced the Spanish into a defensive rather than an offensive posture. Ultimately, despite the disheartening military losses to the British discussed earlier in this chapter, the French Republicans' victory over the Spanish in the French colony's northern province became a fait accompli by late 1794.[141]

Toussaint's change in allegiance coincided with a rebellion in Gonaïves by a cadre of Spain's "black auxiliaries" against other Spanish troops and civilians in the town. This revolt, which appears to have transpired on 29 April 1794 and cost dozens of lives, may have reinforced the anxieties of many in the Spanish high command concerning the loyalties of the black troops and officers at this critical turning point in the Franco-Spanish war.[142] These loyalties became even more fractured several months later, when Jean-François was accused of ordering a large massacre in the town of Fort-Dauphin. Located in the northern province of Saint-Domingue, Fort-Dauphin had by the 1780s become an important military base and commercial hub (see figure 2). Its proximity to Santo Domingo facilitated trade, much of it illicit, in French manufactures for Spanish horses and cattle, while its sugar- and coffee-producing littoral made it a thriving market for those products. This proximity to the border, as well as to the commercial nerve center of Le Cap, also led French authorities to station a significant garrison there, even as this town's free population numbered only 560 souls in 1780.[143] These factors made Fort-Dauphin a major prize in the Franco-Spanish war, and it fell to the Spanish on 28 January 1794 following a siege lasting several months.[144]

Five months after the town's fall, Nicolás de Toledo told Don Joseph Antonio Urízar, a member of the high appeals court of Santo Domingo, that their nominal ally Jean-François had two days earlier entered Fort-Dauphin with more than 500 heavily armed followers and proceeded to massacre many "French whites," sparing neither the sick nor the weak. "[We] do not know the origins of this attack, nor the number of French whites sacrificed," Toledo wrote, "only that there are so many [bodies] that there are many streets which one cannot cross."[145] Scholars have answered Toledo's question concerning the death toll with a figure of around 700, but his speculations on Jean-François's motivations for carrying out the killing (assuming that Jean-François did indeed order it) remain unresolved.[146] As Spanish fortunes declined following Toussaint's defection, Jean-François may have come to believe that he had less to lose by committing such an act and may have seen these 700 individuals as embodiments of the French forces that had persecuted him and his fellow slave rebels earlier in the decade. These colonists also might have been unfortunate victims of an atmosphere of intense suspicion in which accusations of disloyalty were often tantamount to a death sentence.[147]

According to a secondhand account by an officer in the 186th French Regiment named Grandet, who recounted what had been told to him by a freedman named Noël who had recently switched allegiances from Spain to France, the Fort-Dauphin area's "Spanish commander" departed the town the night before the killings. Jean-François then entered with 800 "blacks" and Father Vázquez, the curate of Dajabón, who delivered a sermon immediately before the massacre. Grandet placed the number killed at 734, slightly less than the figure of 742 offered by a French merchant called Mirande, who composed a firsthand account of the event following his escape from Fort-Dauphin.[148] While these accounts interpreted the event as a cowardly slaughter of unarmed civilians, Jean-François in an 11 July 1794 letter sought to exculpate himself by presenting the violence as an unauthorized overreaction by some of his men to the threat of French attacks. According to Jean-François, though the doomed French colonists had invited retaliation by having captured and sold several of his officers, the violence was caused by a few of his officers and enlisted men who "without reason and without understanding fired upon all the French Whites against my orders and intentions." Though Jean-François could not "stop their fury and their rage" for several hours, he was able to save "many French people" from death. Despite their differences, most of these accounts agreed on one point: that the Spanish officials in the area who were not part of the black auxiliaries did not intercede to stop the killing. In Jean-François's words, they "abandoned all the posts" before the attack.[149]

Jean-François's accusations of selling captives suggest that part of the controversy that enveloped the Fort-Dauphin violence revolved around the question of whether those once held as slaves in Saint-Domingue were now "owners of their [own] will," to use the phrase of the earlier letter by Gabriel Belair. As discussed earlier in this chapter, Jean-François sold captives to the Spanish in exchange for munitions, even though he denied charges of engaging in slaving in his 11 July 1794 apologia. "I Jean-François would pay with my blood [for] all their Blacks whom I had taken from the Republicans and whom I sold," he declared in this letter.[150] Despite such denials, strong evidence implicates him and Biassou in slaving during the Franco-Spanish war.[151] Moreover, according to Jorge Victoria Ojeda, French officials condemned Jean-François for participating in the "sale of French prisoners or soldiers to different persons from the Spanish part, which was labeled as an action contrary to rights." García apparently refuted these charges, "saying that the Spanish troops (including the auxiliaries) did not capture soldiers, but only enslaved thieves, and those who claimed to be free were treated as such."[152] At stake was not simply the question of whether Jean-François and others had sold other human beings but also the scope of the rights possessed by "those who claimed to be free." After 1795, those held in bondage in Santo Domingo would advance claims to freedom and citizenship on the basis of the 1794 French emancipation decree, which in turn would give rise to disputes that called into question the universality of French Republican abolition and equal rights.

In the immediate aftermath of the Fort-Dauphin massacre, García was nonetheless less interested in such questions of rights and more concerned with disposing of the man who stood accused of such a horrific slaughter. In an October 1794 letter to García, the Republican military commander Étienne Laveaux acknowledged a proposal that García had recently made to exchange Jean-François and fifty of his most trusted subordinates for a number of Spanish prisoners held by the French. Laveaux replied that García would have to sweeten the deal by surrendering fifty additional men before he would accept. The Frenchman also rejected García's more gruesome offer to deliver him the head of Jean-François, insisting that although the black officer was indeed an "Enemy of the Republic," he was more valuable to the French alive than dead due to the "powerful influence of Jean-François over the Blacks." While this deal never materialized, this exchange attests to the importance of Jean-François and other "auxiliary" leaders to the French Republic even (or especially) after Toussaint's switch in allegiance. Indeed, Laveaux stated in his letter to García that a change in the loyalties of Jean-François would be highly beneficial in ensuring that France "conserve its colonies."[153]

Despite the refusal of Jean-François and Biassou to switch sides, the Republic did indeed conserve Saint-Domingue. Led by Toussaint Louverture and Laveaux, the Republicans in the year following Toussaint's defection retook the principal parts of Saint-Domingue that the Spanish had captured and forced this enemy to capitulate in 1795.[154] This dovetailed with French Republican military victories over divided enemies, including Spain, in Europe.[155] On 22 July 1795 in Basel, Switzerland, France and Spain signed the Treaty of Basel, which ended hostilities between the two powers and ceded the Spanish portion of Hispaniola to France. By virtue of the 1794 French universal emancipation act and the cession of Santo Domingo to France, all residents of Hispaniola were ostensibly legally freed from slavery (notwithstanding the persistence of slaveholding British occupation to 1798). But how would those thus freed, as well as their former masters, react to these changes?

Conclusions

The advent of emancipation in Hispaniola was a Dominican as well as a Haitian story. All of the transformative events that transpired on the island in the first half of the 1790s—including the Ogé affair, the successful struggle for legal racial equality among the free population, the 1791 slave revolt, and the Franco-Spanish war—emerged partly from the intertwined histories of both sides of the island. While these events were also partly caused by political, intellectual, and military developments in other parts of the Atlantic World, the slave societies of the two parts of Hispaniola—and the long histories of resistance to enslavement in each—formed the local context for these episodes.

Jean-François and Georges Biassou experienced firsthand this linkage between the local and the international. Their fate became a delicate political issue once news of the cession of Santo Domingo reached the island, as Spanish colonial authorities became caught between the obligation to reward these men and their followers for their military services and racially charged fears that they would directly or indirectly incite insurrection among free and enslaved nonwhites in disparate parts of the Spanish empire. Though many of the former black auxiliaries received modest pensions, they were sent to places as far-flung as Honduras, Yucatan (Mexico), Panama, and Trinidad, as well as Florida, Spain, Cuba, and Santo Domingo as a result of policies designed to split them up and reduce their supposed threat. Biassou relocated to Florida, while his old rival Jean-François followed a complicated itinerary, ultimately ending up in the southern Spanish city of Cádiz.[156] Although they had gained their freedom as well as material rewards and military ranks by defending the oldest colonial empire in the Americas, these exiles found mixed receptions in different parts of this empire due to the revolution that they had helped make.

In claiming to be the "king of the counter-revolution," Georges Biassou at once defended something very old and helped to create something very new. In the act of affirming the viability of freed individuals such as himself as political actors, Biassou's words and actions undermined race-based subordination and hierarchy. His bold statement of political inclusion is emblematic of the ways in which slaves, freed individuals, and free-born nonwhites created and advanced their own ideas of political legitimacy during the period and draws attention to dynamics that would recur in the years to come.

CHAPTER TWO

The Courage to Conquer Their Natural Liberty

Conflicts over Emancipation in French Santo Domingo, 1795–1801

On the evening of 30 October 1796, a Sunday (the day of the week often chosen by slave rebels in the Americas), approximately 120 "African cultivators" from the Boca Nigua plantation in Santo Domingo rose up in revolt with the alleged "horrible plan" to kill the plantation's director, Juan B. Oyarzával, and all of the other whites there.[1] Organized around an elaborate hierarchy headed by a "queen" named Marie-Anne, these insurgents used drums to incite potential followers to action and often resorted to more forceful recruitment measures if this failed. Employing a type of guerrilla warfare characterized by the tried-and-true Caribbean pattern of retreat to the mountains, the rebels initially succeeded in forcing Oyarzával and his partisans to flee to nearby Santo Domingo city by setting fire to buildings and canefields. Their dramatic stand proved futile, however, as they were eventually routed by the forces of Santo Domingo's governor, Joaquín García, who oversaw the capture of many of the insurgents and the execution of the ringleaders.[2]

In July 1795, slaveholding Spain had ceded Santo Domingo to the French Republic by the Treaty of Basel. As discussed in chapter 1, the French National Convention had decreed the abolition of slavery in the entirety of France's domains on 4 February 1794, and the wording of the Treaty of Basel and that of the general emancipation law together imply that slavery became illegal in Santo Domingo upon this cession.[3] Nonetheless, servitude was apparently not eliminated by the stroke of a pen. The French and Spanish authorities who crafted the two most informative extant reports on the Boca Nigua episode framed it as a slave revolt, more than a year after apparent emancipation. The author of one of these reports, Philippe-Rose Roume, the French government's principal civilian official in Santo Domingo (who later extolled the virtues of "Our immortal Revolution" in a letter to Dominican officials), even bestowed the highest praise upon García and other Spanish authorities for their swift repression of this revolt while condemning the "crimes" that the *cultivateurs* had supposedly committed at Boca Nigua.[4]

Boca Nigua, located near Santo Domingo city, was the largest and most profitable plantation in the former Spanish colony. Concentrating principally on sugar, it was coveted for its productive capacity by a succession of Spanish and French authorities. Nonetheless, these facts alone do not adequately explain the elision of emancipation in these accounts. While the report of the judge Manuel Bravo y Bermudez, who commanded the military force that put down the uprising, explicitly labeled the rebels "slaves," Roume in his own account substituted the word "*cultivateur*" for "slave" and depicted the insurgents as enslavers who forced other laborers on the plantation to join their uprising on pain of becoming "reduce[d] to slavery."[5] A student of slave revolts in the Americas lacking specific knowledge of the situation in Santo Domingo under French rule might be forgiven for reading these reports as quintessential examples of colonial administrators' responses to a slave rebellion.[6]

The Boca Nigua affair and other episodes, such as the French efforts to subdue what authorities still termed "maroons" along parts of the island's colonial border after 1795, suggest that emancipation was in many ways invisible in French Santo Domingo.[7] Nonetheless, the conflicts that ensued when numerous men and women advanced claims to their rights as French citizens against those who would hold them as slaves came to encompass not only the legality of slavery in that colony but also the perceived moral legitimacy of enslavement itself. Santo Domingo became a critical battleground in the political and philosophical conflicts over the terms and meaning of liberty and citizenship that transpired in Hispaniola and beyond during the second half of the 1790s.

Was there an emancipation in Santo Domingo after 1795? This in turn was closely related to another question: to what extent did the end of legal slavery represent a genuine departure from the past? In fact, much continuity existed in both parts of the island between the slave regime and what followed. In French Saint-Domingue, the legal consignment of most freed people to the roles of plantation laborer or soldier impelled many onetime slaves to pursue freedom on their own terms via armed resistance, flight, and other means. Some of these individuals sought this freedom across the border in Santo Domingo, even as those still in bondage in the eastern part of the island often found that their conditions were very similar to what they had known under slavery.

This contested colonial border remained a concern even after 1795 and constituted an important site of conflicts over sovereignty during the

French and Haitian Revolutions. As the Boca Nigua correspondence suggests, Spanish authorities managed to hold onto a substantial amount of power in Santo Domingo from 1795 to 1801 despite the formal cession of the colony to France. Faced with more pressing concerns elsewhere, the militarily overextended French Republic stationed only a few officials and apparently very few or no troops in this colony;[8] much French administrative correspondence from this period tellingly still refers to Santo Domingo as the "Spanish part" of the island. All this enabled Governor García and other Spanish officials to retain most of their local civil and military authority until the occupation of Santo Domingo by Toussaint Louverture's armies in early 1801.

During the ancien régime and into the revolutionary era, moreover, conflicts over imperial versus local sovereignty in both parts of the island continually intersected with questions concerning the regulation, and then the dismantling, of slavery.[9] Slavery had indeed been an important consideration in the intricate diplomatic negotiations in which Spain and France engaged in 1795 on the matter of sovereignty over Santo Domingo and other territories. Theory and practice were not one and the same, however, as became clear in the Boca Nigua rebellion and other violent conflicts that transpired over the extent of freed Dominicans' rights.

While scholars have devoted considerable attention to the complicated application of French universal emancipation in such places as Saint-Domingue and Guadeloupe, this matter in Santo Domingo has not attracted the same scrutiny.[10] Several factors account for this relative scholarly neglect, including the lesser emphasis that French authorities placed on Santo Domingo relative to other places and the strikingly distinct historiographical traditions of Haiti and the Dominican Republic. While Saint-Domingue was the more lucrative prize for the many factions that competed for power on the island, their comparative inattention to Santo Domingo in fact made it a crucible in contests over the nature of freedom and equality. Rather than existing as a mere blank spot on a map beside revolutionary Saint-Domingue, Santo Domingo was a central theater in the unfolding of French Republican emancipation.[11] Santo Domingo's peculiar status after 1795— and the status of the thousands of people whom many still claimed as slaves there—had significant implications for the central questions that emerged from and drove one of the great revolutions in world history.

In some ways, Santo Domingo's political situation during this time was not so different from that of other parts of the French empire, such as

Martinique and Réunion (a colony in the Indian Ocean), where foreign invasions and local opposition combined to thwart the application of the 1794 emancipation decree.[12] Nonetheless, several features distinguished Santo Domingo from these other places: its physical proximity to Saint-Domingue, the epicenter of revolutionary ferment in the Caribbean; Santo Domingo's lack of a prior history of French colonization; and the many connections that Santo Domingo shared with the possessions of Spain, its longtime colonial master. These facts—along with the conspicuous absence in Santo Domingo of plantation infrastructure on any appreciable scale since the sixteenth century—make its story under French rule quite distinct.

For both formally freed Dominicans and the numerous Dominguan ex-slaves who ventured across the border for political and economic reasons, the proper application of French Republican law to Santo Domingo was no arcane diplomatic exercise. The stakes included access to a plot of land to call one's own; autonomy from the tyranny of the plantation; and, most fundamentally, control over one's own person and labor power. Moreover, as the situation of Dominican former slaves became tied to developments across the border in Saint-Domingue and across the Atlantic in France, the inability—or unwillingness—of Republican authorities to enforce emancipation law threatened to destroy the French Republic's credibility by undermining its professed values and their most radical manifestation.

In recent decades, a number of scholars have convincingly presented emancipation in many parts of the Americas as an ongoing process rather than the culmination of a series of political and military struggles.[13] French authorities' treatment of the Boca Nigua uprising, quasi-independent "maroon" communities, and the seemingly intractable problem of illegal slaving in Santo Domingo exposed some of the political, social, and racial fissures of this process there. At the same time, these issues generated an abundance of impassioned if somewhat grandiloquent affirmations of liberty and equality from the pens of French officials, pages that now fill cartons of documents in Paris and Aix-en-Provence.

While one scholar has labeled the first years after the cession a "long and curious twilight period" in Santo Domingo characterized by the effective retention of Spanish law and the institution of slavery, the more optimistic French administrators imagined that French rule would usher in not a twilight but a dawn—that of the implementation of universal emancipation in Santo Domingo.[14] Ultimately, the epistolary and armed conflicts that arose in the context of the confused political situation in Santo Domingo challenged the political and presumed moral bases not only of the enslavement of Dominicans but also of the concept of a slave society itself.

The Constitutional and Diplomatic Contexts
of Santo Domingo's Political Crisis

The tumultuous political climate of the 1790s in the Atlantic World involved a complicated interplay of radical new ideas and centuries-old practices. Since the sixteenth century, the Americas in general and the Caribbean in particular had been sites of frequent colonial conflict and gamesmanship. This did not change appreciably in the revolutionary era. Nonetheless, the military conflagrations of the 1790s and the exchanges of territory that they often occasioned depended to a great degree on thousands of freed individuals who had won their liberty through military conquest and political activism.[15] Furthermore, in the wake of the French emancipation decree of 1794, territorial exchanges now had potentially crucial implications for the boundaries of citizenship and slavery.

In this light, bringing Santo Domingo under French rule involved much more than a simple change in legal jurisdiction; it also entailed the political conversion of its inhabitants from Spanish subjects and slaves into free French citizens. In an assessment of the situation in Santo Domingo that he presented to the French government in 1797, Roume confidently predicted that if his readers were to follow his recommendations to reduce taxes on the colony's impoverished residents and to send "wise and illustrious" French settlers there, then within three years, "our new brothers" in Santo Domingo would become "perfect [French] republicans."[16] In Roume's eyes, one particular subset of these "new brothers" merited special attention: the colony's newly freed population. Roume suggested that in order to integrate them into the French polity, priests in Santo Domingo would "accustom the landowners and the cultivators [the former slaves] to the regime of liberty." In their efforts to achieve the "reintegration of the former slaves to the indispensable rights of humanity," these clerics would be aided by the "paternal regime" and "good education" that freed Dominicans had received from their former masters.[17]

What were the precise terms by which these "new brothers" might become "perfect republicans?" The scope of citizenship rights of the inhabitants of France's overseas possessions and of the metropole itself represented one of the great political questions of the 1790s, and France's political transformations in this era were closely linked to those of its *outre-mer* (overseas) territories. In 1794–95, France underwent the fall of the Jacobin-dominated government headed by the infamous Committee of Public Safety and the subsequent creation of a new political order led by the five-member Executive Directory.[18] This political crisis at home was intimately tied to a sea change in overseas governance, as the 1795 French constitution that created the Directory also proclaimed the principle of legal integration in an attempt to more forcefully incorporate France's various holdings into a single legal regime.[19]

The underlying idea of this document was simple: France's colonies constituted an "integral part" of the French polity, and as such were to be governed by the same corpus of laws that applied in France itself.[20] This had extremely important implications for the matter of citizenship rights. Under a single set of laws, no legal distinctions separated the inhabitants of the colonies from those of mainland France: all were French citizens with the same rights, including the right not to be enslaved or consigned to a distinct legal status based on perceived color or purported ancestry. This marked a radical shift from the legal paradigm that had prevailed under the ancien régime in which the presence of different legal situations based on geography had constituted the principal framework for confining slavery to the colonies.[21]

The application of this new legal order to Santo Domingo was fraught with conflict. For many, the fate of the "integral part" doctrine was closely tied to that of emancipation: a return to the old geographically based legal segregation might portend the relegalization of slavery and/or the racial caste system. The doctrine's application in Santo Domingo thus held signal importance not only for freed persons but also for the legal and political bases of the French Republican emancipationist project. Tellingly, in a missive to Napoleon dated 28 April 1800 in which several prominent Dominican planters and political leaders decried the "perils" of "suddenly calling the slave to an indefinite liberty," these individuals proposed that France apply a set of "particular laws" to Santo Domingo that would place it under a legal order separate from that of either Saint-Domingue or France—the precise opposite of legal integration.[22] Until its dismantling in the constitution of 1799, legal integration thus became closely connected to universal emancipation;[23] developments in Santo Domingo presented formidable challenges to both.[24] Writing from Le Cap, Julien Raimond, the former activist for legal racial equality who went on to occupy influential posts in revolutionary Saint-Domingue, told Napoleon on 19 August 1800 that the promulgation of the 1799 French constitution had provoked rumors among the "Blacks" in Hispaniola that "the Spanish Part of the Island would be shortly returned to Spain, and that an army would then arrive to reestablish slavery."[25]

The principal document that set the formal terms of Santo Domingo's incorporation into the French empire was the Treaty of Basel, signed on 22 July 1795 by representatives of France and Spain in the Swiss town of that name. The tensions between the provisions of this treaty that pertained to the cession and the "integral part" doctrine proclaimed two months later gave rise to complex legal and political disputes that tested French resolve to defend the liberty of those held in bondage in Santo Domingo. Article IX of the treaty established the fact and conditions of Santo Domingo's cession to France; its two most important components were a clause that allowed Dominicans to migrate with their belongings to a Spanish colony elsewhere within one year of the treaty's signing and a provision that stipulated the replacement of Spanish military units with French ones, to occur at the earliest possible moment.[26]

Diplomats entrusted with negotiating the terms of Spain's surrender to France in 1795 had confronted the issue of the political status of three Spanish territories claimed by France: Santo Domingo, the vast Louisiana territory, and Guipúzcoa, a rugged Basque province in the Pyrenees. While the geopolitical and economic stakes involved in the possession of each area varied, the contentious negotiations that France and Spain undertook with respect to their montane European frontier were closely tied to those that concerned the Caribbean.[27] "The Guipuzcoans are not mature for liberty as we conceive of it," wrote the French diplomat Bourgoiny to Paris in a 20 March 1795 letter. "They would surely be bad French citizens. Their customs, their language, [and] their prejudice would make their amalgamation with the [French] Republic very difficult not to say impossible: and it is our principle to consult and not to force the wish of peoples to incorporate them to us."[28] This letter attests to a central contradiction within the French Republic: while professing adherence to ostensibly universal values, many French authorities simultaneously claimed that certain groups possessed deeply ingrained traits that rendered them unfit for French Republican citizenship, at least before a process of education, adjustment, or conquest.[29]

In the Caribbean, such anxieties became infused with the toxin of racism, which was in turn closely linked to the question of the applicability of the 1794 emancipation edict. In their deliberations over the possible transfer of Santo Domingo and Louisiana to France, French and Spanish officials had grappled with the potential implications of a change in political authority for each colony's slave system and enslaved population.[30] According to a letter by Roume to the French minister of the navy dated 31 December 1795, the Spanish Marquis d'Iranda, who owned the Boca Nigua plantation, had proposed granting Louisiana to France instead of Santo Domingo on the grounds that the French "regime of equality" would reduce Santo Domingo's profitability by liberating the "unfortunate cultivators."[31] By contrast, in a series of instructions issued to Bourgoiny on 6 May 1795, political leaders in Paris contended that Spain would prove less reluctant to relinquish Santo Domingo than Louisiana due to the "dangers to which the liberty of our blacks exposes" Spain's assets in Hispaniola.[32]

Following the signing of the Treaty of Basel, questions concerning the rights of those claimed as slaves in Santo Domingo, that colony's potential profitability, and an array of issues rooted in the old Franco-Spanish disputes on the island continued to influence political reform projects undertaken by French Republicans vis-à-vis Santo Domingo. In October 1797, the Council of Five Hundred (part of the French legislature) followed the logic of the "integral part" doctrine in decreeing a reorganization of the island's political structure that was to reflect the revolutionary division of France into *départements*.[33] The north, west, and south provinces that had comprised prerevolutionary Saint-Domingue became transformed into *départements* bearing these names, while the former Spanish colony to the east would henceforth consist of the *départements* of Samaná and Inganno. Samaná's jurisdiction was to include much of Santo Domingo's north, while Inganno would encompass the south and southeast, including Santo Domingo city. In an attempt to impose a greater degree of administrative control over the eastern part of the island, the Council of Five Hundred also ordered the establishment of several tribunals in locales including Santo Domingo city, the northern city of Santiago, and the eastern town of Seybo.[34]

Subsequent measures further promoted Paris's goal of integrating both parts of the island into a new political and legal arrangement. On 15 January 1798, the council ordered that the number of deputies elected to the *corps législatif* (the French legislature) by citizens in Hispaniola would be determined according to departmental organization, as each of the island's five *départements* could send one deputy to the *corps* in the month of *Germinal*, year 6 (21 March to 19 April 1798). This reform also brought Dominican towns such as Neyba and Dajabón under the jurisdiction of one of the three Saint-Domingue *départements*.[35] While political schemes formulated in France thus established the parameters of the integration of both colonies into a new legal order, the forms that such attempted reorganization would take on the island were conditioned by the long-running disputes over political boundaries that remained unresolved in the postcession years. In a 19 October 1800 letter to Napoleon, the French minister of foreign relations articulated several reasons why Governor García might be willing to relinquish the authority that he still possessed if granted a suitable opportunity. These reasons included Santo Domingo's poverty and administrative expenses, the possibility that García "feared the propagation of the principles proclaimed in the French part on the liberty of the blacks," and the frequency of cross-border trading. Underlying all of these matters were recurrent "violations of territory" in spite of the 1777 Treaty of Aranjuez (discussed in chapter 1) that had supposedly resolved the border issue and the persistence of the "desertion of discontented blacks" across the old boundary line.[36]

This invocation of an ancien régime treaty and the old issue of fugitive "blacks" crossing the border hints at the extent to which the island's "long" eighteenth century informed political programs devised in revolutionary France. In a report submitted to Paris on 26 March 1795, the French diplomat Bourgoiny had enumerated a long list of grievances that he planned to address to his Spanish counterpart. Among these was the assertion that most of Santo Domingo's land was worked by "our fugitive blacks" from Saint-Domingue, who had been encouraged by the Spanish to immigrate and cultivate the land in violation of repeated accords between the two nations for the swift extradition of black fugitives. Bourgoiny further insisted that the Spanish had demonstrably failed to make proper use of this labor force. Only the French, with their superior capital and enlightened economic policies, could in his estimation fully harness the potential of this colony to produce large quantities of sugar, coffee, cotton, and other cash crops.[37]

Closely entwined with the border question was that of the geographical reach of French Republican rights—and restrictions on these rights. Should emancipation stop at the Republic's borders as they had stood in the spring of 1795? This idea emerged as a possible compromise between the goals of defending emancipation and promoting commerce with the slaveholding territories that surrounded the French Caribbean's outposts of abolition. One tract on commerce between France and Spain dated July or August 1795 argued that Santo Domingo ought to remain under Spain because it would generate more wealth as a meat-producing colony under the "regime of Slavery of the Blacks" than it would by employing universally free labor. By this line of reasoning, Dominican traders could exchange their meat for assorted French manufactures (a continuation of the common pre-1789 practice), which in turn would enable these French products to legally reach other Spanish colonies in accordance with Spain's notoriously strict commercial regulations.[38] Napoleon would later revisit the idea of confining general emancipation and slavery to distinct geographical areas in his protracted deliberations on which labor system(s) would prevail in his domains.

Santo Domingo's situation brought to the fore a number of other complicated questions: Should the drive for profit trump the rights of the inhabitants of France's newly acquired lands to their persons and to enjoy the fruits of their labor? Did a conflict between these goals even exist, or, conversely, did the removal of the coercion and deprivation of enslavement actually enhance workers' productivity? Framed in various ways, these questions were all subsets of one central issue: could or should a new political unit be configured without slavery? Slaves in Saint-Domingue had offered their own emphatic answer to this question. When freed people in Santo Domingo recognized the limitations of emancipation there, they too asserted their rights in ways that varied from relocation to open rebellion. The heavy-handed French response to the largest of these revolts and to other challenges to the persistence of servitude revealed some of the deficiencies of the efforts to incorporate Santo Domingo into an order of legal integration and emancipation.

Debates over Emancipation and Citizenship in Santo Domingo

In a letter to the minister of the navy composed two days after the start of the Boca Nigua revolt, the French official Roume praised the plantation director Oyarzával in the highest terms, depicting him as a virtuous defender both of the "regime of general Liberty" and of profit maximization on his plantation.[39] Those who rebelled at Boca Nigua evidently had other ideas. Following the promulgation of the general emancipation decrees of 1793–94, Roume and many other French administrators strove to reconcile the objectives of re-creating a profitable plantation system and upholding the "regime of general Liberty." As the case of Boca Nigua attests, their solutions often involved forms of force that in some ways recalled the days of slavery. Nonetheless, the cession of Santo Domingo to France provoked a series of political and philosophical disputes among French and Spanish officials over the justice of enslaving one's fellow human being.

In the course of his varied assignments in Hispaniola, Roume devised seemingly contradictory ways to address these problems. In order to implement the new legal order organized around the "integral part" doctrine and the Treaty of Basel in Hispaniola, the French Directory had chosen to follow the precedent of sending a Civil Commission to the island, this time with five members. Among those selected were the architect of Dominguan general emancipation, Léger-Félicité Sonthonax; Julien Raimond; and "Particular Agent" Roume, in whom the Directory invested the task of overseeing Santo Domingo's transfer to France. Despite his prior administrative experience on the island, Roume did not accomplish this objective. He also amassed a decidedly mixed record on upholding emancipation in the eastern part of the island.[40]

Boca Nigua was in fact one in a series of servile revolts that transpired in Santo Domingo during the revolutionary years. These uprisings took place in the shadow of the upheaval in French Saint-Domingue, and events in the neighboring colony appear to have influenced some of these insurgents.[41] In the case of Boca Nigua, both Roume and Judge Bravo suspected the hand of Dominguan former slaves (specifically three men who had once been allied with the ex-slave leader Jean-François) in instigating the revolt.[42]

Yet in spite of such allegations, the successful struggle against slavery in the western portion of the island did not occasion a significant immediate change in Santo Domingo's governance or in the condition of its "slaves." As we have seen, priorities elsewhere led the French to station only a skeleton crew of administrators in Santo Domingo; French officials' continued reliance upon Spanish authorities to run both Santo Domingo's few plantations and the colony's central government impeded the prospects for radical social change.[43] "The Minister [of the navy] is also asked to inform the French government; not only of the merit and indomitable courage of our cocitizens from Haiti [Spanish landowners and authorities], but also of the necessity . . . to only proceed with the Frenchification [*francisation*] of the Country with all appropriate prudence," counseled Roume in his account of Boca Nigua.[44]

What precisely would this "Frenchification" entail? In Saint-Domingue at this time, French authorities were attempting to enforce labor regimes that sharply circumscribed the rights of *cultivateurs* and sought to ensure their continued subordination. French officials in Santo Domingo likewise aimed to curtail the liberties of the newly freed in the hopes of reviving the long-dormant plantation complex. Roume and his colleagues in Santo Domingo indeed appear to have equated the Boca Nigua insurgents with the restive *cultivateurs* who they perceived to threaten authority in Saint-Domingue.[45] After all, the French Republican regime could hardly expect to establish a profitable plantation system in Santo Domingo if it could not control the labor force on its largest plantation. Yet Santo Domingo's cession also elicited a concerted effort on the part of some French officials, Roume included, to create in that colony a more egalitarian political and social order.

In its 24 December 1795 instructions to Agent Roume, the Directory had charged him with winning over "our new cocitizens" in a bid to curb emigration from Santo Domingo and secure the support of the elite. Were freed individuals to be considered among these "new cocitizens?" These instructions were quite unclear on this matter. While condemning the "horrible [former] right of the slavery of one man over another," these orders contended that French emancipation law did not constitute an "infraction of the right of colonial property" except in the case of those who were "blinded by vile interest." Entreating the "free slaves" (*esclavos libres*) of Santo Domingo to refrain from "abus[ing] their freedom," these orders asserted that the Spanish had treated their slaves "with a humanity worthy of winning their friendship." Moreover, the Directory took pains to promise land and other material benefits to Dominican former slaveholders who had suffered a "real [economic] loss" as a result of the liberation of their slaves.[46]

This rather timid and equivocal defense of emancipation left ample room for conflict. In the wake of the signing of the Treaty of Basel, a thorny legal problem arose that tested the boundaries of Republican emancipation: whether refugees departing Santo Domingo after 1795 could legally transport with them human beings whom they claimed as slaves under Article IX of the Treaty of Basel, which as discussed earlier in this chapter allowed Dominicans up to one year after the treaty's promulgation to migrate to a

Spanish colony with their belongings.[47] Those opposing such forced emigration held that the inalienable rights of the new French citizens who were unjustly claimed as slaves precluded anyone from declaring them to be his or her property, even in the case of flight to an area where slavery was still the law of the land.

In a correspondence dated 30 September 1795, Agent Roume outlined this legal conundrum and sided with the antislavery position. Forcefully condemning slavery as a "violation of natural law" that had become unlawful in all French domains following the 1794 emancipation decree, Roume argued that the "natural right" of "liberty" superseded the "civil right" of property. Roume correctly anticipated a conflict wherein the "Spanish Property Owner" would attempt to transport his or her alleged "Slave" out of Santo Domingo as "one of [his or her] Goods" in defiance of the latter's claims to possess the right to remain in the colony as a "French citizen." Roume proposed a back door solution to the problem: freed Dominicans could simply travel to Saint-Domingue and hide out there during the year allowed by the Treaty of Basel for Dominicans' emigration with their properties.[48] Such conflicts made Santo Domingo a battleground over what Jeremy Popkin calls "the deadlock over the rival rights claims generated by the institution of slavery"—a deadlock that became heightened, rather than weakened, by revolutionary upheaval and the advent of constitutional guarantees of individual rights in the Haitian Revolution and other contexts.[49]

The "alleged Slaves of Santo Domingo," Roume insisted in a 24 January 1796 letter to the minister of the navy, "knowing that they can remain on the island as French citizens, do not wish to permit their so-called Owners to transport them with them like vile herds of cattle."[50] Faced with assertions to freedom and citizenship on the part of freed persons, Dominican landowners and authorities adopted a variety of strategies to protect their perceived interests. In a 1795 report, the French vice admiral Truguet presciently predicted that fear of the "effects of the liberty of the blacks" on their social and economic position would impel many Dominicans to try to escape with their claimed possessions, including their "blacks." This development would exacerbate what the vice admiral judged to be France's fundamental problem in Santo Domingo: that France could only realize the "inestimable advantage" of fulfilling this colony's economic potential when authorities successfully compelled its "Blacks" to perform agricultural labor. These concerns led Truguet to propose the swift appointment to Santo Domingo of an "Agent of the Republic," who would reassure property owners that their fears of "anarchy" were misplaced.[51] In his appeal to former slaveholders rather than to the colony's freed residents, as well as in his explicit claim that "Black" labor was essential to stimulate agricultural production, Truguet suggested that no radical change in Santo Domingo's social order was in the works.

The rights of the formerly enslaved in Santo Domingo nonetheless became the subject of a spirited debate between Étienne Laveaux, a key French Republican military leader who was serving as governor of Saint-Domingue, and Santo Domingo's Governor García. As a self-professed "Apostle of Liberty," Laveaux took García to task for his perceived hypocrisy in promoting the Spanish king as the fount of liberty in the 1793–95 Franco-Spanish war and then subsequently claiming that Spain had not abolished slavery. To García's assertion that preventing refugees from leaving Santo Domingo with their "slaves" would lead to their "ruin," Laveaux's retort was simple: free soil trumped property rights. According to Laveaux, no individual could claim another as his or her property in French Santo Domingo.[52]

García's response, dated 19 December 1795, drew upon the centuries-old Spanish-American practice of conferring manumission upon certain individuals for services deemed advantageous to imperial objectives. García argued that the liberties granted in the recent Franco-Spanish conflict were no different and that individual manumissions did not in any sense portend the eventual end of slavery in an entire polity.[53] By this line of argumentation, in Santo Domingo and other Spanish colonies, some would remain in a state of perpetual bondage, implying that emigration with "slaves" was entirely justified.[54] In a letter to the Spanish prime minister Manuel de Godoy composed twelve days earlier, García had, moreover, presented slavery as the "most useful and beneficial asset" to Dominicans and accused his Saint-Domingue counterpart and other Frenchmen of undermining the institution by recklessly disseminating "Printed Decrees about the general Liberty of the Blacks." Such actions could, García fretted, incite unrest or rebellion among Santo Domingo's "slaves."[55]

Behind the Laveaux-García exchange was the central question of the Haitian Revolution: Could a polity exist entirely without slaves—or ought it to? For Laveaux, García, Roume, and many others, the success of emancipation in Santo Domingo had implications far beyond that colony. The competing visions of a free society versus a land where some remained enslaved represented nothing less than a conflict over the viability of human bondage itself.

Joseph Antonio Urízar, a member of Santo Domingo's high appeals court, recognized this. In a one-hundred-page apologia of the slave regime in Santo Domingo, Urízar engaged with the liberal ideas of the French and Haitian Revolutions and sought to reconcile the power of these discourses with his own conviction that slavery must endure in his land. In his 25 June 1795 "Discourse on the Modification, and Limits of Slavery," Urízar urged his fellow Dominican administrators to adopt "certain prudent and tactful measures so that the bad example and corruption [of Saint-Domingue]" would not spread to Santo Domingo. Explicitly confronting the arguments that "all men are naturally free" and that the "right of peoples" (*derecho de gentes*) meant that no human being ought to be enslaved, Urízar responded that while "all peoples concur that men by nature are born free," the exigencies of Spanish law and especially of the interests and property rights of slave owners demanded that slavery be maintained.[56]

While Spanish and Spanish-American thinkers and political figures had since the first decades of colonialism in the Americas grappled with issues concerning the rights of subject populations, Urízar confronted the liberationist discourses of the twin revolutions that had upended slavery in the neighboring colony and threatened the social and racial order in Santo Domingo. Many of Urízar's Dominican peers came to similar conclusions on the question of slavery, though with less evident deliberation. According to a report issued by a French government commission to the minister of the navy dated 26 December 1796, "several residents" of Santo Domingo had presented to the Spanish king a request that the Treaty of Basel be annulled on the grounds that it would deprive these individuals of "their properties founded on Slavery."[57] In another correspondence to the minister of the navy, one Jean-Baptiste Formy contended that Dominican "slave-owners" did not wish to become "Republicans" due to their opposition to the "Liberty of the Blacks." Thwarting such entrenched opposition to abolition and taking effective possession of the colony would require "extraordinary forces" on the part of the Republic.[58] In an undated letter, Laveaux was even blunter. "The Spanish have put them [freed Dominicans] into slavery," Laveaux lamented. "They have put them under the torture of the whip, [and] they have rendered them even more unfortunate than before."[59] Such assertions undermined the optimistic predictions of officials such as Roume, who in a 5 August 1796 communiqué to his colleagues on the Civil Commission had declared that Dominicans "all know that slavery is incompatible with our principles" and that one "Proclamation" of amnesty to them was worth more than an army of 50,000 men.[60]

Entreaties that French officials directed to the ex-slaves themselves sought to assuage anxieties that the regime of emancipation and the "integral part" principle were doomed to fail. The anonymous author of one tract that was probably written around the time of Santo Domingo's cession insisted upon the necessity of informing the "blacks" of Santo Domingo that the "[French] government" intended to grant them "Complete Liberty." This author further suggested that the French colonial government ensure that ex-slaves be paid a portion of plantation revenues and that it issue a Spanish-language proclamation declaring these former slaves "French citizens." Most urgently, Spanish authorities must recognize the freedom of these "blacks [who were] formerly their Slaves" and put an immediate halt to their "Kidnap[ping] By force."[61]

More importantly, in a 3 June 1796 proclamation that he issued in both French and Kreyòl (the island's lingua franca), Sonthonax prohibited on pain of imprisonment the mere suggestion that "liberty has not been irrevocably granted, [and] that the intention of the French government is to place back into irons men who should never have had to bear them." "The French Colonies are integral parts of the Republic, and are subject to the same constitutional law," Sonthonax affirmed. Moreover, by translating the "sacred law" of February 1794 (the emancipation act) into "all of the languages that are spoken" on the island, Sonthonax endeavored to spread the gospel of French Republican emancipation to the island's remotest corners.[62]

Yet Sonthonax, it must be recalled, had designed the restrictive labor codes that sought to keep ex-slaves on their old plantations or in the military. In the Haitian Revolution, the fusion of new ideas of economic freedom with liberationist political discourses paradoxically gave sanction to new forms of repression, such as these labor regimes. In the wake of Adam Smith's 1776 publication of *The Wealth of Nations*, the notion that people were naturally driven to pursue their own self-interest, which could in turn benefit society as a whole, was rapidly gaining currency in some parts of the world. These ideas, in combination with the perceived imperative to maximize plantation revenues, gave rise to the argument—first articulated by Sonthonax and later espoused by Julien Raimond, Roume, Toussaint, and others—that industriousness and participation in export labor markets were essential determinants of one's worth as a free citizen.[63]

Historian Thomas Holt has persuasively contended that both the end of chattel slavery in the British world and Britain's later relinquishing of formal domination over most of its colonies were "framed in ways that masked a new coercion even as [they] yielded new opportunities for self-determination."[64] Similarly, in both parts of Hispaniola during the 1790s, French authorities advanced arguments that couched the continuation of hierarchical and coercive labor relations within the guise of free labor. For instance, the municipal administration of Le Cap insisted to Sonthonax on 21 August 1797 that "free hands are better suited to cultivate tropical soil than enslaved hands."[65] In fact, Louis Dufay, one of the delegates sent by Sonthonax to Paris in 1793 to defend the latter's emancipation order, had in his famous speech to the National Convention on 4 February 1794 employed a similar logic—framed in similar language—to persuade the legislators to outlaw slavery. "You will see that your colony of Saint-Domingue, cultivated by free hands, will be more flourishing" and "produce more for the metropole [France] than before [in the times of slavery]." In other words, under a free labor system, the drive to earn money through one's sweat and toil, which would then be spent on French commercial goods, would both strengthen French political and economic power and improve the former slaves' lives.[66]

Nonetheless, key French officials did not trust freed people to become productive citizens (as defined by the former) without strict external restraints. In a 24 December 1795 letter to a "French citizen in Santo Domingo" named Francisco Gascue, for instance, Roume had declared that the new regime of general liberty would stimulate greater agricultural prosperity than had been possible under slavery, as the "joy" of labor and the *cultivateurs'* newfound ability to claim a share of its fruits would create powerful new incentives for them to maximize their productivity. Yet in the same breath, Roume proposed importing "Unfortunate Slaves" from Africa and manumitting them in Hispaniola; he argued that a period of temporary indentured servitude was necessary to pay off their debts and habituate them to life as free and industrious French citizens.[67]

Such contradictions were not mere abstractions for those newly freed from slavery. Faced with the repressive labor regimes and onerous military duties that pervaded postemancipation society in Saint-Domingue, many Dominguan freed people attempted to migrate to Santo Domingo. This elicited harsh reprisals from some French officials. On 21 July 1798, the Directory's main agent in Saint-Domingue, General Gabriel Marie Theodore Joseph d'Hédouville, issued an *arrêté* (order) targeting what he viewed as a "formal invasion of the territory belonging to the [French] Republic."[68] (See figure 3.) The alleged perpetrators of this "invasion" were neither foreign soldiers nor malefactors such as pirates. Rather, Hédouville's targets were French citizens whose "crime" was nothing more than attempting to move within an island that was theoretically unified under Republican rule. Hédouville's response to these migrants' efforts to relocate to the "open land" of Santo Domingo was to empower the military to forbid any further settlement (or "usurpation" of land) in Santo Domingo by Dominguan migrants who did not possess a proper land title.[69]

These tactics were not unique to white administrators from the metropole, as both Toussaint and his adopted nephew, General Moïse, pursued similar policies. On 19 October 1799, Toussaint in a letter to Roume asserted that "a great number of our cultivators take refuge in the Spanish part," which weakened Saint-Domingue's labor force and therefore constituted an "abuse" that must be suppressed.[70] Despite his popularity among freed Dominguans, Moïse shared Toussaint's opinion on this matter. In a 14 October 1799 missive, Moïse urged Roume to "take measures" to stem the "desertion" of many Dominguan migrants to Santo Domingo, since their absence from Saint-Domingue was detrimental to both agriculture and the military. Moïse suggested as a solution the establishment of a "gendarmerie" that would serve the twin functions of stopping such unauthorized migration and protecting the *cultivateurs* from becoming victims of slaving to Havana, Caracas, and assorted other locales within the Spanish empire.[71] By voting with their feet, these *cultivateurs* sought to attain their own version of liberty, which collided with the political and economic agendas of black and white French colonial officials.

These conflicts over migration bespeak the importance of the political, physical, and psychological border bisecting Hispaniola in the events of the postcession years. This importance is evident in a comparative context. Recent microhistorical scholarship on border communities in the American Civil War has offered rich "on-the-ground" depictions of this war that are often in tension with conventional conceptual binaries associated with the conflict. In the words of Edward Ayers, "the nation redefined itself on the landscape of the border, the heart of the nation where North and South meet."[72] Similarly, in the first great abolitionist struggle in the Americas, the experiences of the freed migrants escaping French Republican emancipation by fleeing to a colony still substantially governed by proslavery authorities, as well as those of multilingual "maroon" communities straddling

FIGURE 3 "El ciudad[a]no. Heudoville habla al mentor de los Negros sobre las malas resultas de su revelión." Illustration of General Hédouville speaking with a black officer (possibly Toussaint Louverture) "on the bad effects of their [the blacks'] rebellion." From Dubroca, *Vida de J. J. Dessalines, gefe de los Negros de Santo Domingo* (Mexico, 1806). Courtesy of the John Carter Brown Library at Brown University.

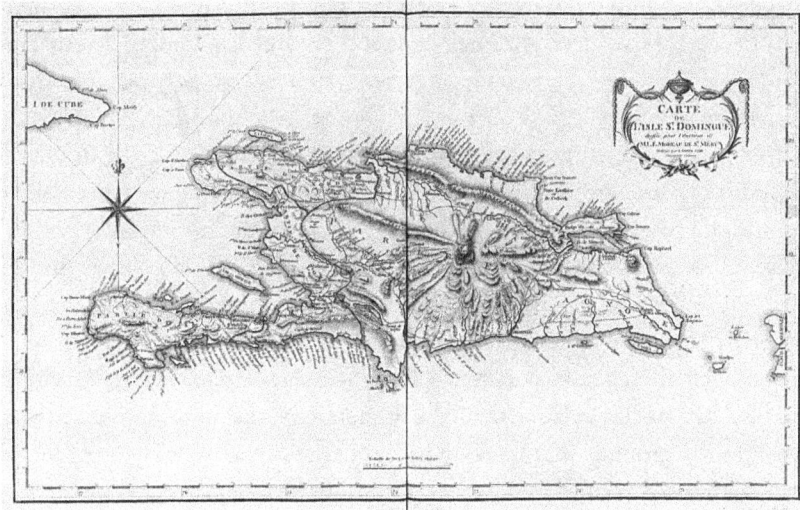

FIGURE 4 "Carte de l'Isle St. Domingue dressée pour l'Ouvage de M. L. E. Moreau de St. Méry Dessinée par I. Sonis." A map of Hispaniola from 1796. Note the prominence of the colonial border. Courtesy of the John Carter Brown Library at Brown University.

Hispaniola's border, complicate distinctions between slavery and emancipation, as well as between "French" and "Spanish." With the advent of revolution and slave emancipation in Hispaniola, long-standing quarrels over the border intersected with new conflicts over slavery and the relationship between colony and metropole. (See figure 4.) In revolutionary Hispaniola, the border held an assortment of meanings: beacon of (relative) freedom, frustrating focal point of conflict over the extradition of fugitives, military boundary, target for contraband, and even a sort of safety valve for tensions within Saint-Domingue.[73]

Though Hispaniola was hardly the only territory to experience civil strife or boundary disputes in the 1790s, its status as the epicenter of the era's great struggles over slavery and racism imbued its border problems with a special significance. In particular, the ambiguities of nationality and citizenship on the island—illustrated by the widespread persistence of "Spanish" identifiers referring to Santo Domingo in French- and Spanish-language colonial sources during the entire fourteen-year period of French rule and the travel restrictions on French citizens concerning Santo Domingo—became closely connected to the question of the rights possessed by those who were now formally free.[74]

The legal limbo faced by those claimed as slaves in Santo Domingo after the cession is a case in point. Their situation in some ways resembled that of other "slaves" caught between legal jurisdictions whose only claim to freedom in many cases rested on the 1794 French abolition law. The French scholar Agnès Renault has closely examined struggles over the limits of freedom in Santiago de Cuba, where thousands of refugees from Saint-Domingue relocated during the Haitian Revolutionary period. Many of these refugees sought to circumvent the 1794 emancipation edict by impelling fellow French citizens to migrate with them from Saint-Domingue to slaveholding Cuba. While these purported masters usually "totally ignored" the emancipation decree's existence, there was at least one instance in which Spanish authorities in Cuba denied a French refugee's ownership claim to a child on the grounds that this boy had obtained his liberty by the order of general emancipation.[75]

Did many French and Spanish authorities and others "totally ignore" the French Republican emancipation law in Santo Domingo, which unlike Cuba had technically come under French rule? The evidence suggests that some forms of servile labor persisted in Santo Domingo despite the initial fervor of Roume, Laveaux, and others. Numerous archival documents, for instance, refer to "slaves" in Santo Domingo after 1795. In a report dated June or July 1797, the French fortifications director, Charles Vincent, stated that impoverished free Dominicans in Montechristi shared their few possessions with their "Slave[s]."[76] Moreover, according to another report that was probably written by Vincent around the same time, the social and economic relations that were embedded in slavery caused would-be masters to insist that the extension of the French "decree of general liberty" to Santo Domingo would lead to their "inevitable ruin." This report's author further argued that "the day of the refusal of the Blacks to obey their master, would be the day of their destruction," as these purported masters—"terrible men"—would not hesitate to retaliate.[77] In a 12 December 1795 letter to Don Eugenio de Llaguno y Amirola, the high court official Urízar had denounced the "printed material" and "verbal exhortations" that Laveaux and other partisans of the French Republic had directed at "our Black slaves" and boasted that the latter were impervious to these influences. "Our fortune, and Providence have been able to dispel all of their attempts [to sway these 'slaves']," Urízar proclaimed. "The most admirable thing being that our slaves are those who detest them [the French entreaties] the most ... generally they all excuse themselves to their liberties, and they prefer our slavery, singing its praises."[78]

When confronted with challenges from below, such as protest, sabotage, flight, or open rebellion, slaveholders and those who claimed this status in Hispaniola and elsewhere often resorted to two contradictory tactics: to deny that those claimed as slaves could possess the agency to take such initiatives (rendering such a possibility "unthinkable" in Michel-Rolph Trouillot's well-known terms) and to express fear that the perceived contagion of unrest would spread.[79] After 1795, some Spanish officials attempted either to attribute unrest among servile laborers to external actors or to simply deny that a problem existed at all. Such intransigence provoked arm-twisting from French Republican authorities, who were themselves often ambivalent about those whose freedom they claimed to protect. In a tacit admission that his earlier exhortations on the elimination of slavery in Santo Domingo had not achieved the intended result, Agent Roume in a letter to the Municipal Administration of Montechristi dated 22 March 1800 urged his interlocutors to view "your former alleged Slaves" as "friends" who were "interested, as are you, in the maintenance of public order and the prosperity of the colony."[80]

Observers gave varying estimates of the number of "slaves" in Santo Domingo. In a 26 June 1800 letter to "citizen Perregaux," the Marquis d'Iranda claimed that 10,000 to 12,000 "Slaves" lived among Santo Domingo's population of approximately 150,000 individuals of "diverse castes."[81] One report on Santo Domingo stated that most of the colony's "ten thousand slaves" tended to animals or worked in the cities. According to this report, the "free population" of Santo Domingo numbered around 50,000, the majority of whom were "of color or mixed."[82] Given the dearth of official statistics until the Napoleonic regime of 1804–09, such reports constitute virtually the only extant sources on the "slave" population's numbers in Santo Domingo during the revolutionary era.

Irrespective of its size, however, this population played an important role in the political conflicts unfolding on the island. In October 1798, General Hédouville removed Toussaint's trusted subordinate, General Moïse, from his post as commander of Republican military forces in Fort-Liberté (formerly Fort-Dauphin) and replaced him with an officer named Grandet. Moïse in turn accused Grandet of working against emancipation by capturing fugitives from Santo Domingo who had fled across the border and returning them to those who claimed to be their masters.[83] (Ironically, this is exactly what the French themselves had long pressured the Spanish to do with Dominguan slaves, with limited results.) In a 12 September 1798 letter to Moïse, the gendarmerie commander Étienne Albert had condemned Grandet for fomenting disorder in the Fort-Liberté area and told Moïse that a "Spanish army" had begun to "arrest all their blacks who are in the French part."[84]

As a former slave leading an army composed mostly of fellow freed-men, General Moïse had reason to be suspicious of hostility from various quarters toward general emancipation. "Since the emancipation of the slaves and the decree of 16 Pluviôse [4 February 1794], the inhabitants of the former Spanish part keep their cultivators . . . in the most severe servi-tude and treat them with more cruelty than ever before," Moïse contended in a 9 October 1798 letter to Hédouville. In this correspondence, Moïse accused Grandet of complicity in the efforts of many Dominicans to re-capture the ex-slaves whom they still considered to be their "property"; part of Moïse's case rested on Grandet's alleged attempts to arrest "vagabonds" in the area.[85]

If these Dominican fugitives lived in a liminal space at the interstices of slavery and freedom, then the situation of the "maroon" communities who often lived near the island's colonial border was perhaps even more precari-ous. In the late 1790s, Republican authorities attempted to integrate into the French political order the members of the best-known of these communi-ties: an enclave straddling the border that the source record typically refers to as "Maniel."[86]

The Borderland "Maroons"

"The citizens of Maniel, who saw in each Frenchman an enemy of their lib-erty, while the horrible reign of despotism and aristocracy lasted, Can now only see in each of us a brother and a defender, since we have decided to give men of all countries, and especially the African people, the full enjoy-ment of the sacred and enduring rights of the human race." So spoke Roume, who hoped that the political transformations in France and Saint-Domingue would facilitate the incorporation of those from Maniel—who were, after all, potential soldiers and plantation workers—into the Republican sphere. By presenting France as the sole guarantor of the "sacred and enduring rights of the human race," Roume marginalized the types of liberty that those from the enclave had carved out for themselves.[87]

The cession of Santo Domingo to emancipationist France raised the question of the continued viability of "maroon" communities after emancipation. In an undated letter to the minister of the navy, an official named Minuty argued that the prerevolutionary practice of appointing a French agent to Santo Domingo to assist in the recapture of "Black maroons" was "illusory" and "useless" in the present context given the general emancipation decree and the subsequent cession of Santo Domingo.[88] Nonetheless, the basic contours of the relationship between colonial authorities and these communities remained much the same after 1795.

While scholars have long debated the role of maroons in enabling the great slave uprising of 1791, the situation of the "maroons" after emancipation—and the challenges that they posed to the emancipationist enterprise—have not attracted the same attention.[89] French and Spanish slave law had both dealt harshly with fugitive slaves,[90] and the relative autonomy of maroon communities, the fact that many were located near the border, and their inclusion of fugitive slaves from both parts of the island had provoked numerous disputes between the French and Spanish colonial governments before 1789. After 1795, French officials in Santo Domingo adopted a model that the Spanish had developed in their dealings with Maniel and other such communities: the combination of the carrot of resettlement and inducements to proclaim loyalty to the colonial state and the stick of military incursions.

Though the "integral part" doctrine enshrined emancipation and racial equality in French law, Roume now used this doctrine to justify subduing those who had won their freedom by other means. In an *arrêté* issued on 16 August 1796, Roume declared that quasi-independent political "order[s]" such as Maniel were "incompatible" with an indivisible French Republic. He also argued that "the totality of the island ha[s] become an integral Part of the territory of France." Roume appointed a delegation to communicate his wishes to the members of this community and to "instruct" them on "their rights and duties" as French Republican citizens—an especially pressing matter given the perceived threat of their co-optation by either British or royalist French factions. Roume nonetheless characterized these "maroons" as a "respectable population of African citizens who had the courage to conquer their natural liberty" and who "have found themselves needing to be constantly on guard against both governments [French and Spanish], which has Produced a type of Small independent State, Located at the limits of the two colonies."[91]

In his attempts to control those who had "had the courage to conquer their natural liberty," Roume employed the same Spanish priest whom Dominican authorities had entrusted with the spiritual instruction of those from Maniel and their resettlement in Catholic *poblaciones* (settlements). In a 16 August 1796 letter to this priest, Juan Bobadilla, Roume called upon him to "conquer for the French Republic the hearts" of the "African population" of Maniel—a task that would be facilitated by the "absolute trust" that these individuals placed in Bobadilla. "His Catholic Majesty, in ceding to us the Spanish part of Saint-Domingue, ceded to us the Land that this population [of Maniel] inhabits; and we cannot permit them to form a state *independent of our laws, on a portion of our own territory*," declared Roume.[92] By enlisting Bobadilla—who had on 25 January 1790 deemed it necessary to "achieve the perfect civilization and reduction to Christian life of those [Maniel inhabitants] who for so long have groaned under the harsh servitude of heathenism"—Roume allied himself with a man who had long worked to undermine the precarious independence that the Maniel inhabitants had forged.[93] Whether the stated ideological justification was the achievement of a Christian "perfect civilization" or the realization of French Republican liberty, each colonial government sought to incorporate the residents of this community into a centralized state.

The revolutionary upheaval nonetheless appears in some instances to have undermined attempts to assert state authority over these communities. In a report written in Santo Domingo on 8 February 1811, a man named Juan Caballero stated that Spanish authorities led by a judge, a battalion lieutenant, and the priest Bobadilla had in the late 1780s persuaded some maroons to form a town called San Cristóbal del Naranjo at the foot of the Baoruco Mountains in southwest Santo Domingo, where Bobadilla regularly administered the holy sacraments. Yet upon Santo Domingo's cession to France in 1795, the intrusion of many French "*negros y mulatos*" (blacks and mixed-race persons) led to the dissolution of San Cristóbal del Naranjo and the dispersion of its residents into the mountains.[94] Though a French colonial official would boast in early 1798 that "the former insurgents of Maniel" had placed themselves "under the Tricolor [French Republican] flag," those from Maniel and other such communities would later challenge the political and military supremacy of both Toussaint Louverture and his Napoleonic successors on the island.[95]

Conflicts concerning these so-called maroon communities after 1795 hint that parts of the island's terrestrial border contained transcultural and semiautonomous spaces that at least partially defied state political, military, and ideological control. In many respects, portions of these borderlands retained this character well into the twentieth century.[96] Fundamentally, the "problem" of Maniel and other such enclaves in the 1790s and early 1800s challenged not only the boundaries of the Republican nation-state and of French emancipation but also the conventional periodization demarcating the colonial and revolutionary eras in Hispaniola.[97] From the vantage point of these communities, the Haitian Revolution appears much less a struggle over liberty, racial equality, and ideology within the French empire than a continuation of the long-standing interimperial efforts to suppress these communities' autonomy.

Ultimately, the Boca Nigua revolt, the question of emigration with "slaves," the political and philosophical debates over emancipation in Santo Domingo, and the conflicts over Maniel attest to the islandwide nature of the great struggles concerning the 1794 French emancipation decree and the "integral part" doctrine. In the years following the cession of Santo Domingo, the insular character of the Haitian Revolution became explicitly articulated in the political vision of Toussaint Louverture, who endeavored to unify the entire island under his rule. Santo Domingo factored centrally into Toussaint's military and political strategies, and the former Spanish colony also became critical to contests over Toussaint's limited vision of emancipation. These struggles would further draw together the histories of the island's two colonies in new and unforeseen ways.

CHAPTER THREE

Santo Domingo and the Rise of Toussaint Louverture, 1795–1801

On 26 January 1801, the forces of Toussaint Louverture, a former slave fighting under the banner of liberty, marched into the city of Santo Domingo. Finding relatively little armed opposition, they proclaimed their governance over the city, as well as the entire former Spanish colony, in the name of the French Republic. At this pivotal moment, the colony's inhabitants found themselves at the center of the era's great conflicts over slavery, the legitimacy of racial hierarchies, and the relationship between colony and metropole.

Though Toussaint's capture of Santo Domingo city in 1801 altered the island's trajectory, the invasion was in fact the culmination of a series of military incursions that Toussaint had made into the colony of Santo Domingo since 1795. These in turn were enabled in part by Toussaint's knowledge of Santo Domingo gained through his service in Spain's armies in 1793–94. Having risen from Spanish "auxiliary" to indispensable leader in the French Republican campaign for the island, Toussaint, along with the thousands of warriors who served under him, wrested numerous strategically crucial Dominican posts from British, Spanish, and royalist French enemies in the second half of the 1790s. Their efforts served both to bring these areas under French Republican control and to augment Toussaint's rapidly growing power. In their reshaping of the colonial border, these military episodes also left a lasting legacy for the island's political geography. Finally, they posed an important if limited challenge to the practice of holding one's fellow human beings in bondage.

As Toussaint became more powerful, he came to embrace a goal that had eluded all before him since the late seventeenth century: the union of the entire island of Hispaniola under a single political regime, in practice as well as on paper. This brought him into conflict with Philippe-Rose Roume, Paris's principal agent in Santo Domingo, who, in accordance with the wishes of the Directory and subsequently the Consulate (Napoleon's regime), sought to thwart Toussaint's ambitions in Santo Domingo. In the six years following Santo Domingo's cession, two opposing visions for Hispaniola's political future clashed: Toussaint's of an island united under his rule and that of

Napoleon and Roume, who saw the status quo of partition as the best way to limit Toussaint's authority.[1] Though Toussaint would initially triumph in this struggle, the Napoleonic vision of division would more accurately characterize the island's history in the two centuries following Toussaint's brief reign in Santo Domingo.

Santo Domingo was integral in interconnected imperial crises that had profound implications for the history of the Caribbean and the hemisphere. Toussaint's fleetingly successful yet ultimately ill-fated attempt to bring the island under his rule helped to shape an integrated Franco-Spanish history of geopolitical conflict and factional warfare that eventually morphed into an anticolonial struggle.

Santo Domingo in the Defeat of the British

In a missive to his rival General Gabriel Hédouville dated 5 September 1798, Toussaint Louverture dreamed of a hemisphere without slavery. If France could only vanquish its foes in the Caribbean, Toussaint declared, then it might realize its supreme goal: "the maintenance and the propagation of universal liberty" in "all of the Americas."[2] Nonetheless, much as Toussaint might have imagined eventual emancipation in the United States or the Spanish and Portuguese colonies to the south, he had to attend to matters much closer to home. There was indeed much to attend to, as these years seemed to inflict one disappointment after another on defenders of emancipation. (Among these adverse developments, it can be argued, were Toussaint's own repressive labor regimes, which he strengthened and expanded at the turn of the century.) Though interspersed with fleeting triumphs, successive political setbacks for the causes of abolition and revolution in France culminated in the rise of Napoleon in 1799 and his dissolution that year of the short-lived French constitution of 1795 that had erased distinctions in citizenship rights for all the inhabitants of that nation's realms.[3]

The cause of universal liberty also faced grave threats in Hispaniola itself. Though the defeat of Spain in 1795 represented a victory for French Republican emancipation, Toussaint and other French leaders still had to contend with the thousands of British troops who occupied a number of sensitive parts of the island. With their domination of the seas, numerous bases in the Caribbean, and strongholds in the key Dominguan towns of Môle St-Nicholas, Jérémie, and Saint-Marc, the redcoats posed a formidable threat to the diverse factions that fought under the French tricolor flag.

The confusion surrounding Santo Domingo's political status exacerbated this menace. As we have seen, notwithstanding the Treaty of Basel's stipulation that "the King of Spain . . . cedes and abandons . . . to the French Republic the entire Spanish part of the isle of Saint Domingue, in the Antilles," much of the old Spanish colonial administration, including Governor Joaquín García, stayed on, struggling for power with the few French officials who claimed authority in Santo Domingo.[4] This situation kept Santo Domingo in a political limbo in which its residents could not be certain who their true rulers were. It also made the island more susceptible to foreign invasion, as its spacious and poorly defended eastern portion offered the British a potential staging ground for attacks on Saint-Domingue. As one Spanish diplomat noted in a 1797 letter to the French minister of foreign relations, the "extraordinary and unexpected delay" of Santo Domingo's transfer to France had rendered it vulnerable to British designs.[5]

For many French Republicans, both this British threat and the presence of many Dominguan settlers in Santo Domingo doubtless increased the perceived stakes involved in securing effective control over that colony, especially since many of these migrants were probably traders who had long engaged in brisk commerce in cattle along the old borderlands (particularly in the central area near Mirebalais).[6] Farther north, vulnerable Dominican towns abutted the coveted sugar zones of Saint-Domingue's economic heartland.

The vagaries of European geopolitics added a further layer of complexity to these events in Hispaniola. Shortly before the signing of the Treaty of Basel, France had made peace with Prussia in this same Swiss town in April 1795, while the Dutch followed suit the next month. This left the British, Austrians, and a small Italian kingdom called Piedmont-Sardinia as the French Republic's principal foreign enemies. During a French military campaign in northern Italy in 1796–97, an obscure Corsican commander named Napoleon Bonaparte defied the orders of the Directory by carving out a new republic in Italy and delivering part of Venice to the Austrians as part of a diplomatic deal unsanctioned by his superiors—actions not dissimilar to those undertaken by Toussaint in his own rise to power, ironically in defiance of Napoleon after 1799.[7]

In the first year of Napoleon's Italian campaign, Spain's rulers opted to renew their former alliance with France by the Treaty of San Ildefonso, signed on 19 August 1796. Per the logic of contemporary geopolitics, this agreement dissolved the tenuous peace that the Iberian power had briefly enjoyed with Britain, and a new war between the two commenced in October of that year.[8] Both the strengthening of the French Republic in Europe and the Franco-Spanish alliance added new dimensions to the series of small wars fought in Hispaniola between the Spanish, French royalists, the British, and assorted French Republican politico-military units. Among the latter, the two most important were the semiautonomous domain in the southern province/*département* of Saint-Domingue under André Rigaud and that led by Toussaint Louverture, who during the earlier Franco-Spanish war had established a stronghold in the western Dominguan provincial town of Gonaïves. Although Paris had delegated the Civil Commission that included Agent Roume and Julien Raimond as its designated authority in Saint-Domingue following that war, most of the real power lay in the hands of Toussaint and Rigaud.

At the end of the Franco-Spanish war, Toussaint had been merely one among many competing Republican military leaders; three years later, he personally negotiated the departure of British forces from the island. In the intervening period, his military victories against this enemy earned him many accolades, of which the most notable was his promotion by the civil commissioner Léger-Félicité Sonthonax to the post of commander-in-chief of all French military forces in Saint-Domingue following a major victory over the redcoats in Mirebalais in 1797.[9] Toussaint's numerous conquests in Santo Domingo during these years also helped to cement his authority and that of the Republic on the island.

Toussaint's campaigns against the British in Santo Domingo centered on the localities of Bánica, Las Caobas (or Lascahobas), San Juan de la Maguana, and Neyba in the colony's center-west and southwest. This terrain constituted a choke point that connected northern Saint-Domingue's sugar zones with the crucial post of Mirebalais and the fertile Dominican interior. The British occupied these towns in successive military advances from late 1796 to the middle of 1797.[10] Nonetheless, by this latter date, John Simcoe, who had been appointed governor for the island by London, commanded only 14,800 men, who opposed Toussaint's armies of 15,000 to 20,000.[11]

For the British, this disadvantage in manpower became compounded by perhaps an even greater weakness: continued reliance upon slavery. As discussed in chapter 1, the British offered enslaved men on the island eventual liberty and meager provisions in exchange for risking their lives for British imperialism.[12] Several thousand men accepted this grim trade-off: the Dominguan "black corps" serving the British numbered 6,700 men as of late 1796, of whom around 5,000 were unfree.[13] Yet by choosing to enslave around 70,000 people while depending on the military service of bondsmen, the British in many senses had the worst of both worlds.[14] Their refusal to proclaim general abolition translated into an inability to claim the moral legitimacy that emancipationist France utilized so effectively in its military campaigns in the Caribbean. Moreover, pervasive racism within the British military administration alienated many potential allies.[15] At the same time, the use of slave soldiers undermined the slave society that the British were trying to preserve, as it weakened plantation discipline and provided guns and training to men who would in many cases end up among Toussaint's forces.[16]

Toussaint took full advantage of the British refusal to relinquish dependence on slave labor. On an island where rivals constantly hurled accusations at each other of secretly harboring wishes to restore slavery, the politically savvy Toussaint recognized the potency of such claims against an adversary whom he could credibly accuse of employing forced servitude. In one detailed recounting of his military exploits dated 9 April 1797, Toussaint proclaimed that ousting the British occupiers in Mirebalais would liberate "thousands of unfortunates," whose suffering just happened to occur in a zone that was the "key" that linked Saint-Domingue's three provinces and the "former Spanish part" to each other.[17] Other high Republican officials echoed Toussaint's concerns. In a 28 June 1796 letter to Sonthonax, General Donatien Rochambeau (who briefly served as the "Commandant in Chief of the Spanish part of Saint-Domingue") accused the British of retaining slavery in Puerto Plata and Samaná (in Santo Domingo's north), where they had established footholds. According to Rochambeau, the British "have sent Emissaries into the interior of the country [Santo Domingo] to permit on their part the maintenance of the Catholic religion, [and] the conservation of Slavery and of properties, if [the colony's] inhabitants wanted to rally to the Side of Great Britain." In Rochambeau's estimation, this siren song would prove all the more seductive to these areas' inhabitants due to the pervasive "prejudices that the Spanish always have about the difference of Colors."[18]

Perceptions of racially motivated Dominican opposition to French rule may have stemmed in part from incidents such as the capitulation of Bánica to the British in August 1796. In a 17 September 1796 statement before Agent Roume, a French-born settler named Pierre-Claude Clément, who had lived in the parish of Bánica for eighteen years, provided a vivid description of Bánica's surrender to the British by its former governor Domingo Figueré. Though most of Bánica's residents (including Figueré) swore an oath of loyalty to the British in a local church, Clément refused to do so, which led Figueré to issue an order for his capture "dead or alive." In Clément's reading of the situation, these Bánica residents' "fear of black troops" (and more specifically, "black republican troops") helped to drive them into the arms of the British. "If White Republicans came to take possession [of Santo Domingo], then we would be able to count on the fidelity of the majority of [Santo Domingo's] inhabitants," Clément related through Roume, "but if blacks come, and above all only blacks," then the Republic's support among Dominicans would quickly evaporate.[19]

For many inhabitants of Santo Domingo, the British offered two attractions that the French Republicans did not: the maintenance of slavery and a royalist political order. Though Santo Domingo's Spanish-speaking residents were not, of course, all of like mind, many found common cause with the British despite the antagonism between the two European metropoles after 1796 and the exhortations that Toussaint and other French leaders directed at them to pledge their loyalty to France. As the news of Santo Domingo's cession became known on the island, many Dominicans had sided with Britain against France, welcoming British ships into their ports, pledging allegiance to the British in exchange for protection, and enlisting in the military forces of France's nemesis.[20] In a 31 July 1796 letter to the Spanish commander in Bánica, Toussaint claimed that a "great number" of Las Caobas residents had defected to the British.[21] Three days earlier, Toussaint had argued that French forces' assumption of effective control over Santo Domingo was necessary in order to thwart both English and Spanish designs on the island.[22]

In the wake of the recent war with Spain, persistent suspicions that many Dominicans harbored proslavery inclinations and were conspiring with France's enemies against general emancipation undermined relations between Dominicans and French authorities. Nevertheless, many residents of Santo Domingo served in French armies after 1795. In an account of recent military events written for Toussaint on 16 October 1798, Moïse commented on the mixed benefit that "Spanish" recruits brought to the French. While acknowledging the military asset that a "large Spanish Cavalry" that was "assimilated" to French forces in the northern border area represented for the Republic, Moïse warned that many members of this cavalry might retain their loyalty to Spain, the "Sworn Enemy nation of the Liberty of the Blacks."[23]

Dominican officials for their part made overtures to their French counterparts when it suited their interests. On 20 July 1797, the commissioners Raimond and Sonthonax related that Governor García had requested in a recent letter that they deploy a number of troops to the northern Dominican towns of Montechristi and Dajabón to take military possession of these strategically crucial places. According to the commissioners, García had requested these troops in order "to oppose an invasion by the English" of the island; the French for their part apparently had their own interest in seizing Montechristi to secure much-needed cattle via the old Dominican cattle trade. In response to this entreaty, these French officials sent an officer named Grandet to assume control over these areas. In addition to replacing Spanish troops with French ones in accordance with the Treaty of Basel, Grandet had orders to oversee the administrative and judicial reformation of these posts. This would entail the replacement of Spanish "public functionaries" with French administrators, with all official correspondence to be henceforth written in French. Nonetheless, "Spanish civil laws" were to remain in force in these areas unless they contradicted the French constitution of 1795.[24] In this moment, the blend of Spanish and French authority in Santo Domingo intersected with the war being waged for control of Hispaniola.

As this war progressed, both the British and the French invested a significant amount of manpower in Santo Domingo. In January 1798, Toussaint deployed a force of 11,000 men serving under Moïse with orders to march from Fort-Liberté in Saint-Domingue's north to Las Caobas, where they were to subdue a unit of English and Spanish soldiers that included a number of "black troops" in the service of the English.[25] Moïse captured Las Caobas on 6 February 1798.[26] This triumph helped to break the back of the British occupation by closing off a vital interior transit route. Moreover, Toussaint's incorporation of Hincha and Las Caobas into the French Republican sphere during this conflict changed the island's political geography by bringing these areas under French (and then Haitian) governance.[27]

By the conclusion of the battle in Las Caobas, the tide of war had begun to turn decisively against the redcoats. The combination of military setbacks, defections to French ranks, disease, and pressing matters elsewhere conspired to convince many British leaders on both sides of the Atlantic that Hispaniola represented a monetary sinkhole whose costs far outstripped the meager benefits that Britain had derived from its military presence on the island. Casualties suffered by the British in their wars against the French on other Caribbean islands, such as Martinique and St. Vincent, bolstered the argument for British military disengagement from this region. Indeed, even the most ardent defender of an aggressive British expansionist policy in the Caribbean would have found it difficult to defend an enterprise that cost the lives of 60,000 British troops in the region in the 1790s.[28] Shortly after General Thomas Maitland assumed command of British forces in Hispaniola in March 1798, discussions between British and French representatives commenced on the terms of a British withdrawal.

Developments in both parts of the island accelerated this process. In the month of Maitland's arrival, Toussaint penetrated a set of British forts that had kept the French out of Arcahaye on Saint-Domingue's west coast, which severely weakened Britain's position in the area. He achieved similar successes in Santo Domingo. In a 4 March 1798 letter to Roume, Toussaint recounted his victories in retaking Neyba, San Juan, Las Caobas, and other key parts of Santo Domingo, condemning in the strongest terms those who had betrayed the French Republic by serving the "Freedom-killing project" (*projet Liberticide*) of the British. According to Toussaint, these conquests (especially that of Las Caobas) had helped to secure Mirebalais for the Republicans and to draw together disparate parts of the island under his rule.[29] "In a word," Toussaint declared in the memoirs that he composed shortly before his death in a French prison cell in 1803, "none of the fortifications that the English had in this part [Saint-Domingue] could resist me, nor those of Neiba, San Juan de la Maguana, Bánica, and other spots occupied by the Spanish. All these I handed over to the republic."[30]

Despite Toussaint's ominous implied threats of retaliation, the extrication of remaining British troops from the island was achieved mostly without further bloodshed. In the spring and summer of 1798, Toussaint and Maitland agreed upon terms for the surrender of Britain's three remaining significant posts in Hispaniola: Port-au-Prince in the west, Jérémie in the south, and Môle Saint-Nicolas in the north. Both in its results and in the means by which it was achieved, this great power's military exit from the island reflected and augmented Toussaint's power. The departure of Toussaint's last remaining foreign nemesis was accomplished without the consultation, much less the approval, of the indignant General Hédouville, who as the Directory's principal representative in Saint-Domingue theoretically outranked Toussaint. Toussaint's military victories against the British, in combination with his adroit political maneuvering, enabled him to expel from the island first Sonthonax and then Hédouville, who in late October

1798 found himself on a ship departing Hispaniola, having little to show for his brief time there other than assorted correspondences containing high-minded rhetoric about liberty, a strengthened black army command, and a bruised ego.

Britain's defeat ultimately signaled Toussaint's emergence as a de facto independent statesman. His trade agreements with Britain and the United States, for instance, sought to ensure markets for the island's plantation goods and to secure continuing access to provisions, weapons, and munitions.[31] The war with the British also helped to establish an enduring French/Haitian power base in Santo Domingo whose legacies still resonate on the island today. In the immediate term, however, Toussaint's triumph led to a new and particularly brutal military phase of the revolution.

Santo Domingo and the War of the South

"It is painful for us, after having, by our sensible, laborious and reasonable conduct, served the general good, to see ourselves faced with slander, oppression, and as the prey of our old despots." Fresh from his triumph over the British, Toussaint in this address to "all good Frenchmen" of Saint-Domingue expressed his unwillingness to rest on his laurels, lest his many enemies succeed in killing or deposing him. Years of war and political intrigue had made Toussaint quite suspicious of those around him, as evidenced in his assertion that a number of would-be assassins were preparing to first dispatch him and then "pass as saviors of the Colony."[32] Though this discourse served a distinct political purpose, Toussaint's anxieties were not entirely unfounded. Following the expulsion of the British, his onetime ally André Rigaud would become his most formidable foe. In their war of attrition, both men would claim the mantle of "savior of the colony," yet the conflict would leave a divisive legacy for the Haitian nation.

Hardened by years of combat against external enemies, the French Republican armies in Saint-Domingue turned on each other after the departure of the British, coalescing into two principal factions led by Toussaint and Rigaud. As the noted Trinidadian scholar C. L. R. James might have observed, internecine warfare among victorious liberation forces following the common enemy's defeat would later become a recognized pattern (indeed, almost a trope) in twentieth-century Third World decolonization. As with so many other matters, the Haitian Revolution in a sense provided an important early example of this phenomenon. Both of these belligerent groups professed loyalty to the French Republic and its ideals, trading accusations of treason and of concocting malicious plots to reestablish the despised institution of slavery on the island.

Though the battle against the British had forced Toussaint, Rigaud, and Roume into a fragile coexistence, this alliance broke down soon after the last British troops left the island. Any hopes of a lasting peace after years of carnage were soon thwarted by a confluence of circumstances. These included the bitter rivalry that emerged between two ambitious leaders as well as animosities between Toussaint's predominantly *nouveau libre* (newly free) following (based primarily in Saint-Domingue's north and west) and the partisans of Rigaud, who had established a stronghold in the colony's southern province earlier in the 1790s. Many officers and plantation owners under Rigaud were *anciens libres* (those of African descent who were further removed from slavery than the *nouveaux libres*).[33]

These tensions stemmed from long-standing social and economic antagonisms. Earlier in the eighteenth century, a wealthy *gens de couleur* class had arisen in the southern province, based partly on entrepreneurship in indigo. This class formed much of the bulwark of support for Rigaud, a Bordeaux-educated military officer who commanded the southern province for much of the 1790s.[34] Under Rigaud's postabolition plantation regime, he rented abandoned plantations to private citizens, who employed the labor of *cultivateurs* under restrictive conditions that closely resembled the harsh labor code of Sonthonax. This served to reproduce the old inequalities between the predominantly *ancien libre* former masters and the *nouveau libre* ex-slaves. Quite simply, in the words of Laurent Dubois, these former slaves "saw the ghosts of slavery in the new order."[35]

In the vicious conflict between the partisans of Toussaint and Rigaud, christened by scholars the "War of the South," Toussaint harnessed the frustrations of these ex-slaves—and the loyalty of a black landowning class that had arisen in the postabolition north and west provinces—in his determined effort to conquer the recalcitrant southern zone. This war involved the commission of atrocities by both sides throughout Saint-Domingue and culminated in Rigaud's defeat and exile from the island in the summer of 1800. While the scholarly literature has usually focused on this conflict's complex racial and political dynamics as well as the sheer devastation inflicted by Toussaint's forces (most notably those under the command of General Jean-Jacques Dessalines) in the south, this war also intersected with the question of Santo Domingo's status and Toussaint's wish to rule that colony.

Due in part to Saint-Domingue's economic importance, many outside parties had a perceived stake in the outcome of the War of the South. While the North Americans and the British lent their support to Toussaint, Spanish authorities and other elite Dominicans generally favored his rival. Supporting Rigaud, after all, might aid in destabilizing French Saint-Domingue, Cuba's great rival, while undermining Toussaint, whose designs on the eastern portion of Hispaniola were rightly feared by Dominican leaders.

At the center of these intrigues was Antoine Chanlatte, a military officer and *homme de couleur* sent to Santo Domingo by Agent Roume, whose disagreement with Toussaint over the question of the status of Santo Domingo exacerbated the political rivalry between the two men. Chanlatte worked both diplomatically and militarily to weaken Toussaint's position. According to an anonymous letter to the minister of the navy dated 13 August 1800, Chanlatte collaborated with Spanish officials in Santo Domingo to send a deputy to Paris (one presumably unsympathetic to Toussaint) to discuss the issue of sovereignty over the colony. At the same time, Chanlatte sought to deliver "abundant munitions" from the Spanish to Rigaud, "his friend, [to] attack Toussaint."[36] According to Pierre Pluchon, the Spanish in Santo Domingo "openly" supported Rigaud over Toussaint, which became apparent in an angry August 1800 letter to Roume in which Toussaint accused the Spanish of offering aid in men, munitions, and arms to his enemy.[37]

Both the Spanish authorities in Santo Domingo and Rigaud naturally wished to preserve their power, while Toussaint felt that the realization of his own political ambitions necessitated dispatching both. This led to a degree of cooperation between these adversaries of Toussaint. This collaboration nonetheless had its limits, as Governor García and other Spanish authorities were astute enough to recognize the imbalance of power between the forces of their favorite, Rigaud, and those of Toussaint. According to a 19 October 1800 report, if the defeated Rigaud had fled to Santo Domingo, then he would have received a cold reception by García due to the latter's fear of retribution at the hands of Toussaint.[38] This did not prevent Rigaud from soliciting munitions and other assistance from Spanish officials in nearby Cuba, an effort that he hoped would be facilitated by these officials' anxieties concerning the revolution in Hispaniola. In a 30 June 1800 request for military aid addressed to Havana's captain general, the Marquis de Someruelos, Rigaud waxed melodramatic, insisting that Toussaint was determined not only to remove Saint-Domingue from the French orbit but also (with British aid) to bring about the loss of all of Spain's New World colonies.[39]

The Haitian Revolution lent itself to hyperbole, and Rigaud appears to have known how to manipulate the fears of white Spanish administrators. Nevertheless, Toussaint did lead a formidable military force. Though he had entered into a secret accord with the British general Maitland in 1798 to desist from supporting any seditious movements in Jamaica, Toussaint's massive army could threaten neighboring governments—as García was to discover in early 1801. This army, however, could not survive on its own. Though he conducted his diplomacy as if he ran an independent state, Toussaint was acutely aware of his vulnerability to and dependence on the powers that quite literally surrounded him.

Most notably, Toussaint's lucrative commerce with the United States was integral to his ability to arm and outfit his thousands of troops. According to historian Sigfrido Vázquez Cienfuegos, in September 1800 Toussaint received in Le Cap 20,000 rifles, 10,000 pairs of pistols, 500 chairs, and 60,000 pounds of gunpowder via trade with the United States. As they nervously observed these exchanges, Santo Domingo's leaders feared that Toussaint might use these weapons against them.[40]

They had reason to be concerned, especially given Toussaint's crushing victory over Rigaud earlier that summer. In his war against Rigaud, Toussaint had benefited from a policy devised by the U.S. Congress that rested on a distinction between formal sovereignty and effective control in both parts of Hispaniola. In 1798, the United States had declared an embargo on trade with France in retaliation for repeated attacks by French privateers on North American vessels; this was the so-called Quasi War. Nonetheless, aware of the profits that its traders had long derived from commerce with Saint-Domingue (which by the late eighteenth century had become "the United States' second-largest trading partner after England"[41]), Congress created a special exclusion to this trade interdiction that permitted commerce with those parts of the French empire that were judged to have separated themselves from direct French control. This provision became known as "Toussaint's Clause" because it chiefly concerned Saint-Domingue.[42]

According to a 9 June 1800 report by Chanlatte, the U.S. government excluded the port of Santo Domingo from Toussaint's Clause (thus legally barring its citizens from trading there) on the grounds that it had come under French sovereignty per the 1795 Treaty of Basel yet had not fallen under

Toussaint's effective control.[43] Toussaint thus benefited from the trade permitted by the relatively sympathetic Adams administration, while Dominicans were denied the benefits of legal trade with North Americans, at least through the main Dominican port. This may have served to further weaken Dominican authorities' military position as well as their ability to offer arms to Rigaud. While internal dynamics drove the War of the South, external forces, such as trade and diplomacy, influenced the strength of each belligerent party.[44]

Rigaud struck first in the War of the South. In June 1799, his forces took two key towns near the border of the southern and western *départements* of Saint-Domingue, Petit-Goâve and Grand-Goâve, which helped convince Alexandre Pétion, an influential military leader and future president of Haiti, to join Rigaud. A series of uprisings associated with Rigaud throughout Saint-Domingue then provoked Louverture, along with his trusted officers Henry Christophe and Jean-Jacques Dessalines, to brutally crush these movements, after which they carried out an invasion of the south. Despite Toussaint's threefold manpower advantage over Rigaud (45,000 men under Toussaint versus 15,000 serving Rigaud), it took several months of protracted "scorched earth" warfare—and a U.S. blockade of southern Dominguan ports—to defeat Rigaud, who fled from Saint-Domingue in late July 1800.[45]

Rigaud's fall made Toussaint the most powerful individual on the entire island. "Far from restricting himself to military functions," Chanlatte lamented in a report dated 20 June 1800, Toussaint "has extended his authority to all of the branches of social organization. It has been a long time since anything has been done outside of his influence."[46] On 19 February 1799, General François Kerverseau, whom the French metropolitan government had appointed to serve as the "Commissioner of the Executive Directory in the Former Spanish Part of Saint-Domingue," had composed a frank letter to the minister of the navy in which he similarly expressed dismay at Toussaint's growing power.[47] By this time, Toussaint's subordinate, Moïse, controlled the districts of Montechristi and Dajabón in the former Spanish colony's north, and Toussaint's ambitions concerning the rest of that colony were, in Kerverseau's eyes, becoming ever more readily apparent. While Kerverseau dismissed rumors that Toussaint was planning a large-scale invasion into Santo Domingo as "simple conjecture," Kerverseau vowed to employ all means at his disposal to prevent such an incursion. He assured his superior that the "Spanish government" in Santo Domingo would "safeguard, if necessary, by arms, the possessions that remain under its protection and its responsibility until the [full execution of the] legal taking of Possession" of Santo Domingo by France had transpired.[48] Such legal and diplomatic niceties stood in marked contrast to the military situation on the ground. According to a report presented to the "Consuls of the Republic" in September or October 1800, Toussaint had possessed nine parishes in Santo Domingo as of the previous *Germinal* (22 March to 20 April 1800), and he also had imprisoned numerous Dominicans in Port-au-Prince.[49]

These words of caution and resignation rang true for a succession of French administrators (including Sonthonax, Hédouville, and his successor, Roume), who between 1797 and 1801 found themselves on long, lonely voyages from Hispaniola back to France, whiling away the days of the passage contemplating how they would explain to authorities in Paris their failure to subordinate the ex-slave Toussaint to the will of a global military power. Meanwhile, the thousands of freed men and women who comprised the bulk of Toussaint's power base were becoming increasingly apprehensive as their once-trusted leader, intent on maximizing plantation revenues, imposed restrictive labor regimes modeled substantially on that of Sonthonax that tied the former slaves to their old plantations or the military. Toussaint also parceled out many abandoned plantations to his loyal officers and even invited back many of the refugee planters who had once held the *cultivateurs* in bondage.[50] All this led some of these discontented ex-slaves to engage in periodic armed resistance that Toussaint swiftly crushed.[51]

Toussaint's ability to thwart these varied challenges to his authority depended on a masterful command of the arts of war and politics, a willingness to employ brute force, an indefatigable intensity (Toussaint reportedly slept only a few hours per night), and a powerful charisma enhanced by skillful appeals to the ideals of liberty and equality. Toussaint shared many of these qualities with Napoleon, whose military conquests in the 1790s in parts of Europe and the Middle East paralleled Toussaint's martial triumphs in Hispaniola.[52] Napoleon's ability to translate his military victories and professed loyalty to revolutionary ideals into widespread political support enabled his coup d'état of 18 *Brumaire* year VIII (9 November 1799), which overthrew the Directory and replaced it with a regime headed by Napoleon known as the Consulate.[53] Toussaint's assumption of authority over France's most prized colony around the same time made him Napoleon's most formidable ally—and potential adversary—in the Caribbean. Aware of their interdependence and of the other's power, both men maintained a cautious coexistence in the final years of the eighteenth century. Nonetheless, a fateful combination of geopolitical shifts and a collision of egos unraveled this entente and led Bonaparte to make the catastrophic decision to try to oust Toussaint rather than continue their old relationship. Fear of a Napoleonic invasion force in turn factored centrally into Toussaint's decision to invade the capital of the former Spanish part of Hispaniola. Both episodes proved to be quite costly for these men, and both transpired within the political context of emancipation's dismantling in the French world.

Toussaint's Invasion of Santo Domingo City

Except perhaps in the most lopsided conflicts, a military intervention is a calculated risk. In addition to military and civilian casualties, decision makers often consider the potential economic costs versus gains, the allegiances of the target zone's population, and the implications of all of these matters for the invader's international political standing. While Napoleon's deployment of military force to depose Toussaint in late 1801 and early 1802 owed largely to the perceived economic and strategic imperative to reassert metropolitan control over the island, the motivations behind Toussaint's invasion of Santo Domingo city a year earlier are less immediately apparent. Why did Toussaint divert thousands of his best troops to the enterprise of conquering the nerve center of an impoverished territory that had long been neglected by its old colonial masters? Why did he add this burden to his already overflowing agenda of consolidating his authority over Saint-Domingue, ensuring the loyalty of diverse and often antagonistic sectors of the population, rebuilding the Dominguan economy, and navigating the treacherous waters of international diplomacy?

The answer, quite simply, is that Santo Domingo mattered in all of these areas. Toussaint came to view the submission of Santo Domingo as vital to furthering his interconnected objectives of increasing plantation production and of ensuring his own political survival. Wresting parts of Santo Domingo from the British had given him a foothold in this colony; with the dispatching of Rigaud, Toussaint saw the Spanish administration in Santo Domingo city as the final obstacle to the realization of his wish to unite the entire island under his authority. In invading Santo Domingo city, Toussaint also sought to realize the economic potential of a colony that offered the plantation entrepreneur twice as much land as Saint-Domingue, augment his army with Dominican recruits, enhance his credibility as a champion of emancipation by stamping out the widespread illegal slaving of French citizens that transpired in Santo Domingo, and forestall the potential landing of a military expedition from mainland France in the former Spanish territory.[54]

Of these objectives, the final was the most salient. Mounting tensions with Napoleon exacerbated Toussaint's anxieties concerning a possible French invasion of the island through its eastern part, where several of Toussaint's prior adversaries had disembarked. In 1796, Moreau de St Méry (who would later join Napoleon's Colonial Ministry after the 1799 coup, serving alongside other proponents of slavery[55]) had written that Santo Domingo was "open and defenseless," exposing neighboring Saint-Domingue to "all manner of attacks and abuses."[56] Two years later, Toussaint's rival, General Hédouville, had entered Hispaniola via Santo Domingo. Then, in April 1800, a new Civil Commission with orders from Paris to prevent Toussaint from taking control of Santo Domingo arrived in that colony on the frigate *L'Africaine*.[57] Both Toussaint and his enemies thus understood the strategic importance of Santo Domingo and the stakes involved in controlling it. Toussaint "wishes to enlist in his army the blacks of the Spanish part and [add] to his coffers the considerable funds that are located there [in Santo Domingo]," wrote the anonymous author of a letter to the minister of the navy in August 1800. "With these forces he believes that he can prevent the French from disembarking on the island, and he will stop at nothing to achieve this objective."[58] One observer from Baltimore likewise remarked that Toussaint intended to "conquer the Spanish part of St Domingue" partly out of determination to "prevent, if he can, the landing of French troops, which he presumes should arrive and attack him from that side."[59]

In one telling indication of the primacy of such strategic concerns in Toussaint's decision to invade Santo Domingo city, the Dominican scholar Emilio Cordero Michel, who has written favorably of Toussaint's occupation of the eastern portion of the island to the point of hyperbole, stated that the "real reason" for Toussaint's invasion and occupation of Santo Domingo in 1801 was his wish to "consolidate his politico-military regime."[60] The major secondary works that treat this subject concur that Toussaint's worries about a possible French invasion strongly motivated his conquest of Santo Domingo city. In their histories of the Haitian Revolution, both C. L. R. James and Laurent Dubois emphasize the strategic factors impelling Toussaint to take Santo Domingo. These included Toussaint's desire to consolidate his power and control all of the island's ports in order to thwart the arrival of hostile forces.[61] Moreover, according to Carolyn Fick, Toussaint was attuned to the rise of disconcerting reaction in France and the imminent possibility of a French invasion of Saint-Domingue, and his actions in Santo Domingo amounted to a preemptive strike.[62] Madison Smartt Bell in his biography of Toussaint also highlighted the ominous political circumstances that appeared to threaten both French Republican emancipation and Toussaint's rule, including Napoleon's accession to supreme authority and the promulgation of the 1799 French constitution.[63] Finally, according to Philippe Girard, Toussaint's agents in France had informed him in 1800 that an expedition was assembling there to attack Saint-Domingue by way of Santo Domingo. Though false, the allegations "convinced Louverture to seize Santo Domingo before France could land troops in that colony."[64]

In articulating his rationales for invading Santo Domingo city, Toussaint also pointed to threats to French citizens' freedom that had emerged on the island itself. Human trafficking through Santo Domingo posed a special challenge to the project of French Republican emancipation, as the weak French political and military presence in that colony exacerbated the difficulties of enforcing the law. In the assessment of Toussaint's adversary Chanlatte, many Dominicans were conspiring to delay the effective "taking of possession" of Santo Domingo by France to "buy time to kidnap the blacks who are on the estates or domestics to transport them to the lands of slavery."[65] In a 29 October 1799 letter to Roume, Toussaint had condemned the abuses perpetrated against many "French cultivators" in Santo Domingo and urged Roume to put a stop to illegal slaving there.[66] Roume in turn sought the support of officials in other lands in his efforts to combat this trafficking. In a 23 February 1800 letter to the Cuban official Someruelos, Roume claimed that many "black French citizens" were being captured from Hispaniola and sold "as slaves" in Cuba. Invoking both the French emancipation decree of 1794 and the renewed Franco-Spanish alliance, Roume demanded that Someruelos promptly ensure the freedom of all captive French citizens in Cuba.[67]

When it became clear that Roume could not suppress these violations of the emancipation law, Toussaint characteristically decided to take the matter into his own hands. In an impassioned missive to Roume dated 18 January 1800, Toussaint decried the frequent sales of "black French Citizens" through Azua (in southern Santo Domingo) to points elsewhere and insisted that many "Spaniards" engaged in this "despicable trafficking." Consequently, "it seems to me that to save the French of this part [Santo Domingo] and preserve the black Citizens from slavery, it is necessary to take a part" of Santo Domingo—specifically, Azua and other locations of such enslaving.[68] Professions of antislavery were closely linked to Toussaint's desire to enhance his political power. While Toussaint's sympathies with the plight of these captives may have been genuine, he operated in a larger context in which imperial warfare and struggles over emancipation were intimately connected.[69]

Within this militarized context, the overseers of emancipation in Hispaniola made its fruits contingent upon grateful service to the Republic. The professed goal of rescuing hapless victims of enslavement by perfidious enemies fit in well with such political narratives of state-centered liberation. The problem of slaving also highlighted uncomfortable intersections between past and present. "On the nineteenth of the previous month," wrote Chanlatte (then a brigade general in Santo Domingo) to Roume on 21 January 1800, "a Black Citizen (as we still have the humiliating necessity here to distinguish Colors) notified me that the Citizeness Thérèse, woman of color had sold to a Spaniard named Miguel Pérez, a black Citizeness named Flore, attached to her service."[70] Chanlatte's perceived "humiliating necessity" constitutes an early example of a dilemma that postemancipation societies would confront over the following two centuries: whether to use terms associated with inequality and stigmatization in the effort to eradicate vestiges of past injustice.[71]

In his efforts to shore up his legitimacy at home, in France, and abroad, Toussaint engaged in his own way with the changing legal landscape. With more than 10,000 men at his command, Toussaint could have quickly and easily overrun the paltry Spanish defenses guarding Santo Domingo's capital city long before his eventual invasion. He nonetheless exhibited a concern with legal protocol epitomized by his obsession with obtaining formal authorization from Roume to assume command over Santo Domingo.[72] Toussaint relentlessly pressured Roume to acquiesce to the black general's takeover of Santo Domingo, while insisting to other French authorities that such a transfer of power would at long last fulfill the Treaty of Basel.[73]

Roume had his own ideas concerning the former Spanish colony's governance. In line with his superiors' wishes, he repeatedly refused the Dominguan general's demands that Roume issue an *arrêté* sanctioning a new Louverture regime in Santo Domingo. Roume advanced several legal, economic, and geopolitical arguments to support his position. In letters to

Toussaint, Roume insisted that the metropolitan government had not granted either of them the authority to legally govern or administer Santo Domingo, whose poverty would in any case place heavy burdens on a treasury already strained by armed conflicts on several continents. Roume furthermore contended that no such transfer of power in Santo Domingo ought to occur until the "troubles" that afflicted the island had subsided.[74] The inhabitants of Santo Domingo "did not refuse to become French," General Kerverseau echoed, "but they did not claim to render themselves subjects of Toussaint; it was not to Toussaint but to the [French] Republic that the King of Spain ceded this portion of the Isle."[75]

Toussaint was undeterred by such claims. After his efforts to cajole Roume into issuing the *arrêté* through diplomatic means failed, Toussaint adopted a more forceful approach. According to Chanlatte, Toussaint deployed a force of 7,000 to 8,000 "blacks" to Le Cap to compel Roume "on pain of pillage and fire" to grant the authorization. "They demanded of him [Roume] with the tone of revolt distribution of lands, complete liberty to work how and where they wish and for their benefit, [and] finally an order for the taking of possession of the Spanish part."[76] These men were only successful in winning the last of these demands. In another report, Chanlatte asserted that Toussaint had "promised" these 8,000 or so followers the "Spanish part," and when these individuals had cornered Roume, they demanded that he "grant the cultivators ownership over half of the land" and the ability to "enjoy completely the benefit of liberty . . . to work for their profit instead of working for that of the landowners."[77]

Evidently motivated by such hopes for a more capacious liberty, these several thousand individuals forced Roume to issue the long-awaited *arrêté* on 27 April 1800.[78] "I will never sign the death order of these peaceful inhabitants of the Spanish part," Roume had supposedly declared right before signing the order. "Since I face the alternatives of being sacrificed or of requesting this taking of possession [of Santo Domingo], my choice is made, France will avenge me!"[79] Though Roume issued a second *arrêté* on 16 June 1800 that annulled the previous one, Toussaint appears to have taken little notice of this. Frustrated by Roume's continued obstinacy, Toussaint detained his adversary in an undignified residence in Dondon (northern Saint-Domingue) in November 1800 and then deported him to Philadelphia nine months later.[80]

In his efforts to take Santo Domingo, Toussaint also faced opposition from other quarters. On 22 July 1800, the five-year anniversary of the Treaty of Basel's signing, a group of Dominicans composed a petition to García in which they denounced the French regime as "only a friend and protector of the slaves" and asserted that Republican officials had armed onetime bonds-men and formed gendarmerie units from them.[81] Furthermore, on the eve of Toussaint's incursion into Santo Domingo city, elite Dominicans addressed several petitions to Spanish officials requesting that the colony's effective transfer to France be deferred until a more propitious moment.[82] In one such petition to the Spanish king, prominent citizens of Santo Domingo city argued that several forces made such a delay necessary: the "disorder and anarchy that reign in the part of the island under France"; Toussaint's "quite openly declared intentions" to sever ties with France; his purported practice of pressing "whites" into forced labor; and his alleged pillaging of many Dominicans' houses and other properties.[83]

The racial overtones of this petition serve as a reminder that race was ever-present in the contest between Toussaint, metropolitan French author-ities, and Dominican officials for supremacy in Santo Domingo. Despite the successive triumphs against institutionalized racism and slavery that had culminated in the proclamation of the "integral part" doctrine in the 1795 French constitution, vestiges of the old racist order persisted into the revolutionary era and became more pronounced as the 1790s drew to a close. Planters and other conservative groups, for instance, helped pass two regressive measures in 1798. The first segregated white troops from "black or colored" fellow soldiers in France, while the second critically undermined the voting rights of most *cultivateurs* and tied them to their plantations on pain of losing citizenship rights.[84]

In Hispaniola, struggles over such policies were entwined with the ques-tion of the status of Santo Domingo and the issue of race relations in that colony. The man entrusted with enforcing in Hispaniola the restrictive vot-ing rights law just discussed, the hapless General Hédouville, had shortly after arriving in Saint-Domingue in 1798 substituted white soldiers for their black counterparts in certain important parts of the colony. He had also ar-gued that in the name of ensuring "tranquility," it was necessary to use only "European troops" to take Santo Domingo.[85] Moreover, on 12 August 1796, no less a champion of racial equality than Julien Raimond had informed Roume that although their Civil Commission had initially possessed the "determination" to refrain from sending any commander who was "black or of color" to the colony of Santo Domingo, circumstances might force Rai-mond and his colleagues to send such a commander. Raimond contended that this "determination was dictated to us out of consideration for and deference to the Spanish."[86] In an 18 August 1796 letter to his fellow civil commissioners, Roume had likewise insisted that while events had obliged this commission to deploy a multiracial force of troops to the "frontier Posts" bordering Santo Domingo, this body would not dare to send an exclusively black force under a black leader.[87] Such concerns led the fortifications director, Charles Vincent, to declare in 1797: "A great difficulty that will result from the Entrance of the Republicans in the Spanish part [of the island], will come thus, without a doubt, from the changes that should be necessarily introduced by the Regime of Blacks. . . . One should say frankly that the only way to reassure the inhabitants [of Santo Domingo] on this point, would be to prohibit at the moment of the taking of possession, if such a thing is possible, and only provisionally, all French Blacks from traversing the Spanish part, as all Spanish Blacks are from coming here."[88]

This statement's hesitant and ambivalent tone holds as much importance as its words. In positing a distinction between "French" and "Spanish" "Blacks" and in defending strict (albeit purportedly temporary) territorial limitations on their movement, Vincent mapped race onto the island's contested political geography.[89] The Napoleonic regimes that succeeded Toussaint in Santo Domingo would place such constructions at the center of their brutal campaigns of reenslavement.

Toussaint devised his own strategies to respond to such racial anxieties. Shortly after forcing Roume to issue his *arrêté* granting the black general authorization to take control of Santo Domingo, Toussaint sent the white general Pierre Agé on a diplomatic mission to meet with Governor García, with whom he was to arrange for the long-delayed effective transfer of authority over Santo Domingo to the French Republic, represented by Toussaint. In a letter to Chanlatte dated 27 April 1800, Toussaint elaborated that Agé would be aided by a contingent of "white troops" along with many of the "French inhabitants" of Santo Domingo city.[90] According to a 28 May 1800 letter from Edward Stevens, the chief U.S. consul in Saint-Domingue, to Secretary of State Timothy Pickering, Toussaint had sent an armed schooner (which was later captured near Puerto Plata by a British ship) from Le Cap with "70 white soldiers" under General Agé to Santo Domingo in response to the fears of the "Spaniards" regarding "the Domination of the Blacks."[91]

Following García's rejection of Toussaint's demands, the latter began to assemble a large military force that would succeed where Agé's diplomacy

had failed. This brought Toussaint into direct conflict with the metropolitan government to which he continued to pledge allegiance. In the year following his November 1799 coup, Napoleon tried to maintain the de facto
political status quo of division in Santo Domingo in response to two principal concerns: engagements in numerous other theaters of war and a firm
intention to limit Toussaint's power. In a 19 October 1800 report to Napoleon, the French foreign minister outlined the military, strategic, and racial concerns that had resulted in the "taking of semi-possession" of Santo
Domingo instead of the total fulfillment of the terms of the Treaty of Basel.
In this official's estimation, few (white) French soldiers in either Europe or
the Caribbean were available due to the "war on the [European] continent,
the losses of our navy, and the troubles in the western part of St Domingue."
The Republic also hesitated to establish a substantial military presence in
Santo Domingo because "the inhabitants of the ceded territory would have
viewed with dread the reunion [of the two parts of the island] by troops of
color, and it was not possible then to send white troops there." The foreign
minister thus advised Napoleon to "leave to the Spanish the task of defending this territory" in order to circumvent Roume's 27 April 1800 *arrêté* by
which "the General Toussaint-L'ouverture would be required to take possession of it [Santo Domingo] with a certain number of white troops."[92]
Accordingly, on 20 November 1800 the minister of the navy instructed
Toussaint to "not undertake anything" in the "former Spanish part" of the
island.[93]

Toussaint took little heed of these orders, entering the city of Santo Domingo on 26 January 1801 at the head of approximately 10,000 troops.[94] His
forces quickly subdued the 1,500 men that the Spanish in Santo Domingo
had deployed against him.[95] Toussaint divided his forces into two divisions:
one under Moïse, which invaded the northern part of the colony of Santo
Domingo, and another assigned to the southern part led by Paul Louverture, the Dominguan general's brother. Toussaint maintained the political
division of Santo Domingo into the *départements* of Samaná and Inganno
that the Directory had ordered several years earlier. He appointed a general
named Clairvaux to administer Samaná and Paul Louverture to oversee
Inganno.[96] On 5 February 1801, Toussaint declared that elections on the island would be organized around municipal administrations that would send
deputies to departmental assemblies, which would in turn elect representatives to a Central Assembly that would sit in Port-Républicain (the renamed
Port-au-Prince) and that would answer to Paris.[97]

"The invasion of the Spanish part [by Toussaint] has completely changed the political situation of France in St. Domingue," General Kerverseau wrote to the minister of the navy in September 1801. In capturing Santo Domingo city, Toussaint had, according to Kerverseau, closed off the last port on the island through which metropolitan French administrators or military units could enter, deposed an "allied Government" that had maintained a measure of "good order" and "internal and external security," undermined the quiescence of a formerly "peaceful population [that was] accustomed to subordination to order and obedience," and taken over a "vast country" that had once served as an "avenue" through which continental French forces could enter all the *départements* in Saint-Domingue.[98] Moreover, in putting García and his ruling cadre on boats to Venezuela and Europe, Toussaint definitively severed Santo Domingo from the Spanish orbit, which helped to pave the way for the short-lived Dominican independence movements twenty years later.[99]

Toussaint's intervention in Santo Domingo city also helped to precipitate a new crisis of empire in the French world. "This taking of possession [of Santo Domingo] was but the final act of the tragedy that unfolded in the Colony to lead to independence," lamented Chanlatte in 1801.[100] This invasion indeed appears to have constituted a tipping point in Napoleon's disastrous decision to deploy a military expedition whose failure would lead to the creation of independent Haiti. Toussaint's conquest of Santo Domingo city thus at once contributed to the emergence of the first emancipationist independent nation in the hemisphere and set an important precedent for the Spanish-American independence wars later in the century. Santo Domingo was at the intersection of French and Spanish imperial crises that transformed the geopolitics of the Caribbean and the hemisphere in the first third of the nineteenth century.

Conclusions

"The question is not to know if it is good to abolish slavery, but if it is good to abolish liberty in the free part of Saint-Domingue. I am convinced that the island would belong to the English, if the blacks were not attached to us by the interest of their freedom." In a riposte to the proslavery arguments of the former Saint-Domingue intendant François Barbé-Marbois, Napoleon in a speech before the Council of State on 16 August 1800 had advocated a plan that would retain slavery in territories such as Martinique (where a

British occupation had kept the institution intact after 1794) while preserving formal emancipation in places such as Saint-Domingue and Guadeloupe, where emancipationist regimes had come to power. "My policy is to govern men as most want to be governed," Napoleon continued. "I believe that this is the manner of recognizing the sovereignty of the people . . . thus, I will speak of liberty in the free part of Saint-Domingue; I will confirm slavery in Ile-de-France [an Indian Ocean territory where planters had retained slavery in violation of the 1794 emancipation law], [and] even in the enslaved part of Saint-Domingue [Santo Domingo]; allowing myself to soften and limit slavery, where I will maintain it; [and] reestablish order and introduce discipline, where I will maintain liberty."[101]

In his decision making regarding the labor regimes that would exist in his domains—and in fashioning colonial policy more generally—Napoleon had to manage an array of competing priorities and interests. On the one hand, an influential planter lobby (whose stamp was evident in the discriminatory 1798 laws detailed earlier in this chapter) sought to appeal to Napoleon's wishes to harness the productive potential of his overseas holdings and to wrest control over these territories back from upstarts like Toussaint. Nevertheless, Napoleon was also keenly aware that abolishing slavery had enabled the French Republic to remain a viable power in the Caribbean. After protracted vacillation, Napoleon (who assumed the title of First Consul of the Republic upon taking power) ended up crafting a delicate compromise that in some ways anticipated the disastrous "free state"/"slave state" division at the heart of the sectional crisis in the antebellum United States. Years later, he would come to regret abandoning this proposal in favor of the attempted restoration of slavery in some of the "free" territories.

Napoleon's rivalry with Toussaint proved crucial in the former's eventual decision to change course. As discussed earlier in this chapter, the first consul's efforts to maintain the status quo in the "enslaved part" of Hispaniola owed largely to his determination to prevent Toussaint from unifying the island under his rule. In secret instructions to the rear admiral Joseph Cambis (his main agent in Santo Domingo) dated 14 January 1801, Napoleon had outlined a vision for that colony's governance that built upon his peculiar concept of "recognizing the sovereignty of the people." While instructing Cambis to "remind the inhabitants of the Spanish part, as well as the current administrators . . . that this country [Santo Domingo] is henceforth French," Napoleon declared that "the intention of the Government [is] to never reunite the two parts [of the island] under one single government." Paris "will govern the French part with and by the blacks, [and] it will govern the Spanish part according to the norms of the country," Napoleon elaborated. The first consul distilled these principles into two concrete objectives that he ordered Cambis to pursue: to "oppose, by all means, the encroachment of an army of blacks within the boundaries of the Spanish part"; and to "reassure all the white landowners [in Santo Domingo] on the views of the French Government, which, aware of the catastrophes in the French part, will not grant unlimited freedom to men even less likely to make good use of it."[102]

This freedom would become a pivotal concern in Toussaint's yearlong occupation of Santo Domingo that commenced twelve days after Napoleon issued these instructions. The liminal status that formally freed people occupied in Santo Domingo under Toussaint underscores the complexity of the French and Haitian Revolutions. While it may be tempting to follow Bonaparte and label Santo Domingo the "enslaved part" of the island in this period and Saint-Domingue the "free part," the primary source record argues for a more nuanced interpretation. In particular, Toussaint's occupation of the eastern part of Hispaniola would further bring together the struggles for freedom of onetime slaves in both parts of the island.

In 1801, Toussaint would attempt to remake Santo Domingo into a prosperous colony that would buttress his power on the island by serving as a sort of economic and strategic insurance policy against a French metropolitan invasion. He justified his actions in the name of freed people's rights. While proclaiming all Dominicans to be free French citizens, Toussaint nonetheless could not escape from the hegemonic ideal of a plantation economy based on a tightly controlled labor force. The following chapter will illustrate how his transformative reign paradoxically became a captive of the models of the past.

CHAPTER FOUR

Uprooting the Tree of Liberty?

Toussaint Louverture in Santo Domingo, 1801–1802

In defeating me, they have only cut down the trunk of the tree of liberty in Saint-Domingue, but it will grow back as its roots are deep and numerous.
—Toussaint Louverture

This famous pronouncement on the resilience and ultimate triumph of liberty over repression, said to have been uttered by the Haitian Revolution's central figure upon his capture and exile to France in 1802, encapsulated in twenty-six French words the struggle for freedom that shaped that revolution and its arguably largely unfulfilled promise over the following two centuries. Indeed, the assertion that the "roots" of the liberty tree (a potent French Revolutionary symbol) were in Saint-Domingue rather than (or in addition to) France attests to the importance of Hispaniola in the political, social, intellectual, and economic transformations of the late eighteenth and early nineteenth centuries.[1] At the same time, the powerful imagery of thwarted quests for freedom followed by the aspiration for renewal strikes a chord with the numerous challenges that have confronted the nation of which Toussaint Louverture was in many ways the founder, while still resonating with the persistent hope that a better future might yet lie ahead.

In the years following his shift in allegiance from Spain to the French Republic in the spring of 1794, Toussaint came to anoint himself the principal defender of general slave emancipation in Saint-Domingue. Nonetheless, in an article casting Toussaint as a "black Talleyrand," Philippe Girard emphasized Toussaint's apparent reluctance to extend his policy of emancipation beyond Saint-Domingue. Citing the examples of his complicity in thwarting a Jamaican slave conspiracy in 1799 as well as his debatable commitment to emancipation in Santo Domingo, Girard asserted that Toussaint "pursue[d] abolitionism in one country only."[2] The extant evidence on Toussaint's reign in Santo Domingo, however, suggests a somewhat different interpretation.

Rather than pursuing emancipationist policies in Saint-Domingue and ignoring or undermining struggles for liberty in other places (at least within

Hispaniola), Toussaint decreed essentially the same labor codes in Santo Domingo as he did in Saint-Domingue: a set of restrictions designed to bind laborers (most of whom were ex-slaves) to certain enterprises. In Saint-Domingue this usually translated into the plantation; in Santo Domingo, Toussaint aspired to replicate the colony's few productive plantations in an effort to finally fulfill this territory's economic potential. Toussaint's policies in Santo Domingo were driven by a narrow vision of liberty and an overriding concern with establishing a profitable plantation economy.

Diverse groups of people—ranging from Haitian politicians and ordinary citizens to both Haitian and foreign scholars—have for the past 200 years closely analyzed and interpreted Toussaint Louverture's place within Haitian history and the precedents that he set as the country's first real leader, even though he never actually led any formally independent state by that or any other name.[3] Neither scholars nor other parties by contrast have devoted comparable attention to his place in Dominican history, despite his prominent role in Santo Domingo during this critical period.[4]

Scholars such as Richard Turits have presented as a major theme in Dominican history the state's mostly vain attempts (until the twentieth century) to impose an export-oriented plantation economy upon a reluctant peasantry.[5] Cast in this historical tradition, Toussaint was one of numerous Dominican leaders who pursued such a model, as his political and economic vision of a unified Hispaniola envisaged the implementation of a lucrative plantation complex across the entire island.

As we have seen, this vision took shape against the backdrop of the dissolution of the doctrine of legal equality between continental France and the overseas territories in favor of the older principle that the colonies required "particular laws," as set forth in Napoleon's 1799 constitution. Toussaint in a sense took this concept of "particular laws" to its logical conclusion by imposing his own legal order in Hispaniola. Most notably, Toussaint's 1801 constitution bestowed upon the black general the title of governor-for-life over the island and affirmed the abolition of slavery in both colonies.[6]

Toussaint pursued three principal objectives in Santo Domingo. First, as a devout Catholic, Toussaint imposed Catholicism as the state religion in Hispaniola, actively repressing manifestations of other faiths, especially those associated with the African roots of the ex-slave population. Second, he promoted an economic model based on large-scale plantation production. Finally, he built this on labor restrictions that envisioned the *cultivateurs* as subordinated units of labor, albeit with certain enumerated rights, including a modest share of plantation profits. The conflicts that transpired when the *cultivateurs* resisted these measures reflected a recurring phenomenon in postemancipation Caribbean history: the antagonism between authorities' and planters' quests for plantation profits (created by a substantial docile labor force) and peasants' own preferences for smaller-scale agricultural production that would afford them much more autonomy than working on sizable plantations.[7]

While many of these peasants would have likely defined liberty substantially in terms of access to land and a livelihood free from exploitation, Toussaint and many other French authorities emphasized the duties of free citizens to render plantation and military labor to the Republic. Thomas Holt reminds us that freedom, like all concepts, is and was "a historically particular and socially constructed phenomenon" and that consequently, "the struggle to define the content of freedom was at bottom a contest for social power, a struggle at once intellectual and political, social and economic."[8] Conceptualizing Toussaint's reign in both Santo Domingo and Saint-Domingue as such a "contest for social power" can help to reconcile the ostensibly contradictory aspects of Toussaint's governance. Toussaint decreed a restrictive labor regime for Santo Domingo in order to create virtually ex nihilo a profitable plantation economy in this colony that would generate revenue to support his political ambitions—and his military defense of general emancipation against powerful slaveholding foreign powers or even a possible invasion from France. Though he found himself significantly constrained by external forces, Toussaint did have some real choices, and his decisions profoundly influenced the subsequent histories of both parts of Hispaniola.

Toussaint's Religious Policies

"The [French] Republic does not need your goods; it only demands your heart."[9] In a 4 January 1801 proclamation to all of the inhabitants of the colony of Santo Domingo, Toussaint defended his impending conquest of the capital city and promised good governance in an effort to counteract what he knew would be a somewhat skeptical reception of his accession. Declaring that he and his emissary to Santo Domingo, Pierre Agé, had acted in strict conformity with the terms of the Treaty of Basel, Toussaint insisted to his audience that his true intentions in that colony were to "assure your happiness, [and] reestablish public tranquility and good order."[10] In his bid to gain Dominicans' allegiance, Toussaint employed rhetoric similar to that used by other French Republican administrators when addressing other potentially recalcitrant colonial populations during this era. This rhetoric was characterized by a mix of appeals to liberty and reassurances concerning the protection of property and the maintenance of order, which these officials hoped would win over diverse groups that had distinct and often competing interests.[11]

Toussaint could not, of course, please all of the factions on the island, and when he had to make a difficult decision, he often favored the interests of wealthier groups over those of the *cultivateurs*. This owed to a variety of personal, pragmatic, economic, and structural factors. As Carolyn Fick has written, Toussaint's preference for an economic path centered on the plantation stemmed from both the constraints that he faced in "such a precarious environment as the late eighteenth-century Atlantic world, still dominated by the imperial powers of Europe," and the emergence of an "unbridgeable gap between the state structure [in Saint-Domingue], which was a military one, and the rural agrarian base of the nation."[12]

In his occupation of Santo Domingo, Toussaint appears to have perceived a similarly "unbridgeable gap" between his own professed Roman Catholic faith and the mixed African and Christian beliefs that many of the island's inhabitants held. Toussaint keenly understood both the institutional and social power of religion on an island where multiple African, European, and indigenous faiths had long interacted under the suspicious eye of a succession of slaveholding regimes that had all promoted official state Catholicism. More recently, as discussed in chapter 1, religion had constituted a powerful unifying force among the slave rebels in the early 1790s, while Catholic priests had served as key intermediaries between black insurgent leaders and the Spanish before and during the Franco-Spanish war.

Toussaint now moved swiftly to assume control of institutional religion in Santo Domingo, overseeing the appointment of priests and creating several new parishes in the Santiago de los Caballeros area in the north.[13] Toussaint also declared Catholicism to be the state religion on the island in his 1801 constitution (which a French Republican official stationed in Caracas denounced as antithetical to "French tolerance") and repressed religious practices that he deemed subversive.[14] In a 4 January 1800 decree, for instance, Toussaint had outlawed nocturnal dances and meetings on pain of corporal punishment based on his allegation that a number of malefactors had sought to "divert from his [illegible] labors, the peaceful cultivator, in encouraging the violent passion of liberty that he has for dances, principally for that of Vaudoux."[15]

This emphasis on labor discipline would characterize Toussaint's governance in Santo Domingo. In his efforts to redirect the energies of the "peaceful cultivator" toward the construction of a viable plantation economy in Santo Domingo (and the resuscitation of such an economy in Saint-Domingue), Toussaint came to rely upon labor codes that undermined the liberty that he claimed to promote.

"The Land Only Awaits the Aid of Arms to Work Its Treasures"

"[Toussaint] bragged to me of the wealth that one would find [in Santo Domingo] and the great means that this country would provide him so that his authority [would be] finally exclusively respected on the entire island," wrote General Antoine Chanlatte in a 20 June 1800 report to the minister of the navy.[16] Such a prediction would seem to contradict the trope of a colony characterized by poverty and neglect—an image supported by Chanlatte's assertion in this same report that Santo Domingo represented a significant burden on the treasury of New Spain, which disbursed 300,000 to 400,000 *gourdes* annually to the Caribbean colony to subsidize its administrative, judicial, military, and religious costs.[17] Though Toussaint indeed knew Santo Domingo's impoverishment from firsthand experience, he also understood that it had once rendered substantial plantation-derived profits to its overlords and that it might do so again. Toussaint became determined to exploit Santo Domingo's productive potential by creating a plantation system supported by constrained labor, capitalistic agrarian policies, and reduced customs duties on key cash crops, such as sugar and coffee.

The near-total absence of an infrastructure that might enable the large-scale production of such crops must have been quite a shock to a man born and raised in what was in his day the world's wealthiest plantation colony. Relatively rich in land yet comparatively poor in labor and especially capital, Santo Domingo had long been forced to import the plantation staples that many of its neighbors exported. In its first years under French rule, the colony's only notable export products were tobacco, Acajou wood (or mahogany), and *tafia* (rum). These, in addition to the sale of animal products, such as meat and hides, constituted its main sources of revenue.[18]

Toussaint's ambitious plans to reverse this state of affairs were not quite as far-fetched as they might initially seem. After all, he also faced the enormous task of rebuilding the plantation economy of a devastated Saint-Domingue after nearly a decade of war, and he succeeded remarkably well.[19] In pursuing his political and economic goals, Toussaint consciously or unconsciously modeled many of his efforts upon the prescriptions of a relatively obscure Dominican clergyman, who, oblivious to the coming revolutionary turmoil, had in the late colonial era sought to replicate Saint-Domingue's successful plantation complex across the border in his own land.

In the 1780s, a priest named Antonio Sánchez Valverde had provided a blueprint for developing Santo Domingo that would profoundly influence the economic models pursued by administrators there for decades to come. Mindful of the wealth that France had derived from its coveted Caribbean possessions (especially Saint-Domingue), Sánchez Valverde proposed to overhaul the Spanish colony's economy in the image of its neighbor's. In a sustained argument to the Spanish Crown contained in his tract *Idea del valor de la isla española* (Idea of the Worth of Hispaniola), Sánchez Valverde contended that the "key" to exploiting the "most fertile" land of Santo Domingo was the massive importation of African slaves. Until the Spanish followed the French example and undertook this initiative, Santo Domingo's wealth would remain but "a treasure hidden in the bowels of the earth."[20] Though it is unclear whether Toussaint himself actually read or was directly familiar with Sánchez Valverde's ideas, they influenced many chroniclers and authorities in revolutionary Hispaniola. As an amateur scholar and astute observer of Caribbean affairs, Agent Philippe-Rose Roume, for instance, had read the expansive *Description* of Santo Domingo penned by M. L. E. Moreau de St Méry, who in turn had drawn significantly upon Sánchez Valverde's work.[21] Perhaps drawing inspiration from this priest's arguments, Roume had told several colleagues in late 1797 that the agricultural production of Santo Domingo could, with the appropriate guidance, surpass that of Saint-Domingue within fifty years.[22] Occupying a precarious if powerful position and aware of the necessity to raise funds for his military and state apparatus, Toussaint appears to have believed that a much more accelerated timetable was needed. Despite—or perhaps in part because of—the revolutionary upheaval, administrators such as Toussaint found much to emulate in the Valverdean vision.

The ideas that shaped Toussaint's policies in Santo Domingo were also derived from his own experiences in Saint-Domingue and his observations on the relationships between economic and political power that had emerged in colonial times. The maintenance of political control had a reciprocal and circular relationship to restrictive labor policies under Toussaint: the cash crops produced under these labor codes generated revenues for Toussaint, which he used to fund his army and administration. These tangible manifestations of his power then served to enforce his harsh labor policies.[23]

Toussaint's economic agenda in Santo Domingo also impelled him to court the support of that colony's equivalent of Saint-Domingue's *grands blancs* (the plantation- and urban-based white elite class). In addition to promising to uphold property and order, Toussaint favored plantation entrepreneurs with economic measures designed to create incentives for the cultivation of the same cash crops that had produced such great wealth in Saint-Domingue as well as in Jamaica, Barbados, Brazil, and elsewhere.

These preferences underlay two key orders issued by Toussaint in February 1801 on labor relations and agriculture in Santo Domingo. Evidently driven by a philosophy that favored the concentration of wealth in relatively few hands, these orders explicitly targeted the smallholding practices of many former slaves.

Emphasizing that agricultural production in Santo Domingo was "very different than in other countries," Toussaint set forth in a 7 February 1801 *arrêté* a series of steps designed to promote his economic vision. In this order, Toussaint forcefully denounced the "abuses" committed by "cultivators" in Santo Domingo who bought up small plots of land and then cultivated this land for themselves in small groups. Since this practice led these individuals to "abandon the plantations," it accelerated in Toussaint's eyes the "ruin" of these enterprises. In response, Toussaint set a minimum amount of land per legal concession (fifty *carreaux* or 150 to 200 acres).[24] He also put in place formidable bureaucratic obstacles to land ownership, stipulating that prospective buyers had to present themselves before certain authorities, who would then decide whether to approve the sale based on a number of factors spelled out in the order. These included whether the proposed buyer was "attached" to a plantation and how many *cultivateurs* he would employ.[25]

In a proclamation that Toussaint delivered to all of the residents of the "former Spanish part" of the island on 8 February 1801, he explained the economic and philosophical rationales behind the restrictive measures issued the previous day. Lamenting that except for some modest sugar cultivation, Santo Domingo was "without agriculture," Toussaint called upon

Dominicans to "imitate" the French with respect to plantation production and accordingly required them to plant staple plantation crops, including coffee, cotton, sugar, and cacao. Judging it necessary to procure a sizable and acquiescent labor force to cultivate these crops, Toussaint also ordered Dominican *cultivateurs* to be "attached" to their plantations, declaring: "I have never thought that liberty was a license, that men [who] became free could give themselves with impunity to laziness [and] to disorder." While he affirmed that these *cultivateurs* had a right to basic protection of their persons as well as to their quarter of the plantation revenues, Toussaint insisted that they must be "subordinated," for their own good as well as for that of the colony. "Everywhere the land only awaits the aid of arms to work its treasures," Toussaint proclaimed in a statement that had strong echoes of Sánchez Valverde's prescriptions of nearly two decades earlier.[26] While various observers over the past two centuries have seen in Toussaint the realization of the Abbé Raynal's famous prediction of the coming of a "black Spartacus," Toussaint's labor and economic policies in Santo Domingo suggest that, at least in this colony, he may have had more interest in fulfilling the vision of Sánchez Valverde than that of the Abbé Raynal.[27]

In the ensuing weeks, Toussaint issued other decrees that contained a mixture of economic incentives for traders and planters and restrictions on the autonomy of freed people. Declaring that "with arms, intelligence, and activity, laborious men are assured, on such fertile land, to be paid a hundredfold for their efforts and their work," Toussaint on 12 February 1801 reduced import and export duties in both of Santo Domingo's *départements* of Samaná and Inganno from 20 to 6 percent to stimulate production and trade. In this order, he singled out cash crops, including sugar, coffee, cacao, and tobacco, whose production in his mind served "the state" (*la chose publique*).[28] This fixation on plantation agriculture led Toussaint to ban or marginalize potentially competing forms of production. On 5 March 1801, Toussaint prohibited all woodcutting of mahogany except for that which served the "internal construction of the Colony," ostensibly in the name of curbing deforestation.[29] Toussaint's relentless pursuit of his economic vision caused him to brush aside criticisms of his policies such as that offered by a French official in Caracas who predicted that this ban on woodcutting would hinder Santo Domingo's economic development.[30]

All of these economic measures constituted part of a larger project: the political unification of Hispaniola under Toussaint's governance. In March 1801, Toussaint consecrated this vision in a constitution that aimed

to permanently institutionalize his political authority. Drafted by a multiracial delegation comprised of men from both colonies, this document named
Toussaint governor of the island "for the rest of his glorious life" while at the
same time refusing to formally break with the mother country, asserting
that "all men [on the island] are born, live and die free and French."[31] Yet
as before, this freedom would be sharply circumscribed. Rather than seizing the opportunity to outline a more capacious vision of freedom, the
architects of this constitution not only reiterated but broadened Toussaint's
earlier labor measures; by implication, the charter also affirmed their application to Santo Domingo.[32] Moreover, the framers inscribed into this document Toussaint's preference for the export of plantation crops by banning
their importation into the island.[33]

In the labor codes that he had promulgated in 1798 and 1800, Toussaint
had adopted the core components of the labor regulations that the civil
commissioners Léger-Félicité Sonthonax and Étienne Polverel had devised in 1793–94: workers were to be bound by law to their plantations; they
would collectively earn a quarter of plantation revenues; and military and
domestic service constituted the only legal means by which able-bodied individuals could escape plantation work.[34] Toussaint's two main innovations
on these earlier decrees by way of his 1801 constitution were the intensifica-
tion of this "militarization of agriculture" and the extension of these labor
rules to Santo Domingo.[35]

Though Santo Domingo's dramatically different economic situation might
have suggested the wisdom of employing a labor system distinct from that
which prevailed in Saint-Domingue, Toussaint appears to have sought to
impose similar labor regimes in both places. The general himself later
justified his labor codes as a necessary means to "make [ex-slave laborers]
appreciate the price of liberty without license," to "prevent the corruption
of morals," and to promote the "general happiness of the island" and the
"interest of the republic." "I had indeed succeeded," Toussaint boasted in
his memoir, "because you could not see in the entire colony [Saint-Domingue]
a single man without occupation and the number of beggars had diminished."[36]

Unfortunately, much of the extant evidence on the effects of Toussaint's
labor policies in Santo Domingo is contained in quite tendentious tracts
that were sometimes written by those who opposed him. In a May 1801 report, Toussaint's adversary Chanlatte accused him of employing the "most
severe violence" to "[call] all blacks, without distinction" to agricultural

labor in both parts of the island.[37] Moreover, two British correspondences from the 1820s offer lurid portraits of the state of agricultural labor under Toussaint in the two colonies. In a letter to Secretary George Canning written in Port-au-Prince on 9 September 1826, British consul general Charles Mackenzie detailed the "decidedly coercive" clauses of Toussaint's constitution concerning labor and contended that although the "cultivators" were supposed to receive a quarter of plantation revenues, they were given "in reality much less" than this share.[38] In a report submitted to the Earl of Dudley a year and a half later, Mackenzie claimed that atrocities evocative of the days of slavery, such as caning and live burials, had survived under Toussaint.[39] Those claiming to have been subjected to these labor practices were perhaps even more polemical. In an account of his experiences as a French colonist in the Samaná peninsula (northern Santo Domingo), Armand Hardouin compared Toussaint to the Roman emperor Nero and accused him of forcing "the Spanish of all classes and colors" to perform "public labor."[40]

Many years ago, C. L. R. James labeled Toussaint's imposition of restrictive labor policies in Saint-Domingue a "change from the old to the new despotism."[41] Across the border in Santo Domingo, Toussaint's determination to transform a long-neglected outpost of empire into a prosperous export colony led him to repress ex-slaves' practices of cultivating small-scale landholdings that had deep roots in both Dominguan and Dominican history. While the different stages of plantation development that characterized the two colonies by 1789 translated into distinct patterns of peasant and slave cultivation, the peasantries of both grew out of enslaved populations who had found in subsistence agriculture an escape from the dehumanization of the slave regime.

As Michel-Rolph Trouillot has demonstrated, slaves' cultivation grounds in colonial Saint-Domingue had acquired a profound "ideological significance" for their symbolic as well as economic value, since they represented a rare area in which the slaves exerted a degree of control and autonomy.[42] Richard Turits has argued that a similar phenomenon occurred in Santo Domingo. "Deeply rooted in peasants' moral economy," Turits contends, "was a right to the land. Especially in the historical context of slavery, an independent means of subsistence became associated with freedom—autonomy from economic subordination to and control by others as well as from the vagaries of market and central state forces."[43] In the Haitian Revolution, these historical developments converged as both Dominican and Dominguan freed peasants determinedly sought this "autonomy from economic subordination." Indeed, the "abuse" involving small-scale cultivation in Santo Domingo that Toussaint had vehemently decried in his 7 February 1801 order may well have had its roots in these same practices and inclinations.

The advent of revolutionary conflict in Hispaniola in the 1790s led formally free men and women to adapt old tendencies to new circumstances. As we have seen, numerous freed people from Saint-Domingue had attempted to migrate across the old colonial boundary after 1795, often seeking to escape the "free" labor regimes in the western portion of the island. In so doing, they built on well-worn patterns in which ex-slaves and their descendants in Santo Domingo had carved out spaces of greater economic and personal autonomy as poor but free ranchers and farmers. "What is surprising but nonetheless true," Chanlatte had declared in a report dated 9 June 1800, "is that the slaves even in the Spanish part have preferred their state [of bondage] to the facility that they had to go to the French part where liberty awaited them."[44] What Chanlatte interpreted as a rejection of freedom in fact may have been an illustration of these individuals' quests to attain liberty on their own terms by consciously or unconsciously following the example of Dominican peasants who for centuries had created and preserved their own versions of freedom in *el monte*, the Dominican countryside. Chanlatte indeed admitted that many French citizens "of all colors" often "frequented" Santo Domingo in order to "seek asylum" from various "persecutions" that they had experienced in Saint-Domingue.[45]

While Haiti's foundation by onetime slaves has been commemorated by everything from the large statue of the "unknown maroon" in Port-au-Prince to contentious debates over the role of Vodou in the 1791 slave revolt, no comparable official or mass awareness of the Dominican slave past has emerged.[46] Yet in its own way the Dominican peasantry—and by extension, the nation as a whole—was also the "offspring of slavery," in the words of the Dominican intellectual Pedro Francisco Bonó.[47] Indeed, as in the Haitian case, genuine liberty for freed Dominicans came to encompass much more than an escape from the juridical status of slave. Equally crucial was the ability to cultivate a plot of land, however small, and to benefit from its fruits in proportion to the amount of labor invested. Trouillot has argued for the case of Haiti that such a fundamental right to land and its products became "the terms under which freedom was first formulated in the history of the nation"; this also applies to a large extent to Santo Domingo.[48]

Perhaps partly due to his status as a relatively privileged coachman during his time in bondage, Toussaint appears not to have held such sentiments; if he did, he did not act upon them. For their part the freed individuals who lived in Toussaint's Santo Domingo were part of what Turits has termed an "exceptional and enduring Caribbean peasantry" that successive Spanish, French, Dominican, and Haitian regimes attempted to subordinate to their economic and political agendas. These efforts mostly failed until the long twentieth-century dictatorship of Rafael Trujillo.[49] Thus, for all of his successes in rising from slavery to the pinnacle of power in Saint-Domingue and in outfoxing and overpowering the armies of the world's most powerful empires as well as numerous internal foes, in the context of Dominican history Toussaint was but another leader who failed to create a plantation economy. While the short duration of his reign accounts for part of this failure, other factors include the resistance of the *cultivateurs* and many Dominicans' unwillingness to work with or especially for this onetime slave.

As the starting point of the European colonial enterprise in the Americas, Hispaniola had been the first territory to experience the range of labor systems that the Europeans implemented in their conquered lands. This inheritance framed Toussaint's seemingly contradictory choices. As Philippe Girard and others have noted, since the time of Columbus an array of "semi-free" labor arrangements had developed throughout the Caribbean, which offered some precedents for French Republican authorities' attempts to fashion labor codes that maintained a subordinated labor force without reducing the workers to chattel.[50] In his own efforts to devise such a system, Toussaint's predispositions led him to confuse the *cultivateurs'* preference for smaller-scale agricultural production on their own terms with indolence, as he equated productive labor exclusively with the types of plantation and military work that had proven so vital to the success of colonial French Saint-Domingue. The struggles between Toussaint and these ex-slaves in both parts of the island challenged the boundaries of emancipation.

The Question of Slavery under Toussaint in Santo Domingo

Toussaint's record on upholding emancipation in Santo Domingo was mixed. On the one hand, in addition to his restrictive labor rules, Toussaint adopted measures designed to defend Santo Domingo's few plantations from "maroon" communities. Nevertheless, Toussaint also undertook efforts to protect those whom many Dominican emigrants claimed as their slaves, following the earlier initiatives of Roume. While Emilio Cordero Michel has argued that Toussaint won the support of the "popular masses" in Santo

Domingo with his affirmation of emancipation and his appointments of nonwhites to high offices, the evidence for this is lacking.[51] At the same time, Toussaint did not simply institute a "new type of Slavery," as the exiled Agent Roume asserted in a September 1801 letter.[52]

Toussaint nonetheless confronted numerous accusations that he wished to impose slavery in new guises. "Is there on the entire island," General François Kerverseau had asked rhetorically on 15 December 1800, "a single black person who, however beaten down he may be . . . to please Toussaint, would want to accept new irons?"[53] As in Saint-Domingue, Toussaint understood the importance of asserting his control over the existing plantation infrastructure in Santo Domingo, a circumstance that exacerbated such polemical denunciations of the controversial leader. In his 15 April 1801 recounting of Toussaint's takeover of the Boca Nigua plantation, a Dominguan tax collector argued that shortly after assuming power in Santo Domingo, Toussaint had declared Dominican refugees to be "émigrés" and distributed their possessions among his chieftains.[54] Most notably, the general had "seized the superb plantation of M. Oyarzaval" and confiscated the "most Precious" items there. This transfer of authority did not, however, improve plantation laborers' conditions. "The system of equality and liberty that had made the French the first nation in the world," this official proclaimed, "is not at all appropriate for this country. I repeat again that this System has not destroyed slavery there, it has only changed the color [of the plantations' managers;] the black brigands, who have been installed there, alone reign there as tyrants." Despairing that this new arrangement retained the brutality of slavery while eliminating the strict labor discipline that had made pre-1789 Saint-Domingue "so flourishing and so superb," the tax collector concluded that "the lack of arms, laziness, libertinage, and all the crimes that follow from this precipitate [Saint-Domingue's] destruction, and upon seizing the Spanish part, one has just dealt [Saint-Domingue] the final blow."[55]

Since Santo Domingo's plantation infrastructure was so meager and Toussaint's reign there was so brief, these plantation takeovers did not produce the same degree of economic and social change that they did in Saint-Domingue. Toussaint nonetheless strove to protect Santo Domingo's few productive enterprises from so-called maroons. In a 22 September 1798 letter to Hédouville, Toussaint had written favorably of the commandant in the Dominican town of Neyba, held in high esteem by many Dominican landowners due to his "influence" over the "blacks" of the nearby transfrontier community of Maniel. Many of these landowners had complained to

Toussaint of "incursions" and "pillage" of their "plantations" committed by individuals from Maniel.[56] Yet Toussaint's tough labor policies may in fact have augmented these communities' numbers, for according to Adolphe Cabon these labor rules exacerbated "*marronnage*" (flight), which Toussaint reframed as "vagabondage."[57]

Like his onetime adversary Roume, Toussaint could not accept a viable independent polity in Hispaniola that existed outside of either the political sphere of the French Republic or the social and economic world of the plantation. This led him to employ a mixture of military and diplomatic tactics devised to bring those from Maniel under his direct control. Due to the "powerful considerations of the restoration of agriculture" that alone could return Saint-Domingue to its "former splendor," Toussaint had demobilized several hundred soldiers in 1798 and reassigned them to agricultural labor while redeploying about one hundred other troops to Neyba to serve under an officer named Mamzelle, who had the "trust of the blacks of Maniel." Toussaint made these decisions in order to bring these "blacks," who had become virtually "independent," into the Republican fold so that they would obey the Republic's "beneficent laws."[58]

Maniel presented a direct challenge both to Toussaint's claims to be the foremost defender of liberty on the island and to his projects of political centralization and economic overhaul. While the inhabitants of this "maroon" community in a sense transcended the 1793–94 emancipation decrees, the plight of others on the island who faced enslavement by those who ignored these decrees presented Toussaint with continual challenges. In a report to the minister of the navy dated 17 May 1801, Toussaint's friend Charles Vincent, the fortifications director, stated that while "the black man, enjoy[s] all his rights in the French part," if he found himself in the "Spanish part" he could "be sold and embarked to be transported to another Colony."[59] The most convincing evidence of Toussaint's inability to fully eradicate enslavement from Santo Domingo nonetheless comes not from those with whom he had close contact but rather from those who departed from the island seeking to take their "slaves" with them.

Bondage and Flight from Santo Domingo

Like most revolutions, the upheaval in Hispaniola produced its share of exiles whose economic losses, psychological and social displacement, and real as well as perceived political persecution run throughout the pages of seemingly innumerable correspondences and reports. Though scholars of the Haitian Revolution have largely focused on the waves of Dominguan refugees who fled events such as the 1791 slave revolt, the destruction of Le Cap in June 1793, and the collapse of French rule in Saint-Domingue in late 1803, the transfer of Santo Domingo to France produced its own cohort of emigrants who often relocated to lands remaining in the Spanish empire, such as Cuba and Puerto Rico.[60] Since 1795, French officials had pressured their Spanish counterparts to help suppress this outmigration, with limited success. On the final day of 1795, Agent Roume had informed the minister of the navy that a Don Joaquín Pueyo, who had served as the mayor of Santiago de los Caballeros for twenty-five years, held such sway among the city's population that French officials had asked him to intervene to prevent some "men of color" and "free blacks" from departing for Cuba. Roume also related that Pueyo was "considered as the protector of the free [people] and the slaves of African blood" in Santo Domingo.[61] Half a decade later, Toussaint imposed an outright ban on all emigration from Santo Domingo except for that of some government officials and military units. Toussaint presumably adopted this measure in response to the accelerated emigration provoked by his capture of Santo Domingo city in 1801.[62]

On 20 May 1802, one such refugee, Don Pedro Abadia, composed a detailed letter to a Monsieur Thermite, the commander of the frigate *La Poursuivante*. Writing from Aguadilla, Puerto Rico, Abadia described himself as "the unfortunate attorney of the most beautiful plantation in the Spanish part of St-Domingue" who had been "chased from this country by the bloodthirsty and hypocritical Toussaint Louverture." Professing his loyalty to the Napoleonic forces that were engaged in a war to reconquer Hispaniola, Abadia insisted that he would without hesitation provide useful information to this expedition's leader, General Charles Victor Emmanuel Leclerc, in order to prove his "devotion to our new mother country." Abadia nonetheless seems to have acted less out of any newfound sense of patriotism than out of material and familial motivations. As a relative of this plantation's director, Juan B. Oyarzával, and as an official charged with overseeing the production of *aguardiente* (sugar cane brandy) who had experience punishing slaves who had allegedly attempted to steal this product, Abadia eagerly awaited the end of the "reign of the black despot" so that he could return to the Oyarzával plantation with his "200 blacks."[63]

Were these "blacks" claimed by Abadia enslaved or free? As had some of his Republican predecessors, Toussaint confronted the question of whether the purported property rights of Dominican emigrants trying to depart the island with their "slaves" superseded the rights of the latter. High-ranking Spanish officials generally sided with the purported slaveholders, as is evident in a 16 September 1801 letter by a Pedro Ceballos, who praised the "prudent" measures that Governor Joaquín García had adopted "in favor of the Owners of Slaves" that permitted these individuals to emigrate with these "Slaves" in accordance with the "liberty" that the Treaty of Basel had given them to do this.[64]

An intriguing series of petitions, preserved in the *Audiencia de Santo Domingo* collection in the Archivo General de Indias (Seville), provides further insight into these conflicts. In the years following the signing of the Treaty of Basel, many Santo Domingo refugees had composed petitions to representatives of the Spanish Crown in the colonies and in Europe requesting material assistance, such as a stipend, a pension, or land. Many of these petitioners had also advanced claims to "slaves" in Santo Domingo in spite of the French Republican emancipation law. While numerous such petitions contain implicit evidence of the perpetuation of servitude under Toussaint, others document Toussaint's partially successful efforts to halt the emigration of "slaves" from Santo Domingo.

As discussed in chapter 2, the controversy over emigration from Santo Domingo with purported slaves had begun soon after word of the cession reached the island. This in turn had impelled petitioners such as Doña Josefa de Coco y Landeche to seek official aid in preserving their dominion over their "slaves." On 8 February 1796, Coco y Landeche, an indigent widow and owner of a sugar plantation, had addressed a petition to Spanish authorities in Santo Domingo pleading for assistance in immigrating to Cuba with her family as well as with several "Blacks" whom she had in her "service."[65] The determination of many others like Doña Josefa to emigrate with those whom they claimed as their slaves appears to have made the latter a substantial proportion of the Dominican emigrant population. According to Carlos Esteban Deive, Toussaint estimated that 3,000 captives had departed Santo Domingo by 1801; this figure represents a fifth of the 15,000 slaves who had lived in the colony in 1789.[66] Emigration on such a scale would seem to have jeopardized Toussaint's hopes of building a plantation economy in Santo Domingo, which led him to try to stop this emigration. According to a letter by Cuba's Marquis de Someruelos to another Spanish official dated 2 November 1801, a widow named Doña Ana Baptista had attempted to emigrate from Santo Domingo to Cuba with nine children and eight "slaves." She was forced to "abandon" these "slaves" because authorities in Santo Domingo did not permit her to "embark" them.[67] In a similar case, Toussaint's government prohibited the Dominican refugee José de Labastida from taking his six "slaves" with him when he departed Santo Domingo for Maracaybo (in modern Venezuela).[68]

Did Toussaint simply want to preserve scarce labor, or did this interdiction also reflect genuine sentiment in favor of protecting these would-be slaves? As with his earlier opposition to slaving in Santo Domingo, a mixture of entwined economic, political, and humanitarian motivations appears to have driven Toussaint to take action against this emigration. Toussaint's compassion for his fellow freed people was difficult to disentangle from his desire for political supremacy on the island and his wish for "arms for the cultivation of the land," in Deive's words.[69] Above all, though, Toussaint understood the economic stakes involved in the question of this emigration. An 1804 cadastral survey carried out in Santo Domingo by the Napoleonic regime that governed there from 1804 to 1809 noted that the "capital representing the tributes" fell by "twelve hundred thousand francs" upon Toussaint's invasion of Santo Domingo city. The main reason for this loss, according to the survey, was the departure of many *cultivateurs* whom numerous emigrants had taken to Cuba and Puerto Rico. In a blunt assessment of the impact of such migration, the survey's authors concluded that the loss of this labor had turned Santo Domingo into a "wasteland," devoid of the revenues that otherwise would have accrued.[70]

Toussaint had mixed success in stopping this emigration with "slaves." According to one account, a militia lieutenant named Alexandro Ynfante tried to leave Santo Domingo with his purported slaves after having spent ten months there under Toussaint but was thwarted by Toussaint's prohibition against taking these "slaves" out of the colony on pain of "severe penalties."[71] These "severe penalties" nonetheless had not prevented him from holding these people in servitude for ten months on Toussaint's watch. Moreover, on 8 July 1804, another refugee named Domingo Díaz Paez composed a petition from Santiago de Cuba relating that he had owned property in Santo Domingo and had fled Toussaint's occupation of that colony with several captives.[72] In a petition for land and slaves to facilitate his resettlement in Cuba, Tiburcio Josef Esterlín, who had served on the high appeals court in Santo Domingo city, wrote that he had left behind coffee and cacao plantations along with about eighty men and women claimed as slaves when he departed from the colony.[73]

Deive has argued that Toussaint's 1801 invasion had two contradictory effects on Santo Domingo's "slaves": while it emboldened many of them to flee or to simply refuse to accompany their would-be masters on ships departing from Santo Domingo, it also enabled numerous individuals to emigrate from the island with their purported human property.[74] Some of these petitioners indeed provided evidence of the exploitation of these political disruptions by these "slaves." According to a petition composed by the refugee Francisco de Arredondo, the "black government" had provoked his "slaves" to flee from his control.[75] Furthermore, a report composed by the members of the Real Audiencia (high appeals court) of Santo Domingo (which had relocated to Cuba) discussed the situation of the lawyer José Antonio Ilinojosa, who in his flight from Santo Domingo to Cuba lost the equivalent of 900 pesos when his two "blacks" refused to join him.[76] Nonetheless, Toussaint's measures against enslavement in Santo Domingo appear to have not significantly altered the quotidian situation of the majority of those claimed as slaves in that colony.

Toussaint proved more successful in the arena of high politics. His 1801 invasion decapitated the Spanish political apparatus in Santo Domingo, bringing a dramatic and sudden end to a process that had proceeded very slowly since the signing of the Treaty of Basel. Governor García arrived in Maracaybo on 22 February 1801 as part of a party of 1,803 political leaders, administrators, military officers, soldiers, family members, and servants. The official record of the expedition that included García (who sailed on the Danish ship *Eliza*), created in Maracaybo on 21 March 1801, noted that its members had fled the regime of the "black General of the French Colony Tousaint [*sic*] Louverture." Among these 1,803 people were 360 "Slaves" who thus comprised 20 percent of the total.[77] The situation of these "Slaves" evinces the success of many Spanish colonial officials and would-be slaveholders in circumventing French Republican emancipation and preserving ties of servitude. Though they had lived through a transformational slave revolution, slavery was business as usual for these transplanted colonists and authorities.

Ultimately, while Toussaint did not impose slavery in Santo Domingo, neither did he completely fulfill his and the French Republic's promises of genuine emancipation and equal citizenship in that colony. His adherence to formal emancipation went beyond the (initially) more limited visions of his onetime rivals Jean-François and Georges Biassou. Moreover, his attempts to eliminate slaving in Santo Domingo—even if limited in efficacy and partly qualified as a justification for his invasion and as a means by which to retain labor power—serve as evidence of his commitment to abolition. Although he could be fairly described as a Machiavellian political figure, he also stood for the premises that nobody should be enslaved and that the old system of institutionalized racism could no longer endure. In this, Toussaint was truly ahead of his time. Nonetheless, in his efforts to replicate the Dominguan plantation complex in the neighboring colony, Toussaint looked backward to the repressive labor policies of his predecessors, which in turn had emerged from the world of the plantation in which Toussaint had been raised. His failure to depart from the plantation model in Santo Domingo undermined emancipation there and widened the divide between Toussaint and the island's freed population—a divide that would prove fateful when the metropolitan French invasion of the island that Toussaint so feared finally materialized.

Conclusions

Writing from Philadelphia on 2 December 1801, Roume informed the minister of the navy that travelers from Bordeaux were spreading rumors that the "Consuls of the Republic" had ordered Toussaint to oversee the reestablishment of "colonial slavery" in Hispaniola, naming him "Captain General" and investing him with a full range of "military and civilian" powers.[78] Though rumors of an impending attempt to restore slavery had merit, the first consul had in fact become opposed to Toussaint's accumulation of power and had consequently outfitted a huge military expedition to overthrow him and restore direct metropolitan French rule to the island.[79]

By the middle of 1801, Toussaint appeared to possess virtually unquestioned authority over Hispaniola, yet his grip on power was less secure than it seemed. On the one hand, his military supremacy had assured a relatively easy conquest of Santo Domingo, as he had disregarded repeated metropolitan instructions to first not undertake and then to renounce his takeover in Santo Domingo. His subordination of three officials sent by Paris to check his power in 1801 repeated the well-established pattern that had played out in his earlier expulsions of Sonthonax, Hédouville, Roume, and others.[80] Nevertheless, Toussaint faced hostility in Paris and increasing distrust among the freed population on the island. Toussaint's vulnerabilities became painfully evident when Napoleon's troops landed on his shores a year after the black general's conquest of Santo Domingo.

Though Toussaint continued to profess loyalty to France, many inside and outside Napoleon's government increasingly came to perceive his actions as motivated by a secret wish to win independence. As early as February 1799, the "Particular Agent" Desforneaux had warned that Toussaint's "insatiable ambition" fueled his determined pursuit of a "system of personal independence" that necessitated a swift and forceful response from Paris.[81] Moreover, according to Girard, Napoleon's most reliable informants on the island during the critical early months of the new century, Chanlatte and Kerverseau, had from their posts in Santo Domingo issued "warnings about Saint-Domingue's slow slide toward independence" that "made more of an impression on Bonaparte than the conflicted debates on emancipation in Parisian circles ever did."[82]

Toussaint's intervention in Santo Domingo city had raised questions in metropolitan circles regarding the canny governor's loyalty and legitimacy; his promulgation of the constitution naming him governor-for-life later that year represented all the proof that many needed that he amounted to nothing more than a "usurper" with a thinly disguised "opposition to the current system of the metropole [France]," as one exiled Saint-Domingue colonist living in Philadelphia put it.[83] "The taking of possession of Santo Domingo," echoed the French ambassador Louis-André Pichon in a letter from New York, "is but the prelude to the resistance that [Toussaint] proposes to make to the forces of the Metropole."[84]

Across the Atlantic in Paris, those who controlled the reins of power had reached the same conclusions. In late 1801 Napoleon, who had risen to the most prominent position among these leaders, organized military expeditions to Hispaniola as well as several other overseas territories with the aim of strengthening metropolitan rule. While he targeted several leaders whom he deemed a threat to his authority, Napoleon appears to have reserved a special ire for Toussaint, whose sins in the Corsican's eyes were numerous. In addition to several major perceived affronts to Napoleon's authority such as those just discussed, many lesser demonstrations of the Dominguan general's power—including a curious order that Dominicans construct an "*Arc de Triomphe*" in Toussaint's honor—seemed to directly challenge the claims to supremacy of Bonaparte, for whom the outward manifestations and accoutrements of power mattered a great deal.[85] Nonetheless, such slights were only part of a confluence of circumstances that contributed to Napoleon's decision to deploy the expedition to Hispaniola. Notably, in addition to the influence of the planter lobby, an ephemeral Franco-British peace temporarily removed the military threat of France's main rival in the Carib-bean.[86] This led Napoleon to believe that he now had free rein to crush Toussaint and other perceived challengers to his authority. In an oft-cited letter that Napoleon appears to have taken to heart, General Kerverseau wrote to the first consul in September 1801 that no nation as great as France should "receive laws from a rebel negro in one of its own colonies."[87] Bonaparte's fatal miscalculation that deposing Toussaint was a superior al-ternative to negotiating and collaborating with him precipitated the war of Haitian independence, which lasted from early 1802 until November 1803.

Once the die had been cast, Napoleon acted swiftly. As part of a lengthy series of instructions to his brother-in-law General Charles Leclerc, whom he had appointed to lead the expedition to Hispaniola, Napoleon on 31 Oc-tober 1801 declared, "If the political goal [of the expedition] in the French part of Saint-Domingue should be to disarm the blacks and make them cul-tivators, but free, we should in the Spanish part disarm them as well, but place them back into slavery."[88] This followed a decree that Napoleon had issued two days earlier in which he had declared Toussaint's occupation of Santo Domingo to be "null and void" and ordered all "Ecclesiastic, civil and military divisions" to remain under "Spanish authority" until the metropoli-tan French government came up with a clear plan for administrative and judicial reorganization in the colony.[89]

"I am a soldier. I have no fear of men, I only fear God. If it is necessary to die, [then] I will die as an honorable soldier who does not have anything to regret." Toussaint uttered these words in a 20 December 1801 speech to the residents of Saint-Domingue that Pierre Pluchon cites as the turning point marking the moment when Toussaint publicly declared his intention to militarily oppose Napoleon's forces.[90] About a month later, in late January 1802, the Leclerc expedition entered the island through its eastern part, just as Toussaint had feared.[91] Toussaint's soldiers fought hard to retain every inch of ground, yet they were hindered by defections (such as that of Gen-eral Pierre Agé, whom Toussaint had sent to lead the diplomatic mission to Santo Domingo in 1800), conflicts within their own ranks, and the early loss of vital posts such as Le Cap, which burned to the ground in February 1802.

In this same month, the enemy targeted Santo Domingo city. Napoleon had appointed General Kerverseau, who knew the former Spanish colony well, to lead the division assigned to wrest its capital city from the hands of Paul Louverture. Kerverseau's 400 men and two frigates were seemingly no match for the 1,600 men who defended Santo Domingo city.[92] The Leclerc expedition's overall troop commitment to the eastern part of the island indeed appears to have been disproportionately slight, as evidenced in a 17 February 1802 letter to Bonaparte in which Leclerc stated that he had only 1,000 men stationed in the "Spanish part" out of a total of more than 14,000 soldiers.[93] This, in addition to the rebel forces' determination to defend the liberty that they had "conquered through much blood and fire," may explain why Leclerc's men seized the city of Santo Domingo only when Paul Louverture was duped into surrendering after receiving a false letter ordering him to yield to the invaders.[94] Following a three-week siege, Santo Domingo city finally fell on 21 February 1802.[95]

After the fall of Santo Domingo city, Toussaint's military position steadily worsened. A series of defections by his major chieftains decimated his ranks and placed him in an increasingly vulnerable position. Most notably, the surrender in April 1802 of one of his most important generals, Henry Christophe, broke the back of his military campaign and impelled him to approach General Leclerc to discuss terms of surrender. At a meeting in Le Cap later that spring, Toussaint and his second-in-command, Jean-Jacques Dessalines, met with Leclerc and Christophe and signed an accord that sent Toussaint back to his old plantation as a retired general and incorporated his former troops into Leclerc's forces.[96] In a letter to Toussaint dated 3 May 1802, Leclerc acknowledged his former adversary's submission to the "arms of the republic" and entreated Toussaint to trust him and to distance himself from those who had "sought to mislead [Toussaint] about the true intentions of the French government."[97] In truth, it was Leclerc himself who proved to be duplicitous. In June 1802, he tricked and captured Toussaint and then proceeded to send the Dominguan leader and his family to France, where the Haitian Revolution's greatest figure would die in an isolated prison cell in the Jura Mountains in April 1803.[98]

Napoleon is famously held to have bitterly regretted his choice to combat Toussaint instead of continuing their fragile alliance; this mistake perhaps cost him at least as much geopolitically as his better-known debacle in Russia. "What might [I] not undertake," Napoleon ruefully reflected at the end of his life, "with an army of the twenty-five to thirty thousand blacks [whom Napoleon might have enlisted had he reconciled with Toussaint], in Jamaica, the Antilles, Canada, the United States even, and the Spanish colonies?"[99] Some less famous exiled Dominican leader might well have expressed similar sentiments. Toussaint's opinions on economic development (and, to a lesser extent, political organization) converged to a remarkable degree with those of many of his numerous enemies in French and Spanish elite circles. If more of these individuals had been able to find common ground with the Dominguan leader, then the historical trajectories of both parts of the island might have been very different. As a firm adherent of a Valverdean plantation-oriented economic model based on a subordinated labor force who nonetheless generally managed to retain the allegiance of thousands of armed ex-slaves, Toussaint could have been a very useful part-ner for these elites.

In his assessment of Toussaint's life and legacy, Pluchon claimed that by virtue of two deeds—his defense of formal emancipation and his defiance of the might of Napoleonic France and its armies—this famed leader "tran-scends the petty borders of political maneuvering, to enter the universe of myths and symbols."[100] Notwithstanding two centuries of myth making, the weight of historical evidence concerning Toussaint's rule in Santo Do-mingo mostly does not accord with the image of the martyred hero that he wished to create for both contemporaries and posterity. Yet Toussaint cer-tainly understood the power of "myths and symbols"—especially that of the tree of liberty, which became a popular symbol of renewal and the promise of a new beginning in the French and Haitian Revolutions. Like all symbols, it could nonetheless acquire quite distinct meanings in specific situations. Surveying the human and material devastation wrought by Dessalines's armies in Saint-Domingue's southern province in the civil war of 1800, Toussaint is alleged to have remarked, "I said to trim the tree, not uproot it."[101] In Santo Domingo, Toussaint in some senses uprooted the tree of lib-erty, yet in other respects he put down the roots for the 1822 Dominican abolition of slavery. His rule thus left a paradoxical and contested legacy for subsequent Dominican (and Haitian) history.

CHAPTER FIVE

The Shame of the Nation

*The Force of Reenslavement and the Law of Slavery
under the Regime of Ferrand, 1804–1809*

On 10 October 1802, General François Kerverseau composed a frantic "proclamation" that detailed the plight of "several black and colored children" from the French ship *Le Berceau* who "had been disembarked" in Santo Domingo. According to the "alarms" and "foolish speculations" of various rumor mongers in that colony, these children had been sold into slavery with the complicity of Kerverseau. As Napoleon's chief representative in Santo Domingo, Kerverseau strove to dispel the "sinister noises" and "Vain fears" that had implicated him in such atrocities, insisting that "no sale [of these people] has been authorized" and that any future sale of this nature would result in the swift replacement of any "public officer" who approved it. Kerverseau concluded by imploring his fellow "Citizens" to "distrust those who incessantly spread" these rumors and to instead "trust those who are charged with your safety; who guard over you while you sleep, and who attach to the prosperity of this country, and to Yours, their happiness and their Glory."[1]

Would Kerverseau clear his name? Would these children be fated for a life of bondage, or would they be able to enjoy the right to grow into free men and women? In late 1801 and early 1802, Napoleon had deployed a military expedition to Hispaniola with the aim of reasserting metropolitan control over the island. According to widespread rumors, this expedition had also become committed to the hidden goal of the restoration of slavery by the fall of 1802.[2] Keenly aware of the ferocious opposition that metropolitan French forces would encounter should the island's freed population get wind of the second of these motivations, the expedition's leaders did their utmost to discredit these rumors suggesting an impending return to slavery. This lent a special urgency to the *Berceau* incident, impelling Kerverseau to shore up the French Republic's emancipationist credentials by denying all wrongdoing and promising harsh punishments for all would-be enslavers.

Ultimately, these determined efforts proved futile, as the "common wind" of information disseminating from diverse locales brought word not only of episodes such as the landing of the *Berceau* but also of France's successful restoration of slavery in Guadeloupe and the preservation of the institution in Martinique, which had spent most of the emancipation era under slaveholding British rule.[3] In addition to demonstrating the intense concern that French officials, including Kerverseau, had for their own credibility in light of these pervasive fears of reenslavement, the *Berceau* incident illustrates Santo Domingo's involvement in networks of captivity and coerced migration that became especially pronounced during a decade that witnessed fundamental challenges to both the transcontinental slave trade and slavery itself.

The French words *Le Berceau* translate to "The Cradle"; Hispaniola in late 1802 was nonetheless fast becoming a graveyard of both French Republican emancipation and Napoleon's grand designs to reassert French imperial power in the Americas using Saint-Domingue as a base. Seeking to prevent the death of his own career or worse, Kerverseau forwarded to his superiors seven documents detailing the facts of the *Berceau* affair. While these papers suggest that the embattled general had entrusted the children in question to a man named Cornet who would care for them as free people, they also hint at the existence of an illicit slaving enterprise that involved Santo Domingo.[4]

Unsurprisingly for a clandestine slaving operation, the ship's exact itinerary is unknown, but the evidence from Kerverseau's dossier indicates that the ship transported several dozen captives, most of them from Martinique, Guadeloupe, and French Guyana, and that it may have passed through Aruba, Saint Croix, and Puerto Rico before arriving in Santo Domingo.[5] Extant hospital records from Santo Domingo list eighteen people from the crew of the *Berceau*, including five from Cayenne (French Guyana), two from Saint-Domingue, six from Martinique, four from Guadeloupe, and one from Africa.[6] Indeed, much to the presumed chagrin of Napoleon's agents in Hispaniola, the ship appears to have literally imported into Santo Domingo sobering evidence of the destruction of French emancipation in other parts of the Caribbean. On 30 October 1802, the governor of Puerto Rico, Ramón de Castro, had advised the French expedition's leader, General Charles Leclerc, that he had learned via a "subject interested in tranquility" residing in Santo Domingo that a commander named Broit (of the *Berceau*) had tried to sell "eighty-five to ninety-five blacks" from Guadeloupe in Santo Domingo, dumping several there "due to illness and other reasons" and taking the remainder with him in order to try his luck at various other ports.

The Puerto Rican governor assured General Leclerc of his willingness to help to "contain this political Epidemic, avoid its spread and havoc, [and] apprehend and punish vigorously the guilty parties and their accomplices."[7]

Leclerc and Kerverseau confronted two related problems: quarantining this "political epidemic" and relocating the seventeen or so black "prisoners of War" from this ship who found themselves in Santo Domingo. In Kerverseau's judgment, these captives could not stay indefinitely in Santo Domingo upon release from its hospital where they currently resided. "Foreign Governments do not even want to admit them as slaves," lamented Kerverseau in a letter to Leclerc dated 4 November 1802. Kerverseau proposed employing them as sailors on French ships, "where they could serve usefully," or sending them to Aruba or even Buenos Aires.[8] Though he strove to dispose of these captives as expeditiously as possible, Kerverseau called others as witnesses to testify on the circumstances of their captivity and forced transit. The remarkable series of "*déclarations*" that survive in the archival record serve as evidence of a striking irony: that a prominent military official serving a government that was progressively abandoning general emancipation invited captives to offer eyewitness accounts to assist an investigation into slaving. One such witness, a "*nègre créole de la Martinique*" (black creole from Martinique) named Jean-Charles, claimed to have been captured from a Danish ship by the British off the coast of St Thomas and sent to Martinique, where he was placed on the *Berceau* and shipped to Santo Domingo.[9]

Jean-Charles and his fellow captives found themselves in the middle of the reversal of the hemisphere's first empire-wide experience with general emancipation. Following the Napoleonic expedition's defeat in late 1803 and the formation of independent Haiti on 1 January 1804, one of the vanquished force's generals named Jean-Louis Ferrand established a regime in the eastern part of the island that sought to erase the emancipationist past and to place thousands of freed people back into bondage. In the face of this massive project of attempted reenslavement, those claimed as slaves or vulnerable to enslavement devised a multitude of ways to pursue their own versions of freedom.

These individuals operated within a multilayered legal context shaped not only by a decade of revolution but also by the hybrid French-Spanish legal situation in Santo Domingo (discussed further in chapter 6) and by the legacies of the old legal regime of slavery. In his attempts to institute a coherent legal framework in Santo Domingo, Ferrand sought to improve upon the failures of Leclerc and his successor, General Donatien Rocham-beau. According to one report to Paris composed on 25 February 1803, upon disembarking on the island, "the General in Chief [Leclerc] had ... the double task of reestablishing [in Saint-Domingue] legitimate authority by the force of arms and by that of Laws. The Second [task] was perhaps still more difficult than the first, since it was necessary to complete it in the tu-mult of the Camps."[10]

In societies predicated upon the forced servitude of some of their mem-bers, conflicts often emerged between these two pillars of "force of arms" and "laws." Though "existing relations of force," in Rebecca Scott's words, ulti-mately undergirded master-slave relations in American slave societies, the incoherence of laws built on the premise of transforming human beings into property enabled some slaves in many parts of the hemisphere to exploit certain statutes or provisions to improve their condition or to win their free-dom.[11] Moreover, some slaves even managed to influence the evolution of slave law in some places by asserting claims such as the right to purchase oneself from bondage.[12]

Ferrand's enterprise in Santo Domingo made the inchoate nature of slave law even more apparent. Ferrand seems to have operated largely indepen-dent of the direct orders of Napoleon,[13] and the general in any event had a very dubious legal mandate to reimpose slavery in Santo Domingo, as it is not clear whether slavery was ever explicitly reestablished in law by the French under Napoleon in the former Spanish colony. As discussed in chap-ter 4, Napoleon on 31 October 1801 had instructed General Leclerc to place Dominican blacks "back into slavery," but no known legal mechanism backed up this order. The French scholars Jean-François Niort and Jérémy Richard have argued that any measure restoring slavery at this time would have been illegal by virtue of being in contravention of the 1799 French con-stitution, while only an act passed by a legislature would have the "same ju-ridical force" as the 1794 emancipation act.[14] Bonaparte's legislature on 20 May 1802 in fact passed a law composed of four short articles that did little more than confirm slavery in those areas where it had been maintained de facto. The law's four articles are worth quoting in their entirety:

> First Article: In the colonies returned to France in execution of the
> Treaty of Amiens of 6 Germinal Year Ten [27 March 1802], slavery
> will be maintained in accordance with the laws and regulations prior
> to 1789.

Article 2: This will also be the case in the other French colonies beyond the Cape of Good Hope.

Article 3: The trade in Blacks and their importation in the said colonies will take place in accordance with the laws and regulations in force before the said date of 1789.

Article 4: Notwithstanding all of the preceding laws, the colonial regime is subject for ten years to the regulations that will be made by the government.[15]

In simply stating that "slavery will be maintained" in those colonies that Britain had "returned" to France by the Treaty of Amiens (Saint-Lucia and Martinique), this measure thus did *not* legalize the reestablishment of slavery in Saint-Domingue, Guadeloupe, or Guyana, which had come under emancipationist governments after 1793. It was also silent on Santo Domingo. Thus, the murderous campaign conducted by Napoleon's general Antoine Richepance had questionable legal sanction for reenslaving thousands of people in Guadeloupe, as did Ferrand for his attempted restoration of slavery in Santo Domingo.[16]

Niort and Richard have, moreover, unearthed surviving copies of a "consular order" that Bonaparte issued on 16 July 1802, which stipulated that "the colony of Guadeloupe and dependency will be governed in the manner of Martinique, Saint Lucia, Tobago, [and the] eastern colonies, by the same laws that were in place in 1789." Scrupulously avoiding the use of the word "slave," this order made no mention of either Saint-Domingue or Santo Domingo. What is more, Niort and Richard have contended that the order may not have carried legal weight even in Guadeloupe. They insisted that "the reestablishment of slavery, and more generally of the old segregationist and discriminatory order in Guadeloupe [after 1802] rested, for 46 years, on a legality that was more questionable than that of the law of 30 floréal an X (20 May 1802)."[17] One can advance a similar argument concerning Ferrand's efforts to restore slavery in Santo Domingo. Except for Napoleon's 16 August 1800 "enslaved part" speech to the Council of State discussed in chapter 3 and his 31 October 1801 order to Leclerc, I have not uncovered an executive order, a law, or even correspondence from Napoleon's government that authorized or explicitly endorsed the reestablishment of slavery in Santo Domingo.

This uncertainty over Ferrand's legal mandate vis-à-vis slavery contrasts greatly with the situation in Haiti, whose laws unequivocally rejected the institution (notwithstanding early leaders' reliance upon forced labor). Ferrand's conflicts with the young Haitian nation underscore the interconnected histories of both sides of the island in the years immediately after the establishment of Haiti. Conceptualizing this period through an islandwide lens offers several new perspectives on Haitian and Dominican history. First, it enables one to contextualize the militarism of both regimes sharing the island in this era: that of early Haitian leaders as partially a response to a brutal campaign of reenslavement, and that of the Ferrand regime as a reaction both to the massacres of whites carried out by Haitian leaders in 1804 and to a justified fear of Haitian invasion.[18] Second, it encourages comparisons between the repressive policies of each of the island's regimes, while highlighting the intertwined struggles of the citizens of each for a more genuine liberty. Finally, it reflects the centrality of the larger geographical and geopolitical contexts within which these regimes operated.

In 1802, Kerverseau and Leclerc had desperately tried to silence rumors of a return to slavery, which did not allay islanders' well-founded suspicions regarding the expedition's true goals. After 1804, Ferrand attempted a different type of silencing: the erasure of emancipation by re-creating slavery in law, on the ground, and in the written record. In this respect, Ferrand anticipated a later act by authorities in Louisiana that "effectively silenced the very existence of the abolition that had taken place in the French colony [Saint-Domingue] in 1793–1794," in the words of Rebecca Scott.[19]

Yves Bénot has shown that the abandonment of emancipation by Napoleon's Consular government provoked considerable opposition in metropolitan France among those who condemned slavery, racism, and colonialism (though not always all three together).[20] In Santo Domingo, a different form of opposition emerged: that of freed people who sought to preserve their liberty. Thomas Holt noted years ago that "it is from ex-slaves that we may well learn much of what it means to be free."[21] This statement can be expanded to add that formally freed people who lived under the threat of reenslavement also can convey political lessons on freedom that have purchase in our own time. The very uncertainty of their condition, as much as the abject deprivation that they so feared, doubtless gave them a visceral appreciation for liberty. It is their actions—often in vain, occasionally with success—that kept alive the legacy of French Republican emancipation in Santo Domingo.

The Establishment of Ferrand in Santo Domingo

On 28 April 1803, a beleaguered General Donatien Rochambeau argued in a missive to the minister of the navy that "we now have to endure the war of the White Color against the two others."[22] Rochambeau's depiction of the final year of the Haitian war for independence as a race war converged with the reactionary turn of the metropole regarding slavery and legal racism. In 1796, accusations of racism had contributed to the ouster of Rochambeau from the position of "Commandant in Chief of the Spanish part of Saint-Domingue" that he had briefly held that year.[23] In the changed political context of 1803, by contrast, this man's prejudices and ruthlessness fit in well with the mission of reinstituting metropolitan rule at any cost.[24]

The most significant such cost was the lives of tens of thousands of men, women, and children who perished from violence, disease, or privation.[25] Napoleon's determination to control Hispaniola led him to deploy to that island a massive invasion force on which he staked the future of French imperialism in the Americas. According to one estimate, France sent 47,286 men to the island between 4 February 1802 and 21 May 1803.[26] By comparison, this was more than twice the population of Le Cap at its height in the late 1780s and 16,000 more than the entire white population of Saint-Domingue on the eve of the revolution.[27] It was also only slightly less than the entire population of the colony of Santo Domingo in 1808, according to one census.[28] Though Saint-Domingue was the main prize, its neighbor also merited the belligerents' attention. This owed in part to the strategic imperatives that had impelled Toussaint Louverture in January 1801 to capture the former Spanish colony's nerve center in an unsuccessful effort to prevent the Napoleonic expedition from landing in that colony. As he formulated plans to use a reconquered Saint-Domingue as a beachhead for French imperial expansion in the Western Hemisphere, Napoleon grasped the necessity of holding onto Santo Domingo and subduing potential and actual enemies there.[29]

"The possession of this part [Santo Domingo] is essentially necessary for the execution of the orders of the Government," Toussaint's old foe General Antoine Chanlatte had written in an undated report advising the French government on military strategies for the island's reconquest. "The locality offers great means to maintain oneself without much force and to oppose the bands of Toussaint in case he fights against national authority; and when the Republic will make itself known there, each Spaniard interested in defending his life, his possessions and his family will become a soldier who will be worthy of the name of French republican."[30] Asserting control over Santo Domingo initially required deposing the Louverture regime, which General Kerverseau had accomplished in February 1802. The more difficult mission would nonetheless come later: the subjugation of thousands of what were characterized as "Maroons" in Santo Domingo, whose destruction Napoleon had mandated in his instructions to Leclerc.[31]

These "maroons" posed several challenges to the expeditionary force. As we have seen, former fugitive slaves who lived in semiautonomous communities apart from the plantations and urban centers had long resisted the political and economic projects of a succession of Spanish and French leaders, from the early colonial governors to Toussaint Louverture. The Leclerc-Rochambeau expedition now targeted them as a special military threat; of particular concern was these communities' apparent absorption of many of Toussaint's former soldiers into their ranks. In fact, in the summer of 1802, when most of the key members of the old Louverturian military leadership either had been deposed or had joined the Napoleonic armies, the "maroons" constituted the only substantial opposition to Napoleon's troops on the island.[32] Not coincidentally, those from these enclaves also often found themselves the victims of the expedition's harshest measures. In mid-1802, for instance, Leclerc's soldiers were ordered to shoot any armed "maroon" on sight—including women—while their superiors often held public hangings of captured rebel leaders, especially those deemed maroons.[33]

The mountainous borderlands between the two colonies were a strategic flashpoint that formed the backdrop for many of these conflicts between the "maroons" and the invaders.[34] In one proposal dated 5 March 1802, a petitioner named Lavassor had advocated splitting Hispaniola and other French territories into two areas: a "white" zone in the mountains and a "black" zone on and near the plains and lowlands. Lavassor supported this proposal by citing the "maroon" activity that the mountains supposedly facilitated and by asserting that Santo Domingo's "immense and uncultivated plains" could be worked by multitudes of blacks, until such time as the whole of "Africa is exhausted."[35]

While such grand schemes no doubt motivated some of Napoleon's partisans, events on the island ultimately dictated the war's outcome. In 1802 and early 1803, forces under General Kerverseau conducted expeditions against the "maroon" community of Maniel in the borderlands. Despite his frustration at an initial lack of manpower, Kerverseau used the same carrot-and-stick policies that his predecessors had, with rather more emphasis on the stick.[36] On 24 April 1802, the French general Boudet informed Rochambeau (who had just succeeded Boudet as commander of all French forces in Saint-Domingue's west and south) of the potential links between the Maniel residents and the rebels. Warning Rochambeau that the "insurgents" could seek refuge in Maniel and augment this group's numbers (which he estimated at around 1,200), Boudet communicated his intention to send a "deputation" that would "open relations" with those from Maniel, which he hoped would bring them to the French side and stop their alleged killings of whites.[37] Three months later, a commander in Neyba named Joseph Ruiz wrote to Rochambeau that "a great quantity of Blacks from the Army of Toussaint took refuge there [in Maniel] with their arms; [and] that seven or eight [fugitives] arrive there each day, and that they organize companies." What is more, according to Ruiz a ship had recently disembarked near Petit-Trou, Saint-Domingue, to trade powder and munitions with the inhabitants of Maniel in exchange for mahogany. Most urgently, Ruiz reported that several "Blacks" from Rochambeau's own division had attempted to travel to Maniel with false passports and that despite Ruiz's order that all "French cultivators" in the area return to their plantations, many had instead gone to Maniel.[38]

Those from Maniel nonetheless appear to have had less success defending themselves against the Leclerc-Rochambeau expedition than they had had against Toussaint and earlier leaders. According to an "Order of the Day" dated 26 March 1803, Kerverseau had "taken the important position of Maniel," "killing and dispersing" its residents.[39] Recounting these events in a report that he composed in Mayagüez, Puerto Rico, in February 1804, Kerverseau related that he had attacked Maniel with a force of 600 "Spaniards" and 200 "French blacks or mulattos." After a pitched battle in which those from the enclave were "vanquished by fear more than by our arms," all of their encampments were "reduced to Ashes" and a garrison was stationed there to prevent new "maroon" communities from forming. "Such was the end of this republic of Brigands who for about a century lived by Hunting, pillage and piracy," declared the white general.[40]

This victory was short lived. The defeat of Maniel could not offset the effect of successive setbacks at the hands of forces under Toussaint's former general Jean-Jacques Dessalines, who carried on the struggle of his deposed mentor following a period of combat in the armies of the invaders.[41] In October 1802, around the time of Dessalines's defection back to the rebel side, yellow fever claimed the life of Leclerc, who was replaced by Rochambeau as commander of the expedition.

Hardship was indeed the lot of most officers and enlisted men fighting on the metropolitan French side. For instance, by 23 September 1802, Kerverseau, though holding the rank of general, was listed as commanding a mere 651 troops, who formed part of a diminished expeditionary force of 24,519 men. This precipitous decline in troop strength owed in part to the effects of disease, which had by one account destroyed half of Santo Domingo's "garrison" in six weeks.[42] The survivors faced a bleak struggle for self-preservation. By late June 1803, Kerverseau commanded only 479 men, out of 17,055 in the entire expedition.[43] According to an official report, a scant 7,000 men remained in French service on the island as of 21 August 1803, with 2,000 to 3,000 dying per month. In this dire assessment, without external assistance, the French fighting force would be reduced to zero in three months.[44]

This desperation contributed to the assortment of well-documented atrocities committed by Rochambeau and his men during his year at the helm of the expeditionary force, of which perhaps the most notorious was the importation of war dogs from Cuba (though the tactic had in fact been initiated by Rochambeau's predecessor).[45] As its military position steadily eroded and the body count kept rising, Rochambeau's force also perpetrated lesser known outrages, such as the forcible military recruitment of both urban and rural residents of Santo Domingo in the hope that more acclimated troops might bolster the strength of the expedition.[46] While "Spanish" troops served various French regimes throughout the period of French rule over the island's eastern part, in 1803 the recruitment of such troops apparently became more heavy-handed.[47] In October 1803, on the eve of the French expedition's final defeat, Dr. Pedro Francisco de Prado warned his fellow Dominicans that a new threat had replaced that of the "ominous cloud of blacks" who had sought to take the city of Santo Domingo. These Dominicans were now threatened by the "oppressive yoke" of metropolitan French military presence. Kerverseau's enlistment of troops whom he then stationed in various border areas drew particular ire. According to Prado, Kerverseau issued two declarations to Dominicans in an effort to stop the resulting desertions.[48] A 7 June 1803 letter by Kerverseau to several military commanders and "notables" in Santo Domingo decried the "disastrous effects of the desertion that has reduced an army of more than two thousand men to less than four hundred, and delivered the border to the Enemy."[49]

Such impressment proved particularly disastrous in the countryside. Pierre Quantin, a general under Rochambeau, wrote a series of letters to his superiors that revealed what happened to Dominican peasants ensnared by the invasion force. Quantin commanded the crucial border post of Fort-Dauphin,[50] which had been wrested from those fighting against the expedition on 1 December 1802.[51] In January 1803, Quantin—who was listed as commanding 844 troops as of 20 February 1803—reported to Rochambeau that two or three "Spaniards" were dying every day.[52] Two months later, on 4 March 1803, Quantin informed Rochambeau that sixteen deserters had probably returned to their ranches (*hattes*).[53] In sharp contrast to his superior's starkly racialist language, Quantin candidly noted that soldiers "of all colors" were dying under his command.[54]

These developments may have helped lead to Quantin's replacement by General Jean-Louis Ferrand by 20 June 1803.[55] Born in Besançon, France, in 1758, Ferrand had participated in the revolutions in the Thirteen Colonies and in France before joining Napoleon's ill-fated expedition of reconquest.[56] (See figure 5.) Ferrand had apparently arrived on the island just after Leclerc's death, as a list of military officers dated 22 December 1802 referred to him as a brigade general who had "Disembarked" on 24 November of that year.[57] For all his military experience, Ferrand faced two great obstacles: the superior strength and morale of the enemy and his own hubris. The former cost him his command of Fort-Dauphin, which fell to the rebels on 12 September 1803; the latter cost him his life five years later.

By the time Fort-Dauphin fell, many of the expedition's survivors had already begun to contemplate returning to France, and a chaotic evacuation was already underway in the Dominguan town of Jérémie.[58] Ferrand, however, refused an opportunity to escape the island on a British ship, deciding instead to retreat to the Cibao area (northern Santo Domingo). He then settled in Santo Domingo city on 16 December 1803.[59] Within weeks, Ferrand's men who chose to stay the course, along with the surviving garrisons from Jacmel and Croix-des-Bouquets, Saint-Domingue, and a contingent of French soldiers in Cuba, had relocated to Santo Domingo, which "became the single largest concentration of French troops in the Greater Antilles" during the Ferrand years, according to Philippe Girard.[60] Thousands of civilians from various parts of Saint-Domingue, often with empty stomachs and little more than the proverbial shirts on their backs, joined these soldiers in a mass exodus eastward. Once in Santo Domingo, many onetime

FIGURE 5 "Général Ferrand. Il mourit victime de l'ingraditude." Portrait of General Ferrand from 1811 captioned "He died the victim of ingratitude." This portrait was published by Gilbert Guillermin, an officer who had served under Ferrand. Courtesy of the John Carter Brown Library at Brown University.

residents of France's former crown jewel bided their time in anticipation of a new French expedition that never arrived.

After Dessalines proclaimed the independence of Haiti in early 1804, he memorably claimed to have "avenged America."[61] As Ferrand and his crew of just a few hundred men strove to establish a government in Santo Domingo city, they embarked upon a different sort of vengeance: violence against those who in Ferrand's mind had overthrown Saint-Domingue's legitimate French masters and replaced them with a barbaric regime.[62] At its core, the underlying logic behind the policies of the Ferrand regime was the desire to crush the new Haitian state and reestablish a rejuvenated French plantation colony on its ruins. In pursuing this enterprise, the regime would be met with the determined opposition of those who refused to allow the emancipationist past to be completely erased.

A Demographic and Economic Portrait of Santo Domingo under Ferrand

In a 3 August 1813 report, a man named Carlos de Urrutia called upon the "liberal hand" of an "enlightened Government" to finally realize the economic potential of a colony that had languished in poverty for centuries. Despite the presence of a relatively prosperous tobacco industry based in the north, as well as an overabundance of pigs, cattle, and other animals whose meat and hides brought in revenue, Urrutia believed that Santo Domingo still lacked the resources and the farsighted policies to cultivate the real money-makers of the day, such as sugar, coffee, and cacao. He accordingly suggested reforms to economic governance there that would place Spain's oldest colony on track to claim a more exalted place in the empire.[63]

Urrutia's prescription in many ways echoed that of Sánchez Valverde of nearly thirty years earlier, and its very issuance implies repeated past failures to implement a profitable plantation system in Santo Domingo. The Ferrand regime, which fell four years before the writing of this letter, indeed proved no more effective than prior governments in improving Santo Domingo's economy. Far from exercising a "liberal hand" over Santo Domingo, Ferrand based its fortunes on a formula that bore a resemblance to that of Toussaint: the combination of economic incentives for plantation production with repressive labor policies. Ferrand nonetheless differed from the late Dominguan general in one crucial respect: as an unabashed buyer and seller of human beings, Ferrand harbored no qualms about endorsing open enslavement in the land that had pioneered American plantation slavery.[64] As Fernando Picó has observed, for Ferrand and most other Caribbean leaders in these years, "a world without slaves was inconceivable."[65]

The brutality of Ferrand and many former Saint-Domingue colonists toward Haitians and nonwhite Dominicans was rooted in more than just nostalgia for the old slaveholding order. Many French-speaking inhabitants of Santo Domingo in the Ferrand era were survivors of massacres of whites in Haiti ordered by Dessalines in 1804.[66] Their accounts of the slaughter of loved ones and compatriots by the Haitians may well have encouraged the racist violence of Ferrand and his high command, many of whom had themselves survived a crushing military defeat at the hands of men and women who had been deemed property or second-class citizens less than a decade and a half earlier.

One such white refugee, Norbert Thoret, told a harrowing tale of his captivity in black-ruled Haiti and the killings of many fellow whites there. Thoret, a French-born tailor who had served in this capacity in the Napoleonic expedition to Hispaniola of 1802–03, found himself compelled to ply his trade for Dessalines in independent Haiti and forbidden from leaving the country. According to Thoret, on Dessalines's orders, more than 4,500 whites were "pitilessly slaughtered" in Haiti, including women and children. After escaping such a fate largely due to his professional skills and some opportune circumstances, Thoret managed to flee Haiti with the assistance of several "blacks" (who were later slaughtered by "Spaniards" in Santo Domingo). He then lived in Santo Domingo under Ferrand for thirty-two months, where he reestablished himself as a tailor and purchased a plantation and "slaves" with his earnings.[67] Thoret's account offered seemingly irrefutable proof of Haitian barbarism to men like Ferrand who sought to reimpose slavery, even as Ferrand's own policies—most notably, his orders sanctioning the capture and enslavement of Haitians—factored prominently in Haitian aggression toward the fledgling French regime to the east.[68]

Thoret may have served as a model for the type of white plantation entrepreneur that Ferrand wished to attract in order to develop a viable plantation economy in his colony. On the eve of the cession of Santo Domingo, most of the colony's few relatively lucrative plantation and ranching enterprises had been under the control of the Spanish colonial administration by virtue of either their owners' inability to meet financial obligations or the forced transfer of religiously held properties occasioned by the Jesuits' expulsion from Spain's American domains in 1767. These enterprises' status from 1795 until Toussaint's invasion of Santo Domingo city in 1801 appears to have remained largely unchanged. As discussed in chapter 4, Toussaint seized several such enterprises (most notably the Boca Nigua plantation) during his brief reign, after which Kerverseau in 1802 claimed these properties based on France's assumption of Spain's assets and prerogatives in this land as stipulated in the Treaty of Basel.[69] Kerverseau had also tried to direct the energies of several Dominican plantations toward the production of *tafia* (rum) for his troops. For instance, he ordered on 12 October 1803 that thirty-four *cultivateurs* be "taken" from their current plantations and reassigned to labor on the *tafia*-producing San Nicolás plantation.[70]

Ferrand would considerably expand upon these efforts to impose direct state control over potentially lucrative assets. Two comprehensive listings of property that came under the French "national domain" administration were produced by the state to document these transfers. These records confirm the portrait of a colony with few productive enterprises and a small labor force, yet they also hint at continual conflicts over the conditions and fact of servitude.

As Urrutia's letter suggests, Santo Domingo underwent little substantial economic change during the Ferrand period, as it continued to rely upon ranching, tobacco production, and the limited cultivation of plantation crops, such as sugar and coffee. Ferrand instituted a policy of granting money to the owners of productive enterprises in proportion to their coffee and sugar output; in at least one case, such financial incentives also reflected the size of the subordinated labor force.[71] Ferrand also attempted, with limited success, to entice white exiled planters from the former Saint-Domingue to Santo Domingo.[72] Despite such measures, the scope of cultivation in Santo Domingo remained small. According to one estimate, as of 1 January 1808, only 8,506 *carreaux* (about 28,000 acres) of Santo Domingo's land were planted in sugar, and just 2,231 *carreaux* (7,362 acres) of land were devoted to tobacco.[73]

The scale of individual enterprises mirrored this larger picture. A national domains survey dated 21 January 1804 listed four plantations and three cattle ranches; two of the plantations were planted in sugar, one in cacao, and one in assorted provisions. Two of these plantations were listed as having labor forces of around fifty *cultivateurs*, while another had twenty-one laborers and the fourth had none listed.[74] An 1806 cadastral survey contained many of the same data, with the notable exception of a substantially smaller number of laborers; the survey's creators attributed the decrease to Dessalines's failed 1805 invasion of Santo Domingo, discussed later in this chapter. Upon this incursion, two of the three "blacks" on the L'Espérance ranch "followed the rebels [Haitians] in their flight."[75]

While these laborers had apparently rejected servitude in French Santo Domingo and sought a different life in independent Haiti, others became the subject of claims that implicitly elided the French emancipation edict of 1794. According to a set of "Observations on the nature of national Domains of the eastern part of St Domingue," a plantation manager named Gabriela Sánchez had violated French authorities' claims to all property associated with her plantation by "embarking" for Havana with twenty "cultivators" who had been "attached" to the estate in the year 1800.[76] Were these "cultivators" property? In advancing a claim to these laborers, the Ferrand government implicitly tried to re-create "slave" as a coherent category by taking as a given the legitimacy of demanding the "restitution" of human beings as property, in spite of the French emancipation law that had been in force when Sánchez took these captives with her to Cuba.

Some of those who could not escape the reimposition of servitude found that certain aspects of associational life enabled them to improve their condition. As in many other parts of Latin America, Catholic brotherhoods had become part of the social fabric in colonial Santo Domingo, as they offered members of various statuses and conditions numerous forms of social, material, and spiritual support.[77] Under Ferrand, some "slaves" appear to have found a degree of autonomy through these groups, even as the number of such organizations in Santo Domingo seemed to drop sharply in the wake of Toussaint's invasion in 1801.[78] The 1806 cadastral survey listed "61 blacks" among the colony's "rural Properties" who were part of the "Brotherhood of St Antoine" (Confrérie de St Antoine) located in the city of Santiago. "These blacks have always lived in a state of independence," this survey noted, "which has never permitted [officials] to collect any goods from them."[79]

According to a census of the colony's population published in 1808, urban "slaves," who could presumably more easily avail themselves of the opportunities offered by these brotherhoods, constituted a significant proportion of the unfree population. Among the 7,052 souls whom this census designated as "Slaves" (*Esclaves*), 35 percent were listed as residing in Santo Domingo city and Santiago, the colony's two main urban areas, though this figure likely reflects an urban bias in the collection of data. This census divided the colony's population into four distinct categories based on race and condition: "European Whites" (*Blancs Européens*), "Whites of the Country" (*Blancs du Païs* [*sic*]), "Creoles of color" (*Créols* [*sic*] *de couleur*), and "Slaves." While both classes of whites together accounted for just over a quarter of the population, the "Creoles of color" group encompassed 60 percent of the total. Those claimed as slaves represented 15 percent of the entire population—the same proportion as in 1789, though the population of the entire colony had halved in these two decades according to this census, falling from around 100,000 to just over 50,000.[80]

Francophone migrants constituted a substantial portion of this population, at least according to census data for Santo Domingo city. In such a census dated 18 November 1808, 3,875 inhabitants were listed as "French" (*Français*), while the remaining 3,891 were labeled "Spanish" (*Espagnols*). The census takers listed a quarter (24.7 percent) of the city's "French" population as "black" (*nègre* or *négresse*), while applying this label to only 13 percent of the "Spanish" population.[81] While such perceptions of fused color and national identities perhaps served to heighten the regime's concern with "French" blacks whom its leaders associated closely with Haiti, the Dominican historical context also shaped the colony's demography and the ideas of race that prevailed in the Ferrand period.

As discussed in chapter 1, for instance, Santo Domingo's distinct history of negligible plantation infrastructure, a weak colonial state, and a host of other forces had enabled the emergence of a free African-descended majority long before the Haitian Revolution. Moreover, the phrase "*Blancs du Païs*" used in the comprehensive 1808 census bears a striking resemblance to the term *blancos de la tierra* (whites of the land), which according to Richard Turits emerged in colonial Santo Domingo to describe "people of African origin who were better off [than others] and who lived with privileges [that were] in principle reserved for whites."[82]

Given that the colony's ruling cadre were veterans of the Leclerc-Rochambeau expedition who modeled many of their policies on the racist laws promulgated in late colonial Saint-Domingue, this perception of such a large free "colored" population very likely alarmed them. After all, even at the height of the legal onslaught on the rights of the *gens de couleur libres* in Saint-Domingue, they had constituted no more than 10 percent of the total population in 1789.[83] "If I were to disarm all who are not white," Kerverseau had stated in late 1802, "I would disarm nine tenths of the Spanish Part."[84] Having been a leading officer in the service of an expedition that had fought under explicit orders to "not allow any blacks having held a rank above that of captain to remain on the island," Kerverseau had confronted in Santo Domingo a long tradition of relative nonwhite mobility.[85] In a 22 October 1802 letter, Kerverseau had instructed a subordinate to exercise "great surveillance" over the *cultivateurs* of Santiago and to "purge" the countryside of the "most seditious" and send some of these to Puerto Plata.[86] Though he would depend on black and mixed-race soldiers in his military campaigns as had his predecessors, Ferrand likewise sought to disenfranchise and subordinate nonwhites. In this, he conformed to the official racism emanating from the metropole, enhanced by his hatred and fear of the emancipationist state next door.

Legal and Political Conflicts over Enslavement and Citizenship Rights

In a correspondence to Napoleon written on 5 February 1805, a group of Dominguan refugees in Santiago de Cuba denounced the "cowardice" of France's "enemies" who had "betrayed, evacuated, and delivered Saint-Domingue to a miserable handful of freed people and rebel slaves, who only have the energy and courage of a blind and cowardly ferocity."[87] During a time of substantial regression to the legal racism of the prerevolutionary era in the French world, French migrant enclaves in places such as Santiago de Cuba and Santo Domingo became hotbeds of such vitriol, even as many in the Francophone sphere resisted the destruction of the more egalitarian order of the 1790s.[88] In spite of such resistance, the fact of slave revolution in nearby Haiti, as well as Dessalines's killing of many French whites who remained there after 1803, shaped the decisions that the leaders of the French occupation of Santo Domingo made in their efforts to fashion a new slaveholding society. In this respect, the close proximity of Haiti reinforced the resurgence of racism in French law and colonial policy.

Though ideologies of racial inferiority had emerged in close connection with plantation slavery in the French Caribbean and beyond, antislavery and antiracism had often diverged in the writings of many eighteenth-century French abolitionists and in the discourses of numerous individuals in the revolutionary era, as support for one did not necessarily imply acceptance of the other.[89] Nonetheless, the years 1790 to 1802 in the French world can be conceptualized as an arc across which struggles against legalized racism and slavery yielded landmark legislative triumphs, peaking in 1795, only to reverse direction after that year. The subsequent erosion of these gains again drew racism and slavery closely together.

After 1802, Napoleon coupled his repudiation of the 1794 emancipation decree with an array of racist laws that left the hard-won gains of the early 1790s in tatters. These included the reinstatement of assorted ancien régime regulations that had aimed to closely monitor the activities of persons of African extraction in France, the reinstitution of the requirement that blacks carry identity cards while in the metropole, prohibitions on mixed-race persons' entry into France, and a ban on interracial marriage.[90]

In line with the actions of their leader, authorities in various French territories passed laws that similarly targeted the rights of those of African ancestry and that sought to limit the means by which those claimed as slaves could gain their freedom.[91] Ferrand for his part enforced a distinction between "French" blacks, whom he associated with Haiti and considered especially subversive, and "Spanish" blacks, deemed somewhat less dangerous.[92] The line separating "French" and "Spanish" blacks ran through the ancien régime to the revolutionary era and into the post-1804 period.[93] Ferrand's actions in this respect closely resembled those of his counterparts in other parts of the Americas, as Cuban officials generally sought to bar the settlement on that island of free and freed men of African descent from Saint-Domingue, while North American authorities passed laws designed to halt or greatly reduce the entrance of what they termed "French Negroes" into the United States.[94]

Ferrand issued an assortment of other racially discriminatory orders, some implicitly in response to claims making by both those claimed as slaves and those deemed to be of African descent who were able to prove their freedom. These laws included curfews, racially based exclusion from emigration and immigration programs, antivagabondage measures, and even discrimination in treatment for illnesses.[95] In a 27 February 1806 order, Ferrand also banned the bestowal on any "persons of color" of inheritance exceeding the value of one hundred *gourdes* that was against the interests of "absent rightful heirs."[96]

These discriminatory measures were closely linked to fears of a Haitian invasion. In early 1804, Ferrand related in a note to his subordinate Vives his anxieties concerning a "quantity of blacks and people of color of both sexes, refugees from the French part [Haiti], who are continually in idleness and who will surely become dangerous especially if the Brigands [Haitians] invade the land." Ferrand then ordered Vives to gather information on and put to work those among this group who did not have any "means to subsist" or who were "slaves who find themselves here without their masters."[97] These efforts culminated in a 15 September 1804 order by Ferrand to create a comprehensive registry that recorded the following information for all "French blacks and people of color" over twelve years old: names, ages, status ("free or slave"), and "from which neighborhood and plantation they come," in addition to their present place of domicile. Ferrand also proposed either employing "French black and colored slaves" in "useful jobs" or loaning them out.[98] (Ferrand's obsession with monitoring nonwhites is also evident in a December 1804 order that a subordinate conduct a "*contrôle*," or inspection, on a number of men belonging to two military companies. This inspection was to ascertain "if these men were free or enslaved, before departing the French part," as well as other information, such as their comportment during Toussaint's reign in Santo Domingo.)[99]

Toward the end of the ancien régime, a ministerial order had declared that the "first stain" ascribed to blacks by many whites "extends to all of their descendants, and . . . cannot be erased by the gift of freedom."[100] In the spirit of this order and another from the same era that had mandated the arrest and imprisonment of all "Black slaves who try to pass for free" in Port-au-Prince, the Ferrand government imposed all manner of restrictions on the mobility of nonwhites, seeking to enslave those who could not prove their freedom and to disenfranchise those who could.[101] In particular, this entailed policing the line between "slave" and free, which Ferrand attempted via measures such as a 31 December 1807 decree that those wishing to create État Civil records in their names must present a "title of liberty" and an order requiring all "People of color" intending to sell dry goods to provide written proof of their liberty and pay a deposit.[102]

The intended parallels to the prerevolutionary order became explicit in one letter that Ferrand composed to the "Notables of Santo Domingo" on 15 September 1804. In his discussion of a work program aimed at "French blacks and people of color," Ferrand stated that the program "is a means to occupy the Vagabonds, and to persuade those, who believe themselves [to be] independent, that we consider them in the State in which they were before the revolution, and from which they have been removed to the detriment of the Colony."[103]

The legal scholar Vernon Palmer has written that "history tends to show that the stronger the fear of insurrection, the more likely restrictive laws will be passed targeting free people of color."[104] While the Ferrand regime's legislative record amply supports this assertion, a look back at the notarial archive hints that the law also represented a terrain for contestation over rights.

During the Ferrand years, a number of formally freed men and women created several dozen notarized acts that recognized their free status. The language of many of these acts (which are the focus of chapter 6) displayed ambiguity concerning the scope of citizenship in Santo Domingo. A discernible tension existed between two statements that appear repeatedly in these acts: that the freed subject would live like "other freed people" and that she or he would have "all of the rights" of *"anciens libres"* (the formerly free, i.e., those who had never been slaves).[105] This tension was rooted in the bitter political and legal history of colonial Saint-Domingue. As discussed in chapter 1, the 1685 *Code Noir* had granted ex-slaves virtually equal rights to those born free, yet by the 1780s, due to racist laws and pervasive informal discrimination, living like "other freed people" often meant enduring political disenfranchisement and innumerable quotidian humiliations.

In their struggle against these laws, activist *gens de couleur libres* from Saint-Domingue had devoted scrupulous attention to law and to the effective manipulation of language. John Garrigus observes that "the first free colored spokesmen in revolutionary Paris—a merchant and a planter—were so skilled at legalistic argument that historians have mistakenly described them as 'lawyers.'"[106] Three notarial acts from French Santo Domingo hint at the continued salience of language in conflicts over rights there in the Ferrand era. In the 19 August 1803 act of the sale of Rozine *dite* Alzire to her mother, Rosalie *dite* Dufay, discussed in the introduction to this study, Rosalie had been labeled a *"mulâtresse libre affranchie"* (free freed mulatto), but the word *"affranchie"* (freed) had been crossed out. This 1803 document then declared that Rozine would enjoy "all of the rights ... attached to The Class Of Free men."[107] The 12 December 1805 Santo Domingo city manumission act for the adolescents Zénon and Solon, moreover, noted that they would "enjoy liberty from this day forth, as the other freed people enjoy it in this Colony, by virtue of the edict of the month of March 1685 [the *Code Noir*]."[108] Finally, in a record created in Santo Domingo city on 30 April 1804, a notary initially marked a woman called Louise-Félicité *dite* Agard as a "slave," but then struck this word and replaced it with the phrase "Legally acquired property."[109]

Of course, the mere invocation of the *Code Noir* in such acts in no way implied its wholesale and faithful application, any more than had been the case in colonial Saint-Domingue. Nonetheless, the code's provisions of equality and the history of activism associated with them—in addition to its other clauses affording slaves some basic rights—represented implicit if not explicit grounds for the advancement of claims to greater rights by both "slaves" and free persons who were targeted by Ferrand's racist laws.[110] During the Ferrand period, some of those held in bondage in Santo Domingo stretched the boundaries of the law, forcing authorities to address their claims to switch "masters," to reunite with a captive relative who had been transferred to another location, or to escape from servitude altogether.

Some "slaves" struck against their predicament by provoking or exploiting disputes over their purported ownership. In a 28 July 1808 letter to a Don Juan Castillos, Ferrand described a conflict concerning the ownership of a "black creole" named Manuel Aldaña, who was detained in a prison in Seybo. While Feliciana Cabrera, a native of Hincha who had migrated to Seybo, claimed to have "lost" (*perdu*) this would-be slave in Hincha, a man named Jean Lemdez also asserted his rights over him. Lemdez meticulously assembled a dossier of evidence to prove his case, including a notarial act of his purchase of Manuel from Thomas Figueredo, a native of Bánica, created by the notary Antonio Pérez. Other documentation traced the purported ownership of Manuel back to a Dionicio Hernández, whose succession had reportedly transferred Manuel to his brother Santiago. Ferrand requested that Santiago Hernández appear before Castillos in order to show one or more "titles of property" over Manuel so that the matter might be resolved.[111] Buried in this voluminous paper trail is Manuel's own agency: the pivotal word "lost" implies that he may have become a fugitive, creating this dispute over his ownership by his attempts to escape from bondage.

More direct evidence of flight appears in a 3 September 1807 letter that a woman named Ana Victoria Lasapelo wrote to the commandant in chief of the Western Subdivision in Santo Domingo. In it, she implored her interlocutor to apprehend a "Slave" named Mauricio who had departed with the "Brigands" (Haitians), offering to provide proof of ownership if requested.[112] On what legal basis did this unspecified written proof of Mauricio's servile status rest if, as is likely, he had been freed by the 1793–94 emancipation edicts (and their putative extension to Santo Domingo via the Treaty of Basel)? Would his settlement in Haiti invalidate his purported master's claims on his person? Implicit in the assertion that this document superseded his actions was the attempted re-creation of slavery in the documentary record.

This document serves as a reminder that the reimposition of slavery in Santo Domingo entailed quasilegal as well as military force.

In some instances, those claimed as slaves in Santo Domingo under Ferrand subverted the legal logic of French Caribbean slavery by obliging authorities to call them to testify in contentions over purported ownership.[113] In early 1805, a woman made a claim to recover her daughter Anastasie, who had been taken from the Cambariva plantation by a Nicolás González and sent to Puerto Rico in exchange for the *"petit nègre"* ("little black") Juannico. Anastasie's mother insisted to the "Captain General" (presumably Ferrand) that her daughter and Juannico be returned to their original residences. Ferrand requested that both Juannico and Anastasie's mother appear as declarants before a government commission in order to resolve the problem.[114] In a somewhat similar case, Ferrand wrote to a military commander in Samaná on 4 June 1808 concerning the alleged slave Nicolás, who was currently held in prison there. Nicolás had advanced a claim to belong to the family of a man named Sosa against the opposition of a Julián Vallejos. Ferrand ordered Nicolás to appear in Santo Domingo city so that authorities could determine his "legitimate owner."[115]

Ferrand employed his own legal tools in his most draconian policy: the capture and enslavement of Haitians. In an *arrêté* issued on 6 January 1805, Ferrand authorized those living near the Haitian border to enter that country and "make prisoners" of Haitians under fourteen years of age, who would become the "property" of their captors. Females under twelve years old and males under ten could not be returned to Haiti but could be either "attached" to a plantation or sold. Ferrand entrusted his commandant Joseph Ruiz, the veteran of the war against Maniel, and other trusted subordinates with the task of issuing official certificates affirming these captives' ownership and their capture in the "territory occupied by the rebels."[116] Furthermore, Ferrand stated in a letter to Ruiz that Haitian males in Santo Domingo over fourteen years of age should be shot.[117]

Extant notarial records confirm that Haiti indeed became a target for human traffickers from the other side of the border in that nation's early years. On 3 February 1808, Pierre Senabrier sold a woman named Marie-Catherine to a buyer named Chadefand for 144 *gourdes*. Marie-Catherine had initially been "captured among the Brigands [Haitians]" before being sold twice. A 26 December 1807 certificate created by her first owner, Anastacio Valdez (appended to this notarial act), affirmed that Marie-Catherine had been "captured in the enemy part [Haiti]" before coming into Valdez's possession.[118] Moreover, on 11 September 1808, a man called Espaillat sold four children to Ferrand's second-in-command, General Joseph Barquier. Three of them had been "captured among the rebels" according to certificates mentioned in the notarial act.[119] Such certificates and notarial acts represent an effort to reinscribe slavery into the legal record.

Slaving in Santo Domingo under Ferrand rested on a mix of opportunism and violent antipathy toward the new nation of Haiti. This in turn entailed a wholesale rejection both of the revolutionary emancipation decrees and of emancipations granted by onetime slaves-turned-military officers. In one 8 November 1804 letter to his subordinate Peralta, Ferrand rejected even the limited manumissions that Jean-François and Georges Biassou had offered in the early 1790s. Insisting that these men had never had the "right" to liberate anybody, Ferrand declared that all "French black and colored slaves" who had been granted their "liberty" by either of these freed leaders did not have a valid claim to freedom and thus must be "considered as Slaves." By contrast, Ferrand argued that the former "Spanish Slaves" who had received their liberty from the "King of Spain" due to service in colonial armies ought to remain free.[120] In this letter, Ferrand implicitly responded to would-be slaves' potential efforts to attain liberty, accepting only a narrow range of claims to free status. Though Ferrand in this letter apparently tacitly accepted the ancien régime idea that the monarch was the ultimate arbiter of legal condition, some of his other actions disregarded royal authority and instead recalled that most ancient of bases for enslavement: capture in war. In a 2 October 1808 letter to several of his subordinates, Ferrand explicitly stated that captives taken from Haiti in battle would legally belong to their captors.[121]

Fear of their citizens' enslavement at the hands of the Ferrand regime or a French invasion force from beyond the island contributed to several measures undertaken by Haiti's first leaders, including enlisting thousands of citizens in the construction of a series of forts (the most famous of which was Henry Christophe's Citadel) and conducting military incursions into Santo Domingo in 1804–05.[122] After both sides traded victories in battles over the strategic northern city of Santiago in 1804, Dessalines launched a 20,000-man expedition to capture Santo Domingo city in February 1805.[123] (See figure 6.) This invasion attempt met with defeat despite Dessalines's sevenfold manpower advantage over Ferrand due to the fortuitously timed arrival of a French naval force under Admiral Missiessy and the British reluctance to assist Dessalines.[124]

DESALINES

Primer Emperador de Hayti en dia de Gala.

FIGURE 6 "Desalines Primer Emperador de Hayti en dia de Gala." Portrait of Jean-Jacques Dessalines, "First Emperor of Haiti." From Dubroca, *Vida de J. J. Dessalines, gefe de los Negros de Santo Domingo* (Mexico, 1806). Courtesy of the John Carter Brown Library at Brown University.

According to Thoret, Ferrand, faced with the Haitian siege of Santo Domingo city, proclaimed the following to its inhabitants: "The blacks will not hesitate to attack us. There is none among us who does not know of the incredible cruelties that they have committed against our unfortunate compatriots," a clear reference to the Haitian massacres of whites the year before. "The same fate shall befall us, if we fall into their hands."[125] Dessalines, for his part, cited his enemy's own atrocities to defend his aggression. In a 12 April 1805 address to his citizens following the failed attack, Dessalines justified his invasion of the "former Spanish part" of the island partly on the basis of the "decree issued by Ferrand, on the date of 16 Nivose, year III"—the notorious order sanctioning the capture and enslavement of Haitians. Dessalines also accused the "Spanish" of collaborating with the "freedom-killing endeavors" of the French and called upon his fellow Haitians to "live or die as free men," distributing among them numerous copies of the 6 January 1805 enslaving order in an effort to rally them around the flag.[126] Emilio Cordero Michel has argued that Ferrand's 6 January 1805 declaration was indeed a major reason why Dessalines led his invasion into Santo Domingo, as the decree represented ample evidence that "the project of Ferrand . . . included not only the reconquest of Haiti but also the reestablishment of slavery as he had already done in Spanish Saint-Domingue [Santo Domingo]."[127] Deborah Jenson likewise rightly contends that the 6 January decree "was the most incendiary possible challenge to Dessalines and the viability of black freedom and independence."[128]

Though the Ferrand regime built on precedents from both the ancien régime and the revolutionary era, the rulers of Napoleonic Santo Domingo felt especially compelled to react to the presence of Haiti, fusing the external threat of "rebel" armies with internal concerns in a way that bears more than a passing resemblance to early Haitian leaders' resort to forced labor on the grounds of defending against a French invasion.[129] As Rebecca Schloss has observed, the birth of independent Haiti exacerbated the tendencies of French authorities on both sides of the Atlantic to associate nonwhites with criminality and subversion. There was an acute fear that "a network of *gens de couleur* roaming the Atlantic would incite rebellion and bring the downfall of France's remaining West Indian colonies."[130] These developments transpired during a decade that was marked by both dramatic challenges to enslavement and human trafficking in some areas and the retrenchment of these practices in others.

Santo Domingo in Circum-Caribbean Circuits of Captivity

In spite of events such as the abolition of slavery in Saint-Domingue and the end of the legal British Atlantic slave trade in 1807, the decades following the Haitian Revolution witnessed the resurgence of plantation slavery in Cuba, Louisiana, and Brazil, a phenomenon that Dale Tomich has termed the "second slavery."[131] These developments stemmed from a confluence of technological breakthroughs, policy shifts, the collapse of Saint-Domingue's plantation complex, expanding industrial demand for plantation products, and other factors. Cuba in particular profited from the fall of French Saint-Domingue (at least from the vantage point of planters and politicians). Slavers on the Spanish island legally imported 325,000 Africans from 1790 to 1820 (an average of more than 10,000 per year), while both the number of sugar mills and the average output of sugar per plantation roughly doubled from 1790 to 1806. By 1820, just sixteen years after the independence of Haiti, Cuba had become the world's largest sugar producer and the new crown jewel of a Spanish empire that was disintegrating elsewhere. These developments had profound reverberations for the subsequent history of the island.[132]

Though Santo Domingo was never as integral in the transatlantic slave trade as Havana, the former was a central battleground in struggles over the terms of bondage and liberty—and the viability of slave status across imperial and colonial boundaries—in the decade to 1810. Santo Domingo's long-standing political links to Cuba and Puerto Rico had facilitated illegal slaving between these places during the emancipation period. Following the *Berceau* incident in the fall of 1802, Santo Domingo became even more implicated in far-reaching circuits of captivity that unsettled distinctions between slavery and freedom.[133] In his trading of Haitian captives to places with long-established slave-based economies (such as rice-producing South Carolina) and in his sales of captives from slaving vessels that shipwrecked on Santo Domingo's coasts, Ferrand himself participated in networks of captive trading that operated on the margins of the law.

Ferrand's shocking order to Ruiz, commanding him to execute male Haitians over fourteen, attests to a dilemma that he shared with many other authorities in the Americas: the wish to accrue profit by maximizing the size of the servile labor force, counterbalanced against the fear of an uprising. Largely cut off from sources of servile labor outside of the island, Ferrand resorted to trafficking in Haitians—while trying to eliminate those whose knowledge of freedom and warfare might pose a threat. Hence the chilling focus on the seizing of children.

Ferrand sought to export some of these captives to South Carolina in exchange for slave-produced rice, as a way to pass on some of his risk to his North American counterparts while tapping into one of the most lucrative plantation economies in the antebellum United States.[134] In a 4 December 1804 letter to the Superior Council of Santiago, Ferrand related that a ship that he had deployed to Charleston, South Carolina, containing a number of "black Brigands" had recently returned to Santo Domingo with a quantity of rice obtained in exchange for the captives. Ferrand estimated his revenue at 1,000 to 1,200 *gourdes*.[135]

These exchanges underscore the primacy of trade and diplomatic relations with the United States to the Ferrand regime. Ferrand's own service in the American Revolution had given him firsthand knowledge of the hemisphere's first independent nation, whose trade had proven vital to the economy of Saint-Domingue/Haiti during the latter's colonial and revolutionary eras.[136] Furthermore, though foreign trade data for Ferrand-era Santo Domingo are presently unknown,[137] Ferrand doubtless understood the importance of profitable commerce between his colony and the United States, which had acquired a massive new territory and the key Caribbean port of New Orleans the year before Ferrand established his regime in eastern Hispaniola.[138]

This trade was in turn connected to the complex politics of foreign recognition of a state born of an anticolonial *and* antislavery war. In the first two years of Haitian independence, no doubt to the consternation of Ferrand, the United States was the most important commercial partner to Haiti.[139] Nonetheless, the confluence of pressure from France, racial anxieties, geostrategic considerations, and perceived legal and political uncertainties as to whether Haiti was still a colony of France led the United States government to criminalize trade with the new nation in 1806. This trade remained explicitly illegal until 1808 and then arguably illicit under embargo legislation until 1810.[140] The trade's relegalization after this date, however, did not translate into prompt official diplomatic recognition of Haiti by the United States. Due in large part to Southern opposition, this step would have to wait until 1862, following the departure of the Confederate states from the Union.

Ferrand's anti-Haitian foreign policy contributed to the diplomatic nonrecognition of the new nation in the Caribbean. As Julia Gaffield and Deborah

Jenson have shown, Ferrand's policy of deploying privateers to attack foreign ships suspected of trading with Haiti, his government's military confrontations with the Haitians, his multitude of laws and decrees, and even the Napoleonic contingent's very presence in Santo Domingo gave credence to the impression among foreigners not only that France was still actively fighting to reconquer Saint-Domingue/Haiti but that the European nation still possessed a valid claim to its lost territory.[141] (Ferrand also deployed agents to Curaçao and St. Thomas who, despite convincing these islands' governors to ban trade with Haiti in 1804 and 1806, respectively, had only limited success in suppressing the trade itself.)[142]

In the words of an unadmiring contemporary, the U.S. senator Samuel White, Ferrand launched a "war of proclamations" against the Haitians (and against nonwhites in Santo Domingo).[143] This was part of a legal strategy that exploited pervasive racism among white foreigners as well as the legal principle that third-party nations could recognize a former colony's independence only when the old colonial power had formally relinquished its claim over the territory, which did not happen for Haiti until 1825.[144] One U.S. Supreme Court justice no doubt echoed the sentiments of many fellow citizens—along with numerous others—in his assertion that "France has not yet relinquished the contest [with Haiti], and until she does, I think that all ports of the island are still ports of France."[145]

Ferrand's privateering was motivated not only by his fierce anti-Haitian sentiments but also by concerns of a more material nature. In spite of the captives-for-rice trade with South Carolina, the cash-strapped Ferrand government lacked adequate sources of revenue. It therefore relied to a considerable degree on the proceeds of ship captures to finance its administrative and military costs, justifying many interceptions on the high seas as retaliation for foreigners' alleged trading with Haiti.[146] If these ships contained captives who could be sold for the profit of the state, then so much the better. The records of the board that Ferrand entrusted with adjudicating ship capture cases, known as the Commission des Prises de Santo Domingo (Santo Domingo [Ship] Captures Commission), contain details on the sale of "slaves" procured from the seizures of vessels that straddled the thin line between legal and illegal trafficking. On 9 February 1804, the ironically named *Good Hope*, a captive-trading vessel with a largely British crew and British captain sailing under the Danish flag, shipwrecked near the Dominican town of Higüey. According to the commission's records, the ship had stopped at St Croix, where the captain claimed to have lived for six years, and then proceeded to sail first to Havana and subsequently to Santo Domingo. This captain's luck finally ran out in the latter locale, as the 18 March 1804 judgment of the commission mandated the confiscation of all of the ship's purported cargo—including its 185 "Blacks"—and these captives' sale for a total of 81,400 francs.[147]

Following the legal abolition of the British Atlantic slave trade by a 25 March 1807 Act of Parliament, attempts to ferret out such secretive slaving vessels sailing under foreign flags gave rise to a complex military and juridical infrastructure. The British and the signatories to their antislaving treaties (such as Brazil), for instance, set up "mixed commissions" that adjudicated cases involving the capture of suspected slavers.[148] While the raison d'être of the Commission des Prises may at first appear to have been quite distinct from that of these "mixed commissions," telling similarities existed between the two bodies. Namely, the decisions of both could accrue revenue for state authorities by exploiting the labor of captives, whether labeled "slaves," "liberated Africans," or something else.[149]

Those who sought to eliminate slaving in the Napoleonic-era Caribbean faced several formidable challenges, including the difficulties of policing the seemingly innumerable ships that plied circum-Caribbean and Atlantic routes as well as the presence of eager buyers of human flesh in places such as Santo Domingo. Whatever their legal status may have previously been, these *Good Hope* captives found themselves sold into something closely resembling slavery in processes that combined the use of force with legal and bureaucratic procedures that re-created slavery in the written record as well as on the slave ship. On 8 December 1806, a businessman from St Thomas named H. Abendanon sold to another businessman resident in Santo Domingo city named Payra Ferry 187 "new blacks" (*nègres nouveaux*), who had been sold in a public auction of captives from the *Good Hope*. The vessel was listed as having been shipwrecked in Higüey and captained by a "Biscoe."[150] Furthermore, on 4 September 1808, the merchant Mauger sold a seventeen-year-old African-born boy named L'Éveillé to another merchant named René Pichaud. L'Éveillé came into the seller's possession by purchase in a "public sale" in Samaná of items that had come from the capture of the Danish ship *Only Son*.[151]

While Kerverseau had grappled with the question of how best to dispose of the *Berceau* captives, Ferrand had no qualms about selling off captives who had found themselves shipwrecked on Dominican shores. In a 27 February 1804 letter to the commandant of Higüey, Ferrand requested that his subordinate send to Santo Domingo city those individuals remaining in Higüey who had been among the 103 "blacks" who had been aboard a ship from Puerto Rico that had wrecked near Higüey. Ferrand promised to pay fifteen *gourdes* for each "head" that residents of the Higüey area sent to Santo Domingo city.[152] In instructions that he gave to another subordinate named Villavicencio dated 20 July 1807, Ferrand clarified that his earlier statement on the Higüey "blacks" had been an order, not a suggestion, demanding an inquiry as to whether any of the "Blacks coming from the Vessel shipwrecked, about four years ago, on the coasts of your district" had been hidden from the central government by residents of Higüey.[153] Ferrand's distinctly personalistic approach to resolving such matters is evident in a letter that he wrote to another official on 17 August 1807 in which he ordered that a "*nègre Bossal*" (African-born black) living in Seybo who may have "come from some ship [that had] perished on the Coast" be sold the following day in a "public sale, for the account of the Government."[154]

Officials charged with resolving these slaving cases often responded to geopolitical concerns in their decision making, as the outbreak of the Napoleonic Wars had made colonial rivalries even more salient. One incident involving a slave-trading ship called the *Joseph* illustrated how shifting geopolitical winds could affect the lives of those held in servitude. In an 8 April 1806 letter to the minister of the navy, Ferrand recounted the story of the *Joseph*, a vessel that was "evidently English" but sailed under the Swedish flag. After loading its human cargo in Africa, this ship had made a stopover in St Barthélemy, where it had switched flags. It then traveled toward Havana with its "thus disguised cargo" after having "boarded around a Hundred Blacks on another Swedish Vessel." A French corsair called *La Fortune* captured it en route. Though the captain of the *Joseph* requested the "intervention" of Spanish authorities by virtue of being arrested in the territorial waters of Cuba, the governor of Baracoa (Cuba) turned the case over to a French tribunal in Santo Domingo that he deemed to be the sole authority competent to judge the legality of the *Joseph's* capture. After deliberating on the matter, the "Administrative Commission of Santo Domingo" judged this capture to be legal, basing its decision on a 1778 law stipulating that any ship with an "enemy owner" could not be considered neutral.[155]

The application of this ancien régime statute elided the emancipation period, asserting a property right in human beings that was assumed to exist despite the uncertain legality of slavery in French Santo Domingo. While Kerverseau's preoccupation with saving his own skin in the *Berceau* episode had stemmed from a concern to not present its captives as slaves, in the case of the *Joseph* different colonial authorities took as a given the right to hold people as property—even as they disputed specific means of exercising this supposed right. Nonetheless, the illicit itineraries of these slavers serve as an apt reminder that enslavement required the exertion of force regardless of any legal sanction. Both Ferrand and these contrabandists devised their own solutions to navigate the tensions between the force of enslavement and the law of "slavery"—a tension that had existed in the French world since at least the promulgation of the *Code Noir*.

Conclusions

In a report to the minister of the navy dated 6 March 1801, a Saint-Domingue official had condemned Toussaint Louverture's rule as the "shame of the nation," yet this label more aptly applies to the Napoleonic campaigns of reenslavement.[156] Ferrand's attempts to place thousands of people into bondage encountered the determined opposition of "slaves," who devised novel ways of manipulating the law of "slavery" in their efforts to evade the force of reenslavement. Those who fought back against Ferrand's racist laws drew upon a heritage of resistance to enslavement and racial repression forged over several centuries by slaves and freed people from both parts of the island.

Though Ferrand tried to re-create slavery as a legal construction, in the written record, and as a lived reality, many "slaves" in Santo Domingo utilized the legal tools of the Napoleonic state and built on the successful struggle for freedom in independent Haiti. Santo Domingo under Ferrand ultimately represents a crucial case in the legal history of race and slavery in the Americas, as many "slaves" and others who challenged the project of reenslavement left traces of an alternative history in the archival record. Among these traces are 103 notarized freedom acts created by freed men and women who in some respects carried on the torch of liberty that Napoleonic France had abandoned, even as many of their number implicitly acquiesced to the bondage of others. These acts and the stories behind them form the basis of chapter 6.

CHAPTER SIX

They Always Knew Her to Be Free

Archiving Liberty in French Santo Domingo, 1804–1809

On 30 July 1803, the *citoyenne* (citizen) Adelaïde Faury presented herself before the notary Derieux in Santiago, Santo Domingo. Faury, a merchant from Fort-Dauphin, had traveled to the notary's office in order to deposit what was perhaps the most important document in her life. Created by *citoyenne* Faury's former master, Magdeleine Garçon Magagues, and a French consular official in Norfolk, Virginia, this earlier document (appended to Derieux's 30 July 1803 act) had declared, "From this day forward, September 1st, [in the year] seventeen-hundred and ninety-four, I grant liberty to my aforementioned servant [slave] Adelaïde Faury of Fort-Dauphin."[1]

Citoyenne Faury's story spans the arc of general emancipation and the subsequent reemergence of slavery that characterized the two decades after 1789 in France's Caribbean colonies. As is evident in the preceding paragraph, Madame Garçon had granted Faury her freedom in 1794, the same year when the French Republic proclaimed the abolition of slavery throughout its domains. Madame Garçon, who was probably one of the hundreds of slaveholding refugees from Saint-Domingue who brought their purported human property with them to numerous circum-Caribbean and Mid-Atlantic ports, such as Norfolk, thus removed Faury from the scene of the revolutionary turmoil to which she would subsequently return.

Uprooted from the site of the first large-scale general slave emancipation in the Americas before she could benefit from the institution's dismantling there, *citoyenne* Faury won her liberty in slaveholding Norfolk, only to then feel obliged to document her status as a free woman after her return to Hispaniola and her establishment as a merchant there.[2] Her odyssey provides further evidence that the first French universal emancipation in many ways represented an ambivalent rupture with much continuity with the past.[3] Nonetheless, confronted with a Napoleonic regime determined to reenslave thousands of people who had been formally freed in Hispaniola in the 1790s, men and women like *citoyenne* Faury creatively maneuvered within this challenging legal and political setting. As the several dozen surviving acts created by French notaries that recognize or grant the freedom of at least one individual in French Santo Domingo suggest, purported slaves and freed people skillfully exploited small openings in the repressive social and legal order.[4]

The present chapter rounds out the political history recounted in chapters 1 through 5 by presenting a much more fine-grained snapshot of some of the ways in which freed persons in Santo Domingo under the slaveholding regime of General Jean-Louis Ferrand (1804–09) strove to secure their freedom. The strategies employed by such individuals who came before French notaries in Santo Domingo during this era can be grouped into three principal types. Those fortunate enough to possess tangible proof of their juridical freedom (such as a manumission act or a baptismal record) deposited these artifacts of liberty with notaries. Others with the means to do so purchased themselves from their "masters," while some freed individuals with the right connections called upon witnesses to vouch for their freedom. These strategies often worked together.

The uncertainties surrounding these individuals' legal condition became compounded by the unstable political situation. Would the Ferrand regime collapse? Would the French again abolish slavery as they had in 1793–94, or would Napoleon's troops retake Haiti, thereby crushing the one abolitionist nation in the hemisphere? Nobody knew for sure. Nor was it immediately evident whether French or Spanish law (or some combination of the two) might prevail in a given dispute. While the principal laws governing matters such as enslavement, manumission, and the rights of freed people in the Spanish-American world largely derived from the *Siete Partidas* (Seven Divisions), a wide-ranging compilation of laws promulgated in thirteenth-century Castile, France by contrast lacked a coherent legal framework concerning slavery in its overseas possessions until 1685, when legal scholars working for Louis XIV devised the *Code Noir*. This comprehensive reorganization of French colonial slave law attempted to strike a delicate balance between maintaining discipline among slaves and ensuring certain minimal standards concerning humane treatment and the rights of manumitted persons that were more often honored in the breach. Though slave laws in both French Saint-Domingue and Spanish Santo Domingo had influenced each other in the prerevolutionary era—indeed, Spanish Dominican jurists had self-consciously adopted key aspects of the French *Code Noir* in their late colonial slave code in an effort to emulate the brutal opulence of Saint-Domingue—the two colonies uneasily sharing Hispaniola had developed distinct legal codes and cultures of slavery by 1789.[5] France's failure to fully assert control over Santo Domingo after its cession in 1795 contributed to the emergence of a complicated hybrid legal situation there wherein officials and other parties drew upon both French and Spanish law.[6]

The itinerant notaries who redacted these records strove to navigate this confused legal terrain. Following Santo Domingo's cession to France, several French Republican notaries left their posts in Saint-Domingue to serve the Dominguan migrant community across the border in Santo Domingo. One of their number intriguingly drafted his acts in French on the letterhead of the Spanish king and was referred to in these documents as the "*Écrivain du Roy et Seigneur Don Carlos IV de la ville de Bayajá*" ("Writer of the King and Sire Don Carlos IV in the City of Bayajá").[7]

Both the Francophone and Spanish-speaking worlds had long employed notaries as guarantors of the legal validity of agreements contracted between citizens.[8] According to Julie Hardwick, as indispensable "mediators of oral and literate cultures," notaries were the main gatekeepers to the world of literate power both in mainland France and in the colonies.[9] The early modern French, moreover, "found the acts that notaries wrote to be crucial safeguards" of transactions ranging from marriage contracts to loans and sales to wills.[10] The omnipresence of slavery in France's overseas colonies dramatically enhanced the importance of these "crucial safeguards" for the numerous men and women whose formal separation from perpetual servitude often rested on a piece of paper procured in precarious circumstances. In sum, securing a notarized act attesting to one's legal condition of freedom provided a degree of insurance against enslavement in French Santo Domingo, though only a small fraction of those vulnerable to enslavement there were able to obtain such records.

The individuals who sought these freedom acts constituted part of a heterogeneous populace that comprised Saint-Domingue transplants, Spanish speakers whose roots in the colony long antedated the cession, and a small number of North American traders and Dutch and Danish smugglers.[11] Intriguingly, few freed people or freedom granters appear in these records as having lived in Santo Domingo, while a notable proportion of the freed subjects had an ascribed African provenance (28 percent of subjects with a prior residence listed were so designated). "*Congo*" was the most common geographical label in this subset (five of sixteen cases), which presumably reflected the demographic predominance of West Central Africans in Saint-Domingue in the late eighteenth century.[12]

The thousands of Dominguan refugees who resettled in Santo Domingo brought with them mentalities and practices forged in the profoundly gendered slave society of eighteenth-century Saint-Domingue. Perhaps most notably, women and children had constituted about two-thirds of all subjects of manumission in the entire history of French Saint-Domingue. This owed to forces such as the familial and sexual dynamics of this society and certain provisions of the *Code Noir* manumitting slave women who married their masters and liberating slaves who were beneficiaries of a will.[13] These factors may help to explain the striking fact that around 77 percent of the freed subjects of these 103 acts were women. In their quests for freedom in the hostile environment of a militarized revanchist slaveholding regime in Santo Domingo, these women tapped into the long history of what Malick Ghachem calls "feminized resistance to slavery" in the old Saint-Domingue.[14]

Many Saint-Domingue refugees in Santo Domingo and elsewhere anticipated an imminent French reconquest of Haiti and the resumption of business as usual within a reconstituted plantation society.[15] Dominguan migrants in Santo Domingo indeed frequently attempted to preserve social and familial networks that had developed in Saint-Domingue, while the freed people among them drew upon these networks in their campaigns for a permanent and enduring liberty. It is not accidental that just under a fifth (17 percent) of all the freedom acts involved the granting or recognition of freedom for at least one of the subject's children, while in 11 percent of all 103 acts, the subject was the freedom granter's own child. Claims such as the one filed by a Dominican to an African-born purported slave-turned-"maroon" who was captured in Cuba, and one made to a captive who was sold in St Thomas, Curaçao, and Santo Domingo between 1805 and 1807, hint at Santo Domingo's role in broader Caribbean and Atlantic prosopographies and histories of migration, emancipation, and reenslavement.[16] Nominally part of a French Republic, and then French Empire, that had repudiated the nation's commitment to emancipation, Santo Domingo in the Ferrand era was nonetheless profoundly influenced by the eight-year emancipationist period.[17]

The dismantling of emancipation and of the more racially egalitarian legal order of the 1790s translated into the widespread application of racial labels in the notary's office.[18] In the emancipation era, notaries had generally eschewed racial terms in favor of the designation *citoyen/ne* (citizen), but in late 1803 and 1804, this trend dramatically reversed, at least within the notarized freedom acts created in French Santo Domingo. The usage of *citoyen/ne* in these records all but ceased by November 1804, as freed subjects were increasingly accorded racial labels and the freedom granters were often listed as *le sieur* or *la dame* (roughly "Sir" and "Madam").[19]

Before proceeding, a word of caution is in order. In many cases, it seems, freed persons' strategies to win these liberty acts reflected more of a determination to secure freedom for themselves and their relatives than a wholesale rejection of the slave system. In particular, some of those who employed such strategies or who sought to ensure the transfer of property to those freed from bondage did so at the cost of continued servitude for others.[20] Fundamentally, the existence of dozens of notarized "slave" sales in the extant documentary record from French Santo Domingo, combined with the small number of freedom acts relative to the "slave" population, serve as reminders that the attainment of freedom was the exception rather than the rule among those held in bondage there.[21]

Yet even when qualified with these realities, the strategies employed at the notary's office in French Santo Domingo provide evidence that the Napoleonic program of reenslavement was every bit as contentious and unrealized as the enterprise of "emancipation" that had preceded it.

The Presentation of Documentation of Free Status

"All creatures in the world naturally love and desire liberty, and much more do men, who have intelligence superior to that of the others, and especially such as are of noble minds, desire it."[22] This statement comes not from an Enlightenment-era tract on abolitionism but rather from the *Siete Partidas*. Though it sanctioned human bondage, this code held slavery to be "contrary to natural reason," from which it followed that the law ought to favor liberty.[23] In contrast, colonial legislation in late eighteenth-century French Saint-Domingue had sought to impose a stringent burden of proof on those of African descent to document their free status.[24] After the collapse of emancipation, French authorities in Santo Domingo reverted to this underlying presumption of slavery, which impelled the subjects of these notarial acts to marshal documentation that would reduce the risk of enslavement at the hands of an opportunistic or vengeful would-be master.

On 3 September 1804, almost eight months to the day after Jean-Jacques Dessalines declared Haitian independence, another former slave called

Marie-Jeanne came before a notary in the last real bastion of French power in Hispaniola, the city of Santo Domingo, in order to register and deposit a manumission act. Created in Mirebalais on 2 December 1794 by the *citoyen* Girard, this document stated that in recognition of the "good and loyal services" that Marie-Jeanne had rendered to Girard as a governess and as a wet nurse to three of his children, she would no longer have to live in slavery.[25] This woman must have been quite familiar with the disconnect between metropolitan law and on-the-ground reality, since in December 1794, the theoretically free soil of Saint-Domingue had been partially occupied by military forces of the slaveholding British and Spanish empires, which circumscribed the application of the 4 February 1794 French emancipation decree, as we saw in chapters 1 and 3.[26]

Given that they had to interact with officials who were in the employ of a slaveholding state that sought to turn back the clock on emancipation, many freed people in Santo Domingo sensed that the mere invocation of this law of general emancipation might not constitute sufficient proof of their own free status. After all, authorities' acceptance of this claim would "upset the entire applecart," to use Rebecca Scott's words, since it would imply that most of Santo Domingo's captives had a valid legal claim to their liberty.[27] Freed people thus scrambled to assemble all documentary evidence of their attainment of freedom. The records that these individuals zealously guarded included sacramental documents, such as baptismal and marriage acts, as well as civil records, such as manumission papers. Within a single notarial act from Ferrand-era Santo Domingo, one or more such documents might be appended, each duly certified by both its creator and the Santo Domingo notary who redacted the final notarial act.

Beginning in 1802, many freed people in Hispaniola and elsewhere had responded to the presumed repeal of the French emancipation law by seeking to exploit the legal channels of manumission. According to Philippe Girard, "in Saint-Domingue [after 1802] panic-stricken *nouveaux libres* begged their former masters to let them buy their freedom, while *anciens libres* lined up in the courts to get their old emancipation papers notarized."[28] The Napoleonic regimes that followed did little to assuage such anxieties.[29] Emblematic of the Ferrand regime's renewed presumption of slavery was the 31 December 1807 order (discussed in chapter 5) that Ferrand issued requiring the subjects of all État Civil records created henceforth in Santo Domingo to show a "title of liberty" in order to prove their legal condition of freedom. Furthermore, in a letter to the commandant of Seybo dated 12 September 1807,

Ferrand rejected the claim of a man called Jacques (surname illegible) to have granted liberty to an unnamed woman. Ferrand declared that in the absence of a proper *"rectification"* of her freedom, this woman was to remain a "slave." He then proceeded to ask the Seybo commander to send her to him so that she could be sold.[30]

According to Kathryn Burns, notarial records are "always in implicit dialogue with an imagined litigious future."[31] For the freed woman Henriette *dite* Pommeau and many others, such a future entailed avoiding the fate of the unfortunate woman who had lacked a written *rectification* of her manumission. On 28 June 1805, Henriette deposited in the notary Pierre-Joseph-Jean-Baptiste Antoine Funel de Seranon's Santo Domingo city notarial office a document created and signed in 1803 by Michel, a notary from Le Cap who had attested to Henriette's having produced several witnesses affirming that her former master had freed her in approximately 1787. Claiming to have lost her original manumission papers during the destruction of her hometown by the "rebels," Henriette drew upon her social contacts and access to notarial services to produce these two written testaments to her legal freedom.[32] Faced with the prospect of a possible return to servitude, Henriette determinedly sought to transform the "messy specifics" of her manumission and life as a freed woman in the tumult of revolutionary Saint-Domingue into a "legally valid form" that would help to protect her against reenslavement.[33]

Another woman who acted with foresight was Margueritte Bonne. On 24 December 1801, Bonne had procured from the notary Michel in Le Cap a document stating that her former master, Morel, had drawn up with this same notary a manumission act in her name dated 6 April 1790. Consultation of this notary's registry had revealed the existence of this 1790 manumission act despite its destruction in the great June 1793 fire in Le Cap. By the summer of 1803, Bonne had migrated to Santo Domingo as part of the wave of French refugees who fled the collapse of French Saint-Domingue. Upon arriving she prudently appeared before the notary Derieux in Santiago on 8 August 1803, depositing Michel's 1801 attestation of her manumission.[34]

For those fortunate enough to bear such evidence of their freedom, no piece of paper was too old or too tattered to submit in their own defense. On 18 August 1807, Louise *dite* Letort deposited in a Santo Domingo city notary's office an "extremely damaged" manumission act from the year 1739 that had freed her and her mother Rose.[35] In the summer of 1806, the "*mulâtresse libre*" (free mulatto) Marie-Magdeleine, whose mother was listed as coming from the "*côte de Guinée*" (African coast), similarly presented to the notary Funel de Seranon a manumission act in her name from 1728.[36] This act hinted at a multigenerational story of enslavement and liberation in which those subjected to bondage sought to use to their advantage the systems of law and written documentation that had often aided their oppressors. Having lived through most of Saint-Domingue's history under French rule, Marie-Magdeleine knew all too well the power of written documents in substantiating one's claims to the legal status of free person.

In manipulating the legal levers of this slaveholding society, the subjects of these notarial acts employed every resource at their disposal. While some utilized the documentary evidence of freedom that they possessed, others who had managed to accumulate the funds sought recourse in the age-old practice of self-purchase.

Self-Purchase

Since at least the time of the Romans, laws in slaveholding societies had sometimes included certain means by which those in bondage could purchase their freedom. Perhaps no aspect of slave law better encapsulated the absurdities of transforming a human being into a "person with a price."[37] In tacitly acknowledging slaves' volition, capability for rational decision making, and desire for their freedom, the practice belied the presumed lack of full personhood inhering in many legal frameworks for enslavement.[38] At the same time, it did not challenge (indeed, it depended on) the premise that one could assign a monetary value to a fellow person. In plantation societies, such as eighteenth-century Saint-Domingue, masters and colonial authorities grew to fear the implications of such a route to freedom. As these anxious authorities had implicitly recognized in their laws seeking to restrict this type of manumission, self-purchase involved much more than a simple exchange of money for a change in legal status.[39] Behind each formulaic legal act of self-purchase lay multiple hidden conflicts and negotiations; behind each sale price lay one human being's assessment of another's purported economic worth.

Illustrative of this is the self-purchase of Marie-Elizabeth *dite* Justine. On 8 June 1807, the notary Funel de Seranon redacted an act that formally recognized Marie-Elizabeth's purchase of her own freedom. According to this document, this woman's "good conduct" and the constant "affection" and "attachment" that she had shown her former purported master, Bernard Leglise Dupoux, had convinced the latter to reduce her purchase price to 300 *gourdes* despite her higher "value."[40] While would-be masters employed the language of "good conduct" in order to inscribe in these records the fiction of the manumitted person's grateful acceptance of the former's voluntary and benevolent exercise of his or her power to liberate, this elided a much more complex reality.[41]

In accumulating her purchase price and buying her freedom, Marie-Elizabeth situated herself within a deep islandwide history of resistance to enslavement. The sedimentation of legal systems in French Santo Domingo entailed a complex interplay between two quite distinct legal and extralegal traditions of self-purchase that had evolved in both parts of the island during the centuries of colonial slavery. Though some slaves in both colonies had managed to procure the funds for self-purchase through a variety of sources, including hiring out their labor, selling the products of their cultivation grounds, and even prostitution, the legal and political context in each colony differed significantly. As with so much else, one central force behind this divergence was the two lands' markedly different trajectories of plantation development; another was pronounced variations in local laws and their interpretation and enforcement. For a variety of economic, social, and political reasons, administrators in colonial Saint-Domingue had from the early eighteenth century imposed much legislation that aimed to significantly impede access to manumission through self-purchase and other means. By contrast, the relative lack of such laws (and their often infrequent enforcement) in Santo Domingo had facilitated the development of certain practices by which slaves could buy their own freedom for an agreed-upon price. Some of these customs appear to have acquired legal backing over time.[42]

While the frequency of self-purchase in colonial Santo Domingo remains unknown, evidence suggests that it was a recourse chosen by some slaves in their escape from bondage.[43] Intriguing clues further hint that practices of self-purchase that had evolved there during the colonial period continued into the era of emancipation. In a 26 June 1800 correspondence to a *citoyen* Perregaux, the Marquis d'Iranda (the absentee owner of Santo Domingo's largest plantation) had defended a state of affairs in which thousands of the colony's inhabitants still occupied the status of "Slave." "The Slaves there [in Santo Domingo] are under the protection of a magistrate," Iranda asserted.

"They cite before him [the magistrate] their master when they have just motivations to bring a complaint, and they can also buy themselves, reimbursing him [the master] the price of their acquisition."[44]

These developments reflected a Spanish-American slave regime in which certain legal and customary barriers to a master's absolute control over a slave had emerged, including the presence of local officials entrusted with defending slaves in legal disputes and forms of self-purchase that involved gradual self-ownership through payment in installments.[45] These aspects of slave society became inscribed in both local regulations, such as the 1784 *Código Negro*, issued by authorities in Santo Domingo, and a royal *cédula* (decree) governing slavery promulgated five years later.[46]

The situation in Saint-Domingue was rather different. As discussed in chapter 1, authorities in that colony in the late eighteenth century had passed a spate of laws seeking to sharply reduce both the numbers and the political rights of its *gens de couleur libres*. These officials' predecessors, however, had in fact adopted measures against self-purchase much earlier. According to Malick Ghachem, colonial administrators' concerns about the ease of self-purchase in Saint-Domingue—which they considered especially threatening to social order due to slaves' allegedly frequent resort to prostitution to raise the necessary funds—had resulted in a 1711 law that required authorities' written permission for all future manumissions. Manumissions based solely on a master-slave agreement, in other words, would henceforth be illegal. As early as 1711, then, Dominguan administrators (followed two years later by the king) had rejected the absolute inviolability of the master's property rights over his or her slave.[47]

Such anxieties are evident in the writings of Moreau de St Méry. In his tract on the history of the Spanish part of the island, the chronicler had presented manumission in Spanish Santo Domingo as a gendered and destabilizing phenomenon. He insisted that the presumed ease of manumission (especially self-purchase) had long served to undermine order there in much the same way that it supposedly had in French Saint-Domingue. For Moreau, self-purchase in Santo Domingo had produced a sizable group of "vagabonds" and destitute women whose only means of subsistence was "shameful commerce."[48] Such characterizations grew out of a long history of casting racial prejudice in colonial French Saint-Domingue in gendered terms and framing cross-racial sexual activity as a menace to the social order. Indeed, in an effort to counteract "stereotypes of racial pollution and effeminate vice," the (male) *gens de couleur libres* activists of the 1780s and early 1790s had often affirmed their "filial piety and obligations as husbands and fathers" and "virtue and virility," in the words of John Garrigus.[49]

Despite such impassioned denunciations of self-purchase, only 7 percent of all extant notarial freedom acts from French Santo Domingo mentioned this practice. Confusion over the exact terms of self-purchase, along with the difficulties involved in raising the funds, may help to explain its relative infrequency there, though the comparatively small sample size imposes certain limitations on what can be generalized or extrapolated.[50] The terms of the exchange as laid out in most of these notarial acts were typically fairly straightforward: the "slave" paid off his or her price to the purported master in one lump sum, upon which the latter formally relinquished all rights over the newly freed person.[51]

One exceptional case nonetheless suggests that more complex forms of self-purchase also existed in French Santo Domingo. Toward the end of 1805, a woman named Catherine bought her freedom from the merchant Mathurin Chinon for the sum of 1,760 francs, which were listed as "coming from her peculium."[52] The Roman legal framework upon which both the *Siete Partidas* and the *Code Noir* were largely based contained stipulations for such a path to freedom. According to Peter Temin, in ancient Rome the *peculium* was "money 'owned' by slaves, with which to purchase freedom." In other words, slaves could accumulate funds (to which the master could not lay claim, even though the law technically forbade slaves from owning property), which they could devote toward their self-purchase.[53]

While such possession and manipulation of resources by slaves and those claimed as such stretched the juridical limits of enslavement, some individual cases pushed the boundaries of slavery (and freedom) still further. Over the course of twelve days, the *citoyenne* Louise-Félicité *dite* Agard won her freedom, lost it, and then regained it in a saga that illustrated that freed individuals sometimes could not rest assured that they were safe from reenslavement even after they had gained that precious scrap of paper stating that they were not human property in the eyes of the law. On 5 May 1804, Louise-Félicité deposited before a notary in Santo Domingo city a document dated 30 April 1804 declaring that she had paid her former "master," Dominique Cerice Vigneron, 500 *gourdes* for her liberty.[54] Nonetheless, just a few days later, Vigneron revoked the 30 April 1804 freedom act, only to then create a second document that same day that reemancipated his former "slave." Whence this dramatic about-face? Perhaps the financial aspect of their relationship entered into this matter, as the second act in favor of Louise-Félicité mentioned the 500-*gourde* payment whereas the revocation did not.[55] What is evident is that Louise-Félicité's self-purchase was no simple monetary exchange. As Laurent Dubois has shown in his study of ex-slaves in 1790s Guadeloupe, people such as Louise-Félicité "actively used and reshaped documentation" in order to assert their political and social identities as "citizens rather than as objects."[56]

In responding to such initiative, the Ferrand government sought to regulate the terms of manumission in order to bolster its control over the colony and the servile population. In a 5 December 1807 letter to his subordinate Agustín Franco de Medina, General Ferrand addressed the difficult situation of an unnamed "*nègre*" in Puerto Plata (northern Santo Domingo) who claimed that he had gained his liberty seven years before by paying fifty *gourdes* to his former master. On unspecified grounds (possibly penury), this man had petitioned for an exemption from having to pay the comparable sum required for the "*ratification*" of his liberty. Ferrand rejected this man's argument that held Franco to be the responsible party in the granting of this ratification, insisting instead that only he (Ferrand) held such authority.[57] Implicitly following the 1711 precedent, Ferrand asserted his authority to determine this man's legal condition.

Nevertheless, demands advanced by "slaves" for a path to liberty via self-purchase pushed Ferrand to address their concerns by proposing a carefully regulated mechanism for this. In the letter to Franco quoted in the preceding paragraph, Ferrand informed his underling that "a quantity of Slaves" who belonged to the "former convents of the country [Santo Domingo]" had put forth demands to be able to purchase their freedom. Moreover, according to Ferrand, other "Slaves" in the Cibao area shared with those of the convents the "same desire" for liberty. In search of a means by which to grant some of these demands that would accrue profit for the state and not undermine the slave system or his own authority, Ferrand granted Franco permission to establish a system of self-purchase. Self-purchases under this system had to conform to the following prices: 150 *gourdes* for each "head" (*tête*) who was sixteen to forty years of age, one hundred *gourdes* per "slave" aged twelve to sixteen and over forty, seventy-five *gourdes* for "slaves" aged eight to twelve, and fifty *gourdes* for children under eight years old. As before, Ferrand claimed final authority over the ratification of all manumissions that might ensue.[58]

Though Ferrand tried to impose a system that treated human beings like cattle, he acknowledged that the "desire" of these "slaves" for freedom had impelled him to propose an arrangement that provided certain limited avenues to escape from enslavement. As Dominguan authorities had done in the early eighteenth century, Ferrand at once sought to set the financial and legal terms of manumission while at the same time tacitly recognizing the will of these captives. In calling witnesses to attest to their freedom, some freed people in French Santo Domingo exploited another fissure in the edifice of repression.

Calling Witnesses

On 21 June 1805, a woman from Le Cap called Marseille *dite* Migniac appeared before a Santo Domingo city notary, claiming to have lost her original freedom papers in a fire (probably one of the burnings of her hometown during the revolutionary years). In the absence of such a record, she called four witnesses, including a pharmacist and an administrative official, who supported her claims to be a free woman. One witness declared that he had known Marseille since 1788, that he had observed her "enjoying her State of Freedom," and that she was "considered as [other] formerly Free, and Freed [people] were" by others whom both Marseille and this witness knew. Moreover, this same witness had "never heard" that this woman was "in the Bonds of slavery." Another witness stated that Marseille had once owned a coffee plantation and slaves in Mornet, Saint-Domingue, before she fled to the colony of Santo Domingo during the revolutionary upheaval.[59]

Therefore, by virtue of her prior ownership of this plantation and servile laborers, her connections with influential citizens, and, perhaps most crucially, these witnesses' concurrence that they "always knew her to be free," Marseille was able to translate her lived experiences on both sides of the island into an official recognition of her legal freedom.[60] The salience of property ownership in these witnesses' testimony, moreover, is evocative of the economic influence of many free women "of color" in the old French Saint-Domingue.[61]

In French Santo Domingo, "free person" and "slave" constituted statuses that were constructed and interpreted in part through others' observations of an individual's social and economic roles and behavior. Such perceptions of an individual's proper or assumed legal condition were historically and contextually contingent, reflecting not only the legal categories themselves but also the socially embedded expectations and experiences that constituted the somewhat malleable yet powerful "scripts" for who and what an enslaved or free man or woman should be.[62]

Scholars who work with legal documents have long understood the power of the skillfully constructed narrative to influence the outcome of legal proceedings. Such narratives in turn reveal much about the society within which these proceedings transpire. In her well-known study of such matters in sixteenth-century France, Natalie Zemon Davis explored the "possible story lines determined by the constraints of the law and approaches to narrative learned in past listening to and telling of stories or derived from other cultural constructions." Davis argued that some "possible story lines" were more likely than others to shape narratives recounted in the legal record due to the confluence of social convention, legal codes (both as written and as popularly understood), and a host of other factors.[63] In French Santo Domingo, freed persons and their witnesses constructed tales that emphasized some of the salient characteristics of life as a free person as often recognized in a Caribbean slaveholding society: ownership of property including slaves, participation in a social network that included prominent individuals, and enjoyment of a quotidian experience free from submission to a master. In the production of these notarial acts, freedom was created as a social reality via the reaffirmation of these purported aspects of it.

People like Marseille could thus inscribe their own liberty into these legal documents through mobilizing witnesses to confirm their long experience of living as free individuals. This in turn required the exploitation of one's social networks, which were often rooted in his or her former area of residence. It was indeed no accident that one of Marseille's witnesses was from her former home of Le Cap, while two others hailed from nearby Fort-Dauphin. This pattern obtained for numerous other freed subjects, such as a refugee from Léogane (southern Saint-Domingue/Haiti) named Chonne Martin.

On 26 February 1806, Chonne Martin appeared before the notary Funel de Seranon in Santo Domingo city. Having lost, during the "troubles, pillages and fires" of revolution in Saint-Domingue, the original "title of liberty" (*titre de liberté*) that her father and former master, *sieur* Martin, had previously granted her, Chonne found herself "today obliged to justify her state as [a] Free person." In pursuit of this objective, Chonne called four witnesses (all of whom were from the Léogane area), who swore that they had "full and certain knowledge" that the elder Martin had bought Chonne and then proceeded to free her. These witnesses also stated that they had seen Chonne "enjoy [her liberty], in Léogane, before the Revolution."[64] These narratives of her purchase and liberation by her own father, the original manumission act's destruction in revolutionary violence, and her long-standing experience as a free woman could substitute for documentary proof of prior manumission in Chonne's successful bid for the formal recognition of her freedom.

The situations of Chonne, Marseille, and many others reflected the instability of the categories of slave and free person in Hispaniola and the broader Caribbean in this era. This instability was in turn partly rooted in certain legal and customary routes to freedom that had emerged in the Spanish and French worlds. Spanish law had for centuries contained certain means by which one could move from slavery to freedom via an extended period of living as a free person (known as prescription). According to the *Siete Partidas*, a slave who "goes about unmolested for the space of ten years, in good faith and thinking that he is free, in the country where the master resides" would gain his liberty after this duration of time; he could also earn his freedom after living in such a state for twenty years "in some other country" or for thirty as a "fugitive."[65] More recently, in colonial French Saint-Domingue, efforts to evade taxes and legal restrictions on manumission had given rise to a peculiar form of semifreedom christened *liberté de savane* (savannah freedom), wherein many slave-owners had circumvented official manumission by granting unofficial freedom to slaves who often subsequently continued to labor on their old plantations.[66]

Questions of legal status were at the heart of one notable case brought to French authorities near the end of the Ferrand era. On 18 March 1808, a woman named Marie Emilie from Mirebalais came before the notary Barthélemy Vallenet in Santo Domingo city and stated that the "*négresse*" Marie Melie, who had been sold into slavery on 23 February 1808, was in fact "Free by birth" by virtue of being the daughter of a Marianne, who was herself born free. Marie Emilie then proceeded to affirm that Marie Melie had received a proper baptism and that a "great number" of former Mirebalais residents presently living in Santo Domingo city could swear to the veracity of this woman's legal freedom.[67] Her plight appears to have garnered the attention of General Ferrand himself. In a 4 March 1808 letter to a military subordinate in Azua, Ferrand related that a "Marie Emelie" (who was very likely the captive woman from the 18 March 1808 notarial act, notwithstanding the confusion between her name and that of her benefactor) had been sold to a Francisco de Castro by Joseph Dias, a resident of Azua, despite the fact that she "seems to be free by birth, according to certificates that state this and [that] have been submitted to me." In the ensuing dispute over this woman's status and thus the validity of the sale, Ferrand called upon Dias to present himself to him with the "titles" that could prove his legitimate ownership of Marie Melie.[68]

The vertiginous rise of French Saint-Domingue from a neglected backwater in the late seventeenth century to the world's most profitable colony less than a century later would be difficult to comprehend without accounting for the interlocking familial, professional, and social networks that bound together the diverse groups that comprised colonial society.[69] In Ferrand-era Santo Domingo, freed people, "slaves," and their advocates took full advantage of such networks and of the social power conferred by the sacraments of baptism and marriage.[70] Adroit exploitation of these networks and of the markers of free status (both document based and otherwise) improved one's chances both of crossing the line between slave and free and of remaining on the right side of it.

Conclusions

The destruction of universal emancipation in the French empire represented a tragedy of epic proportions. In deciding to abandon general emancipation and to deploy military expeditions to key colonies, Napoleon at once ruined his chances at significantly expanding France's imperial presence in the Americas and condemned thousands of human beings to servitude.[71] The foundation of an aggressively racist slaveholding regime in Santo Domingo in the wake of the defeat of the most important of these expeditions in turn reflected an attempt to negate the legacies of emancipation. These notarized freedom acts nonetheless hint at a much more complicated situation.

The strategies that the subjects of these acts employed were substantially rooted in the slave societies of colonial Santo Domingo and Saint-Domingue, yet their resonance extends far beyond Hispaniola's shores. The individual quests for freedom detailed in these notarial acts represented part of a "broader history of access to rights and to dignity, [a] history rooted in knowledge born from personal and familial experience of vulnerability," in the words of Rebecca Scott and Jean Hébrard.[72] The fragments of life histories contained in these records evince the multiplicity of means by which those in a position of acute "vulnerability" in French Santo Domingo sought to better their condition by exploiting the openings that existed or that they could create. In using the notarial system to archive their freedom, these freed individuals created their own distinct chapter in the history of the Age of Atlantic Revolutions (and Counterrevolutions).

Epilogue

For five years during the first decade of the nineteenth century, the land that would later become the Dominican Republic hosted a project of reenslavement that repudiated a revolutionary emancipationist experiment that had only just begun. However unequal and repressive the regime of emancipation had been in Hispaniola from 1793 to 1802, freed people there had, at least in theory, been able to claim new rights, such as payment for their labor, protection from cruelties such as the whip, and ownership over their own persons. General Ferrand, by contrast, sought a return to the old slaveholding order. The Ferrand period was a powerful counterpoint to a story of slave revolution, emancipation, and the defeat of three empires by former slaves and free-born people of African descent. Nonetheless, continual struggles over bondage in Napoleonic Santo Domingo made this colony a key arena of conflict over the terms of servitude and freedom during an era in which slavery in the Atlantic World faced great challenges but also found fertile new (and renewed) grounds.

Having come to power partly as a result of Napoleon's ill-conceived decision to deploy the Leclerc expedition to Hispaniola, the Ferrand regime collapsed five years later due in large part to an equally infamous decision by Napoleon. Though the loss of Saint-Domingue had crushed Napoleon's aspirations to expand the French empire in the Americas, he crowned himself emperor of France in 1804 and proceeded to deploy conquering armies to diverse parts of the European continent. In early 1808 one of these armies invaded Spain, deposing King Charles IV and installing Napoleon's brother Joseph on the Spanish throne. This created a crisis of political legitimacy that brought partisans of Napoleon into conflict with those loyal to King Charles's son and heir, Ferdinand VII. These developments had profound effects on the Spanish-American colonies, as *juntas* (governing councils) professing loyalty to Ferdinand VII sprang up in many colonies in opposition to Napoleon's agents. The destabilizing influence of these conflicts on the colonial order proved too much for Spain to reverse even after the defeat of Napoleon and the accession of Ferdinand VII to the throne in 1814.[1]

Napoleon's invasion of Spain also provoked strong reactions against "French" settlers in Cuba and Santo Domingo. In 1809 the government of Cuba ordered the expulsion of the French from that island, forcing thousands to migrate to New Orleans and other places.[2] In Santo Domingo, where the French controlled the central government, a succession of anti-Napoleon uprisings beginning in 1808 led to an armed conflict that resulted in the collapse of the Napoleonic regime in July 1809 and a British-negotiated transfer of power over Hispaniola's eastern part back to Spain.

In 1810, a former military officer who had served under Ferrand named Gilbert Guillermin printed in Philadelphia a work that is perhaps the most detailed extant firsthand account of this war. According to Guillermin, "by its topographical position, and the nature of its population, [Santo Domingo] found itself thrust into the center of the fermentation" when many of its inhabitants revolted against the "alleged usurpation of the house of Napoleon, and . . . the imagined oppression under which the Spanish Royal family languished in France."[3]

Politics on the island of Hispaniola during this war were saturated with fear, a circumstance that was worsened by shifting alliances among several parties that all desired the ouster of the Ferrand regime. While officials in Cuba and Puerto Rico deployed troops and sent arms and munitions to assist the Spanish in Santo Domingo, the British entered into an "offensive, and defensive alliance" with Puerto Rico's governor Toribio Montes in 1808.[4] Upon learning of events in Spain, Montes had authorized the capture of French ships, justifying this action as part of the "War" that the Supreme Junta of Seville had declared on Napoleon, according to a 2 August 1808 letter from Montes to Ferrand.[5] Furthermore, the Haitian leaders Henry Christophe and Alexandre Pétion, who were engaged in a conflict that pitted Christophe's northern kingdom against Pétion's southern republic, each sought to exploit the discord in the neighboring territory to gain an advantage over his rival.[6] Pétion, moreover, feared that the victors in this war in Santo Domingo would have designs on parts of Haiti, while Governor Montes instructed General Juan Sánchez Ramírez, the leader of the anti-French resistance in Santo Domingo, to not admit any "French Blacks and mulattos" into any Spanish military units due to anxieties concerning a possible Haitian invasion. Sánchez nonetheless "contract[ed] an alliance with Christophe, who sent him 300 men [serving as] auxiliary troops."[7]

Spanish authorities in Puerto Rico, Cuba, and elsewhere seeking to recruit troops to fight the Ferrand regime knew that they wielded a potent weapon in stirring up anti-French sentiments. Nevertheless, in an early example of a tendency that would recur in the later mainland independence wars, these elites sought to prevent these mobilizations from transforming into a genuine challenge to the social and racial order. They were perhaps mindful of what had transpired in Cuba when the Marquis de Someruelos had deliberately exploited "popular anxieties" to rally many of the island's residents against the French. This had, in Guillermin's recounting, unleashed a wave of unrest that had targeted not only French settlers but also "rich Spanish landowners," whose properties in Havana were sometimes subject to pillage.[8] Salvador Felix, who had been sent by Montes to instigate rebellions in Santo Domingo, tried to walk this thin line. While he succeeded in helping to incite uprisings in Neyba and Azua in late September and early October 1808, he was compelled by necessity to engage in trade with Pétion, exchanging cattle for munitions and arms.[9]

Ferrand was also caught in a vise, as his regime's militant racism was at odds with its need to employ nonwhite soldiers. Throughout its short existence, the Ferrand regime depended on the services of a nonwhite military unit known as the Légion Coloniale (Colonial Legion). In Guillermin's words, "the Légion Coloniale was composed of men of color, and of Free Blacks, who since the beginning of the Revolution have given to the French Government unfailing proofs of their loyalty, courage and Devotion." In particular, the Légion's leaders, Repussard and Savari, had acquired a "reputation for Bravery" in eighteen years of service. "This corps has always formed the avant garde of the columns," Guillermin declared, "and has had the greatest part of the Glory that the Garrison of Santo Domingo acquired in the numerous sorties that it made during the siege of this post."[10] The Légion indeed comprised a sizable portion of Ferrand's armed forces. One military record from 23 September 1804 lists ninety-nine troops (out of 862 total) serving in the Légion.[11] On 1 January 1809, there were 183 men in the Légion out of a total force of 1,361, while the Légion represented just fewer than 14 percent of the troops who were listed as being in the service of the French regime upon its fall in July 1809.[12]

Some men of African descent who served as soldiers and officers in the 1808–09 conflict may have seen this service as an opportunity to improve their lot, as many nonwhite Dominguan soldiers had before them. In an October 1808 letter to two Spanish officers, a "man of color" and military officer named Carreaux lauded the efforts of the Spanish in a recent victory in Azua. "The details of your Victories have strongly interested our compatriots, who ardently wish to see the natives of the country recover their former rights, and Expel a government of usurpers," declared Carreaux in what may well have been a thinly veiled critique of the racist laws of the Ferrand regime.[13]

The combined, if not always concordant, opposition from those oppressed by the Ferrand regime's racial policies, patriotic Dominicans, and external military forces seems to have overwhelmed the Napoleonic government, which by November 1808 was losing the war. Early that month a force of 600 "insurgents," of which 200 were "French Mulattos, or Blacks," defeated a French regiment of 250 men in Azua. By 3 November 1808, according to Guillermin, "all the districts of the East" had witnessed uprisings. The Spanish had around 1,800 troops at this time, of whom 1,200 were infantrymen and the rest were cavalrymen.[14]

Ferrand's misapprehension of the enemy's strength cost him his life and accelerated the demise of his regime. According to a report to Napoleon composed by a man named E. Paillier, who claimed to have been serving with Ferrand on his final mission, Ferrand had assembled a contingent of 600 men (of which half were regular infantrymen, one hundred were "French militia," and 200 "Spanish militia") to attack an enemy force in Seybo led by a turncoat officer whom Ferrand had once entrusted with command of the area. Believing that "all would return to order upon his appearance, and in case of resistance, the dispersion of the rebels would be easy," Ferrand's men were unprepared for the 2,100 soldiers from Havana and Puerto Rico who greeted them in Seybo on 7 November 1808. The ensuing battle quickly became a lopsided affair. For a veteran of a quarter century of warfare, such an ignominious defeat apparently proved too much to bear. After ordering the survivors of his troop to retreat, Ferrand reportedly exclaimed, "I am the victim of my overconfidence," then seized a cartridge from one of his aides before any of his men could react. "He primed his pistols, and, at the moment when it was least expected, he destroyed his head [*il se cassa la tête*]."[15]

Ferrand was succeeded as commander-in-chief by General Joseph Barquier, who could not stave off the regime's collapse. Indeed, by the time of Barquier's accession, it had become evident that the Napoleonic government was facing political as well as military defeat. On 18 December 1808, nineteen deputies formed a "Junta" near Santo Domingo city that recognized Ferdinand VII as the "Legitimate King and natural Lord" and that named General Juan Sánchez Ramírez the "political and military Governor, and interim intendant."[16] At this same time, anti-French forces placed Santo

Domingo city under a siege that prompted a massive evacuation. Guillermin asserted that as of 30 December 1808, 3,300 women and children had fled Santo Domingo city; this almost halved the presiege population of 8,000.[17]

The inability of the French regime to defeat the insurgency owed to a combination of profound anti-French sentiment following Napoleon's 1808 invasion of Spain; the lack of French reinforcements due to military overextension and British naval power; the weaknesses of key leaders, such as Ferrand's overconfidence; and crucial infusions of troops and arms from outside parties to the Spanish side.[18] In particular, the British, based in nearby Jamaica, saw these uprisings as a chance to inflict a crushing defeat on their arch nemesis. In the immediate wake of the collapse of French rule in Saint-Domingue in 1803, British warships sent to blockade French Santo Domingo had offered only halfhearted opposition to Napoleon's forces there due in part to racial anxieties stirred up by Dessalines's massacres of whites. Yet following the decisive British victory over Bonaparte at Trafalgar in 1805, the latter's deployment of two squadrons to disrupt British commerce provoked a battle near Santo Domingo, resulting in a bitter French defeat at the hands of British ships defending Jamaica in early 1806.[19] Three years later, the British actively collaborated with Ferrand's foes, engaging in such actions as transporting a military regiment from Puerto Rico to Santo Domingo on British ships in April 1809. Then, on 11 May, eleven British warships arrived in the harbor of Santo Domingo city.[20]

At this point, the Napoleonic regime's fall was a fait accompli. The British disembarked near Santo Domingo city on 28 June 1809 and penetrated the city walls the following day under the command of Commodore William Pryce Cumby.[21] (See figure 7.) This led General Barquier and his British and Spanish counterparts to begin to negotiate a surrender agreement. On 6 July 1809, the British major general Hugh Lyle Carmichael, the Spanish general Juan Sánchez Ramírez, and Barquier signed an accord for the capitulation of the French in Santo Domingo. This agreement stipulated that French troops must evacuate Santo Domingo city and all other important posts and sail for France within twelve days, British troops were to occupy these posts until this evacuation was complete, and a prisoner exchange was to commence immediately. While this accord allowed all individuals, of whichever "sex, condition, or color that they may be, French or Spanish," to emigrate from Santo Domingo to another Caribbean territory or to the United States at the expense of the British government within ten days, the document contained another provision that could be interpreted as a confirmation of

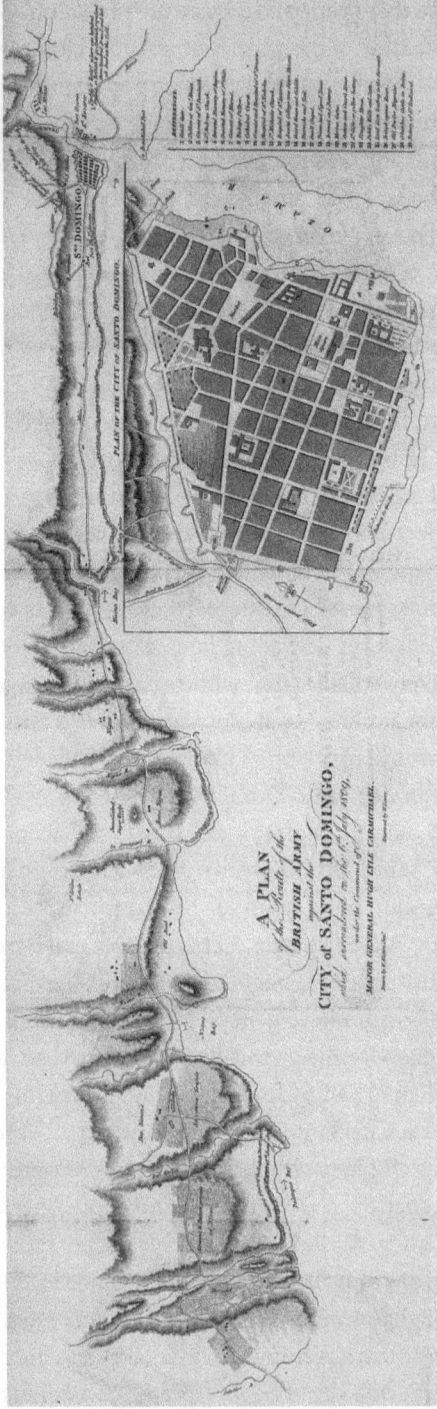

FIGURE 7 "A Plan of the Route of the British Army against the City of Santo Domingo, which surrendered on the 6th July 1809 . . ." A plan of attack for the British against Santo Domingo city, 1809. Includes geographical and topographical features as well as a city plan and a list of important sites in the city and environs. From William Walton, *Present state of the Spanish colonies* (London, 1810). Courtesy of the John Carter Brown Library at Brown University.

slavery: "All individual and personal properties of all Descriptions shall be respected."[22]

Though the fall of the French regime marked the beginning of a brief new period of Spanish rule in the eastern part of the island, it also ushered in a decade of uprisings, conspiracies, and political movements culminating in the short-lived first Dominican independence in 1821 and annexation by Haiti the following year. Santo Domingo's experience as a French colony, moreover, had significant implications for the collapse of Spanish sovereignty over most of the American empire by 1830.[23] The era of French rule in Santo Domingo (especially the confusion over the colony's governance from 1795 to 1801 and Toussaint Louverture's 1801–02 occupation) created a crisis of political sovereignty in what had been Spain's oldest colony, evinced the weakness of the Spanish metropole, and undermined the institution of slavery by facilitating the flight of Dominican "slaves" from the control of purported masters to opportunities for more autonomous cultivation in the countryside.[24] Indeed, notwithstanding the numerous holdovers from the slaveholding order that remained in Santo Domingo after 1795, the efforts to apply the 1794 French emancipation act in Santo Domingo after the cession represented among the most severe legal challenges to the enslavement of Africans and their descendants that had yet emerged in a Spanish-American colony.[25] In this light, Spanish America's nineteenth-century "liberators," who sometimes initially supported gradual emancipation schemes, appear less visionary than their reputations suggest.[26]

Hispaniola was also a critical arena in equally far-reaching French imperial transformations. In 1795, the French Republic had articulated a new vision of empire in promulgating a constitution that declared the colonies to be an "integral part" of a French polity that no longer recognized distinctions in citizens' rights between colony and metropole. Efforts to incorporate Santo Domingo into this new political order gave rise to conflicts that tested the boundaries of this doctrine of legal integration. When Napoleon subsequently dismantled the "integral part" doctrine in his 1799 constitution, which stipulated that the colonies were to once again be subject to "particular laws," he ironically helped to pave the way for Toussaint Louverture's promulgation of his own 1801 constitution. In a sense, the latter document represented a defiant logical extension of the principle of "particular laws" for the colonies. Clashes between these divergent conceptions of empire and the metropole-colony relationship helped to bring about the Haitian war of independence, which resulted in the complete rejection of

colonialism in Haiti and the establishment of the reactionary colonial regime of Ferrand in Santo Domingo.

The crises of empire in the French and Spanish worlds at the end of the
Haitian Revolutionary era (which ought to be reconceptualized as ending
in 1809, not 1804) were intertwined and mutually reinforcing. Just as Napoleon's invasion of Spain dealt the oldest empire in the New World a fatal
blow, the resulting upheaval in the Spanish world not only unseated the Ferrand regime but also weakened Napoleon's power. The removal of the
French beachhead in eastern Hispaniola further reduced the possibility of a
French reconquest of Haiti, which would have had profound geopolitical
implications for Latin American independence and North American expansion. Indeed, according to Fernando Picó, the fall of the Ferrand/Barquier
regime significantly undermined French power in the Caribbean in the early
nineteenth century.[27]

When contextualized within the *longue durée* of Hispaniola's history, some
of the apparent ruptures of the Haitian Revolution begin to appear less pronounced. Emancipation in Santo Domingo from 1795 to 1801, for instance,
involved the harsh repression of "slave" revolts, carrot-and-stick tactics
employed by both French and Spanish authorities against "maroon" communities, and continuing disputes over the old colonial border and over migration
between the two parts of the island. Furthermore, the destruction of institutionalized racism in French Saint-Domingue in the early 1790s (and its return
a decade later) was part of a long history of racial struggle that often transcended colonial boundaries, as the tragic story of Vincent Ogé illustrated.

Yet in other important respects, this revolution was just that: a momentous
break from what had come before. The 1792 French racial equality law
just alluded to, as a case in point, was far ahead of its time in a colonial
world where the color line separated much more than just those who were
potentially "enslaveable" and those who were not. Even more radically, the
uncertain situation of those held in bondage in Santo Domingo after 1795
brought to the fore the Haitian Revolution's central question: Can a viable
polity exist where nobody is held in chattel slavery? Even as he tried to re-
suscitate the plantation economy in Saint-Domingue and to impose a plantation system in Santo Domingo, Toussaint offered an affirmative answer
to this question. Furthermore, despite their participation in slaving during
the Franco-Spanish war in the early 1790s, the slaves-turned-officers Jean-
François and Georges Biassou played important roles in bringing about the
general emancipation decrees in Saint-Domingue in 1793, which in turn

formed the basis for the first empire-wide general slave emancipation in the hemisphere.

On the eve of the French and Haitian Revolutions, Santo Domingo was among the most neglected of Spain's American domains, yet it became deeply involved in an episode whose reverberations in Caribbean, Atlantic, and even global history were profound. Santo Domingo's importance in the Haitian Revolution owed to much more than just the colony's geographical proximity to Saint-Domingue, as patterns of slavery, race relations, resistance to enslavement, and peasant cultivation that emerged from Dominican and transcolonial Hispaniolan history represented vital contexts for this revolution. This book has sought to elucidate these contexts and to show that Santo Domingo was a central theater in the political and social developments of the Haitian Revolutionary era.

The archives of race and slavery in the Haitian Revolution speak in multiple and sometimes seemingly contradictory ways, revealing innovative strategies to secure freedom (which did not always imply freedom for others), flight by freed persons escaping an emancipationist regime to a land under the de facto governance of proslavery authorities, political discourses that framed the greatest slave revolt of its era as a counterrevolution, the invention of a law of reenslavement, and clashes between Dominican and "maroon" lived realities of freedom on the one hand and a French Republican centralizing project on the other. By mining these archives for the voices of slaves and freed persons, this book has not only demonstrated Santo Domingo's importance in this most Atlantic of revolutions but also offered new perspectives on this era's transformations in French and Spanish law, racial ideologies, political geography, and, perhaps most fundamentally, the meaning and scope of freedom.

I have also presented a new point of departure for understanding the past and present of Hispaniola's two modern nations themselves. In the decades following the end of the Ferrand regime, the eastern portion of Hispaniola followed a trajectory distinct from those of its Spanish-American cousins, declaring independence three times (in 1821, 1844, and 1865) from two powers (Spain and Haiti), while independent Haiti experienced a range of political regimes.[28] The struggles over slavery, sovereignty, and race on the island from 1795 to 1844 would later inform both Dominican and Haitian historical memory, often becoming invoked in selective ways to justify antagonism toward the neighboring nation in the twentieth and twenty-first centuries. Yet many of the stories told in this book attest to alternative narratives of cross-colonial and cross-racial cooperation, intertwined "French" and "Spanish" struggles for liberty, and even equal citizenship across the island, as epitomized by the "integral part" doctrine.

The past looms large over the efforts of Dominicans, Haitians, and others to resolve the problems of the present in Hispaniola and in the diaspora, as it always has. This book, a reinterpretation of a critical part of this past, offers new vantage points for understanding the complex politics of the contemporary moment.

For five centuries, the island of Hispaniola has been a crucible in the political, economic, and social processes that have shaped the development of the modern world. From the sixteenth century, when it was the first site of debates over the rights and humanity of indigenous Americans, to the twenty-first, when the precarious situation of Haitian migrants and Dominicans of Haitian descent in the Dominican Republic has raised urgent questions of human rights and the scope of citizenship, this island has held an importance that far outstrips its relatively small size.[29] Though the Haitian Revolution was shaped by decades- or centuries-old phenomena, it forged new concepts of citizenship and liberty, epitomized by its unprecedented challenge to slavery. Slaves and freed people in both parts of the island were at the center of this story. These individuals drew upon the long and interconnected histories of resistance to slavery and racism in both colonies to make visible the potential of French Republican emancipation. They bequeathed powerful legacies for the struggles for equality, liberty, and human dignity that continue to this day.

Glossary of French and Spanish Terms

French Terms

Affranchi (f. "affranchie") ▪ A freed person; a former slave.

Ancien libre ▪ The "formerly free"; a person of African descent who was free before the Haitian Revolution.

Ancien régime ▪ Literally "old regime"; a term for the political and social order in France and its overseas colonies before the French Revolution of 1789.

Arrêté ▪ An order or decree.

Citoyen (f. "citoyenne") ▪ "Citizen"; a political term often used to emphasize egalitarianism under the French Republic in the 1790s.

Code Noir ▪ The principal law code concerning slavery in French overseas territories, promulgated by the regime of Louis XIV in 1685.

Conseil ▪ Council.

Cultivateur (f. "cultivatrice") ▪ Literally "cultivator" or "agriculturalist." This term came to refer to formerly enslaved agricultural laborers in the era of emancipation.

Dame ▪ An honorific title roughly corresponding to "Madam."

Département ▪ Department or administrative unit; the principal subnational form of political organization created in France and then in the colonies during the French Revolution.

Dit (f. "dite") ▪ "Called" or "so-called"; often used to refer to a nickname or other known appellation.

Esclave ▪ Slave.

État Civil ▪ The main legal repository of birth, marriage, and death records both in metropolitan France and in the colonies.

Gens de couleur ▪ People of color.

Gens de couleur libres ▪ Free people of color; those of African descent who were not enslaved.

Gourde ▪ A unit of currency used in revolutionary Hispaniola.

Grands blancs ▪ A term that referred to the upper class of whites in Saint-Domingue, including powerful planters, political and military elites, and the most prosperous merchants.

Homme de couleur ▪ Man of color.

Libre ▪ Free.

Marron ▪ "Maroon" or fugitive slave.

Marronnage ▪ Slave flight.

Mémoire ▪ A report, often composed by a civilian or military official.

Mulâtre (f. "mulâtresse") • "Mulatto." The term generally referred to an individual of mixed European and African ancestry.

Nègre (f. "négresse") • Black person. This term acquired a pejorative connotation in the French Caribbean and was sometimes used as a synonym for *esclave*.

Noir (f. "noire") • Black person. This term was generally less derogatory in connotation than *nègre*.

Nouveau libre • The "newly free"; a person of African descent who was freed in the Haitian Revolution (typically by the 1793–94 general emancipation decrees).

Outre-mer • Literally meaning "overseas," this term referred to France's territories outside of Europe such as Saint-Domingue.

Partie espagnole • The "Spanish part" of Hispaniola (Santo Domingo).

Sieur • An honorific title roughly corresponding to "Sir."

Spanish Terms

Alcalde • Mayor.

Audiencia • High appeals court; also, a regional governing body in the Spanish empire.

Cabildo • Town council.

Cédula • A decree or order.

Cimarrón • "Maroon" or fugitive slave.

Código Negro • The "Black Code" issued in 1784 in Santo Domingo concerning the treatment and governance of slaves.

Cofradía • A Catholic religious brotherhood.

Esclavo (f. "esclava") • Slave.

Hato • Cattle ranch or ranching estate.

Junta • Governing council.

Libre • Free.

El Monte • The countryside in Santo Domingo.

Mulato (f. "mulata") • "Mulatto." As in the French world, the term generally referred to an individual of mixed European and African ancestry.

Negro (f. "negra") • "Black"; a racial term referring to a person of African descent. Sometimes also used as a synonym for *esclavo*.

Pardo (f. "parda") • "Brown"; another racial term referring to a person of African descent.

Siete Partidas • A compendium of laws compiled in thirteenth-century Castile. Among its many other provisions, the *Partidas* contained rules regarding enslavement, manumission, and related matters.

Síndico procurador • A public advocate charged with defending slaves in legal disputes.

Notes

Introduction

1. *Dite* here means "called" or "so-called." See the Glossary of French and Spanish Terms for translations of non-English words used in this work.

2. See act in favor of Rozine *dite* Alzire, 17 October 1806, ANOM DPPC NOT SDOM 705. I retain all original capitalization and punctuation in my translations of material from French- and Spanish-language primary sources, as well as the original orthography in my untranslated transcriptions of this material. All translations in this book are my own unless otherwise indicated.

3. The French Republic decreed the abolition of slavery in all its domains by an act of the National Convention on 4 February 1794. See "Decree of the National Convention . . . That abolishes the Slavery of Blacks in the Colonies," 4 February 1794, CARAN Colonies CC/9a/9.

4. This term implicitly privileges a teleology of the creation of Haiti, in contrast to the term "Saint Domingue Revolution," which is preferred by many French scholars. See Geggus, *Haitian Revolutionary Studies*, 1.

5. The forerunner of most modern historical studies of the Haitian Revolution in English is James, *Black Jacobins*. Some notable contributions published in the past few decades are Geggus, *Haitian Revolutionary Studies*; Dubois, *Avengers of the New World*; Dubois, *Colony of Citizens*; Fick, *Making of Haiti*; Popkin, *You Are All Free*; and Girard, *Slaves Who Defeated Napoléon*. See also Julius Scott's pioneering thesis "The Common Wind." On Santo Domingo/the Dominican Republic in the historiography of the Haitian Revolution and the nineteenth century, see Eller, "Awful Pirates and Hordes of Jackals."

6. My usage of the racial terminology employed in colonial and revolutionary Hispaniola, as both terms of self-identification and labels applied by others, seeks to convey the historical contexts of these terms while recognizing their artificial and socially constructed nature. In the interest of historical accuracy and sensitivity to U.S. readers, I will retain the original French and Spanish racial terms except in cases where currently accepted U.S. terms, such as "black," fit the context. (See the Glossary of French and Spanish Terms for translations of these terms.) Instead of speaking of free persons "of color," for instance, I will use the French *gens de couleur libres* (meaning "free persons of color"), which was a legal and social term for those of African descent who were not enslaved in the French Caribbean. For incisive discussions on the complexities of treating racial terms in historical scholarship, see Dubois, *Avengers of the New World*, 5–6; and Ferrer, *Insurgent Cuba*, 10–12. This study is conceptually indebted to Gary Wilder's formulation of an "imperial nation-state." See Wilder, *French Imperial Nation-State*. The present study is also informed by scholarship produced in the last few decades that has examined the viability of analytical frameworks such as "Atlantic World" and "empire." See, for example, Cañizares-Esguerra and Seeman, *Atlantic in Global History*; J. Scott, "Crisscrossing Empires"; Scott and Hébrard, "Les papiers de la liberté"; Gray, "Papacy and the Atlantic Slave Trade"; Burnard, "Empire Matters?"; Adel-

man, *Sovereignty and Revolution in the Iberian Atlantic*; and Hamnett, "Process and Pattern."

7. Notable examples of such work include Putnam, "To Study the Fragments/ Whole" (quote is from 616); Reis, *Slave Rebellion in Brazil*; Gaspar, *Bondmen and Rebels*; and Farge and Revel, *Vanishing Children of Paris*. On the effects of the Haitian Revolution outside of Hispaniola, see among other works Gaffield, " 'So Many Schemes in Agitation' "; White, *Encountering Revolution*; Sidbury, "Saint-Domingue in Virginia"; several volumes under the editorship of David Geggus, David Gaspar, and others such as Geggus and Fiering, *World of the Haitian Revolution*; and various works by Rebecca Scott, Jean Hébrard, and Ada Ferrer cited throughout this study.

8. Dubois, *Avengers of the New World*, 7. For a contrasting perspective, see Geggus, "Caribbean in the Age of Revolution."

9. Jenson, *Beyond the Slave Narrative*, 107. Emphasis mine. Period sources often render the country's name as "Hayti," but I employ the more conventional contemporary orthography of "Haiti."

10. Sources from the United States and England created in the Haitian Revolutionary era often used the terms "Santo Domingo" or "San Domingo" to refer to either the colony of French Saint-Domingue or to the entire island. I eschew such usages in this book for clarity.

11. The term "Dominican" should not be confused with the identically spelled demonym for the inhabitants of Dominica, an island nation in the Lesser Antilles.

12. Though population figures for Santo Domingo in this era are rather scarce and often unreliable, 15,000 represents a reasonable estimate of the slave population as of 1789. The chronicler Médéric-Louis-Élie Moreau de St Méry estimated that 15,000 slaves lived there among an overall population of 125,000 souls. Moreau de St Méry, *Description topographique et politique de la partie espagnole*, 1:44. In a report dated 1 October 1797, the French official Philippe-Rose Roume also stated that 125,000 people resided in the colony of Santo Domingo; this included 15,000 individuals whom Roume labeled "newly free" (*nuevos libres*). Report submitted by Roume to "French Government Commission in the [Caribbean] Islands," 1 October 1797, in Rodríguez Demorizi, *Cesión de Santo Domingo a Francia*, 279. A copy of this report exists in ANOM CMSM F3 201. In a tract on Santo Domingo written for the Spanish monarch, the priest Antonio Sánchez Valverde estimated that 12,000 to 14,000 slaves lived in that colony as of 1785. Sánchez Valverde, *Idea del valor de la isla española*, 169. The former Saint-Domingue colonist Jean Barré de Saint-Venant offered a figure of 15,000 slaves in Santo Domingo in *Des colonies modernes sous la zone torride*, 207.

13. This work has benefited from several decades of scholarship on "postemancipation societies" in the hemisphere. Among these works, the ones that have most influenced this study are Holt, *Problem of Freedom*; R. Scott, *Slave Emancipation in Cuba*; and Dubois, *Colony of Citizens*. See also R. Scott, *Degrees of Freedom*; Trouillot, *Haiti, State against Nation*; Sheller, *Democracy after Slavery*; and Cooper, Scott, and Holt, *Beyond Slavery*.

14. Kreyòl was the lingua franca in colonial Saint-Domingue. Modern dialects are now spoken in Haiti and several other Francophone Caribbean lands. Kreyòl draws upon French, African languages, and other influences.

15. Ghachem, *Old Regime and Haitian Revolution*, 6. This study builds upon a new wave of legal-historical studies that have examined legal contests that arose outside of the French empire over the legitimacy, applicability, and universality of the 1794 French emancipation law when those claimed as slaves in other lands invoked this law in defense of their freedom. See, for instance, Peabody, " 'Free upon Higher Ground' "; Renault, "Les conditions d'affranchissements"; Palmer, "Strange Science of Codifying Slavery"; and R. Scott, " 'She . . . Refuses to Deliver Up Herself.' "

16. On gender-based pay discrimination under the new labor codes that emerged on the island after abolition, see Fick, "Emancipation in Haiti," 17–20.

17. See especially Colwill, " 'Fêtes de l'Hymen, Fêtes de la Liberté' "; Desan, *Family on Trial in Revolutionary France*; Peabody, "*Négresse, Mulâtresse, Citoyenne*"; Geggus, "Slave and Free Colored Women in Saint Domingue"; Kafka, "Action, Reaction, and Interaction"; and Heuer, *Family and Nation*.

18. On historical and modern Haitian-Dominican relations, see Wucker, *Why the Cocks Fight*; and Matibag, *Haitian-Dominican Counterpoint*.

19. García, "Haitians without a Nation," http://www.bostonglobe.com/opinion /2013/12/30/haitians-dominican-republic-immigration-ruling-leaves-community -stateless/7XLAA20GHC4RV5No9fw26M/story.html.

20. I am, of course, not the first to challenge simplistic tropes of conflict as regards Haitian-Dominican relations. In particular, Eugenio Matibag in *Haitian-Dominican Counterpoint* sought to offer a more complete picture of the island's history comprising not only conflict but also the "interdependencies and reciprocal influences that have shaped each country's identity" (3).

21. I use the phrase "we must first take account" as an allusion to former U.S. Supreme Court Justice Harry Blackmun's famous statement that "in order to get beyond racism, we must first take account of race." See Harvard Law School's tribute to Justice Blackmun, http://www.law.harvard.edu/news/bulletin/backissues/summer99 /article7.html. On racial ideologies in Dominican history, see among other works Candelario, *Black behind the Ears*; Torres-Saillant, "Tribulations of Blackness"; and Turits, "Par-delà les plantations." On the historical roots of race relations in modern Haiti, see Trouillot, "Culture, Color, and Politics in Haiti."

22. Matibag, *Haitian-Dominican Counterpoint*, 3.

23. The literature on contemporary transnational migration concerning the Caribbean is quite expansive; the works that have most informed my own scholarship are Portes and Stepick, *City on the Edge*; and Waters, *Black Identities*.

24. The *audiencia* (regional governing body and high appeals court) based in Santo Domingo city held jurisdiction over much of the circum-Caribbean area, including Cuba and Puerto Rico. According to Eugenio Matibag, Santo Domingo was also an important transshipment point for slaves bought from Portugal and France who were

sent to Jamaica, Cuba, and Puerto Rico. Matibag, *Haitian-Dominican Counterpoint*, 55. On subsidies from New Spain to Santo Domingo, see Chanlatte to Minister of the Navy, 20 June 1800, CARAN Colonies CC/9a/24.

25. Ghachem, *Old Regime and Haitian Revolution*, 31–38. While exact white immigration figures to French Saint-Domingue are unavailable, evidence suggests that many if not most such immigrants were young men. According to Stewart R. King, "the white population [of French Saint-Domingue toward the end of the eighteenth century] consisted largely of migrants, mostly young men in relatively good health." King, *Blue Coat or Powdered Wig*, 44.

26. Generally, the gender ratio in the transatlantic slave trade was skewed toward males, though significant variations existed across time and space. Based on an exhaustive study of French slave trading records encompassing most of the eighteenth century, David Geggus found an overall gender ratio of 179 males to one hundred females, which he called "entirely average for the Atlantic slave trade." Geggus also stated that "males constituted between 60 and 70 per cent of captives in almost all slave trades across the Atlantic." Geggus, "Sex Ratio, Age and Ethnicity," 25. Geggus has also argued that records covering the entire period of French Atlantic slave trading indicate a gender ratio in which two-thirds of the captives were male. Geggus, "French Slave Trade," 122. In a study of 1,740 *engagés* (indentured servants) who departed from a variety of places in France for diverse parts of the Americas between 1682 and 1715, Gabriel Debien found that "the ordinary age is around twenty years." Debien also found only nine women in his entire sample. Debien, *Le peuplement des Antilles françaises*, 38–39. For more information on early labor developments in French Saint-Domingue, see Frostin, *Les révoltes blanches*, chaps. 1–2.

27. Garrigus, *Before Haiti*, 53.

28. Dubois, *Avengers of the New World*, 21–26.

29. Ibid., 26–28; and Garrigus, "Blue and Brown," esp. 237–40.

30. On these conflicts over the militia, see Garrigus, *Before Haiti*, chaps. 4–5; King, *Blue Coat or Powdered Wig*, chap. 4; and Frostin, *Les révoltes blanches*.

31. Dubois, *Avengers of the New World*, 30; and Garrigus, *Before Haiti*, 2–3.

32. Dubois, *Avengers of the New World*, 21. On the economy of French Saint-Domingue before and during the revolution, see also Fick, "Emancipation in Haiti"; Garrigus, *Before Haiti*, esp. chaps. 2 and 6; King, *Blue Coat or Powdered Wig*, esp. chaps. 2 and 6–7; and Lundahl, "Toussaint L'Ouverture and the War Economy."

33. Born into an influential family in Martinique in 1750, Moreau earned a law degree in Paris and became a lawyer in the mid-1770s in French Saint-Domingue. In an effort to improve colonial administration there, he composed several scholarly works in the 1780s, including two multivolume treatises on the history, politics, economy, and environment of both colonies comprising the island of Hispaniola: *Description topographique et politique de la partie espagnole* (2 vols.) and *La description topographique, physique, civile, politique et historique de la partie française* (3 vols.). His prominent role in political struggles in revolutionary Paris led to his exile to Philadelphia, where he

finished and published these two works on Saint-Domingue and Santo Domingo. Dubois, *Avengers of the New World*, 8–11.

34. Moreau de St Méry, *La description topographique, physique, civile, politique et historique de la partie française*, 1:25.

35. Moreau de St Méry, *Description topographique et politique de la partie espagnole*, 1:5 and 2:99.

36. See Guitar, "No More Negotiation," http://cai.sg.inter.edu/revista-ciscla/volume 29/guitar.pdf.

37. While scholars dispute the extent of the indigenous depopulation, its magnitude was undeniably severe. According to Suzanne Austin Alchon, more than 90 percent of the indigenous population of the Caribbean perished within the first sixty years of European colonialism. Alchon, *Pest in the Land*, 64.

38. For evidence of African slaves in Hispaniola in 1503, see Ayala, *Letter to Ferdinand and Isabella*, 45. On the Canary Islands as a prototype for American plantation slavery, see Stevens-Arroyo, "Inter-Atlantic Paradigm"; and Fernández-Armesto, *Before Columbus*, esp. chaps. 6–9. On the history and significance of sugar cultivation, see Mintz, *Sweetness and Power*.

39. Turits, *Foundations of Despotism*, 27–29, 276n13; Deive, *La esclavitud del negro*, 604–5; and Cassá, *Historia social y económica*, 174–75.

40. Moreau de St Méry, *Description topographique et politique de la partie espagnole*, 1:61–66.

41. Barceló, *Código Negro Carolino*, 174.

42. Cassá, *Historia social y económica*, 29 and 195–97.

43. On the *hato*, see Turits, *Foundations of Despotism*, 29; and Silié, "*Hato* and the *Conuco*."

44. Moreau pointed to cattle trading with the Spanish side of the island as one of the main economic roots of French Saint-Domingue. According to Moreau, the first French *hattes* (the French translation of *hato*), founded via trade with Santo Domingo in the late seventeenth century, were important in enabling the establishment of the first sugar plantations in the north of Saint-Domingue, of which there were three in 1698. This also set precedents for continual squabbles between French and Spanish officials over illegal animal trading throughout the eighteenth century. Moreau de St Méry, *Description topographique et politique de la partie espagnole*, 2:99–125.

45. Cassá, *Historia social y económica*, 235.

46. Moya Pons, *Manual de historia dominicana*, 148–53.

47. Cassá, *Historia social y económica*, 258 and 266; Matibag, *Haitian-Dominican Counterpoint*, 56.

48. Cassá, *Historia social y económica*, 29; Matibag, *Haitian-Dominican Counterpoint*, 56; González, *De esclavos a campesinos*, 18–19.

49. Giusti-Cordero, "Beyond Sugar Revolutions" (quotes are from 69–70).

50. Moya Pons, *Manual de historia dominicana*, 155–57.

51. Turits, *Foundations of Despotism*, 26.

52. González, *De esclavos a campesinos*, 34–35; Turits, *Foundations of Despotism*, chap. 1; Turits, "Par-delà les plantations," esp. 51–59; and Turits, "New World of Color." See also Silié, *Economía, esclavitud y población*, esp. chaps. 4–5.

53. Even though the landowning class in Santo Domingo did not attain the same societal dominance as in many other Spanish-American colonies, the cattle trade with Saint-Domingue and elite familial domination over entry-level military positions enabled the entrenchment of what Christine Rivas calls a "moderately comfortable landowning, cattle raising group of nominal whites" who exercised considerable authority. For example, Don Ignacio Caro, a military officer who served under Governor Joaquín García in the 1793–95 Franco-Spanish War (detailed in chapter 1), came from this well-connected elite group. See Rivas, "Spanish Colonial Military" (quote is from 260).

54. Turits, *Foundations of Despotism*, chap. 1.

55. Nouët et al., *La vie aventureuse de Norbert Thoret*, 11. I am grateful to Jeremy Popkin for generously sharing with me a copy of this rare manuscript.

56. Dubois, *Avengers of the New World*, 171–72; Garrigus, *Before Haiti*, 79.

57. Though the expedition's leaders insisted to the ex-slaves that they would uphold general emancipation, Napoleon's armies defended and reimposed slavery in other French colonies, such as Martinique and Guadeloupe; news of these developments quickly reached Hispaniola and gave credence to freed persons' fears there.

58. Moreau de St Méry, *Description topographique et politique de la partie espagnole*, 1:7.

59. Dubois, "Enslaved Enlightenment," 7.

Chapter One

1. Georges Biassou to Governor-General Joaquín García, 24 August 1793, AGS GM 7157, f. 12. Biassou and fellow ex-slave leader Jean-François seem to have dictated all their letters to scribes due to their apparent inability to write. Popkin, *You Are All Free*, 127.

2. Biassou to García, 24 August 1793, AGS GM 7157, f. 12.

3. Coronil, "After Empire," 275.

4. Geggus, *Haitian Revolutionary Studies*, 201. Nonetheless, scholars are starting to devote more attention to such leaders. See among other works Landers, *Atlantic Creoles*, chap. 2; and Ojeda, *Tendencias monárquicas*.

5. On the *gens de couleur libres*, see Garrigus, "Redrawing the Colour Line"; Garrigus, *Before Haiti*; King, *Blue Coat or Powdered Wig*; Garrigus, "Blue and Brown"; and Dubois, *Avengers of the New World*, chap. 3, esp. 60–65. On Ogé and his background, see Garrigus, "Vincent Ogé Jeune."

6. See Turits, "Par-delà les plantations"; Turits, *Foundations of Despotism*, chap. 1; Deive, *La esclavitud del negro*; and Silié, *Economía, esclavitud y población*.

7. Turits, "Par-delà les plantations," 54.

8. Ibid., 58–59. On the service of nonwhite men in the military, see Rivas, "Spanish Colonial Military," 255; and Cassá, *Historia social y económica*, 217–18.

9. Torres-Saillant, "Tribulations of Blackness," 134–35. Colonial legislation sometimes allowed for partial "decolorization" in certain instances while reaffirming racial hierarchy. According to a 1784 slave code, the "cotton cultivator," "even if he be black, or brown [*pardo*]," "can ascend from the fourth generation of his lineage to the hierarchy of whites provided that he and his successors have cultivated [cotton] for twenty years." Barceló, *Código Negro Carolino*, 176.

10. Moreau de St Méry, *Description topographique et politique de la partie espagnole*, 1:58–59.

11. Charles Vincent, "Reflections on Political Economy concerning the three Spanish Jurisdictions of Montecrist, San-Yago and Porto de Plata, relative to their reunion with the [French] Republic," 1797, ANOM DFC 5, no. 913. Emphasis in original. I discuss Toussaint's constitution and its signatories in chapter 4; one of them was named "Carlos de Roxas" or "Rojas."

12. Julien Raimond to Minister of the Navy Castries, 1786, ANOM CMSM F3 91.

13. Sala-Molins, *Le Code Noir*, 200. The article in the original French reads: "*Octroyons aux affranchis les mêmes droits, privilèges et immunités dont jouissent les personnes nées libres.*" On Raimond, see Garrigus, *Before Haiti*, esp. Introduction and chaps. 4–9; and Garrigus, "Opportunist or Patriot?"

14. Garrigus, "Vincent Ogé Jeune," 52–59; Dubois, *Avengers of the New World*, 134–35. See also J. Scott, "Common Wind," 179–80; Deive, *La esclavitud del negro*, 191–200; and Fick, *Making of Haiti*, chap. 5.

15. Report on Ogé affair by Spanish Council of the Indies, 15 July 1791, AGI ASD 1029; Garrigus, "Vincent Ogé Jeune," 57–59.

16. Ogé to Spanish authorities, 12 November 1790, AGI ASD 1029.

17. The problem of fugitive slaves crossing the colonial border dated back to the early decades of French settlement in Hispaniola. In two reports composed in 1685 and 1687, the governor of Saint-Domingue denounced the dozens of runaway slaves who fled to the Spanish part of the island. According to these reports, these escapees' experience of freedom across the border made them more resistant to the French slave system upon their recapture; the governor held several of these former fugitives responsible for killings of whites on the French side. Ghachem, *Old Regime and Haitian Revolution*, 55–58. Furthermore, according to Moreau de St Méry, on 1 December 1710 the rulers of French Saint-Domingue instructed an official named M. Beaussan de Petit-Bois to arrest all "fugitive French blacks" (*nègres fugitifs français*) in Santo Domingo and to bring legal suits against "Spaniards" who had captured these fugitives or "granted them freedom." Moreau de St Méry, *Description topographique et politique de la partie espagnole*, 2:172–74.

18. Moreau de St Méry, *Description topographique et politique de la partie espagnole*, 2:177. According to Melania Rivers Rodríguez, on the eve of the Haitian Revolution in 1789, rumors circulated on the island that French slaves who reached

Santo Domingo would legally gain their freedom. Rivers Rodríguez, "Los colonos americanos," http://rcientificas.uninorte.edu.co/index.php/memorias/article/view Article/229.

19. In addition to the extradition clauses, these accords also proscribed unauthorized settlements by fugitive slaves and others. For instance, one treaty drawn up on 11 December 1766 by the captain general of Santo Domingo, Don Manuel de Azlor, and Saint-Domingue's governor M. de la Valtière stipulated in its first article that all "Black fugitives, called maroons of one or another Nation, will be exactly and in good faith returned . . . paying always the same price of twenty five pesos that the treaty of seventeen sixty two stipulated." Article III stated that the "most appropriate means" were to be employed against "Black maroons, united and fortified in the untamed lands, near the Border" in order to capture them and to "totally destroy their establishments." Article IV prohibited residents of either colony from undertaking any work "on lands beyond the limits that are conceded, nor on uncertain or disputed land" on pain of a one-hundred-peso fine. Franco-Spanish treaty of 11 December 1766, AGI ASD 1101. The Treaty of Aranjuez, signed in 1777 by French and Spanish officials, represented a compilation of earlier accords that attempted to resolve continuing boundary disputes and also mandated the prompt return of fugitive slaves to their masters. See Deive, *Los guerrilleros negros*, 191–94; and Treaty of Aranjuez, 3 June 1777, AGI ASD 1019. For more details on the problem of French settlements on land claimed by the Spanish, see Joseph Solano to Don Julián de Arriaga, 25 November 1774, AGI ASD 1019.

20. Correspondence of Governor Blanchelande, 14 November 1790, ANOM CMSM F3 196; "Tratado de límites," 533. According to Carlos Esteban Deive, the French official Cambefort likewise demanded Ogé's immediate extradition from Santo Domingo in accordance with the "police treaty of 1777." Deive, "Les réfugiés français," 131.

21. García to Don Antonio Porlier, 31 December 1790, AGI ASD 1029.

22. According to Christine Rivas, special military units "patrolled the hinterland to avoid a revolt of the free black population." Rivas, "Spanish Colonial Military," 251.

23. Garrigus, "Vincent Ogé Jeune," 34.

24. García to Don Antonio Valdéz, 25 May 1790, AGI ASD 1028.

25. Report on Ogé affair by Council of the Indies, 15 July 1791, AGI ASD 1029.

26. Garrigus, "Vincent Ogé Jeune," 50.

27. Rivers Rodríguez, "Los colonos americanos," http://rcientificas.uninorte.edu .co/index.php/memorias/article/viewArticle/229.

28. For a discussion of the political and legal dimensions of torture in French Saint-Domingue, see Ghachem, *Old Regime and Haitian Revolution*, chap. 4.

29. Nouët et al., *La vie aventureuse de Norbert Thoret*, 12.

30. Garrigus, "Vincent Ogé Jeune," 60–62. For more on the Ogé affair, see Garrigus, " 'Thy coming fame, Ogé! Is sure' "; Garrigus, *Before Haiti*, 236–49; and Dubois, *Avengers of the New World*, 80–88.

31. Joaquín García to *conde del campo* Alange, September 1791, AGS GM 7149, f. 439.

32. Fick, *Making of Haiti*, 113; Dubois, *Avengers of the New World*, 97–98. On these early leaders and their goals, see Bénot, "Insurgents of 1791."

33. García to Alange, September 1791, AGS GM 7149, f. 439.

34. Marquis de Rouvray to "Spanish commander," 31 August 1791, AGI ASD 1029.

35. Blanchelande to García, n.d., AGI ASD 1029.

36. García to Bajamar, 25 September 1791, AGI ASD 1029.

37. García to Alange, September 1791, AGS GM 7149, f. 439.

38. Neely, *Concise History of the French Revolution*, 132–38.

39. Lacroix, *La Révolution d'Haïti*, 92.

40. Quoted in Deive, *Los guerrilleros negros*, 198–99.

41. Quoted in Popkin, *You Are All Free*, 128. I am grateful to Popkin for sharing with me a copy and transcription of this letter.

42. Popkin, *You Are All Free*, 129–30. Both Catholicism and Vodou, a complex religion that developed in eighteenth-century Saint-Domingue out of a mixture of Catholicism and various African religions, were central aspects of slaves' lives in the French colony. For a discussion of Vodou and its effects on slave resistance and the August 1791 revolt, see Fick, *Making of Haiti*, 41–45 and 91–94.

43. Geggus, "Slave Resistance in the Spanish Caribbean," 139; and Dubois, *Avengers of the New World*, 107–8. Dubois on these pages notes that "Spanish officers" sometimes visited insurgent camps on the border. On the "dechristianization" campaigns in the French Revolution, see Neely, *Concise History of the French Revolution*, 197–200.

44. Declaration of M. Peyredieu to the Municipality of Le Cap, 21 April 1793, CARAN CC D/XXV/46, dossier 439.

45. "Extract from a particular letter from Cap Français, dated 6 March [1793]," ANOM CMSM F3 197.

46. On monarchical ideologies in Saint-Domingue, see Ogle, "Trans-Atlantic King." On the *Code Noir* and royal measures to ameliorate slaves' conditions, see Ghachem, *Old Regime and the Haitian Revolution*, esp. chaps. 3 and 5; and Dubois, *Avengers of the New World*, 106–8.

47. By the 1780s, between 30,000 and 40,000 African captives were arriving in the colony each year from diverse parts of the continent; 300,000 were shipped to Saint-Domingue in the eight years to 1791. Dubois, *Avengers of the New World*, 39; Ghachem, *Old Regime and the Haitian Revolution*, 275. On African political ideas in Hispaniola, see Thornton, "'I Am the Subject of the King of Kongo'"; Thornton, "African Soldiers in the Haitian Revolution"; and Mobley, "'Kongo, ede m kriye.'"

48. Popkin, *You Are All Free*, 11.

49. Count of Gaston, "Summary of the Current Situation in the Colony of St Domingue," 6 December 1791, CARAN Colonies CC/9a/5.

50. Jeannot had been executed in November 1791 by Jean-François for excessive brutality toward captives, and Boukman Dutty had perished in battle that same month.

51. Fick, *Making of Haiti*, 112–17.

52. It is unclear to whom this "Belair" refers. Most likely, this was either Charles Belair, a nephew of Toussaint Louverture, or Gabriel Belair, an officer under Biassou. Ghachem, *Old Regime and the Haitian Revolution*, 272n47; Geggus, *Haitian Revolutionary Studies*, 267n49.

53. Quoted in Piquionne, "Lettre de Jean-François, Biassou et Belair," 206–10. For a translated version, see Bell, *Toussaint Louverture*, 39–41. All quotes are from the Piquionne version.

54. Though David Geggus has called into question the authenticity of the letter, Malick Ghachem, Jeremy Popkin, and Madison Smartt Bell have all convincingly argued that the letter credibly speaks to some of the goals and ideals of the insurgents. For an overview of this debate, see Ghachem, *Old Regime and the Haitian Revolution*, 272–73n50. See also Bell, *Toussaint Louverture*, 42–43; Popkin, *You Are All Free*, 50; and Geggus, *Haitian Revolutionary Studies*, 267n49.

55. For a copy of the 4 April 1792 law, see "Law Relative to the Colonies and to the means to pacify the troubles there," 4 April 1792, CARAN CM D/XVI/16.

56. Popkin, *You Are All Free*, 23. During his two years as governor, Blanchelande had become widely reviled in the colony due to his futility against the slave rebels and his status as a royal appointee. Ibid., 23–25.

57. Fick, *Making of Haiti*, 116–17.

58. Sonthonax, Polverel, and Ailhaud to "Free Men of Saint-Domingue," 24 September 1792, ANOM CD B 277.

59. On these prerevolutionary abolitionists, see Dubois, *Colony of Citizens*, chap. 2. On the opinions and intentions of Sonthonax and Polverel vis-à-vis the question of slavery upon their appointment and arrival in the colony, see Popkin, *You Are All Free*, 87–92.

60. García to Pedro Acuña, 18 November 1792, AGS GM 7157, f. 71.

61. Fernando Portillo y Torres to Pedro Acuña, 25 September 1793, AGI ASD 1110.

62. Gaspar de Casasola to Rochambeau, 9 November 1792, AGS GM 7157, f. 70.

63. Report by Rochambeau on military events in northern Saint-Domingue, 9 November 1792, CARAN CC D/XXV/113, dossier 896.

64. "Variétés: Parallèle entre la situation actuelle du Soldat, et celle de l'ancien régime," *Les Affiches Américaines*, no. 62, 3 August 1791, microfilmed at University of Florida's Special Collections.

65. See Marat, *Chains of Slavery*; and Hammersley, "Jean-Paul Marat's 'The Chains of Slavery.'"

66. Neely, *Concise History of the French Revolution*, chaps. 6–7.

67. Ibid., chap. 6, esp. 140–47; Schroeder, *Transformation of European Politics*, chap. 2. On the "citizen-soldier," see Garrigus, "Vincent Ogé Jeune," 51–52; and Dubois, "Citizen Soldiers."

68. Schroeder, *Transformation of European Politics*, 70. For more details on the decision of Spain's monarchs to abandon their long-standing alliance with France, see Stein and Stein, *Edge of Crisis*, chap. 2.

69. García to Pedro de Acuña, 24 May 1793, AGS GM 7157, f. 129.

70. Dubois, *Avengers of the New World*, 152–53.

71. Vázquez Cienfuegos, *Tan difíciles tiempos para Cuba*, 57–71.

72. Many officers in the Dominican *fijos* (fixed regiments) of 1763 and 1777, for instance, had been veterans of campaigns in Cuba or had been posted to that island. See Rivas, "Spanish Colonial Military," esp. 266–72.

73. See Ferrer, *Freedom's Mirror*, chap. 3. On the Haitian Revolution and Cuba, see also González-Ripoll et al., *El rumor de Haití en Cuba*; Childs, *1812 Aponte Rebellion in Cuba*; Vázquez Cienfuegos, *Tan difíciles tiempos para Cuba*; and Ferrer, "Speaking of Haiti," among other works.

74. I thank Julia Gaffield (personal communication, 23 April 2014) for suggesting this to me.

75. García to Gaspar de Casasola, 19 April 1793, AGS GM 7157, f. 120. The primary source record suggests that García made such an offer of freedom only to French Dominguan slaves, not Spanish Dominican slaves. No primary source that I have found mentions any such offer made to the latter, and García likely would have favored recruiting among the tens of thousands of war-hardened rebel slaves in French Saint-Domingue over arming far fewer Dominican slaves, which could have had a destabilizing effect. The latter scenario is nonetheless possible, given the precedents of other Spanish officials' arming slaves in their own colonies and the simple fact that recruiting among enslaved Dominicans would have bolstered García's manpower. Regardless, given the sheer numbers and military experience of the Dominguan slave rebels, these men surely greatly outnumbered any Dominican slave recruits.

76. Hyacinthe was a young slave who had led a slave rebellion in the western part of Saint-Domingue in 1792. Fick, *Making of Haiti*, 139.

77. García to Pedro de Acuña, 14 May 1793, AGS GM 7157, f. 124.

78. Landers, *Atlantic Creoles*, 71–72. On the military recruitment of slaves in Spanish America, see Landers, "Transforming Bondsmen into Vassals."

79. I thank Cyrus Veeser (personal communication, 30 January 2014) for suggesting this to me.

80. Ojeda, *Tendencias monárquicas*, 57. On these militias, see Rivas, "Spanish Colonial Military."

81. Dubois, *Avengers of the New World*, 146.

82. J. Scott, "Common Wind," 233.

83. The continual rivalry between the leaders of these "black auxiliaries" appears to have been partly related to the distribution of resources by the Spanish high com-

mand. In a letter dated 16 September 1793, Biassou's subordinate Gabriel Belair complained that while Jean-François's men had received "considerable sums" from Spanish authorities, Biassou's forces had only obtained a very small recompense for their "two years" of "fight[ing] without any interest other than for the King." This caused great "envy" among Biassou's men and prompted many of them to "desertion" to the ranks of Jean-François. Belair to Joaquín García, 16 September 1793, AGS GM 7157, f. 21.

84. Lord Dunmore's initial efforts to recruit the slaves of Patriot masters into British armies in Virginia eventually led to the recruitment of 25,000 slaves by both sides in the American Revolution. Dubois, *Colony of Citizens*, 224.

85. Though the Franco-Spanish conflict played out chiefly in Hispaniola, France and Britain vied for supremacy in the eastern Caribbean during these same years, often arming slaves on terms similar to those offered in Hispaniola.

86. Geggus, "Arming of Slaves in the Haitian Revolution," 220. See also Dubois, *Colony of Citizens*, esp. chaps. 7–8.

87. Joaquín García to Pedro de Acuña, 13 January 1793, AGS GM 7157, f. 83. The meaning of "Public Papers" in this letter is unclear; García may have been referring to charters such as the Declaration of the Rights of Man and the Constitution of 1791 and/or to the numerous less famous political pamphlets and treatises emanating from revolutionary France.

88. Letter contained in Monte y Tejada, *Historia de Santo Domingo*, 4:62–63.

89. This reliance upon priests caused some Spanish officials on the island to complain that the conflict with France had become a "war of Pater Noster and Ave Maria." Quoted in Geggus, *Haitian Revolutionary Studies*, 175.

90. García to Acuña, 14 May 1793, AGS GM 7157, f. 124.

91. The thirteenth-century Castilian collection of laws known as the *Siete Partidas* held slavery to be against "natural reason." As discussed in further detail in chapter 6, the *Partidas* enumerated certain rights for the enslaved and prescribed means by which those in bondage might become free. R. Burns, *Las Siete Partidas* (quote is from 4:977, *Partida* IV, Title XXI, Law I). On slavery and the papacy, see Gray, "Papacy and the Atlantic Slave Trade."

92. García to Acuña, 14 May 1793, AGS GM 7157, f. 124.

93. Hyacinthe to Joaquín García, no date, AGS GM 7157, f. 109. On 19 April 1793, García acknowledged receiving an undated letter the previous February from "General Jacinto," which almost certainly is the one quoted here; García in his April letter mentioned Hyacinthe's claim to be a "*cimarrón*." Joaquín García to Ignacio Caro, 19 April 1793, AGS GM 7157, f. 122. The term *cimarrón* referred to slaves who had fled from their masters and is the root of the English word "maroon." For details on Hyacinthe's career and demise in mid-1794, see Fick, *Making of Haiti*, 139–40, 157–58, and 185–86; and Lacroix, *La Révolution d'Haïti*, 481.

94. "Sentimental Letters on the Santo Dom[ingo] revolution. Thursday 8 August 1793, year 2 of the French republic. Sixth Letter To the Rebels," 8 August 1793, AGS GM

7157, f. 13. Julius Scott cites an apparent copy of this document from the *Archivo General de Indias* in "Common Wind," 246.

95. Popkin, *You Are All Free*, 85–95, 145–54.

96. "Proclamation" of Sonthonax and Polverel, 21 June 1793, ANOM CMSM F3 198. For more details on the Galbaud affair, see Popkin, *You Are All Free*; Popkin, *Facing Racial Revolution*, chap. 10; and Dubois, *Avengers of the New World*, 155–59.

97. "Proclamation" of Sonthonax and Polverel, 21 June 1793, ANOM CMSM F3 198.

98. Popkin, *You Are All Free*, 2.

99. Sonthonax and Polverel to National Convention, 10 July 1793, CARAN CC D/XXV/41, dossier 408.

100. Galbaud, "Succinct and Preparatory Narration of My Conduct in Le Cap," CARAN CC D/XXV/48, dossier 459.

101. Dubois, *Avengers of the New World*, 153; and Deive, *Los guerrilleros negros*, 207–9. In addition to their fighting abilities, these new recruits also provided the Spanish with invaluable intelligence on the enemy. For instance, according to Julius Scott, these black troops were the "eyes and ears of the Spanish in Santo Domingo." J. Scott, "Common Wind," 244–45. Indeed, in a 22 October 1793 letter, García acknowledged that "the Chiefs of our black allies were the first ones who delivered to my hands the Proclamation of the Commissioner [Sonthonax]." He was referring to the general emancipation decree of 29 August 1793. García to Alange, 22 October 1793, AGS GM 7151, f. 66.

102. Julien Raimond, "Means to Take Possession of the Spanish Part of St Domingue and to form an armed force to defend it from the English Enterprises," 7 *Vendémiaire an 4* (29 September 1795), CARAN AF/II/64.

103. Popkin, *You Are All Free*, 256–57.

104. Proclamation of Sonthonax and Polverel, 11 July 1793, ANOM CMSM F3 286.

105. Proclamation of Sonthonax, 1 August 1793, ANOM CMSM F3 198; Ghachem, *Old Regime and the Haitian Revolution*, 82–84.

106. Colwill, " 'Fêtes de l'Hymen, Fêtes de la Liberté,' " 128 and 132. Sue Peabody has likewise argued that in utilizing marriage as a form of social control, Sonthonax was motivated by "Republican ideologies of womanhood" that "held that a woman's relationship to the state was mediated through her husband." Peabody, "*Négresse, Mulâtresse, Citoyenne*," 66. Suzanne Desan, moreover, organized her study of the family in revolutionary France around the contention that the family was "an arena of social and political contestation during the French Revolution." Desan, *Family on Trial in Revolutionary France*, 2. See also Heuer, *Family and the Nation*.

107. See Kafka, "Action, Reaction, and Interaction."

108. Sonthonax to National Convention, 30 July 1793, CARAN CC D/XXV/5, dossier 52.

109. "Proclamation" of Georges Biassou, 25 August 1793, AGS GM 7157, f. 15.

110. Popkin, *You Are All Free*, 236.

111. Quoted in Popkin, *You Are All Free*, 276.

112. Popkin, *You Are All Free*, 277.

113. Ibid., 267–70; Dubois, *Avengers of the New World*, 160–63.

114. Sonthonax to Polverel, 10 September 1793, CARAN CC D/XXV/5, dossier 53.

115. Sonthonax argued that the "representatives of this [French] Republic" had "untied the hands of the Civil Commissioners in granting them the power to provisionally change *police [power] and plantation discipline*," citing Article III of a 5 March 1793 decree of the National Convention that had allegedly "delegated" to Sonthonax the authority to make these changes. Sonthonax, "Proclamation in the Name of the Republic," 29 August 1793, ANOM CMSM F3 198. Emphasis in original.

116. Sonthonax, "Proclamation in the Name of the Republic," 29 August 1793, ANOM CMSM F3 198. Emphasis in original.

117. Ibid.

118. Popkin, *You Are All Free*, chap. 10; Dubois, *Colony of Citizens*, 159–68.

119. On 25 February 1793, shortly after the outbreak of war between England and France, a contingent of French planters in London composed an entreaty to Adam Williamson, lieutenant governor of Jamaica, in which the planters "invoke the protection of S.M.B. [the British king]" and "swear loyalty to him" so that he may "conserve the colony [Saint-Domingue]." Capitulation proposal by French planters to Williamson, 25 February 1793, ANOM CMSM F3 285 (subsequently confirmed in Santiago, Santo Domingo, and Jérémie, Saint-Domingue; the version that appears in the archive is a 26 October 1793 reprint from Charleston, South Carolina). See also Dubois, *Avengers of the New World*, 153; and Geggus, *Slavery, War and Revolution*, chap. 3 and 395–99.

120. The British lost 15,000 of the 25,000 troops that they deployed to Saint-Domingue. Geggus, *Haitian Revolutionary Studies*, 20.

121. Geggus, *Slavery, War and Revolution*, 114; Dubois, *Avengers of the New World*, 166–68 and 179; Fick, *Making of Haiti*, 185.

122. García to Alange, 22 October 1793, AGS GM 7151, f. 66.

123. Ibid.

124. García to "the General Commanders, and other Chiefs of our Troops stationed in the North, South and West part," 21 October 1793, AGS GM 7151, f. 68.

125. Proclamation of Joaquín García, 18 October 1793, AGS GM 7151, f. 67.

126. García to "the General Commanders, and other Chiefs of our Troops stationed in the North, South and West part," 21 October 1793, AGS GM 7151, f. 68; proclamation of Joaquín García, 18 October 1793, AGS GM 7151, f. 67.

127. García to the Marquis of Bajamar, 25 January 1792, AGS GM 7157, f. 46.

128. Turits, "Par-delà les plantations," 66n10; and Turits, *Foundations of Despotism*, 36–37.

129. Sonthonax, "Proclamation in the Name of the Republic," 29 August 1793, ANOM CMSM F3 198. Following his 31 October 1793 emancipation proclamation, Polverel promised to issue his own labor code but was not able to do so until 7 February 1794

due to illness. Fick, "Emancipation in Haiti," 18–19. For more information on the labor regimes devised by Sonthonax and Polverel, see Fick, *Making of Haiti*, chap. 7. For an analysis of similar developments in 1790s Guadeloupe, see Dubois, *Colony of Citizens*, chaps. 6–7.

130. Sonthonax, "Proclamation in the Name of the Republic," 29 August 1793, ANOM CMSM F3 198.

131. Ibid.

132. Sonthonax to Polverel, 10 September 1793, CARAN CC D/XXV/5, dossier 53.

133. Kafka, "Action, Reaction, and Interaction," esp. 50–54.

134. Belair to Joaquín García, 10 September 1793, AGS GM 7157, f. 16.

135. Ibid.

136. Dubois, *Colony of Citizens*, 193.

137. Fernando Portillo y Torres to Pedro Acuña, 25 September 1793, AGI ASD 1110.

138. Geggus, *Haitian Revolutionary Studies*, chap. 8; Ghachem, *Old Regime and the Haitian Revolution*, 301–2.

139. Dubois, *Avengers of the New World*, 178–79.

140. Geggus, *Haitian Revolutionary Studies*, 131; Dubois, *Avengers of the New World*, 182.

141. Fick, *Making of Haiti*, 185.

142. Geggus, *Haitian Revolutionary Studies*, 121–23; Dubois, *Avengers of the New World*, 178–79.

143. King, *Blue Coat or Powdered Wig*, 30–32.

144. For an eyewitness account of the fall of Fort-Dauphin, see Knapp, "Items Concerning the Capture of Fort-Dauphin by the Spanish in Saint-Domingue, January 1794," SHAT Xi 71. See also the surrender accord between Don Gabriel Aristizával and the "garrison and inhabitants of Fort Dauphin," 28 January 1794, CARAN Colonies CC/9a/8.

145. Nicolás de Toledo to Joseph Antonio Urízar, 9 July 1794, AGS GM 7159, f. 4.

146. Geggus, *Haitian Revolutionary Studies*, 180; Dubois, *Avengers of the New World*, 180. See also Popkin, *Facing Racial Revolution*, chap. 13.

147. Though the extremely tendentious nature of the few extant firsthand accounts of the massacre makes it quite difficult to separate fact from fiction, one such account suggests that Jean-François may have feared that these French colonists were collaborating with rivals. This account was written by an anonymous French refugee who had fled the burning of Le Cap in June 1793 and then returned to the Fort-Dauphin area, where his family had owned a plantation, in 1794. This refugee claimed that Jean-François and his men "tried to palliate their crime by saying that they had been informed that we [the French colonists] wanted to revolt against them and deliver that part of the island to the English, who were already in possession of other parts. Another excuse given was that Jean-François, outraged at the return of the French proprietors, threatened to start a rebellion of all the Negroes against the Spanish,

unless he was promised that we would be delivered to him to be done with as he chose." Quoted in Popkin, *Facing Racial Revolution*, 263.

148. Account of Grandet on Fort-Dauphin massacre, 7 July 1794, ANOM CMSM F3 199. The Mirande account is discussed in Popkin, *Facing Racial Revolution*, 252–53.

149. "Declaration made by the General Jean-François on all the matters that have been the Cause of the affair that took place on 7 July in Fort-Dauphin," 11 July 1794, ANOM CMSM F3 199.

150. Ibid.

151. In a letter to the French government, a French official named Charles Malenfant asserted that Jean-François had sold many "Blacks" to Cuba and Puerto Rico during this war. Charles Malenfant to French government, undated, CARAN Colonies CC/9a/20. Furthermore, on 29 August 1793, Joaquín Cabrera, the commandant of San Rafael, wrote to Biassou to thank him for hunting down and capturing a "black slave" named André who had fled to French Saint-Domingue. Cabrera to Biassou, 29 August 1793, CARAN Colonies CC/9a/8. Finally, in a 28 February 1803 letter to Colonial Prefect Hector Daure, a naval officer named Vermonnet stated that slavers working under Jean-François had sold 4,742 slave children (*negrillons*) through Santo Domingo to assorted Spanish colonies. Vermonnet estimated that around 100 of these captives went to Cuba, 200 to Caracas, 200 to Campeche (Mexico), 300 to Trujillo (Honduras), and 250 to Grenada. Vermonnet to Daure, 9 *Ventôse an* 11 (28 February 1803), SHAT B7 13.

152. Ojeda, *Tendencias monárquicas*, 79.

153. Étienne Laveaux to Joaquín García, 21 October 1794, AGS GM 7151, f. 463.

154. In 1794, Sonthonax and Polverel were forced to depart Saint-Domingue for France to defend themselves against charges brought by émigré planters that they had usurped legitimate authority in issuing the emancipation decrees. Though Polverel died during the proceedings, Sonthonax won his trial and returned to Saint-Domingue in 1796 as a member of a new Civil Commission. Dubois, *Avengers of the New World*, 180 and 196.

155. Neely, *Concise History of the French Revolution*, 233–35.

156. Geggus, *Haitian Revolutionary Studies*, chap. 12; and Landers, "Rebellion and Royalism in Spanish Florida," 156–77.

Chapter Two

1. "Order of the Provisional Agent [Philippe-Rose Roume] on the Praiseworthy Conduct of the Spaniards [concerning] a Revolt of blacks in the Spanish Part," 9 *Nivôse an* 5 (29 December 1796), ANOM CMSM F3 200. In his report to Santo Domingo's governor, Joaquín García, on the Boca Nigua revolt, the judge Manuel Bravo y Bermudez claimed that the "rebels" numbered 110 to 120, not counting women and children. "Report by the Judge Bravo y Bermudez to the President of Santo Domingo [Joaquín García] on the Revolt of the Blacks of the Plantation of Oyarzábal or

Yranda," 14 December 1796, ANOM CMSM F3 200. Roberto Cassá has estimated that more than 200 "slaves" (his word) were involved in the uprising. Cassá, "Les effets du Traité du Bâle," 206.

2. "Order" of Roume, 29 December 1796, ANOM CMSM F3 200. In his report, Bravo y Bermudez meticulously listed the "blacks" whose dead bodies his troops had recovered in the fighting and described in detail the guerrilla-style combat that pitted his forces against elusive rebels. Bravo y Bermudez to García, 14 December 1796, ANOM CMSM F3 200.

3. The Treaty of Basel stipulated that Spain "cedes and abandons . . . to the French Republic the entire Spanish part of the isle of Saint Domingue, in the Antilles." Treaty of *Bâle* (Basel), 22 July 1795, CARAN AF/III/61. The famous abolition law passed by the French National Convention on 4 February 1794 stated: "THE NATIONAL CONVENTION declares that the slavery of Blacks in all the [French] Colonies is abolished: as a result it decrees that all men, without distinction of color, residing in the colonies, are French citizens, and shall enjoy all the rights assured by the [French] constitution." "Decree of the National Convention . . . That abolishes the Slavery of Blacks in the Colonies," 16 *Pluviôse an* 2 (4 February 1794), CARAN Colonies CC/9a/9. Emphasis in original.

4. Roume to municipal authorities of San Juan de la Maguana, 1 *Floréal an* 5 (20 April 1797), CARAN Colonies CC/9a/20; "Order" of Roume, 29 December 1796, ANOM CMSM F3 200.

5. "Order" of Roume, 29 December 1796, ANOM CMSM F3 200; Bravo y Bermudez to García, 14 December 1796, ANOM CMSM F3 200. See also the 14 December 1796 report that Bravo y Bermudez submitted to García on the Boca Nigua uprising, which is preserved in AGI ASD 1033.

6. Many aspects of the Boca Nigua rebellion appeared in slave revolts in the Americas. These included rebels' appointment of a leader bearing a royal title, the salience of drums, the rebels' guerrilla tactics, and authorities' savage repression of the uprising. While the literature on slave rebellions in the hemisphere is vast, two particularly illuminating analyses of major revolts are Gaspar, *Bondmen and Rebels*; and Reis, *Slave Rebellion in Brazil*. Moreover, in his discussion of the Boca Nigua revolt, David Geggus attempted to place it roughly within a typology of slave rebellions. Geggus, "Slave Resistance in the Spanish Caribbean," 147–49.

7. I thank Laurent Dubois (personal communication, 24 September 2010) for helping me come up with the concept of an invisible emancipation.

8. Schaeffer, "Delayed Cession of Spanish Santo Domingo to France," 51–52.

9. See Ghachem, *Old Regime and the Haitian Revolution*; and Ghachem, "Sovereignty and Slavery."

10. For Saint-Domingue, among the best-known works are James, *Black Jacobins*; Fick, *Making of Haiti*; and Dubois, *Avengers of the New World*. On Guadeloupe, see Dubois, *Colony of Citizens*; and Régent, *Esclavage, métissage, liberté*. David Geggus and Carlos Esteban Deive are among the few scholars who have examined emancipation in

Santo Domingo after 1795. See among other works Geggus, "Slave Resistance in the Spanish Caribbean"; and Deive, *La esclavitud del negro*, chaps. 10 and 19.

11. For such a map, see Curtin, *Rise and Fall of the Plantation Complex*, 159.

12. On Martinique, see Schloss, *Sweet Liberty*; and Geggus, "Slaves and Free Coloreds of Martinique." On Réunion, see Allen, "Constant Demand of the French."

13. Among these works, the ones most directly relevant to this study are Cooper, Scott, and Holt, *Beyond Slavery*; Holt, *Problem of Freedom*; and Ferrer, *Insurgent Cuba*. For the United States, see the successive volumes under the editorship of Ira Berlin, Leslie Rowland, and others, including titles such as Berlin and Harris, *Slavery in New York*; and Berlin, Reidy, and Rowland, *Freedom's Soldiers*.

14. Geggus, "Slave Resistance in the Spanish Caribbean," 140.

15. For succinct accounts of the international political contexts of the upheavals of the late eighteenth and early nineteenth centuries, see Curtin, *Rise and Fall of the Plantation Complex*, chap. 11; and Geggus, *Haitian Revolutionary Studies*, chap. 11.

16. Santo Domingo indeed appears to have attracted a number of French/Dominguan settlers in these years. David Geggus has argued that at the time of the execution of the Boca Nigua ringleaders (December 1796), "French migrants from Saint Domingue . . . outnumbered Spaniards on the [Santo Domingo] city streets." Geggus, "Slave Resistance in the Spanish Caribbean," 146. Furthermore, according to the French General Antoine Chanlatte, many people of "all colors, all principles and all opinions" had immigrated from Saint-Domingue to Santo Domingo partly to escape the turmoil in Saint-Domingue. Report of General Antoine Chanlatte "to the French government and to all of the Friends of National Sovereignty and of order," 20 *Prairial an 8* (9 June 1800), CARAN Colonies CC/9b/2.

17. Report submitted by Roume to "French Government Commission in the [Caribbean] Islands," 1 October 1797, in Rodríguez Demorizi, *Cesión de Santo Domingo a Francia*, 280–81.

18. During the ascendancy and reign of the Jacobins (late 1792 to mid-1794), a radical faction that had formed in 1789, the French National Convention became progressively more radicalized and centralized due to a combination of economic crisis, food shortages, fear of foreign invasion, the rise of charismatic and dogmatic political personalities, internal strife, and other forces. Perhaps most notably, in the famous Vendée rebellion in western France in 1793, a revolutionary army put down a counterrevolutionary movement that rose against military conscription and numerous other grievances. Within this atmosphere of paranoia and suspicion, the Jacobins succeeded in dominating the National Convention at the expense of more moderate factions, such as the Girondins. During the so-called Reign of Terror (September 1793–July 1794), the Jacobins persecuted real and perceived political opponents, suppressed dissent, instituted the new Republican calendar (which briefly replaced the Gregorian one), attacked the Catholic religious establishment, and continued to wage war against foreign enemies. This Jacobin overreach, in combination with infighting, contributed to their fall from power in July 1794. This paved

the way for the rise of the Directory. Neely, *Concise History of the French Revolution*, chap. 8.

19. The enfranchisement of thousands of former slaves by the 1794 emancipation law was an essential factor in the formulation of the doctrine of legal integration. For Anne Pérotin-Dumon, this emancipation edict was the "cornerstone of the assimilationist edifice" of the new French regime. See Pérotin-Dumon, *Être patriote sous les tropiques* (quote is from 19). On "integration" versus "assimilation," see Rogers, "On the Road to Citizenship," 69.

20. Quoted in Dubois, *Avengers of the New World*, 196.

21. On race, slavery, and the law in the eighteenth-century French world, see Peabody, "*There Are No Slaves in France.*"

22. "The Town Council, the President of Justice and the Commandant of the Forces of Santo Domingo" to First Consul Napoleon Bonaparte, 28 April 1800, CARAN Colonies CC/9b/17.

23. Napoleon's Constitution of the Year VIII (promulgated in December 1799) revoked the guarantee of equal rights for the inhabitants of all French domains, proclaiming that the overseas territories would once again be subject to "special laws" based on economic, climatic, and cultural factors. For more on these constitutional and legal changes, see Dubois, *Avengers of the New World*, 241–42; Dubois, *Colony of Citizens*, 352–53; and Schoelcher, *Vie de Toussaint Louverture*, 302.

24. A 29 June 1800 letter conveyed some of the potential implications of the "special laws" for Santo Domingo. Its author, a businessman and legal professional named Cottet, proposed the creation of a "Prefecture" in Santo Domingo, which he claimed was in line with the 1799 French constitution and its "particular laws" for the colonies. According to Cottet, this new prefecture would facilitate the consolidation of French rule in Santo Domingo by means of "rally[ing] around [the prefecture] the rest of the white population." This pointedly exclusionary proposition suggests that the particular laws in Santo Domingo could be seized upon by those who sought to undermine racial equality. Correspondence of Cottet, 29 June 1800, ANOM CMSM F3 202.

25. Julien Raimond to Napoleon, 19 August 1800, CARAN Colonies CC/9b/2.

26. For a copy of this treaty, see Treaty of Basel, 22 July 1795, CARAN AF/III/61; and Vega B., *Los documentos básicos para la historia dominicana*, chap. 10.

27. Peter Sahlins has proposed an "oppositional model of national identity" in which "the proximity of the other across the French-Spanish boundary structured the appearance of national identity long before local society was assimilated to a dominant center." From at least the late eighteenth century, relations between Saint-Domingue/Haiti and Santo Domingo/Dominican Republic often (but by no means always) conformed to this logic, especially on the official level. Sahlins, *Boundaries*, 9.

28. Bourgoiny to Committee of Public Safety, 20 March 1795, CARAN AF/III/61.

29. In an undated refutation of Bourgoiny's claims, an anonymous individual wrote that the Guipozcoans were "the same people" (*le même peuple*) as the French

Basques. "Observations on the Letter of Bourgoiny of 30 Ventôse," CARAN AF/III/61.

30. The Treaty of Basel went through at least one draft before emerging in its final form. Article IX of an initial draft stipulated that both Santo Domingo and Louisiana were to be ceded to France. "Treaty Project between the French Republic and the King of Spain," undated, CARAN AF/III/61. Spain in fact retained Louisiana in 1795 only to formally relinquish this territory to France by a secret treaty signed on 1 October 1800. For a discussion of the importance of developments in Hispaniola for the political status of Louisiana at the turn of the nineteenth century, see Paquette, "Revolutionary Saint Domingue."

31. Roume to Minister of the Navy and Colonies, 31 December 1795, CARAN Colonies CC/9a/20.

32. "Instructions for the Citizen Bourgoiny, Entrusted by the Committee of Public Safety to Negotiate Peace with Spain," 6 May 1795, CARAN AF/III/61. Similarly, the anonymous author of a tract composed in the summer of 1795 on the commercial implications of the peace with Spain preferred the acquisition of Louisiana to that of Santo Domingo because the "free Regime in that colony [Santo Domingo]" made the "provisioning in Blacks" to Santo Domingo next to impossible. Anonymous, "Spain: Commerce, Borders, Alliance," CARAN AF/III/62.

33. In 1789–90, legislators in Paris had voted to replace the old provinces of the ancien régime with new units called *départements*. This reform was meant to create a more rational and uniform administrative system by eliminating overlapping jurisdictions and organizing elections according to a clear hierarchy of municipality, district, and *département*. Neely, *Concise History of the French Revolution*, 97–99.

34. Council of Five Hundred order on administrative reorganization, 9 October 1797, CARAN AD C 518.

35. Council of Five Hundred order on electoral reorganization, 15 January 1798, CARAN AD C 521.

36. French Minister of Foreign Relations to Napoleon, 19 October 1800, CARAN Colonies CC/9b/2.

37. "Report on the Eventual Cession of the Spanish Part of Saint-Domingue to the French Republic," Bourgoiny to Paris, 26 March 1795, CARAN AF/III/61.

38. "Observations on the New Commercial Links between France and Spain," *Thermidor an 3* (19 July–17 August 1795), CARAN AF/III/61.

39. Roume to Minister of the Navy and Colonies, 1 November 1796, CARAN Colonies CC/9a/20.

40. Roume served in both Saint-Domingue and Santo Domingo in a variety of capacities from 1791 to 1801; his colonial experience was a factor in his appointment in 1795 as the Directory's "Particular Agent" in Santo Domingo, where he served for eighteen months. As one of the original civil commissioners sent to Saint-Domingue by the French government in 1791, Roume in a 15 May 1791 letter to Deputy Barnave of the French National Assembly had accepted that body's reaffirmation of

the importance of slavery in the overseas colonies. According to this letter, the fact that nine-tenths of Saint-Domingue's population was enslaved meant that varying "gradations" (*grades*) between white and slave ought to exist, such that people who were at least three "degrees" removed from African ancestry should be able to claim a "white" racial status. Roume to Barnave, 15 May 1791, CARAN W 13. Though Roume's racial views later became more egalitarian, a distinct undercurrent of racial differentiation continued to exist in his correspondence.

41. Scattered revolts broke out in Hincha (in 1793) and in Samaná (May 1795). Reports by Spanish authorities who arrested several insurgents in Hincha alleged that the example of Saint-Domingue had helped to inspire the uprising. See Geggus, "Slave Resistance in the Spanish Caribbean," esp. 140–41. On the 1795 uprising, see Joaquín García to Alange, 17 May 1795, AGS GM 7160, f. 126; and Carlos Esteban Deive's account in *La esclavitud del negro*, 471.

42. Roume portrayed the Boca Nigua rebels as having been "indoctrinated" by three former companions of Jean-François, though rumors abounded that other individuals from Saint-Domingue or even the British might also have helped to incite these *cultivateurs* to revolt. "Order" of Roume, 29 December 1796, ANOM CMSM F3 200. Judge Bravo asserted that his forces had arrested and detained "3 brigands of Jean-François" near the Boca Nigua plantation. Bravo y Bermudez to García, 14 December 1796, ANOM CMSM F3 200.

43. In his report on Boca Nigua, Roume praised the Spanish officials who put down the revolt for enabling the "conservation" of the colony for the French, who would soon take (effective) possession of Santo Domingo. "Order" of Roume, 29 December 1796, ANOM CMSM F3 200.

44. Ibid. Roume's references to "Haiti" several years before that country's birth are a source of curiosity for some scholars. For details, see Geggus, *Haitian Revolutionary Studies*, 212–16.

45. The Boca Nigua revolt did in fact share some features with plantation uprisings that occurred in revolutionary Saint-Domingue, which I discuss in chapter 3.

46. "Instructions to the French Government Agent in the Spanish Part of the Island, Roume," 24 December 1795, in Rodríguez Demorizi, *Cesión de Santo Domingo a Francia*, 29–36.

47. The wording of the relevant part of the treaty is as follows: "The inhabitants of the Spanish part of Saint-Domingue who, by motives of [self-] interest or others, would prefer to transport themselves with their goods in the possessions of His [Spanish] Catholic Majesty will be able to do so within one year after the date of this treaty." Treaty of Basel, 22 July 1795, CARAN AF/III/61.

48. Roume, "Reflections on the Report of Regnier," 30 September 1795, CARAN AF/II/64. In the 25 September 1795 report referenced and rebutted by Roume in his 30 September correspondence, Adjutant-General L. Regnier had defended the alleged right of Dominicans to emigrate with their "slaves" per the Treaty of Basel while also proposing the deployment of several French "commissioners" to Santo Domingo

to "prepare [the colony's inhabitants] to enjoy the Benefits of liberty." Adjutant-General L. Regnier, "Report on the Island of St Domingue for the Spanish Part Presented to the Committee of Public Safety Section of Foreign Affairs," 25 September 1795, CARAN AF/II/64.

49. Popkin, *You Are All Free*, 19. On conflicting rights claims in the Haitian Revolutionary era, see among other works R. Scott, "Paper Thin."

50. Roume to Minister of the Navy and Colonies, 24 January 1796, CARAN Colonies CC/9a/20.

51. Vice Admiral Truguet to Committee of Public Safety, "approved" by the Committee on 11 September 1795, CARAN AF/III/61.

52. Laveaux to García, *Brumaire an 4* (23 October–21 November 1795), AGI ASD 1033.

53. There is an extensive literature on slavery and emancipation in colonial Spanish America. Some recent contributions that discuss questions concerning manumission are Landers, "Maroon Women in Spanish America"; Restall, *Beyond Black and Red*; and Fuente, "Slaves and the Creation of Legal Rights."

54. García to Laveaux, 19 December 1795, AGI ASD 1033.

55. García to "Prince of Peace" [Godoy], 7 December 1795, in Rodríguez Demorizi, *Cesión de Santo Domingo a Francia*, 26–27. According to David Geggus, though French Republican authorities in Santo Domingo toward the end of 1795 distributed copies of the prior year's emancipation edict and affirmed the abolition of slavery on the entire island, these measures only had a limited effect. Geggus, "Slave Resistance in the Spanish Caribbean," 140.

56. "Discourse on the Modification, and Limits of Slavery, Formed by D[on] Josef Antonio de Urízar of the Supreme Council of the Indies . . ." 25 June 1795, AGI ASD 1032. Much of this liberationist language also echoed the *Siete Partidas*, a thirteenth-century Spanish law code that constituted the foundation of slave law (and much else) in colonial Spanish America. I discuss the *Partidas* and their importance in Santo Domingo in further detail later in this book.

57. "The Commission Delegated by the French Government to the [Caribbean] Islands" to the Minister of the Navy and Colonies, 26 December 1796, CARAN Colonies CC/9a/11.

58. "Descriptive Report concerning the Spanish Part of St Domingue as well as [the] French [part]," submitted by Jean-Baptiste Formy to the Minister of the Navy and Colonies, *an* 5 (22 September 1796–21 September 1797), CARAN Colonies CC/9a/15.

59. Laveaux to "Commander in Gonaïves," undated, CARAN Colonies CC/9a/20.

60. Roume to "his colleagues the commissioners delegated by the French government in the [Caribbean] islands," 5 August 1796, CARAN Colonies CC/9a/11.

61. Anonymous, "Notes" on Hispaniola, undated, CARAN AF/III/63.

62. Proclamation of Sonthonax, 3 June 1796, ANOM CMSM F3 200. On the political and social importance of translation between French and Kreyòl in the creation of such documents, see Joseph-Gabriel, "Creolizing Freedom."

63. On the relationship between these new economic theories and abolitionist thought, see Dorigny, *Anti-esclavagisme, abolitionnisme et abolitions*, esp. 17–19.

64. Holt, *Problem of Freedom*, xviii.

65. Municipal administration of Le Cap to Sonthonax, 21 August 1797, CARAN Colonies CC/9a/15.

66. Popkin, *You Are All Free*, 360–61.

67. Roume to Francisco Gascue, 24 December 1795, CARAN Colonies CC/9a/20.

68. Hédouville was a veteran French military officer who had arrived on the island earlier in 1798. He carried orders from Paris to retake control of Saint-Domingue from Toussaint Louverture and André Rigaud, allies-turned-rivals who dominated the island's politics in the second half of the 1790s. Dubois, *Avengers of the New World*, 217. See chapter 3 of the present work for more details on Toussaint and Rigaud.

69. "Order Concerning Establishments formed on the Border that Separates the Former Spanish Part from the French Part of St-Domingue, by Citizens Who Have Not Been Authorized There," 21 July 1798, CARAN Colonies CC/9a/18.

70. Toussaint to Roume, 19 October 1799, CARAN Colonies CC/9a/26. In his attempts to restrict travel between the two parts of the island, Toussaint decreed that such travel required a special passport, which cost more than one that only permitted travel within Saint-Domingue. Regulation of Toussaint Louverture, 15 May 1800, ANOM CMSM F3 202.

71. Moïse to Roume, 14 October 1799, CARAN Colonies CC/9a/26.

72. Ayers, *In the Presence of Mine Enemies*, xix. For a discussion of cross-border slaving and the dilemma of arming slaves in the U.S. Civil War grounded in these same border communities, see Ayers, Thomas, and Rubin, "Black and on the Border."

73. François-Thomas Galbaud, the French governor-general who was involved in the conflict that destroyed Le Cap in June 1793, had contemplated invading Spanish Santo Domingo with a black army and then rewarding these warriors with land in that colony in order to preserve the white-owned plantations in French Saint-Domingue. Popkin, *You Are All Free*, 208.

74. For a discussion of one case involving seven slaves from Jamaica who escaped to abolitionist Haiti in 1817 and its implications for questions of nationality and citizenship in Haiti and the Atlantic World, see Ferrer, "Haiti, Free Soil, and Antislavery."

75. Renault, "Les conditions d'affranchissements," 4. According to Sue Peabody, in suits for freedom brought by Dominguan migrants claimed as slaves in Pennsylvania and Maryland from 1794 to 1808, these purported slaves' lawyers "apparently ignored the cataclysmic innovation of the French and Haitian Revolutions: the emancipation of all slaves" in 1793–94. Peabody, " 'Free upon Higher Ground,' " 268.

76. "Military Reconnaissance of the Four Districts of Ajabon, Saint Yago, Porto-Plate and Montechrist, as well as of the Portion of the Coast that Extends from Fort-Liberté to Porto-Plate Inclusively, Followed by a Project [for] a Defensive System for this Extent of the Coast and of the Country," *Messidor an* 5 (19 June–18 July 1797), ANOM DFC 5, no. 910. Vincent was a veteran French colonial authority who would

later serve as one of Napoleon's main informants on the situation in Hispaniola. He had served in Saint-Domingue since 1786 and became one of Toussaint Louverture's most trusted allies. Bell, *Toussaint Louverture*, 218. For more on Vincent, see Schneider, "Le colonel Vincent."

77. "Reflections of Political Economy on the Three Spanish Jurisdictions of Montechrist, San Yago and Port de Plata, Relative to their Reunion with the [French] Republic," undated, ANOM DFC 5, no. 914.

78. Urízar to Amirola, 12 December 1795, AGI ASD 1033.

79. Trouillot, *Silencing the Past*, chap. 3.

80. Roume to Municipal Administration of Montechristi, 22 March 1800, CARAN Colonies CC/9b/17.

81. Marquis d'Iranda to Perregaux, 26 June 1800, CARAN Colonies CC/9b/17.

82. "Précis on the Current Position of Saint Domingue and the Provisional Measures to Take," undated, CARAN Colonies CC/9a/32.

83. Dubois, *Avengers of the New World*, 222.

84. Étienne Albert to Moïse, 12 September 1798, CARAN Colonies CC/9a/23.

85. Moïse to Hédouville, 9 October 1798, CARAN Colonies CC/9a/23.

86. *Maniel* had been a general term used by Dominican administrators to refer to fugitive slave enclaves; a 1784 slave code for Santo Domingo, for instance, had referred to *"Manieles"* in its section on runaway slaves. Barceló, *Código Negro Carolino*, 233. In the revolutionary era, the term became associated with this one specific enclave.

87. "Order of the Provisional Agent in the Spanish Part of St Domingue on the Independent Blacks . . . of Maniel," 16 August 1796, ANOM CMSM F3 200. A copy of this order is preserved in CARAN Colonies CC/9a/11.

88. Minuty to Minister of the Navy and Colonies, undated, CARAN Colonies CC/9a/21.

89. In *Les marrons de la liberté*, Jean Fouchard argued that maroons played a prominent role in the 1791 slave uprising. Gabriel Debien in *Les esclaves aux Antilles françaises* by contrast downplayed the importance of maroons in this event. For a succinct overview of this historiographical debate, see Fick, *Making of Haiti*, 5–9. David Geggus in *Haitian Revolutionary Studies* (46) called Maniel an "important test case" in determining the precise "connection between marronage [slave flight] and revolution in Saint Domingue."

90. The French *Code Noir* of 1685 had stipulated that a "fugitive slave" shall suffer bodily mutilation for the first two offenses and death for the third. Article XXXVIII of the *Code Noir*, in Sala-Molins, *Le Code Noir*, 166. The Spanish *Código Negro* (Black Code) of 1784 likewise prescribed corporal punishments for enslaved fugitives, levying harsher penalties on those who had joined maroon communities than on those who had not. Barceló, *Código Negro Carolino*, 231–36.

91. "Order of the Provisional Agent on the Independent Blacks of Maniel," 16 August 1796, ANOM CMSM F3 200.

92. Roume to Bobadilla, 16 August 1796, CARAN Colonies CC/9a/11. Emphasis mine.

93. Bobadilla to Don Antonio Porlier, 25 January 1790, AGI ASD 1102.

94. Report of Juan Caballero, 8 February 1811, AGI ASD 1042. According to Carlos Esteban Deive, "French" slaves had constituted much of the population of Maniel before the Haitian Revolution, and after the August 1791 slave uprising in Saint-Domingue, the migration of enslaved Dominguans to this community became even more pronounced. This compelled Governor García and other Spanish authorities to attempt to secure San Cristóbal del Naranjo against the numerous French slaves who sought refuge in Maniel. Deive, *Los cimarrones del Maniel de Neiba*, 68–69.

95. J. Rey-Delmas to Minister of the Navy and Colonies, 5 January 1798, CARAN Colonies CC/9a/19.

96. It is no accident that in his 1937 massacre of thousands of ethnic Haitians, the Dominican dictator Rafael Trujillo targeted the "bicultural frontier" between the two countries, in Richard Turits's words. On the massacre and its effects, see Turits, *Foundations of Despotism*, chap. 5 (quote is from 174); Turits, "World Destroyed, Nation Imposed"; and Turits and Derby, "Historias de terror y los terrores de la historia."

97. Indeed, the case of Maniel seems to support Malick Ghachem's emphasis on "a long eighteenth-century continuity between the colonial and revolutionary periods of Haitian history" that underlies *The Old Regime and the Haitian Revolution* (quote is from 4).

Chapter Three

1. I am grateful to John Garrigus (personal communication, 22 October 2010) for assistance on this point.

2. Toussaint to Hédouville, 5 September 1798, CARAN Colonies CC/9a/23.

3. The erosion of revolution in France in the latter half of the 1790s was the result of multiple forces. The fall of the radical Jacobins in Paris and the rise to power of first the Directory and then the Consulate (the regime that Napoleon instituted in 1799) represented transitions to progressively more conservative regimes. Furthermore, according to many accounts of the Haitian Revolution, the so-called planter lobby steadily gained influence in French metropolitan politics during these years and worked tirelessly to undermine emancipation. See Dubois, *Colony of Citizens*, chap. 14 (esp. 347–53). For an interpretation that downplays the role of the planter lobby in French colonial politics, see Girard, "Napoleon Bonaparte"; and Girard, *Slaves Who Defeated Napoléon*, chap. 2.

4. Treaty of *Bâle* (Basel), 22 July 1795, CARAN AF/III/61.

5. Spanish Ambassador del Campo to French Minister of Foreign Relations, 23 May 1797, CARAN AF/III/62.

6. Bell, *Toussaint Louverture*, 143.

7. Neely, *Concise History of the French Revolution*, 233–37.

8. Schroeder, *Transformation of European Politics*, 162–63.

9. See Fick, *Making of Haiti*, 196.

10. See the long report "on the Open Campaign [on] 13 Pluviôse Year 6 [1 February 1798] Against the Enemies of the French Republic by the Army of St Domingue," 1 February 1798, CARAN Colonies CC/9a/19.

11. David Geggus concludes that Toussaint had 20,000 men serving under him around early 1797. Geggus, *Slavery, War and Revolution*, 221. In a 5 May 1797 letter to the "Captain General of the Province of Venezuela," Agent Roume asserted that Toussaint led a force of 15,000 to 18,000 "Africans" who were "as disciplined and subordinated as the best European troops." Roume to "Captain General of the Province of Venezuela," 5 May 1797, CARAN Colonies CC/9a/20.

12. On this offer of freedom for military service, see "Proclamation of Thomas Brisbane commanding for his Majesty . . . at St Marc, L'Arcahaye, and their dependencies," 7 August 1794, ANOM CMSM F3 199.

13. Geggus, "Arming of Slaves in the Haitian Revolution," 225–26. Geggus estimated that approximately 6,000 former slaves served in this "black corps" on the eve of the British evacuation from the island in July 1798. Geggus, *Slavery, War and Revolution*, 315.

14. This figure is from Geggus, *Slavery, War and Revolution*, 291. It is Geggus's estimate of the enslaved population under the British on the island just before the spring of 1797.

15. On this racism, see Dubois, *Avengers of the New World*, 181–83.

16. According to Geggus, by March 1798, numerous soldiers from the British "black corps" had deserted to the French side. For instance, in the Arcahaye plain, more than 300 enslaved troops left the British to join Toussaint's ranks. Geggus, *Slavery, War and Revolution*, 375–76. See also Dubois, *Avengers of the New World*, 215–17.

17. Report on "the Expedition of the Division General Toussaint Louverture, in Mirebalais," 9 April 1797, CARAN Colonies CC/9a/15.

18. Rochambeau to Sonthonax, 28 June 1796, CARAN Colonies CC/9a/15.

19. Statement of Roume, 17 September 1796, CARAN Colonies CC/9a/12.

20. Geggus, *Slavery, War and Revolution*, 183.

21. Toussaint to the "Commandant for the King of Spain in Banique [Bánica]," 31 July 1796, CARAN Colonies CC/9a/12.

22. Toussaint to [name illegible], 28 July 1796, CARAN Colonies CC/9a/12. In an 11 April 1797 proclamation to the residents of Bánica, Las Caobas, San Juan, and Neyba, Toussaint depicted the English as the "common enemies" of the Spanish and the French. "Proclamation of the Division General Toussaint Louverture . . ." 11 April 1797, CARAN Colonies CC/9a/12.

23. Moïse to Toussaint, "Report on the Unfortunate Events [that have] Taken Place in Fort-Liberté on the 23rd, 24th and 25th of Vendémiaire, Year 7 of the French Republic [14, 15, and 16 October 1798]," 14–16 October 1798, CARAN AF/III/210.

24. Commissioners' order on Montechristi and Dajabón, 20 July 1797, ANOM CMSM F3 201; Schaeffer, "Delayed Cession of Spanish Santo Domingo to France," 55. In a 24 May 1797 proclamation to the residents of Las Caobas, Neyba, Bánica, and San Juan de la Maguana, Toussaint ordered a similar type of reorganization in these areas that he had recently taken from the British. Proclamation of Toussaint, 24 May 1797, CARAN Colonies CC/9a/11.

25. "Attack Plan for the Brigade Generals Moyse and Dessalines," 28 January 1798, CARAN Colonies CC/9a/19.

26. Report submitted to Toussaint on the military situation in Mirebalais and environs, *Germinal an 6* (21 March–19 April 1798), CARAN Colonies CC/9a/19.

27. Cartographic evidence suggests that Hincha was an important border area. One map of the island from the 1770s placed Hincha within a zone that was in dispute between France and Spain. ANOM *Atlas Moreau de St-Méry* F3 296, no. A5. Another map from Year 11 (September 1802–September 1803) included Hincha as part of the "Isle of Saint-Domingue" without a demarcation of the old colonial border. ANOM *Atlas Moreau de St-Méry* F3 289, no. 42.

28. This figure is from Dubois, *Colony of Citizens*, 224.

29. Toussaint to Roume, 4 March 1798, CARAN Colonies CC/9a/18.

30. Louverture, *Memoir of General Toussaint Louverture*, 151–53. In my citations to this source, I rely upon Girard's translations of the original manuscript.

31. On Toussaint's diplomacy, see Bell, *Toussaint Louverture*, 157–60; Dubois, *Avengers of the New World*, 215–26; and Girard, "Black Talleyrand."

32. Toussaint Louverture, "Continuation of the address of the general in chief, TOUSSAINT LOUVERTURE, to all good Frenchmen, to true and sincere friends of liberty, to all its defenders," in 4 January 1799 edition of *Le Citoyen Véridique: Gazette du Port-Républicain*, ANOM CMSM F3 202. Emphasis in original.

33. The term *anciens libres* ("formerly free") generally referred to persons of African descent who either had been born free or had acquired their liberty before the Revolution, while the term *nouveaux libres* ("newly free") indicated those who had gained their freedom in the 1793–94 general emancipations. The most concise overview of the political legacies of these divisions for independent Haiti is Trouillot, *Haiti, State against Nation*. Laurent Dubois cautions against interpreting this war as simply a conflict between these two groups, as many "free-coloreds and whites" fought under Louverture, while a number of "ex-slave leaders" were loyal to Rigaud. Dubois, *Avengers of the New World*, 232.

34. For more details on Rigaud, see Dubois, *Avengers of the New World*, 119 and 196–97; and Fick, *Making of Haiti*, 119–21.

35. Dubois, *Avengers of the New World*, 197; Garrigus, "Blue and Brown"; and Garrigus, *Before Haiti*, introduction.

36. Report to Minister of the Navy and Colonies, 13 August 1800, CARAN Colonies CC/9b/18.

37. Pluchon, *Toussaint Louverture: Un révolutionnaire noir d'ancien régime*, 290–91. In a 26 April 1800 report, Charles Vincent insisted that the "surest means" to end the fratricidal conflict would be the swift deployment of a force of 1,200 to 1,500 men on three warships to Rigaud's stronghold of Jacmel through Santo Domingo city, which was the only port suitable for provisioning these men and preparing them for battle. Vincent, "Considerations on the Means of Ending the Civil War in St-Domingue," 26 April 1800, CARAN Colonies CC/9b/17.

38. Anonymous report on military events in Hispaniola, 19 October 1800, CARAN Colonies CC/9a/28.

39. Rigaud to Someruelos, 30 June 1800, AGI Cuba 1709.

40. Vázquez Cienfuegos, *Tan difíciles tiempos para Cuba*, 50.

41. Girard, *Slaves Who Defeated Napoléon*, 5.

42. For more details on Toussaint's Clause, see Bell, *Toussaint Louverture*, 170–71; and Brown, *Toussaint's Clause*.

43. Report of General Antoine Chanlatte "to the French government and to all of the Friends of National Sovereignty and of order," 9 June 1800, CARAN Colonies CC/9b/2. For a discussion of questions of formal sovereignty versus effective control as concerns independent Haiti, see Gaffield, " 'So Many Schemes in Agitation,' " esp. chap. 3.

44. For a discussion of the importance of diplomacy and foreign policy in the War of the South, see Girard, "Black Talleyrand," 102–10.

45. Dubois, *Avengers of the New World*, 234–36.

46. Chanlatte to Minister of the Navy, 20 June 1800, CARAN Colonies CC/9a/24.

47. François Kerverseau had several tours of duty in Santo Domingo in the revolutionary period. For an overview of Kerverseau's career and a transcription of one of his correspondences regarding Toussaint, see Pluchon, *Toussaint Louverture d'après le général de Kerverseau*.

48. Kerverseau to Minister of the Navy and Colonies, 19 February 1799, CARAN Colonies CC/9b/23.

49. Report to "Consuls of the Republic," *Vendémiaire an 9* (23 September–22 October 1800), CARAN Colonies CC/9b/18.

50. For more on Toussaint's labor regimes, see chapter 4 of the present work and Fick, "Emancipation in Haiti."

51. In a 2 December 1801 letter to the minister of the navy, Roume, writing from exile in Philadelphia, related that he had predicted an "explosion of discontent" on the part of the "blacks" against the "so-called governor Toussaint Louverture." Roume to Minister of the Navy and Colonies, 2 December 1801, CARAN Colonies CC/9b/2. In October 1801, Toussaint put down several plantation uprisings in Saint-Domingue's north, which he blamed on Moïse. This led to Toussaint's execution of Moïse in November of that year. For details on these events, see Dubois, *Avengers of the New World*, 247–48.

52. Following his 1796–97 campaign in Italy, Napoleon undertook an expedition into Egypt in 1798. Though the expedition met with mixed success, it further enhanced Bonaparte's standing and helped to enable his accession to supreme political power in 1799. See Englund, *Napoleon: A Political Life*, 126–40.

53. On Napoleon's rise and fall, see ibid. For a reexamination of the political, legal, and social legacies of Napoleon's European conquests, see Schroeder, *Transformation of European Politics*, esp. chap. 8.

54. In a report to the minister of the navy composed on the eve of Toussaint's conquest of Santo Domingo city, one Saint-Domingue official wrote that the attempts of Toussaint and other "black leaders" to recruit soldiers in Santo Domingo would become frustrated by the fact that the colony contained "only three thousand black slaves, including women, the elderly and children." Saint-Domingue official [name illegible] to Minister of the Navy and Colonies, 16 November 1800, CARAN Colonies CC/9b/18.

55. Dubois, *Avengers of the New World*, 241.

56. Moreau de St Méry, *Description topographique et politique de la partie espagnole*, 2:191.

57. Chanlatte to Minister of the Navy, 20 June 1800, CARAN Colonies CC/9a/24.

58. Report to Minister of the Navy and Colonies, 13 August 1800, CARAN Colonies CC/9b/18.

59. Anonymous report from Baltimore, 30 September 1800, CARAN Colonies CC/9b/2.

60. Cordero Michel, "Toussaint en Saint-Domingue espagnol," 252. On page 255, Cordero Michel claimed that Toussaint's rule in Santo Domingo created a "democratic fervor" and a "democratic period without precedent." In *La Revolución haitiana y Santo Domingo*, 60–61, Cordero Michel contended that under Toussaint's regime "the immense majority of the population of Spanish Santo Domingo lived under a democratic climate and a prosperity never known in its history."

61. James, *Black Jacobins*, 237–40; and Dubois, *Avengers of the New World*, 236–38.

62. Fick, *Making of Haiti*, 204–6.

63. Bell, *Toussaint Louverture*, 186–87.

64. Girard, *Slaves Who Defeated Napoléon*, 42.

65. Chanlatte to Minister of the Navy, 20 June 1800, CARAN Colonies CC/9a/24.

66. Toussaint to Roume, 29 October 1799, CARAN Colonies CC/9a/23. On this slaving, see Bell, *Toussaint Louverture*, 93; and Dubois, *Avengers of the New World*, 237.

67. Roume to Someruelos, 23 February 1800, CARAN Colonies CC/9b/1.

68. Toussaint to Roume, 18 January 1800, CARAN Colonies CC/9b/1. Numerous other letters by Toussaint to Roume and others also attest to the black general's declared intention to halt this slaving. In one letter to Roume dated 26 February 1800, for instance, Toussaint denounced the "freedom-killing commerce" (*commerce liberticide*) that existed in Santo Domingo. Toussaint to Roume, 26 February 1800, CARAN Colonies CC/9b/1.

69. On this point I am influenced by Philippe Girard's argument that "in Louverture's mind international diplomacy and Saint Domingue's political and social developments did not operate on separate planes but were instead interwoven.... Louverture's desire for self-preservation might seem crassly self-serving, but he saw himself and the future of emancipation as inextricably linked. His continued tenure as governor of Saint Domingue was in his eyes not only a matter of personal survival but also a guarantee of freedom for the entire black population of the island." Girard, "Black Talleyrand," 91.

70. Chanlatte to Roume, 21 January 1800, CARAN Colonies CC/9b/1.

71. Scholarship on the histories of race in France and the Francophone world is steadily expanding. For notable recent contributions, see Chapman and Frader, *Race in France*; and Nasiali, "Native to the Republic."

72. Toussaint's attention to legal protocol attests to Malick Ghachem's assertion that "the forms and rituals of law gave shape and content to the [Haitian] Revolution"; indeed, Ghachem cites Toussaint's 1801 constitution (discussed in chapter 4 of the present work) in support of this claim. Ghachem, *Old Regime and the Haitian Revolution*, 214.

73. In a 27 April 1800 letter to General Chanlatte, Toussaint argued that he was deploying General Pierre Agé to Santo Domingo to "make the necessary arrangements for this taking of possession" of Santo Domingo in accordance with the "peace treaty drawn up between this power [France] and the King of Spain." Toussaint to Chanlatte, 27 April 1800, CARAN Colonies CC/9b/18.

74. Roume to Toussaint, 24 January 1800, CARAN Colonies CC/9b/1; Chanlatte to Minister of the Navy, 20 June 1800, CARAN Colonies CC/9a/24.

75. Kerverseau, "Report on the former Spanish part," 13 August 1801, RPUF no. 77.

76. Antoine Chanlatte, "Historical Summary of the Deeds that Preceded the Invasion of the Territory of the Former Spanish Part of Saint-Domingue by Toussaint Louverture," 28 May 1801, CARAN Colonies CC/9b/18.

77. Chanlatte to the French government, 9 June 1800, CARAN Colonies CC/9b/2.

78. Secretary-General of the Agency of the French Government in Saint-Domingue to Minister of the Navy and Colonies, 3 August 1801, CARAN Colonies CC/9b/2.

79. Chanlatte to the French government, 9 June 1800, CARAN Colonies CC/9b/2.

80. Girard, "Black Talleyrand," 112.

81. Petition to Joaquín García, 22 July 1800, in Rodríguez Demorizi, *Cesión de Santo Domingo a Francia*, 552–53.

82. Chanlatte, "Historical Summary," 28 May 1801, CARAN Colonies CC/9b/18.

83. Spanish Ambassador to French Minister of Foreign Relations, 2 December 1800, CARAN Colonies CC/9b/2.

84. Dubois, *Colony of Citizens*, 300–304 (quote is from 301).

85. Ibid., 304; Hédouville to Paris, 31 March 1798, ANOM CMSM F3 201.

86. Julien Raimond to Roume, 12 August 1796, CARAN Colonies CC/9a/12.

87. Roume to "his colleagues on the Commission delegated by the French Government in the [Caribbean] Islands," 18 August 1796, CARAN Colonies CC/9a/11.

88. Charles Vincent, "Reflections on Political Economy concerning the three Spanish Jurisdictions of Montecrist, San-Yago and Porto de Plata, relative to their reunion with the [French] Republic," ANOM DFC 5, no. 913.

89. French Dominguan officials' delineations between "French" and "Spanish" blacks dated back to at least the late seventeenth century. In August 1687, Pierre-Paul Tarin de Cussy, the governor of French Saint-Domingue, had contended that "free Spanish mulattos and blacks" were "so many enemies that we keep among us" due to their "libertinage" that might sow dissension or worse among the enslaved population in the French colony. Quoted in Ghachem, *Old Regime and the Haitian Revolution*, 56. I am grateful to Ghachem and Richard Turits for sharing with me a transcription of this August 1687 report.

90. Toussaint to Chanlatte, 27 April 1800, CARAN Colonies CC/9b/18. A copy of this letter exists in CARAN Colonies CC/9a/26. See also Bell, *Toussaint Louverture*, 182.

91. Stevens to Pickering, 28 May 1800, CARAN 208 Mi 1.

92. French Minister of Foreign Relations to Napoleon, 19 October 1800, CARAN Colonies CC/9b/2.

93. Report of Minister of the Navy and Colonies, 30 January 1823, CARAN Colonies CC/9a/54.

94. Lacroix, *La Révolution d'Haïti*, 253. Scholars have offered a variety of estimates of the total number of troops whom Toussaint commanded around this time and the number who participated in his invasion of Santo Domingo city. Emilio Cordero Michel claimed that Toussaint led 20,000 men into Santo Domingo in 1801. Cordero Michel, "Toussaint en Saint-Domingue espagnol," 252. According to Victor Schoelcher, Toussaint commanded 15,000 men at the time of his defeat of Rigaud in mid-1800. Schoelcher, *Vie de Toussaint Louverture*, 293. Pierre Pluchon, moreover, asserted that 25,000 men served under Toussaint around late 1801. Pluchon, "Toussaint Louverture défie Bonaparte," 175. According to Dubois, Toussaint had 23,000 to 30,000 men as of early 1802. Dubois, *Avengers of the New World*, 262.

95. Bell, *Toussaint Louverture*, 190.

96. Pluchon, *Toussaint Louverture: Un révolutionnaire noir d'ancien régime*, 293.

97. "Proclamation" of Toussaint to the "municipal administrations of the colony [Santo Domingo] and to his co-citizens," 5 February 1801, CARAN Colonies CC/9b/9.

98. "Summary of the Reports on the French Part and the Spanish Part of St-Domingue," submitted by Kerverseau to Minister of the Navy and Colonies, 8 September or 12 September 1801, CARAN Colonies CC/9b/23.

99. In 1821, two Dominican movements arose whose leaders advocated separation from Spain. One group, comprised largely of nonwhites, proposed unification with Haiti, which they hoped would lead to the abolition of slavery and greater social

equality. Another, more conservative, faction perceived the Spanish colonial state to be incapable of maintaining order or creating a prosperous economy, which led them to support a break with Spain but to oppose unification with Haiti. Divisions between these two groups helped to enable the Haitian regime of Jean-Pierre Boyer to annex Santo Domingo in 1822. Turits, *Foundations of Despotism*, 44.

100. Chanlatte, "Historical Summary," 28 May 1801, CARAN Colonies CC/9b/18.

101. As quoted in Roederer, *Journal du Comte P.-L. Roederer*, 15–16.

102. "Secret Instructions for General Cambis," 14 January 1801, in *Correspondance de Napoléon Ier*, 6:573 (document no. 5293).

Chapter Four

1. On the role of Hispaniola and the Caribbean in the French and Haitian Revolutionary era's conflicts over liberty, equality, and citizenship, see among other works Dubois, *Avengers of the New World*; Dubois, *Colony of Citizens*; and Knight, "Haitian Revolution and the Notion of Human Rights."

2. Girard, "Black Talleyrand," 92.

3. While the pioneer of modern Haitian Revolutionary scholarship in English, C. L. R. James, famously portrayed Toussaint as a tragic hero undone by his inability to effectively respond to the concerns of the ex-slaves, historian Pierre Pluchon has been far more strident in his critiques of this leader. Some other scholars have attempted more balanced depictions, highlighting both Toussaint's commitment to general emancipation and his Machiavellianism, ruthlessness, and authoritarian governing style. See among other works James, *Black Jacobins*; Pluchon, *Toussaint Louverture: De l'esclavage au pouvoir*; Pluchon, *Toussaint Louverture: Un révolutionnaire noir d'ancien régime*; Bell, *Toussaint Louverture*; Geggus, *Haitian Revolutionary Studies*, esp. chap. 8; Dubois, *Avengers of the New World*; and Fick, *Making of Haiti*.

4. Nonetheless, those scholars who have addressed Toussaint's occupation of Santo Domingo have often focused on the question of whether he abolished slavery there. For example, Dubois in *Avengers of the New World* (236–38) asserted that Toussaint "envisioned a process of gradual emancipation as the ideal" for Santo Domingo and that for the colony's purported slaves, "[Toussaint's] occupation of 1801 seems not to have brought immediate liberty." Writing in the early twentieth century, Adolphe Cabon reached a somewhat similar conclusion. He contended that although "liberty was given" to "all of the slaves" in Santo Domingo upon Toussaint's invasion, these newly freed persons' "condition was not by that [measure] notably changed, as they continued to depend on their former masters." Cabon, *Histoire d'Haïti*, 4:152. See also Girard, "Black Talleyrand," 110–12.

5. See Turits, *Foundations of Despotism*.

6. Toussaint's memoir suggests that the reimposition of the "particular laws" principle influenced the drafting of his constitution. In this memoir, the general wrote:

"Seeing that the [metropolitan] government was not sending laws or decrees, . . . I invited all the city councils to summon an assembly to appoint deputies" to a constitutional assembly. This assembly was to "make laws specific to the country, advantageous for the government, and useful to everyone's interests: laws based on customs, and the character of the inhabitants of the colony, and the areas of the country." Louverture, *Memoir of General Toussaint Louverture*, 143–45.

7. Some of the best-known works that discuss this subject include Holt, *Problem of Freedom*; R. Scott, *Slave Emancipation in Cuba*; and R. Scott, *Degrees of Freedom*. See also Trouillot, *Haiti, State against Nation*, esp. chap. 1; and Mintz, *Three Ancient Colonies*. For a pioneering article on these matters, see Mintz, "Slavery and the Rise of Peasantries," 213–42.

8. Holt, *Problem of Freedom*, xxi–xxii.

9. "Proclamation" of Toussaint to Santo Domingo inhabitants, 4 January 1801, CARAN Colonies CC/9b/9.

10. Ibid.

11. Illustrative of this is a 20 December 1801 proclamation to the "inhabitants of the colony" of Saint-Domingue in which Toussaint promised to "respect persons and properties" while working for the "triumph of liberty and the prosperity of this island." See Toussaint's address to the inhabitants of Saint-Domingue, in Pluchon, "Toussaint Louverture défie Bonaparte," 173–74.

12. Fick, "Emancipation in Haiti," 23.

13. In a 10 September 1801 order, Toussaint authorized Santo Domingo city authorities to appoint priests to the Santiago area and mandated the creation of four new parishes. Toussaint order on religious organization in Santiago de los Caballeros, 10 September 1801, CARAN Colonies CC/9b/9.

14. Report submitted from Caracas by Pons, "Judge of the Peace and of [Ship] Captures in Santo Domingo," to Minister of the Navy and Colonies, 10 or 18 May 1801, CARAN Colonies CC/9b/18.

15. Order of Toussaint on nocturnal dances, 4 January 1800, CARAN Colonies CC/9b/9. This measure built on ancien régime precedents, such as a "Police Ordinance" for Saint-Domingue dated 7 September 1774 that had prohibited "all nocturnal assemblies and dances or Calindas among the people of Color and free blacks." "Police Ordinance concerning dances and assemblies of blacks and other people of color," 7 September 1774, ANOM CMSM F3 273.

16. Chanlatte to Minister of the Navy, 20 June 1800, CARAN Colonies CC/9a/24.

17. Ibid.

18. See "Descriptive Report concerning the Spanish Part of St Domingue as well as [the] French [part]," submitted by Jean-Baptiste Formy to the Minister of the Navy and Colonies, *an* 5 (22 September 1796 to 21 September 1797), CARAN Colonies CC/9a/15.

19. According to Carolyn Fick, Toussaint increased Saint-Domingue's coffee exports by 1801 to more than twenty times their nadir in 1795 and boosted sugar exports

to more than ten times their 1795 level by 1801. Fick, "Emancipation in Haiti," 27–28. Furthermore, British consul general Charles Mackenzie informed Secretary George Canning on 9 September 1826 that Toussaint had raised agricultural revenue in Saint-Domingue from 8,606,720 *livres* in 1796 to 46,266,300 *livres* in 1802, roughly a fivefold increase. This latter figure, according to Mackenzie, represented a quarter of the colony's 1789 revenue. Mackenzie to Canning, 9 September 1826, CARAN Colonies CC/9a/54. Madison Smartt Bell claims that Toussaint managed to almost double the colony's coffee exports between 1799 and 1801 and to increase cotton and brown sugar exports by a notable margin during those same years. Bell, *Toussaint Louverture*, 203.

20. Sánchez Valverde, *Idea del valor de la isla española*, 168.

21. References to Sánchez Valverde appear repeatedly in Moreau's writing. For example, Moreau mentioned "Don Antonio Valverde" in a discussion of ideas of race in colonial Santo Domingo. Moreau de St Méry, *Description topographique et politique de la partie espagnole*, 1:59.

22. Report submitted by Roume to "French Government Commission in the [Caribbean] Islands," 1 October 1797, in Rodríguez Demorizi, *Cesión de Santo Domingo a Francia*, 290.

23. For more details on this, see Fick, "Emancipation in Haiti"; Fick, *Making of Haiti*, esp. chap. 9; and Dubois, *Avengers of the New World*, chap. 11.

24. According to Fick, one *carreau* of land equaled about 3.3 acres, so fifty *carreaux* would be 165 acres. Fick, *Making of Haiti*, 325. Bell wrote that fifty *carreaux* translated into about 200 acres of land. Bell, *Toussaint Louverture*, 206.

25. Order of Toussaint on land acquisition in Santo Domingo, 7 February 1801, CARAN Colonies CC/9b/18. Toussaint appears to have implemented a similar measure in Saint-Domingue. Fick, *Making of Haiti*, 207. Furthermore, according to Eric Nabajoth, Toussaint decreed on 7 May 1801 that notaries could not register land transactions that included less than sixty-five hectares (160 acres) of land. Nabajoth, "Toussaint-Louverture et la Constitution de 1801," 277.

26. "Proclamation" of Toussaint "to all of the inhabitants of the former Spanish part" of the island, 8 February 1801, CARAN Colonies CC/9b/18. Sánchez Valverde had argued that "the richest Mines do not yield their metal if one does not work [in] them, nor does the most fertile land [yield] all of the abundance of its fruits without arms and the plow." Sánchez Valverde, *Idea del valor de la isla española*, 168–69.

27. On the Abbé Raynal and his predictions of a great slave uprising headed by a strong leader, see Dubois, *Colony of Citizens*, 62–73, esp. 64–68.

28. "Proclamation" of Toussaint on agriculture and commerce in Santo Domingo, 12 February 1801, CARAN Colonies CC/9b/18. A copy of this document is located in CARAN Colonies CC/9b/9.

29. Order of Toussaint on mahogany woodcutting, 5 March 1801, CARAN Colonies CC/9b/9. In a letter to the minister of the navy, the French ambassador Louis-André Pichon in New York claimed that Toussaint built numerous "box beams" (*caissons*)

out of mahogany to protect his arms and munitions from the climate. Pichon to Minister of the Navy, 3 June 1801, CARAN Colonies CC/9a/28.

30. Pons to Minister of the Navy, 10 May or 18 May 1801, CARAN Colonies CC /9b/18.

31. Moïse, *Le projet national*, 72. For the full text of Toussaint's constitution, see Moïse, *Le projet national*, 72–85; and Madiou, *Histoire d'Haïti*, 2:542–55. Among the constitution's signatories were several men from Santo Domingo. According to Antonio del Monte y Tejada, five "Spaniards" were involved in drafting the constitution: Muñoz, Caballero, J. Mancebo, Viart, and Carlos de Rojas. The "French" signatories were listed in Monte y Tejada's account as Borgella, Collet, Raymond, Gaston, Latour, and Nocerb. Monte y Tejada, *Historia de Santo Domingo*, 3:212. In Moïse's text the constitution's signatories appear as "Borgella, président, Raymond, Collet, Gaston Nogérée, Lacour, Roxas, Munos, Mancebo, E. Viart." Moïse, *Le projet national*, 85. Madiou listed them as "Borgella, Président, Raymond, Collet, Gaston, Nogérée, Lacour, Roxas, Mugnos, Mancebo, E. Viart" in *Histoire d'Haïti*, 2:554. On Toussaint's constitution, see also Dubois, *Avengers of the New World*, 242–46; and Girard, *Slaves Who Defeated Napoléon*, chap. 1.

32. Title VI of the constitution outlined Toussaint's labor policies. Article XVI confirmed the application in the entirety of Toussaint's domains of his order of 12 October 1800, which had codified his earlier repressive labor decrees. Furthermore, Article XVII established the conditions for the "introduction [to Hispaniola] of cultivators [who are] indispensable for the reestablishment and the growth of agriculture." Moïse, *Le projet national*, 74. A copy of Toussaint's 12 October 1800 agricultural decree is preserved in CARAN Colonies CC/9b/9.

33. Article XVIII reads: "As the commerce of the colony consists only of the exchange of commodities and products of its territory, in consequence the introduction of those of the same nature as its own [products] is and remains prohibited." Moïse, *Le projet national*, 74.

34. In a "Provisional Regulation" issued in Port-Républicain on 18 May 1798, Toussaint had ordered that all "citizens" who were "attached" to agriculture but who were not presently engaged in either military or domestic service be arrested by the gendarmerie and "subjected to labor." "Provisional Regulation of General Toussaint Louverture," 18 May 1798, CARAN Colonies CC/9a/23. Toussaint extended this decree to all of Saint-Domingue in October 1800, when he formally entrusted the military with the enforcement of his labor regime. Bell, *Toussaint Louverture*, 203. For more details on Toussaint's agricultural labor policies, see a report sent to the French minister of the navy and colonies dated 16 November 1800 in CARAN Colonies CC/9b/18.

35. The quote is from Fick, "Emancipation in Haiti," 26.

36. Louverture, *Memoir of General Toussaint Louverture*, 97.

37. Antoine Chanlatte, "Historical Summary of the Deeds that Preceded the Invasion of the Territory of the Former Spanish Part of Saint-Domingue by Toussaint Louverture," 28 May 1801, CARAN Colonies CC/9b/18.

38. Mackenzie to Canning, 9 September 1826, CARAN Colonies CC/9a/54.

39. Mackenzie to the Earl of Dudley, 10 March 1828, CARAN Colonies CC/9a/54.

40. Report of Armand Hardouin, undated, CARAN Colonies CC/9a/53.

41. James, *Black Jacobins*, 242.

42. Trouillot, *Haiti, State against Nation*, 39. See also Mintz, "Slavery and the Rise of Peasantries."

43. Turits, *Foundations of Despotism*, 27.

44. "Description of the French and Spanish Parts of the Island of St-Domingue by Antoine Chanlatte Brigade General [and] Commissioner of the French Government in the Former Spanish Part of Saint-Domingue," 9 June 1800, CARAN Colonies CC/9b/18.

45. Ibid.

46. Nonetheless, some scholars have explored this aspect of Dominican history in depth. See, for example, Deive, *La esclavitud del negro*; and Silié, *Economía, esclavitud y población.*

47. Quoted in Turits, *Foundations of Despotism*, 25.

48. Trouillot, *Haiti, State against Nation*, 39–40.

49. Turits, *Foundations of Despotism*, 26.

50. Girard, "Napoleon Bonaparte," 589.

51. Cordero Michel, "Toussaint en Saint-Domingue espagnol," 254–55.

52. Roume to Minister of the Navy and Colonies, 25 September 1801, CARAN Colonies CC/9b/2.

53. Kerverseau to Minister of the Navy and Colonies, 15 December 1800, CARAN Colonies CC/9b/23.

54. In the French Revolution, the term "émigré" came to acquire connotations of royalism and counterrevolution. In both parts of Hispaniola in this era, this term was often used to refer to planters who had fled their plantations by those who wished to expropriate their holdings.

55. Tax Collector of Saint-Domingue to Minister of the Navy and Colonies, 15 April 1801, CARAN Colonies CC/9b/18.

56. Toussaint to Hédouville, 22 September 1798, CARAN Colonies CC/9a/23.

57. Cabon, *Histoire d'Haïti*, 4:190.

58. Toussaint to Hédouville, 16 September 1798, CARAN Colonies CC/9a/23.

59. Report of Charles Vincent to Minister of the Navy and Colonies, 17 May 1801, CARAN Colonies CC/9a/28.

60. In what is probably an exaggerated estimate, Roberto Cassá wrote that more than two-thirds of Santo Domingo's population emigrated after 1789. Cassá, "Les effets du Traité du Bâle," 209. According to David Geggus, by the summer of 1796 several thousand residents of Santo Domingo, including almost 800 "black auxiliaries," had emigrated. Geggus, "Slave Resistance in the Spanish Caribbean," 140.

61. Roume to Minister of the Navy and Colonies, 31 December 1795, CARAN Colonies CC/9a/20.

62. Toussaint Louverture, "Proclamation . . . to all of the Inhabitants of the Former Spanish Part," 8 February 1801, CARAN Colonies CC/9b/18. According to Frank Moya Pons, in 1795 emigration from Santo Domingo commenced on a fairly modest scale, but it became much more pronounced in the wake of Toussaint's invasion in early 1801. Moya asserted that virtually all Spanish authorities as well as "French functionaries" departed Santo Domingo after this invasion, and at least 1,988 individuals from Santo Domingo arrived in Venezuela in the first two months of 1801. Moya Pons, *Manual de historia dominicana*, 191–92. See also Deive, *Las emigraciones dominicanas a Cuba*, 91–102. Sigfrido Vázquez Cienfuegos has written that as of 30 November 1803, 1,679 "French emigrants" had arrived in Santiago de Cuba from "Santo Domingo." Vázquez Cienfuegos, *Tan difíciles tiempos para Cuba*, 289.

63. Don Pedro Abadia to M. Thermite, 20 May 1802, SHAT B7 13. For an account of Abadia's punishment in 1796 of the "slave" Benito, who was accused of stealing *aguardiente*, see Manuel Bravo y Bermudez to Joaquín García, 14 December 1796, AGI ASD 1033.

64. Pedro Ceballos to Joaquín García, 16 September 1801, AGI Cuba 1705.

65. Petition of Doña Josefa de Coco y Landeche, 8 February 1796, AGI ASD 1033.

66. Deive, *Las emigraciones dominicanas a Cuba*, 94.

67. Marquis de Someruelos to Spanish Minister of State, 2 November 1801, AGI ASD 1037.

68. Petition of José de Labastida, 14 December 1802, AGI ASD 1037.

69. Deive, *Las emigraciones dominicanas a Cuba*, 93.

70. "General Cadastral Register of all the National Goods recognized until this Day in the Eastern Part of Saint Domingue," 21 January 1804, CARAN Colonies CC/9b/2.

71. Account of military service record of Alexandro Ynfante, 7 April 1804, AGI Cuba 1742.

72. Petition of Domingo Díaz Paez, 8 July 1804, AGI Cuba 1742.

73. Petition of Tiburcio Josef Esterlín, 11 May 1804, AGI ASD 1038. Due in large part to the common association of blacks from Hispaniola with revolutionary violence, those Dominican refugees who succeeded in resettling elsewhere with their captives sometimes faced difficulties incorporating these "slaves" into their slave-holding host societies. For example, according to the intendant of Caracas, many Dominicans were unable to sell or rent out their "slaves" because of these captives' associations with the "past uprising [in Hispaniola]." Correspondence of Andrés Talavera, "General Intendant of the Army and the Royal Treasury of these Provinces [of] Caracas," 26 March 1801, AGI ASD 1037.

74. Deive, *Las emigraciones dominicanas a Cuba*, 93.

75. Petition of Francisco de Arredondo, 29 November 1805, AGI ASD 1038.

76. Report addressed to Don José Antonio Caballero, 4 February 1804, AGI ASD 1038. On the transfer of the *Audiencia* of Santo Domingo to Puerto Príncipe, Cuba, after 1795, see Vázquez Cienfuegos, *Tan difíciles tiempos para Cuba*, 279–83.

77. "State that shows the number of Emigrants who have entered this Port [Maracaybo]," 21 March 1801, AGI ASD 1037.

78. Roume to Minister of the Navy and Colonies, 2 December 1801, CARAN Colonies CC/9b/2.

79. The jury is still out concerning the thorny question of Napoleon's intentions with respect to slavery in Saint-Domingue upon deploying the expedition and during the course of the campaign. On this issue, see Dubois, *Avengers of the New World*, 259–60; and Girard, "Napoleon Bonaparte," 600–615.

80. In a letter to Toussaint dated 17 March 1801, the French government insisted that he recognize the authority of General Cambis, the newly appointed "Commissioner of the French government in the former Spanish part of Saint-Domingue." This letter instructed Toussaint to cooperate with Cambis in the "most faithful execution of the order of 1 Frimaire, year 9 [22 November 1800], which postpones until general peace the [effective] taking of possession of this part of the island, ceded to France by the treaty of 4 Thermidor year 3 [the Treaty of Basel]." Paris to Toussaint, 17 March 1801, CARAN Colonies CC/9b/18. See also a letter that these three officials (Mongiraud, Cambis, and Desperoux) composed to the minister of the navy and colonies on 4 July 1801 in CARAN Colonies CC/9b/18.

81. Desforneaux to "Citizen Merlin, Director," 11 February 1799, CARAN AF/III /209.

82. Girard, *Slaves Who Defeated Napoléon*, 37.

83. Gerbier to Saint-Domingue, 3 August 1801, RPUF no. 75.

84. Pichon to Minister of the Navy and Colonies, 3 June 1801, CARAN Colonies CC/9a/28.

85. On the "*Arc de Triomphe*" order, see Kerverseau to Colonial Prefect François Lequoy-Mongiraud, 9 November 1802, CARAN 135 AP 2, dossier 18.

86. In the spring of 1801, Britain and France began to negotiate a peace treaty. These negotiations culminated in the Treaty of Amiens (March 1802), which ended hostilities between the two nations until the renewal of war in the spring of 1803. For a discussion of the geopolitical circumstances concerning this peace and their influence on Napoleon's decision making, see Girard, "Napoleon Bonaparte," esp. 600–603.

87. Quoted in Dubois, *Avengers of the New World*, 253.

88. Napoleon, "Notes pour servir aux instructions à donner au Capitaine Général Leclerc," 31 October 1801, in Roussier, *Lettres du général Leclerc*, 272. See also Dubois, *Avengers of the New World*, 259.

89. Napoleon's instructions on Santo Domingo, 29 October 1801, CARAN Colonies CC/9a/28. The ANOM contains at least two copies of this decree: in 8 SUPSDOM 390 and in CMSM F3 202.

90. Pluchon, "Toussaint Louverture défie Bonaparte," 174–77.

91. Dubois, *Avengers of the New World*, 262.

92. Napoleon, "Notes pour servir aux instructions," 265; Auguste and Auguste, *L'expédition Leclerc*, 111–12. At the time of Leclerc's initial invasion, Toussaint had

3,000 troops in the entire colony of Santo Domingo out of a total of 16,000 to 18,000. Métral, *Histoire de l'expédition des français*, 33; and Leclerc to Napoleon, 15 February 1802, in Roussier, *Lettres du général Leclerc*, 88.

93. Leclerc to Napoleon, 17 February 1802, in Roussier, *Lettres du général Leclerc*, 94–95.

94. The quote is from Métral, *Histoire de l'expédition des français*, 33. For details on Paul Louverture's surrender, see Dubois, *Avengers of the New World*, 267; and Louverture, *Memoir of General Toussaint Louverture*, 73–75.

95. Auguste and Auguste, *L'expédition Leclerc*, 111.

96. For more information on these events, see Dubois, *Avengers of the New World*, 275.

97. Leclerc to Toussaint, 3 May 1802, ANOM CMSM F3 283.

98. For Toussaint's own account of his capture and deportation from the island, see Louverture, *Memoir of General Toussaint Louverture*, 125–43.

99. Quoted in Bell, *Toussaint Louverture*, 220. Philippe Girard also cites this passage in "Napoleon Bonaparte," 601.

100. Pluchon, "Toussaint Louverture défie Bonaparte," 177.

101. Quoted in Bell, *Toussaint Louverture*, 185.

Chapter Five

1. Proclamation of François Kerverseau, 10 October 1802, CARAN 135 AP 2, dossier 18.

2. It remains unclear when this expedition adopted the goal of restoring slavery; the earliest documentary evidence that I have uncovered in which a high official in this Napoleonic force openly and directly advocated the reestablishment of slavery in Saint-Domingue is from January 1803. Half a year earlier, on 24 July 1802, the expedition's leader, General Leclerc, had written to the minister of the navy, Denis Decrès: "Do not think of restoring slavery for some time. I think I can arrange everything so that my successor has no more to do than to put the government's decree into effect, but after the endless proclamations that I have issued here to ensure the blacks their freedom, I do not want to contradict myself, but assure the First Consul that my successor will find everything ready." Quoted in Champion, "30 Floréal Year X," 233 (Berghahn Books edition). In a 15 January 1803 letter to the minister of the navy, General Donatien Rochambeau (who had assumed command of the expedition in late 1802) went further, arguing that "it is necessary to put the blacks back into Slavery" in order to rescue French Saint-Domingue from its "deplorable state" and to make it once again a "flourishing and productive Colony." Rochambeau to Minister of the Navy and Colonies, 15 January 1803, CARAN Colonies CC/9b/19. See also Girard, *Slaves Who Defeated Napoléon*, chap. 10. Girard claims that Rochambeau argued for the reimposition of slavery on the island as early as 1 January 1803 (225).

3. J. Scott, "Common Wind." For details on the restoration of slavery in Guadeloupe, see Dubois, *Colony of Citizens*, part III. On the situation in Martinique, see Schloss, *Sweet Liberty*, chap. 1.

4. L. Delpech to Kerverseau, *Vendémiaire an 11* (23 September–22 October 1802), CARAN 135 AP 2, dossier 18.

5. See Kerverseau to Leclerc, 11 October 1802; Kerverseau to Leclerc, 14 October 1802; and Kerverseau to Leclerc, 4 November 1802, all contained in CARAN 135 AP 2, dossier 18.

6. Hospital records for *Berceau* sailors, *Vendémiaire-Brumaire an 11* (23 September–21 November 1802), CARAN 135 AP 2, dossier 18.

7. Governor Ramón de Castro to Leclerc, 30 October 1802, RPUF no. 1265.

8. Kerverseau to Leclerc, 4 November 1802, CARAN 135 AP 2, dossier 18.

9. Testimony of *Berceau* captives, *Brumaire an 11* (23 October–21 November 1802), CARAN 135 AP 2, dossier 18.

10. Anonymous report to Minister of the Navy and Colonies, 25 February 1803, CARAN Colonies CC/9b/22.

11. R. Scott, " 'She . . . Refuses to Deliver Up Herself,' " 134. For further discussion of the process of status determination in a context of reenslavement, see R. Scott, "Paper Thin." For analyses of some of the contradictions that emerged in attempts to codify slavery, see R. Scott, " 'She . . . Refuses to Deliver Up Herself' "; and Grinberg, "Slavery, Liberalism and Civil Law."

12. On slaves' roles in the emergence of new legal rights, see among other works Fuente, "Slaves and the Creation of Legal Rights"; Fuente, "Slave Law and Claims-Making in Cuba"; and Gross and De la Fuente, "Slaves, Free Blacks, and Race."

13. According to Norbert Thoret, Ferrand "was long reduced to his own resources" due to the war between France and England that blocked all communication from the former. Nouët et al., *La vie aventureuse de Norbert Thoret*, 67.

14. Niort and Richard, "À propos de la découverte de l'arrêté consulaire du 16 juillet 1802," 40–42.

15. Branda and Lentz, *Napoléon, l'esclavage et les colonies*, 121–22. A copy of this 20 May 1802 law is preserved in *Collection générale des lois*, 924.

16. For details on Richepance's expedition to Guadeloupe, see Dubois, *Colony of Citizens*, chaps. 15–16.

17. Niort and Richard, "À propos de la découverte de l'arrêté consulaire du 16 juillet 1802," 36 and 58.

18. I thank Laurent Dubois (personal communication, 24 September 2010) for suggesting the former point to me.

19. R. Scott, "Paper Thin," 1074. Scott referred here to an 1810 act by legislators and the governor of the Territory of Orleans that recognized purported masters' property rights over those Saint-Domingue refugees claimed as slaves in spite of the universal emancipation decrees issued by French authorities nearly two decades earlier.

20. Bénot, *La démence coloniale*, esp. 93–99.

21. Holt, *Problem of Freedom*, 9.

22. Rochambeau to Minister of the Navy and Colonies, 28 April 1803, CARAN Colonies CC/9a/34.

23. On 27 July 1796, a disgraced General Rochambeau had sailed back to France on the *Berceau* following his removal from this position six days earlier on charges of sympathizing with the Dominican clergy and lay elite and encouraging royalist émigrés to return to Hispaniola. In a report composed on 18 July 1796, the French Civil Commission on the island argued that Rochambeau's arrival in Santo Domingo had been "the object of the wishes and the hope of the noble émigrés, and rich colonists, [who were] all royalists." "Extract of the Registry of the Deliberations of the Commission Delegated by the French government in the [Caribbean] islands," 18 July 1796, CARAN Colonies CC/9a/11. Furthermore, in a letter to the Directory composed in July or August 1796, the Bureau des Colonies (Colonial Office) cited a letter that Rochambeau had supposedly written to the minister of the navy in which he had labeled "men of Color" a "rebel Caste, proud and bastard" and had recommended their expulsion from the island. Bureau des Colonies to the Directory, *Thermidor an 4* (19 July–17 August 1796), CARAN Colonies CC/9a/11. See also report to the Directory, 12 September 1796, CARAN AF/III/62; and "Extract of the Registry of the Deliberations of the Commission Delegated by the French government in the [Caribbean] islands," 21 July 1796, CARAN Colonies CC/9a/11. For Rochambeau's attempted refutation of the charges against him, see Rochambeau to Roume, 21 July 1796, CARAN Colonies CC/9a/11.

24. Nonetheless, as a scion of the old aristocracy with a conservative reputation, Rochambeau earned the ire of many of his own generals in the Napoleonic expedition. For more on Rochambeau, who had served in the American Revolution, see Girard, *Slaves Who Defeated Napoléon*, 224–25.

25. All belligerent parties, along with the civilian population, suffered horrific casualties in the Haitian war of independence. One scholar estimates that Napoleon's decision to reconquer Saint-Domingue cost France 50,000 souls (including sailors and civilians as well as soldiers), while perhaps twice that number of Haitians died as a result of Napoleon's expedition. Girard, *Slaves Who Defeated Napoléon*, 343–44.

26. "State of troops [that have] Arrived in Saint Domingue from 15 Pluviôse year ten to 1 Prairial year eleven," 20 June 1803, ANOM TPC D2C 371. This figure roughly accords with that of 43,800 soldiers that Girard presents in *Slaves Who Defeated Napoléon*, 343, while Laurent Dubois wrote that "ultimately upward of 80,000 fighting men were sent [by the French] to Saint-Domingue." Dubois, *Avengers of the New World*, 251.

27. Population figures are from Dubois, *Avengers of the New World*, 22 and 30.

28. "General State of the Population of the Eastern Part of Saint-Domingue, as of the First of January 1808," 1 January 1808, CARAN Colonies CC/9a/45. This census put the population at 50,089.

29. On Napoleon's strategic designs in the Americas and Saint-Domingue's role in this, see Girard, "Napoleon Bonaparte"; Paquette, "Revolutionary Saint Domingue in the Making of Territorial Louisiana"; and Dubois, *Avengers of the New World*, 304.

30. Chanlatte, "Proposed Means to Establish French Authority in Saint-Domingue that Would Create Respect for the Laws of the Republic in the French Colony and Would Work towards its Reduction," undated, CARAN Colonies CC/9b/18. In the words of Dubois, Napoleon himself had ordered Leclerc to "rally support in Spanish Santo Domingo." Dubois, *Avengers of the New World*, 254.

31. Napoleon, "Notes pour servir aux instructions à donner au Capitaine Général Leclerc," 31 October 1801, in Roussier, *Lettres du général Leclerc*, 268–69.

32. The most famous "maroon" leader of the Haitian war of independence was an African-born former slave called Jean-Baptiste Sans Souci, who resisted both Napoleonic French and Louverturian armies (except for a very brief stint in mid-1802 as a nominal French officer) until his demise at the hands of Henry Christophe. See Trouillot, *Silencing the Past*, chap. 2; and Girard, *Slaves Who Defeated Napoléon*, 196 and 249–50.

33. Girard, *Slaves Who Defeated Napoléon*, 192–99.

34. The Leclerc expedition apparently attempted to militarily close off the border between Saint-Domingue and Santo Domingo to prevent enemy soldiers from seeking refuge in the latter. Louverture, *Memoir of General Toussaint Louverture*, 93 (Girard's comments in note 98).

35. "Report by M. Lavassor on agriculture in the Colonies," 5 March 1802, ANOM CMSM F3 266.

36. As of 30 May 1802, only around 10 percent of the Leclerc expedition's forces (2,556 out of 24,220 men) were assigned to the eastern two-thirds of the island, which was nominally under Kerverseau. Comprehensive listing of divisions in Leclerc expedition, 30 May 1802, ANOM TPC D2C 371. On 16 September 1802, Kerverseau informed Pamphile de Lacroix, the commandant of Cibao, that he did not have the troops or funds to attack those in Maniel. Kerverseau to Pamphile de Lacroix, 16 September 1802, CARAN Colonies CC/9b/23.

37. Boudet to Rochambeau, 24 April 1802, CARAN 135 AP 1, dossier 4.

38. Ruiz to Rochambeau, 12 July 1802, CARAN 135 AP 1, dossier 11. On 10 July 1802, Ruiz had related an order mandating the arrest of these escaped *cultivateurs* and their relocation to Port-Républicain after officials ascertained to which plantation they had belonged. Order on *cultivateurs* in Maniel, 10 July 1802, CARAN 135 AP 1, dossier 11. Ruiz's "distinguished conduct" in the "Maniel expedition" earned him a promotion on 23 December 1803 by Ferrand to the rank of first-class cavalry captain. "Nominations" by Ferrand for promotion, 23 December 1803, ANOM TPC D2C 371. One military report from 26 March 1803 stated that the French invaders had noticed an "immense quantity of provisions" that had been planted in Maniel. "Order of the Day," 26 March 1803, CARAN Colonies CC/9b/22. Moreover, Kerverseau accused

those in Maniel of engaging in trade in meat and arms with the Spanish in Santo Domingo. Kerverseau to Rochambeau, 27 March 1803, CARAN 135 AP 2, dossier 18.

39. "Order of the Day," 26 March 1803, CARAN Colonies CC/9b/22.

40. Kerverseau to Minister of the Navy and Colonies, 10 February 1804, CARAN Colonies CC/9a/37.

41. Following Louverture's surrender in May 1802, Dessalines temporarily allied with the Napoleonic forces. His subsequent defection from the French army in late 1802 helped to ensure the defeat of the expedition. See Girard, *Slaves Who Defeated Napoléon*, chaps. 12 and 13.

42. "General Chart of the Armed Forces in St Domingue," 23 September 1802, ANOM TPC D2C 371.

43. "General Chart of the Armed Forces in St Domingue," 20 June 1803, ANOM TPC D2C 371.

44. "Extract of the Correspondence of the Leaders of Saint Domingue remitted by the Squadron leader," 21 August 1803, CARAN Colonies CC/9b/22.

45. On this tactic and relations between the expedition's leaders and Cuban authorities, see Girard, *Slaves Who Defeated Napoléon*, 105–6 and 238–41.

46. If the account of Frenchman Norbert Thoret, an eyewitness to these events, is to be believed, Rochambeau also resorted to extortion to raise desperately needed funds, killing one merchant's son due to the failure of his brother to procure 6,000 *piastres* within twenty-four hours. Nouët et al., *La vie aventureuse de Norbert Thoret*, 26.

47. Though the precise number of "Spanish" troops employed in French armies in the Leclerc-Rochambeau period is unknown, evidence suggests that the figure may have been in the thousands. In a letter on the strategic and economic importance of parts of the island's borderland, Kerverseau claimed to have deployed "three thousand Spaniards assembled on the Border of the two [Dominican] departments for the defense of the country." Kerverseau to Minister of the Navy and Colonies, 10 February 1804, CARAN Colonies CC/9a/37.

48. Pedro Francisco de Prado, account of French occupation in Santo Domingo, 9 October 1803, in Rodríguez Demorizi, *Las invasiones haitianas*, 85–92.

49. Kerverseau to "the military Commanders, [and] to the notables and municipal Administrators of the Eastern Division," 7 June 1803, CARAN Colonies CC/9b/23.

50. According to military records from this period, the invaders had restored the old name of Fort-Dauphin to Fort-Liberté.

51. Rochambeau to Minister of the Navy and Colonies, 7 December 1802, CARAN Colonies CC/9b/19.

52. Quantin to Rochambeau, 24 January 1803, RPUF, no. 1567; "General Chart of the Armed Forces in St Domingue," 20 February 1803, ANOM TPC D2C 371.

53. Quantin to Rochambeau, 4 March 1803, RPUF, no. 1682. *Hatte* is the French rendering of the Spanish word *hato*, which referred to cattle ranches. For more on the *hato*, see the introduction to this study.

54. Quantin to Rochambeau, 21 February 1803, RPUF, no. 1640.

55. "General Chart of the Armed Forces in St Domingue," 20 June 1803, ANOM TPC D2C 371.

56. For more information on Ferrand's prior military service, see Picó, *One Frenchman, Four Revolutions*, 33–34; and Lacroix, *La Révolution d'Haïti*, 474–75.

57. "Review" of military officers and their salaries, 22 December 1802, ANOM TPC D2C 371.

58. The main inventory of the Rochambeau Papers at the University of Florida contains intriguing hints of such an evacuation. For instance, the entry for document number 2084 (a 16 September 1803 letter from a minor official named Henri Perroud to the "Prefect of the Isle of St Domingue") describes the document as a "Report on the expenses of the evacuation of Jérémie and on the difficulty of providing for the care of evacuees with 250 ill persons in St. Yago [Santiago], Cuba." Monti, *Calendar of Rochambeau Papers*, 279–80.

59. "Extract of the Correspondence of the Leaders of Saint Domingue remitted by the Squadron leader," 12 September 1803, CARAN Colonies CC/9b/22; Kerverseau to Minister of the Navy and Colonies, 10 February 1804, CARAN Colonies CC /9a/37.

60. Girard, *Slaves Who Defeated Napoléon*, 335.

61. Dubois, *Avengers of the New World*, unpaginated epigraph at beginning of book. In a "Proclamation" to his fellow Haitians dated 28 April 1804, Dessalines exclaimed: "Yes, we have rendered to these true cannibals war for war, crime for crime, courage for courage; Yes, I have saved my country—I have avenged America." English translation of Dessalines proclamation of 28 April 1804, CARAN Colonies CC/9b/18.

62. General Kerverseau, writing on 10 February 1804, stated that Ferrand had only 157 men under his command upon traveling to Santiago (northern Santo Domingo) in early December 1803. Kerverseau to Minister of the Navy and Colonies, 10 February 1804, CARAN Colonies CC/9a/37. By 20 July 1804, Ferrand had a total of 854 men in his army, including 224 troops from the "*Légion du Cap*" and nineteen "Spanish artillerymen." "State of the Situation" of troops under Ferrand in Santo Domingo, 20 July 1804, ANOM TPC D2C 371.

63. Carlos de Urrutia to "Secretary of State and the Office of Overseas Governance," 3 August 1813, AGI ASD 1042.

64. I have located two "slave" sales among extant notarial records from Santo Domingo in which Ferrand was a buyer or a seller. In the first transaction, Ferrand sold a woman named Pomette to a Captain Philipe Filoche on 18 October 1807. Then, on 30 May 1808, Ferrand purchased a "*négresse*" (black woman) named Agathe from Captain François Antoine Lavalette. Both sales were for 300 *gourdes*. Furthermore, a 3 April 1809 roster of a military unit listed Ferrand as the (former) owner of five "Blacks" who served in it. See sale of Pomette, 18 October 1807, ANOM DPPC NOT SDOM 1699; sale of Agathe, 30 May 1808, ANOM DPPC NOT SDOM 1700; and "Nominative state of men comprising the free Corps, drawn up according to the

Extract of the review of Commissioners and Serving as payment for the Blacks acquired by the Government to form the Corps," 3 April 1809, SHAT B7 12.

65. Picó, *One Frenchman, Four Revolutions*, 54–55.

66. On these massacres, see Trouillot, *Haiti, State against Nation*, 46; and Dubois, *Avengers of the New World*, 300.

67. See Nouët et al., *La vie aventureuse de Norbert Thoret* (quotes are from 31 and 69).

68. Thoret would have had ample opportunity to share his tales of horror with Ferrand, as Thoret describes meeting Ferrand and establishing a close partnership with the general. See Nouët et al., *La vie aventureuse de Norbert Thoret*, 66–71.

69. Kerverseau's confiscation of these properties also built on the revolutionary precedent of state seizures of the assets of refugees who were deemed disloyal to the Republic or who had simply abandoned their properties in their flight from the island. In a decree dated 14 May 1800, Toussaint had ordered that revenue from plantations with "absent Owners" go to state coffers, with deductions made for the wages of the *cultivateurs*. "Regulation" of Toussaint on plantation revenue, 14 May 1800, CARAN Colonies CC/9a/24. Two and a half years later, in an order dated 23 November 1802, Kerverseau had established the organizational structure of a new "Administration of national domains" for Santo Domingo. A colonial prefect was to oversee the confiscation of properties that had belonged to religious brotherhoods, *cabildos* (town councils), and other entities as well as the proceeds of intestate successions. This national domain administration would be based in Santo Domingo city, but administrators would also be stationed in Santiago, Seybo, Azua, Bánica, and La Vega. Order of Kerverseau on national domains, 23 November 1802, CARAN Colonies CC/9b/2.

70. Kerverseau order on national domains, 12 October 1803, CARAN Colonies CC/9b/4.

71. Order of Sub-Prefect A. P. Tirol on plantation production, 15 December 1803, CARAN Colonies CC/9a/37. In a 29 November 1809 letter to Napoleon, a former subordinate of Ferrand, writing to convince Napoleon to grant a generous pension to Ferrand's widow and children, insisted that Ferrand had devoted all of his fortune of around 200,000 francs to the acquisition of plantations and houses. E. Paillier, report to Napoleon on the service of Ferrand, 29 November 1809, CARAN AF/IV/968.

72. Jenson, *Beyond the Slave Narrative*, 308–9.

73. "State of Agriculture and of Animals of all Types in the Eastern Part of Saint Domingue," 1 January 1808, CARAN Colonies CC/9a/45.

74. "General Cadastral Register of all the National Goods recognized until this Day in the Eastern Part of Saint Domingue," 21 January 1804, CARAN Colonies CC/9b/2.

75. "Summary of the Cadastral Register of the Domains of the French Empire," 1806, CARAN Colonies CC/9a/42. This survey listed five plantations and four cattle ranches.

76. "Observations on the nature of national Domains of the eastern part of St Domingue," undated, CARAN Colonies CC/9a/42. A "Gabriela Sánchez" is listed as owning a plantation near Santiago that was to be auctioned off in June 1807. Announcement on auction of assorted properties, 29 May 1807, CARAN Colonies CC/9a/44. According to the 1806 national domains survey, "the widow of André Lecanda [Gabriela Sánchez], who was entrusted with the management of the Esparza plantation in 1800, exported from it 20 blacks whom she took to Cuba, upon the taking of possession of the Spanish Part by Toussaint Louverture, and that the French Government has the right to demand the restitution of these blacks who belong to it, as dependents of the Esparza succession, that has fallen to it by the substitution of the rights of the King of Spain in St Domingue." "Summary of the Cadastral Register of the Domains of the French Empire," 1806, CARAN Colonies CC/9a/42.

77. Spanish authorities in Santo Domingo had long attempted to regulate religious brotherhoods (*cofradías*) involving slaves while recognizing these organizations' role in promoting Catholicism and providing a social and spiritual outlet that might act as a check on violent resistance to enslavement. Chapter 20 of the *Código Negro* of 1784 proclaimed that the *cofradías* involving slaves in the colony were "useful to the public good [*causa pública*] and to religion and to further soften [*suavizar*] their rustic and crude customs." The *Código* nonetheless limited the number of holidays that the slaves could celebrate in their *cofradías*, forbade slaves from the countryside from interacting with their urban counterparts in *cofradías*, and banned public celebrations and dances by slaves and free blacks except under prescribed circumstances. Barceló, *Código Negro Carolino*, 188–89.

78. "General Cadastral Register of all the National Goods," 21 January 1804, CARAN Colonies CC/9b/2.

79. "Summary of the Cadastral Register of the Domains of the French Empire," 1806, CARAN Colonies CC/9a/42.

80. "General State of the Population of the Eastern Part of Saint-Domingue," 1 January 1808, CARAN Colonies CC/9a/45.

81. "General State of the Population of the City of Santo Domingo on 18 November 1808," SHAT B7 13.

82. Turits, "Par-delà les plantations," 53–58. In a 23 March 1804 letter to the minister of the navy, Kerverseau stated that "all of the great landowners of the Colony [Santo Domingo] are absent, the majority of those who remain there are a [illegible] of free blacks, mulattos, and men of color of all nuances, known by the name of Whites of the land." Kerverseau to Minister of the Navy and Colonies, 23 March 1804, ANOM CMSM F3 283.

83. According to Dubois, in 1789 the number of *gens de couleur libres* in Saint-Domingue had stood at around 28,000, or about 5 percent of the entire population. Dubois, *Avengers of the New World*, 30. John Garrigus has observed that "Saint-Domingue in 1789 was a society whose 30,831 French colonists, already outnumbered

fourteen to one by their slaves, lived alongside at least 24,848 free people of African descent." Garrigus, *Before Haiti*, 2.

84. Kerverseau to Daure, 18 November 1802, CARAN 135 AP 2, dossier 18.

85. Quoted in Dubois, *Avengers of the New World*, 255.

86. Kerverseau to Merck, Commandant of the Department of Cibao, 22 October 1802, CARAN Colonies CC/9b/23.

87. "Representatives of the refugee Colonists of Saint Domingue, in Santiago de Cuba" to Napoleon, 5 February 1805, CARAN AF/IV/941.

88. On these political and discursive struggles in the Francophone world, see Bénot, *La Révolution Française et la fin des colonies*; and Bénot, *La démence coloniale*. On the intellectual history of this era more generally, see Dubois, "Enslaved Enlightenment."

89. For a discussion of these abolitionist writings, see Dubois, *Colony of Citizens*, chap. 2.

90. For details on these laws, see Schloss, *Sweet Liberty*, 24; Heuer, "One-Drop Rule in Reverse?"; and Peabody, "*There Are No Slaves in France*," esp. chaps. 7–8.

91. For instance, Rebecca Schloss has shown that Martinican authorities issued several decrees during these years that aimed to strengthen official control over manumission. These included a ruling that no manumission decree issued in any other colony was valid in Martinique until public officials there ratified it as well as a decree that recognized an individual's freedom only if he or she had obtained a "title of liberty" after the French reoccupation of Martinique in 1802, secured official confirmation of such a preexisting title after 1803, or gained the provisional assent of the colonial prefect for manumission. Schloss, *Sweet Liberty*, 39.

92. On 22 May 1804, Ferrand declared that while "Spanish" inhabitants of the department of Cibao could enter the department of Ozama, most "French blacks and men of color" were prohibited entry. Ferrand to Sandoval, 22 May 1804, CARAN Colonies CC/9a/40.

93. According to Moreau de St Méry, as early as 1697, the governor of French Saint-Domingue had signed an accord with his Spanish counterpart in Santo Domingo that had stipulated that "French blacks" (*nègres français*) who had fled to Santo Domingo were to be returned to their former masters. Both bilateral treaties and unilateral declarations throughout the eighteenth century continued to posit a distinction between "French" and "Spanish" blacks. Notably, the 1777 Treaty of Aranjuez had included a provision that exempted "Spanish blacks" (*nègres espagnols*) from a French rule requiring recaptured fugitive slaves to be sold following a set detention period if no would-be master presented himself or herself. Moreau de St Méry, *Description topographique et politique de la partie espagnole*, 2:172, 179.

94. On the situation in Cuba, see Scott and Hébrard, "Servitude, liberté et citoyenneté," 33. On the United States, see Peabody, "'Free upon Higher Ground'"; and White, *Encountering Revolution*.

95. One such curfew prohibited most "Blacks and Mulattos" from being outside after seven in the evening. Ferrand to Colonel Pichot, 7 January 1808, CARAN Colonies CC/9a/45. During the 1805 siege of Santo Domingo city by Haitian forces, Ferrand instructed the "Notables of Santo Domingo" to compose a detailed listing of families that would be eligible for evacuation, which was to only include "whites, and others considered as such" (*blancs, et autres considérés comme tels*). Ferrand to "Notables of Santo Domingo," 4 March 1805, CARAN Colonies CC/9a/40. Furthermore, in a 26 February 1804 order, Ferrand invited only white Saint-Domingue refugees to settle in Santo Domingo. Ferrand order on refugees, 25 February 1804, AGI Cuba 1705. When undergoing treatment in Santo Domingo's hospitals, "black and mulatto" nurses could not claim any part of their salary, while their "white" counterparts would receive half of their salary in the same situation. Lt. Col. Vives to "Colonial Inspector," 18 March 1806, CARAN Colonies CC/9b/3.

96. Ferrand order on inheritances, 27 February 1806, CARAN Colonies CC/9a/42. Access to inheritance had represented a key means by which Saint-Domingue's *gens de couleur libres* had accrued wealth over the course of the eighteenth century. According to Sue Peabody, though a royal decree issued in 1726 had forbidden slaves and *gens de couleur libres* in the French Caribbean from receiving inheritances from whites, this was not frequently enforced in Saint-Domingue. Peabody, "*Négresse, Mulâtresse, Citoyenne*," 58. On the importance of inheritances in eighteenth-century Saint-Domingue, see Garrigus, *Before Haiti*, chap. 1, esp. 64–72; and Dubois, *Avengers of the New World*, 60–65.

97. Ferrand to Vives, 25 January 1804, CARAN Colonies CC/9a/40.

98. Ferrand to Vives, 15 September 1804, CARAN Colonies CC/9a/40. In a 12 April 1803 letter to local officials in Montechristi and Santiago, Santo Domingo, a presumed authority (probably General Kerverseau) had written that "the number of French refugees, [who are] black and of Color, of the different sexes, has considerably increased." Fearful of the alleged "bad intentions" of these individuals, the letter's author indicated that he would soon order all such migrants to appear before authorities so that the latter could record their names, ages, condition, marital and family situation, and ownership of any property. Letter to officials in Montechristi and Santiago, 12 April 1803, CARAN Colonies CC/9a/35. I have not located either registry in my research.

99. Ferrand to Peralta, 21 December 1804, CARAN Colonies CC/9a/40.

100. Quoted in Ghachem, *Old Regime and the Haitian Revolution*, 100.

101. "Police Ordinance concerning So-called Free Blacks," 19 November 1773, ANOM CMSM F3 273.

102. Ferrand order on Napoleonic Civil Code, 31 December 1807, CARAN Colonies CC/9a/44; order of Ferrand on dry goods sales, 26 December 1807, CARAN Colonies CC/9a/42. The État Civil was the main legal repository of birth, marriage, and death records in both metropolitan France and in the colonies.

103. Ferrand to "Notables of Santo Domingo," 15 September 1804, CARAN Colonies CC/9a/40.

104. Palmer, "Strange Science of Codifying Slavery," 97.

105. According to one notarial act, Louise-Félicité *dite* Agard was to be "freed from the yoke of slavery, and Free, as all the other freed people of the colony, to enjoy, and make use of her Free state . . . and as the former regulations and Laws [illegible] in the colony of Saint Domingue prescribe, concerning the manumission of slaves." Freeing of Louise-Félicité *dite* Agard, 30 April 1804, ANOM DPPC NOT SDOM 699. In the manumission act of Étiennette Eloize, the terms of freedom were as follows: "Étiennette Eloize, [is to] be, and remain from this moment Free, and freed from the bonds of servitude . . . [and] fully enjoy her Liberty, and dispose of her person as all the other formerly Free people, and freed people of the colony." Freedom act of Étiennette Eloize, 28 July 1804, ANOM DPPC NOT SDOM 699.

106. Garrigus, *Before Haiti*, 95. For a useful overview of the role of language in the unfolding of revolution in metropolitan France, see Smith, "No More Language Games." On the variegated legal strategies employed by *gens de couleur libres* in their struggle for equality, see Ghachem, *Old Regime and the Haitian Revolution*, 231–54.

107. *Dépôt* of Rozine *dite* Alzire, 17 October 1806, ANOM DPPC NOT SDOM 705.

108. Freedom of Zénon and Solon, 12 December 1805, ANOM DPPC NOT SDOM 735.

109. Freeing of Louise-Félicité *dite* Agard, 30 April 1804, ANOM DPPC NOT SDOM 699. In the original text: "*Lequel nous a dit, et déclare, que satisfait des soins* [illegible], *et du bon service continuel qu'il a reçu de la citoyenne Félicité surnommée Agard, depuis environ quatorze ans, qu'elle est son esclave, et sa propriété Légalement acquise.*"

110. Aside from the guarantee of equal rights for freed persons (except for the requirement that those freed from slavery show respect for their onetime masters and the possibility of reenslavement for certain offenses), the old code had offered several other potential bases for claims making. These included its stipulation of some avenues of escape from servitude (such as being named the executor in the master's will and marriage to the master) as well as its requirements that masters provide for slaves' basic subsistence and refrain from exceptional cruelty. Sala-Molins, *Le Code Noir*, 142, 194, and 198; Dubois and Garrigus, *Slave Revolution in the Caribbean*, 51–53; and Dubois, *Avengers of the New World*, 61.

111. Ferrand to Don Juan Castillos, 28 July 1808, CARAN Colonies CC/9a/45. On 20 July 1808, Ferrand had asked Lemdez in a letter to come before him with Manuel and the proper "titles" that would prove ownership over Manuel. Ferrand to Lemdez, 20 July 1808, CARAN Colonies CC/9a/45.

112. Ana Victoria Lasapelo to Monsieur P. C. Desile, commandant in chief of the Western Subdivision, 3 September 1807, CARAN Colonies CC/9a/44.

113. The *Code Noir* had effectively denied slaves' word any legal weight in civil or criminal cases. Though a royal ordinance from 1738 had subsequently allowed slave testimony to be accepted as evidence in legal cases if such testimony was essential and no white witnesses were available, slaves were still forbidden from testifying against their own masters. Sala-Molins, *Le Code Noir*, 150; Ghachem, *Old Regime and the Haitian Revolution*, 141.

114. "Commission charged with the examination of the Management of the ex-administrator Nicolás González," Session of 20 *Pluviôse an* 13 (9 February 1805), CARAN Colonies CC/9b/15. The claimant is not named in this document.

115. Ferrand to Castet, 4 June 1808, CARAN Colonies CC/9a/45.

116. Order of Ferrand on capture of Haitians, 6 January 1805, CARAN Colonies CC/9a/40. For more details on this extraordinary measure, see Jenson, *Beyond the Slave Narrative*, 151–52.

117. Ferrand to Joseph Ruiz, 6 January 1805, CARAN Colonies CC/9a/40.

118. Sale of the "*négresse*" Marie-Catherine, 3 February 1808, ANOM DPPC NOT SDOM 1700.

119. Sale of four children, 11 September 1808, ANOM DPPC NOT SDOM 1701.

120. Ferrand to Peralta, 8 November 1804, CARAN Colonies CC/9a/40.

121. Ferrand to "Commandants" and "Notables" in Santo Domingo, 2 October 1808, CARAN Colonies CC/9a/45.

122. On Christophe's Citadel, see Trouillot, *Silencing the Past*, chap. 2; and Dubois, *Avengers of the New World*, 303.

123. Girard, *Slaves Who Defeated Napoléon*, 335–36.

124. Bénot, *La démence coloniale*, 117–28; Picó, *One Frenchman, Four Revolutions*, 41–45. According to Girard, Ferrand defended the city with 700 French soldiers and 2,000 "French and Spanish militia." The arrival of Missiessy's force convinced Dessalines to beat a hasty retreat back to Haiti in spite of his seemingly imminent victory due to fears that the fleet would target Haiti, which was made vulnerable by the concentration of Haitian troops in Santo Domingo. Girard, *Slaves Who Defeated Napoléon*, 336–38. The account of Norbert Thoret corroborates the importance of Haiti's vulnerability to French attack in the Haitian invaders' strategy in Santo Domingo: according to Thoret, the arrival of the French naval force near Santo Domingo convinced Henry Christophe, one of the commanders in the invasion force, that the French might rush "in all haste to the French part [Haiti]." Nouët et al., *La vie aventureuse de Norbert Thoret*, 55. In the ensuing years, Dessalines's successors, Christophe and Alexandre Pétion, made little effort to dislodge Ferrand's regime from the island, except for Christophe's apparent provision of several hundred troops to the anti-French forces in the war in Santo Domingo in 1808–09 (see epilogue). This inaction presumably owed in large part to the bitter enmity between the two men, which Ferrand encouraged by deploying "agents provocateurs to foster ill will" between them. Girard, *Slaves Who Defeated Napoléon*, 336–38.

125. Nouët et al., *La vie aventureuse de Norbert Thoret*, 54.

126. Proclamation of Dessalines to fellow Haitians, 12 April 1805, in Rodríguez Demorizi, *Las invasiones haitianas*, 105–8.

127. Cordero Michel, "Toussaint en Saint-Domingue espagnol," 416–18.

128. Jenson, *Beyond the Slave Narrative*, 152.

129. This forced labor may in fact have contributed to the defeat of Dessalines's 1805 invasion. According to Emilio Cordero Michel, the harsh labor policies of Dessalines, combined with bitter memories of Toussaint's labor restrictions in 1801, instilled in the "slaves of Spanish Saint-Domingue [Santo Domingo]" a "fear" of being "tied to agriculture" by a victorious Haitian state, which in turn led many to refuse to support "the political unification of the island" under Haitian governance. Cordero Michel, "Toussaint en Saint-Domingue espagnol," 432. On Dessalines's labor policies, see Gonzalez, "War on Sugar."

130. Schloss, *Sweet Liberty*, 35. Emphasis in original. Alleged connections between Haiti's civil strife and nonwhites in neighboring slaveholding colonies provoked anxiety among some authorities. According to one report to the minister of the navy composed in January 1806, many "people of color" in Santiago de Cuba had collected 5,000 to 6,000 *gourdes* that were to be given to the faction that opposed Dessalines in Haiti's internal conflict. This caused the report's author to suspect the existence of a "secret mission, on the part of the Mulattos" in France and to urge a "redoubling of surveillance and of precautions" against them even as he admitted that "no proof" existed to substantiate his allegations. Letter to Minister of the Navy and Colonies, January 1806, CARAN Colonies CC/9a/42.

131. Tomich, *Through the Prism of Slavery*, 56.

132. Ferrer, "Speaking of Haiti," 225. Cuba's rejection of the Spanish-American trend of separatism in the early nineteenth century has often been attributed by scholars substantially to elites' dependence on slavery and fears of "another Haiti," while the newly independent "black republic" served as an inspiration to some Cuban slaves and free nonwhites. Ada Ferrer has nonetheless cautioned against a simplistic view of these tropes of "fear" and "hope," contextualizing both within the dissemination of news about Haiti in Cuba, the importance of Haiti in rebellions and conspiracies among nonwhites in Cuba, and the numerous other connections between Haiti and Cuba in the first part of the nineteenth century. See Ferrer, "Cuba en la sombra de Haití"; and Ferrer, "La société esclavagiste cubaine et la révolution haïtienne."

133. Some inhabitants of Santo Domingo in the Ferrand period advanced claims to property rights in individuals who resided in Cuba, Puerto Rico, and other places. For instance, in a 5 October 1807 letter, Ferrand instructed his subordinate Pedro Ruiz to send him several "slaves" living in Puerto Rico who were claimed by would-be masters based in Santo Domingo. Ferrand to Pedro Ruiz, 5 October 1807, CARAN Colonies CC/9a/43.

134. On the rice economy in antebellum South Carolina and Georgia, see Carney, "Landscapes of Technology Transfer." Carney's scholarship has demonstrated that South Carolina and Georgia were key nodes in the Atlantic rice economy, with Afri-

can captives and their descendants providing invaluable knowledge and technology in addition to labor. See Carney, *Black Rice*.

135. Ferrand to Members of the Superior Council of Santiago (Santo Domingo), 4 December 1804, CARAN Colonies CC/9a/40.

136. As noted in chapter 3, French Saint-Domingue had been the second most important trade partner to the United States after England in the late eighteenth century, and U.S. trade and diplomacy influenced internal conflicts in Saint-Domingue, such as the War of the South, during the revolutionary period.

137. Some evidence of American financial assistance to Ferrand nonetheless exists in the primary source record. Thoret claimed that an American captain named Tayarre smuggled 60,000 *piastres* sent by the French government through the British blockade to Ferrand. Thoret also noted, however, that Americans "were numerous in the colony [Haiti]" around 1805. Nouët et al., *La vie aventureuse de Norbert Thoret*, 58 and 67.

138. At least one prominent American businessman, William Walton, lived in Santo Domingo during the Ferrand years. The Baltimore-based Walton was involved in high-level moneylending to the regime as well as negotiations to establish an American consulate in Santo Domingo. He was also involved in a number of "slave" sales in Santo Domingo. Nonetheless, Walton appears to have turned against the French and allied with the Spanish during the 1808–09 rebellion of the latter against the Napoleonic government in Santo Domingo. See Ferrand to French minister to the United States, 11 December 1804, CARAN Colonies CC/9a/40; Ferrand to French minister to the United States, 13 December 1804, CARAN Colonies CC/9a/40; and Gilbert Guillermin, "[Illegible] Journal of the Revolution of the Eastern part of St Domingue beginning 10 August 1808," 1810, note of 21 October 1808, ANOM CMSM F3 121. On Walton's involvement in transactions involving captives, see sale of the *"négresse"* Caroline by Walton to the *"veuve"* (widow) [name illegible], 3 April 1806, ANOM DPPC NOT SDOM 704; and sale of the *"nègre"* Dubin (or Lubin) by Walton to Madame Sophie Sabattrier, 11 May 1807, ANOM DPPC NOT SDOM 735.

139. Gaffield, " 'So Many Schemes in Agitation,' " 228–29.

140. Ibid., chap. 4.

141. Ibid., 9–11; Jenson, *Beyond the Slave Narrative*, 107–15 and 143–58. According to Jenson, Ferrand issued orders in 1805 prescribing the death penalty for any person who either traded with Haiti or came within two leagues of any Haitian port. Jenson, *Beyond the Slave Narrative*, 164–65. For further discussion on the intersections between the issue of the capture of ships accused of trading with Haiti and disputes over the recognition of Haiti among foreign powers (such as Britain), see Gaffield, " 'So Many Schemes in Agitation,' " chap. 3.

142. Gaffield, " 'So Many Schemes in Agitation,' " 27.

143. Quoted in ibid., 257.

144. Jenson, *Beyond the Slave Narrative*, 113–14. In 1825, France agreed to extend diplomatic recognition to Haiti in exchange for an indemnity of 150 million francs. Trouillot, *Haiti, State against Nation*, 50–51 and 61.

145. Quoted in Jenson, *Beyond the Slave Narrative*, 113.

146. According to General Kerverseau in a 23 March 1804 letter to the minister of the navy, "the financial resources of that part [Santo Domingo] are reduced today to captures made by the Corsairs; for in the absolute stagnation of commerce, the products of customs are almost nothing, and in this part's current State of depopulation, it is necessary to count as almost nothing that of the national domains." In this same letter, Kerverseau related that North American, British, and Danish "agents of Commerce" had established themselves in Les Cayes and Jacmel, Haiti. Kerverseau to Minister of the Navy and Colonies, 23 March 1804, ANOM CMSM F3 283. On Ferrand's maritime legal strategies and reliance upon piracy to ensure his regime's survival, see Jenson, *Beyond the Slave Narrative*, chaps. 2 and 4. On Ferrand's competition with French authorities on other islands for the revenue derived from capturing ships suspected of trading with Haiti, see Gaffield, "'So Many Schemes in Agitation,'" 49.

147. "State of Affairs in which the articles came from Santo Domingo, that are subject to observation," undated, CARAN Colonies CC/9a/48.

148. On the political situation between Britain and Brazil with respect to these matters, see Mamigonian, "In the Name of Freedom."

149. Beatriz Mamigonian contends that a principal objective of the British Colonial Office was to transport "liberated Africans" from captured slave ships (and from the British colony of Sierra Leone) to serve as indentured laborers in British West Indian colonies. Ibid., 42. Moreover, Lauren Benton has argued that British legal strategies to enforce the ban on the slave trade were closely tied to the consolidation of the British imperial political and legal order in the early nineteenth century. See Benton, "Abolition and Imperial Law." On indentured labor and comparisons to slavery, see Northrup, *Indentured Labor in the Age of Imperialism*; and Adderly, "'New Negroes from Africa.'"

150. Sale of "blacks" from H. Abendanon to Payra Ferry, 8 December 1806, ANOM DPPC NOT SDOM 705.

151. Sale of L'Éveillé, 4 September 1808, ANOM DPPC NOT SDOM 1302.

152. Ferrand to "Commandant of Higüey," 27 February 1804, CARAN Colonies CC/9a/40.

153. Ferrand to Villavicencio, 20 July 1807, CARAN Colonies CC/9a/43.

154. Ferrand to "Chief of Administration," 17 August 1807, CARAN Colonies CC/9a/44.

155. Ferrand to Minister of the Navy and Colonies, 8 April 1806, CARAN Colonies CC/9a/42.

156. "Précis sent by the Government to fill in Saint Domingue the functions of Receiver General of Contributions [Tax Collector]," to Minister of the Navy and Colonies, 6 March 1801, CARAN Colonies CC/9b/18.

Chapter Six

1. *Dépôt* of Adelaïde Faury, 30 July 1803, ANOM DPPC NOT SDOM 485.

2. For Adelaïde Faury's activities as a merchant, see sale of a hut from Jean-Pierre Cayret to Adelaïde Faury, 28 July 1803, ANOM DPPC NOT SDOM 485.

3. The second and final declaration of universal slave emancipation in all French territories took place in 1848.

4. These records represent the totality of all such documents that survive in the books of French notaries who served in Santo Domingo during the years 1795 to 1809. Eighty-nine of these 103 acts were created under the Napoleonic regime of 1804–09.

5. Chapter 20 of the Dominican *Código Negro* of 1784, for instance, borrowed from the spirit of the *Code Noir* in its stipulations that the act of manumission conferred upon those thus freed "the same effects that natural liberty confers on free-born persons granting [the freed person] the same prerogatives, rights, and privileges [*preeminencias*] as [the free-born]"; and that "the freed person who gravely lacks gratitude, and the recognized obligation and submission to his patron, wife or children, shall be . . . returned to his former condition" of enslavement. Barceló, *Código Negro Carolino*, 205.

6. Proposals and ordinances on judicial reorganization in Santo Domingo starting in 1802 called for a degree of power sharing between "French" and "Spanish" authorities. One proposed judicial reform concerning Santo Domingo dated 10 October 1802 envisioned the establishment of three "Courts of Justice," including two of the first instance (one in Santo Domingo city and the other in Santiago) and an appeals court to be located in Santo Domingo city. Each of these three courts was to have three judges, of which one on each tribunal had to be "Spanish." Proposal for judicial organization in Santo Domingo, 10 October 1802, CARAN Colonies CC/9a/32. Furthermore, on 22 September 1805, General Ferrand issued a decree that called for a comprehensive restructuring of Santo Domingo's judicial infrastructure. This included the creation of a high appeals court that would be composed of half "French" and half "Spanish" judges. The decree also ordered the establishment of courts of the first instance that would have the same proportion of French and Spanish justices. This order invoked Spanish legal precedent and maintained certain Spanish officials, such as *alcaldes*, in their posts while also stipulating the appointment of French judges and other authorities. Ferrand, "Regulation on Judicial Organization of the Eastern Department, Formerly [the] Spanish Part," 22 September 1805, ANOM 8 SUPSDOM 390. "French" Santo Domingo was not the only "mixed" legal situation in the Americas in this era. On the "hybrid legal system" in Louisiana, see Gross and Fuente, "Slaves, Free Blacks, and Race" (quote is from 1704). For an incisive discussion on the complex interaction of French, Spanish, and U.S. slave law in the drafting and implementation of the Louisiana Digest of 1808, see Palmer, "Strange Science of Codifying Slavery."

7. See ANOM DPPC NOT SDOM 1301, book of notary Noël Nicolas Leprestre, 1795–96. In fact, at least two "Spanish" notaries, Manuel Regalado and Antonio Pérez, appear in the extant documentary record as having served in Santo Domingo during at least part of the fourteen years of French rule. A 23 September 1805 decree concerning judicial reorganization in French Santo Domingo stipulated that two "former Spanish Notaries" named Antonio Pérez and Manuel González Regalado were to serve in Santo Domingo city alongside their "French" counterparts Jean-Paul Gaernier, Pierre-Joseph Funel, and Barthélemy Vallenet. Ferrand decree on judicial reorganization, 23 September 1805, CARAN Colonies CC/9c/11. A detailed biographical listing of public officials in Santo Domingo city contains an entry for a notary named Antonio Pérez, born in that city on 26 June 1737, who had served in this function there since 1762. "Nominative Listing of Officers Comprising the Judicial Order in Santo Domingo," 1 March 1808, CARAN Colonies CC/9c/11. A death record for the "notary public" Manuel Regalado dated 5 September 1807 exists in the État Civil, Santo Domingo collection in the ANOM (see the microfilm 85 Miom 95). Kathryn Burns has noted that after the promulgation of the *Siete Partidas*, rivalries between monarchical authority and cities in Castile led to the creation of different types of notarial posts, one of which was "*escribano* [] *del rey*" (one Spanish translation of *écrivain du roy*, or "writer/scribe of the king"). The French notary Leprestre's designation thus may have reflected this Spanish medieval precedent. K. Burns, "Notaries, Truth, and Consequences," 358.

8. The requirements for entry into the notarial profession reflected its importance. Per the *Siete Partidas*, these requirements included being a free man (not a slave), being a Christian of "good reputation," possessing skill in writing, maintaining residency in one's place of employment, and being a layman. R. Burns, *Las Siete Partidas*, 3:759–60 (*Partida* III, Title XIX, Law II). Professional standards for notaries in the French world appear to have been similar. According to a 21 July 1802 regulation issued by the "General in Chief [and] Captain General" in Saint-Domingue, in order to enter the profession, a man must demonstrate attainment of at least twenty-five years of age; proof of "irreproachable morality" by way of certificates "in due form" signed by "Notable Citizens" in the prospective notary's place of domicile; and sufficient knowledge of both old and new laws, the "functions and duties of notaries," and the drafting of notarial acts. This regulation, which proclaimed that the "Notariat" was "the Civil institution upon which the security of families and the fortune of Citizens especially rests," also interestingly required notaries to not violate the "law of 16 pluviôse year 2 [4 February 1794]," which may refer to the act of general emancipation passed by the National Convention on that day. "Regulation [on the] Organization of the Notariat in the French Part of the Isle of St Domingue," 21 July 1802, ANOM 8 SUPSDOM 390.

9. Hardwick, *Practice of Patriarchy*, 5, 43. John Garrigus has likewise argued that the notarial system in colonial French Saint-Domingue provided a "public voice" for poor *gens de couleur libres* and that it constituted a nascent "public space" for free

Dominguans regardless of social status. Garrigus, *Before Haiti*, 94–95. On the relationships between social status and literacy in Saint-Domingue under the ancien régime, see King, *Blue Coat or Powdered Wig*, xxii, 177–78.

10. Hardwick, *Practice of Patriarchy*, 5.

11. Fifty-seven liberty acts out of the 103 listed a place of birth or former residence for the freed subject, while fifty-three contained this information for the freedom granter (former purported master or individual entrusted to act in his or her name). Out of such records, more than 59 percent of the subjects and 81 percent of the freedom granters had lived in Saint-Domingue. Within this subset of cases, Saint-Domingue's three provinces (the north, west, and south) had roughly equal representation.

12. According to Laurent Dubois, the term "Congo" in colonial Saint-Domingue came to encompass people from a large area of West Central Africa, including the kingdom of Kongo and many other locales. These "Congos" constituted 40 percent of total slave imports to Saint-Domingue in the eighteenth century. By the 1780s, they comprised half of the slave population on the coffee plantations in the north and west provinces and 40 percent of the total unfree population on northern sugar plantations. Dubois, *Avengers of the New World*, 40–43. According to David Geggus, "West Central Africa" supplied virtually half (49.2 percent) of African slaves sold to Saint-Domingue on French ships. In this colony's north, the figure was even higher (56.6 percent). Geggus, "French Slave Trade," 137–38. On the political and military impact of those from West Central Africa in Saint-Domingue in the eighteenth century, see Thornton, " 'I Am the Subject of the King of Kongo.' "

13. Garrigus, *Before Haiti*, 40; Peabody, "*Négresse, Mulâtresse, Citoyenne*," 57–58; and Ghachem, *Old Regime and the Haitian Revolution*, 85–86.

14. Ghachem, *Old Regime and the Haitian Revolution*, 188.

15. On French efforts to retake Haiti, see Gaffield, " 'So Many Schemes in Agitation,' " 7–9.

16. For details on the "maroon" Marthone's capture in Cuba and the dispute that ensued concerning ownership of her, see notarial act of 28 March 1806, ANOM DPPC NOT SDOM 704; and act of 21 August 1806, ANOM DPPC NOT SDOM 705. For the sale of the captive from Curaçao, see sale of Lucie, 14 December 1807, ANOM DPPC NOT SDOM 1699.

17. The foundation of the First French Empire and the coronation of Napoleon as its emperor transpired in 1804.

18. Fully 78 percent of these notarized freedom acts included at least one racial marker for the subject; the freedom granter was racialized in just under a tenth of all cases. Of the racial terms used, *nègre* and *négresse* were by far the most common, with half of all records that include racialized subjects employing these words. By contrast, the freedom granters who were racialized predominantly bore the labels *mulâtre* and *mulâtresse* (this was the case in six out of ten such records).

19. The singular exception to the elimination of "*citoyen*" in these records by the end of 1804 is the 18 April 1807 self-purchase of Marie-Claire *dite* Coco from her former purported master *citoyen* Pierre-Nicholas Pitre contained in ANOM DPPC NOT SDOM 735. On the relationships between racial ideologies and the usage of honorifics such as *le sieur* and *la dame* in the eighteenth-century French Caribbean, see Popkin, *You Are All Free*, 34; Garrigus, *Before Haiti*, 186; and Dubois, *Colony of Citizens*, 256. My findings appear to accord with those of Frédéric Régent on the resurgence of racial labels in État Civil records in Guadeloupe following the defeat of rebels there in 1802. According to Régent, "the disappearance of the mention of citizen [in these records] mark[ed] the start of the reestablishment of the color barrier." Régent, *Esclavage, métissage, liberté*, 425.

20. As in pre-1789 Saint-Domingue, testaments in French Santo Domingo sometimes granted "slaves" to racially marked persons who were often themselves the former "slaves" of the testator. See, for instance, the will of *sieur* Étienne Gouin (or Gonin; the spelling is unclear), in which the testator "grants to the so-called [*nommée*] Zaire, *négresse*, for her pains and care for various illnesses the *négresse* named Rosalie his Slave." Will of Étienne Gouin/Gonin, 17 December 1805, ANOM DPPC NOT SDOM 1698. Moreover, when the father of Chonne Martin, a former inhabitant of Léogane (southern Saint-Domingue) whom I discuss later in this chapter, purchased his daughter with the purpose of freeing her, he offered as payment two "*nègres*" named Réchange and L'Espérance. Freedom act of Chonne Martin, 26 February 1806, ANOM DPPC NOT SDOM 704. Finally, as discussed later in this chapter, in pursuit of a notarized freedom act, a woman named Marseille *dite* Migniac called witnesses before a notary who affirmed her ownership over "slaves," among other "property," as evidence of her free status.

21. The same books that contain these notarized liberty acts also hold a large number of "slave" sales. My preliminary count of these sales has tallied at least several dozen, which can constitute a basis for future research. Recall from chapter 5 that an 1808 census put the total "slave" population of the colony of Santo Domingo at 7,052.

22. R. Burns, *Las Siete Partidas*, 4:981 (*Partida* IV, Title XXII).

23. Ibid., 4:977 (*Partida* IV, Title XXI, Law I).

24. Beginning in the 1760s in Saint-Domingue, a confluence of repressive legislation and periodic crackdowns by zealous authorities had led *gens de couleur libres* to scrupulously document their legal condition using every means at their disposal. This hostile climate also compelled many of them to notarize even the smallest sales in order to thwart possible accusations of theft that would not have been so readily made against whites. Garrigus, *Before Haiti*, 84, 167, and 178–79.

25. *Dépôt* of Marie-Jeanne, 3 September 1804, ANOM DPPC NOT SDOM 699.

26. For a succinct overview of "The Great Powers and the Haitian Revolution," see Geggus, *Haitian Revolutionary Studies*, chap. 11.

27. R. Scott, "'She . . . Refuses to Deliver Up Herself,'" 128. For a discussion of the contentious legal disputes that ensued over the 1794 French emancipation law's le-

gitimacy and applicability in the antebellum United States, see Peabody, "'Free upon Higher Ground,'" esp. 268–71. See also R. Scott, "Paper Thin."

28. Girard, "Napoleon Bonaparte," 614. Emphasis in original. Régent has found that fear of the impending reestablishment of slavery provoked similar responses among many freed people in Guadeloupe starting in the spring of 1802. Régent, *Esclavage, métissage, liberté*, 425. The threat of enslavement also impelled some individuals to go to the lengths of creating manumission records for those who had been living as free people as a documentary safeguard against the loss of liberty. On 10 May 1803, the Dominguan colonist Michel Vincent created an act of manumission for his companion, Rosalie, and her four children, despite their attainment of freedom some time before. Rebecca Scott and Jean Hébrard attribute this seemingly odd act to the uncertain political and legal context and to "the symbolic and juridical powers of contractual written documents." Scott and Hébrard, "Servitude, liberté et citoyenneté," 30. See also Scott and Hébrard, *Freedom Papers*, 42–48.

29. Bitter memories of the dismantling of French emancipationist regimes in the Caribbean cast a long shadow over subsequent contests over the terms of freedom in the region. In the 1830s, as the British imposed a system of "apprenticeship" in their slaveholding territories that its architects envisioned as a path to gradual emancipation, many of the formally freed "apprentices" tried to purchase their freedom shortly before the term of apprenticeship was slated to end. David Gaspar attributes this to these freed individuals' suspicions that British abolition might not endure; they apparently based this judgment partly on their knowledge of the brutal overturning of French revolutionary emancipation several decades earlier. Gaspar, "La Guerre des Bois," 123–24.

30. Ferrand to commandant of Seybo, 12 September 1807, CARAN Colonies CC/9a/43.

31. K. Burns, "Notaries, Truth, and Consequences," 372. See also K. Burns, *Into the Archive*.

32. *Dépôt* of Henriette *dite* Pommeau, 28 June 1805, ANOM DPPC NOT SDOM 702.

33. The quotes are from K. Burns, "Notaries, Truth and Consequences," 366.

34. Liberty act of *citoyenne* Margueritte Bonne, 8 August 1803, ANOM DPPC NOT SDOM 485. The *Siete Partidas* contained provisions that mandated scrupulous attention to recordkeeping. *Partida* III, Title XIX, Law X, for instance, required a notary to produce a copy (as close to the original as possible) of a document that a client claimed to have lost and to record this in his register. R. Burns, *Las Siete Partidas*, 3:763–64. Such practices were evidently also important in the French world, as comprehensive registries for every notarial book produced in French Santo Domingo exist in the ANOM (section "DPPC SDOM REP").

35. *Dépôt* of Louise *dite* Letort, 18 August 1807, ANOM DPPC NOT SDOM 735.

36. *Dépôt* of Marie-Magdeleine, 8 August 1806, ANOM DPPC NOT SDOM 705.

37. Johnson, *Soul by Soul*, 1.

38. The ambiguities attaching to slaves' personhood in colonial slave laws in the Americas are also evident in tensions within slaves' dual legal status as both transferable chattel and subjects of certain criminal and disciplinary proceedings and sanctions. Notably, the framers of the 1784 *Código Negro* had stated that "slaves ought not to be considered as purely physical entities incapable of virtue and reason, or as pure automatons only useful for onerous agricultural tasks" even as these framers reaffirmed the viability of holding humans as property. Barceló, *Código Negro Carolino*, 166.

39. According to Sue Peabody, Article XXIX of the *Code Noir* had allowed slaves to accumulate funds to purchase themselves or relatives, though this was contingent upon the master's permission. Peabody, "*Négresse, Mulâtresse, Citoyenne*," 58. For the text of this article, see Sala-Molins, *Le Code Noir*, 148.

40. Self-purchase of Marie-Elizabeth *dite* Justine, 8 June 1807, ANOM DPPC NOT SDOM 706.

41. Just over half (51 percent) of these 103 notarial records included a phrase such as "good services" or "good will" (*bon gré*), making this the most frequently cited reason for manumission among these freedom acts. The underlying logic of manumission for "good services" was an assertion of the would-be master's sovereignty over those whom he claimed as his slaves, and this logic was evident at higher levels of authority as well. Malick Ghachem has argued that the very presence of provisions in the *Code Noir* authorizing manumission without a formal justification and the naturalization of freed people implied the king's power to revoke these privileges at will. Ghachem, *Old Regime and the Haitian Revolution*, 82.

42. For details on these developments in colonial Santo Domingo, see Turits, "Par-delà les plantations," esp. 54–55.

43. In a study currently in progress of manumission deeds from the Dominican towns of Higüey and Bayaguana, Richard Turits has identified so far thirty-eight created between 1702 and 1821. About these cases, he writes: "25 were paid for, mostly but not all self-purchase, 11 were gracioso [not paid for], and 2 are unclear." E-mail correspondence (from 12 July 2010) cited with written permission of author.

44. Marquis d'Iranda to Perregaux, 26 June 1800, CARAN Colonies CC/9b/17.

45. For details on these local officials, known as the *síndicos* in Cuba, see R. Scott, *Slave Emancipation in Cuba*, 74–75. On the practice of self-purchase in installments known as *coartación* that emerged in Cuba, which according to Scott "[in] theory . . . created an intermediate status between slave and free," see ibid., 13; and Fuente, "Slaves and the Creation of Legal Rights." In her study of the French refugee community in Santiago de Cuba, Agnès Renault characterized self-purchase (*rachat*) as an "exceptional phenomenon" whose rarity owed to the combination of high purchase prices and purported masters' unwillingness to relinquish valuable servile labor. Moreover, not a single case of self-purchase that she uncovered there before 1809 involved a *coartado* (individual who purchased himself or herself through *coartación*). Renault, "Les conditions d'affranchissements," 12.

46. According to Richard Turits, local authorities in Santo Domingo drew up a Black Code (*Código Negro*)—the Spanish Indies' first—in 1768, followed by a second version in 1784. Both grew out of efforts to emulate the prosperity of French Saint-Domingue and to strengthen racial hierarchy. The 1784 *Código* in turn served as the basis for the sweeping 1789 royal *cédula* intended to govern the slave populations throughout the Spanish empire, yet due in part to planter opposition, neither was actually implemented. Turits, *Foundations of Despotism*, 36–38. The 1784 *Código Negro* stipulated that a *"procurador síndico general"* (general public advocate) be appointed to defend slaves suing for their freedom and that any master who "without just and rational motive impedes the liberty of his slaves who ought to have the highest security to gain it" pay a fine of twenty-five pesos in addition to legal costs. In chapter 22, the *Código* also established a basis for *"coartación"* by which slaves could pay off their purchase price in installments, and masters could not arbitrarily raise this price or refuse payments toward eventual self-purchase. Barceló, *Código Negro Carolino*, 205–8. The 1789 *cédula* further detailed the role of the *síndico procurador*, who was to ensure that slaves receive adequate food and clothing, assist slaves in cases of alleged abuse by masters, and defend slaves who were charged with crimes. According to Alejandro de la Fuente, in Cuba at least, the actions of the *síndico* "not only sustained customary legal practices such as coartación . . . but also cloaked them with a mantle of legality." Fuente, "Slaves and the Creation of Legal Rights," 665. For a reproduction of the *cédula*, see Ortiz, *Los negros esclavos*, 408–15.

47. Ghachem, *Old Regime and the Haitian Revolution*, 83–84.

48. Moreau de St Méry, *Description topographique et politique de la partie espagnole*, 1:57–58. On these same pages, Moreau asserted that "a slave" (using the feminine form of the noun, *une esclave*) in Santo Domingo could purchase her liberty by "present[ing] to her master 250 piastres gourdes (1,375 liv. tournois)" after which "she is assured of her freedom." She could also buy a child's freedom for an additional sum.

49. Garrigus, "Redrawing the Colour Line" (quotes are from 41).

50. In a recent article, Alejandro de la Fuente wrote that "the significance of coartación goes beyond the number or percentage of slaves who successfully availed themselves of it. As with marronage or revolts—which always involved a small proportion of total slaves—the impact of coartación cannot be reduced to mere statistics." Fuente, "Slaves and the Creation of Legal Rights," 669. This argument also applies to the small number of freed people who appear in these notarized freedom acts from Santo Domingo.

51. For example, on 18 April 1807, Marie-Claire *dite* Coco (who had been living in Mayagüez, Puerto Rico) purchased herself from Pierre-Nicholas Pitre for the sum of 280 *gourdes*. Self-purchase of Marie-Claire *dite* Coco, 18 April 1807, ANOM DPPC NOT SDOM 735.

52. Self-purchase of Catherine, 9 October 1805, ANOM DPPC NOT SDOM 1698. The original wording in French is *"provenant de son pécule."*

53. Temin, "Economy of the Early Roman Empire," 141. According to Alan Watson, a version of the *Code Noir* redacted in 1724 allowed slaves to have a *peculium*; the rules governing this drew substantially from Roman legal precepts concerning fathers' and masters' responsibilities for the liabilities and other obligations of sons and slaves. Watson, *Slave Law in the Americas*, 89. The "right of peculium" (*derecho de peculio*) also appeared in Spanish-American legislation, such as the 1784 *Código Negro*. See Barceló, *Código Negro Carolino*, 199–201.

54. Self-purchase of *citoyenne* Louise-Félicité *dite* Agard, 5 May 1804, ANOM DPPC NOT SDOM 699.

55. Revocation and reinstatement of liberty for *citoyenne* Louise-Félicité *dite* Agard, 11 May 1804, ANOM DPPC NOT SDOM 699.

56. Dubois, *Colony of Citizens*, 257.

57. Ferrand to Medina, 5 December 1807, CARAN Colonies CC/9a/43.

58. Ibid.

59. Witnesses' testimony in favor of Marseille *dite* Migniac, 21 June 1805, ANOM DPPC NOT SDOM 702.

60. Ibid.

61. John Garrigus has observed that "according to one local census from mid-[eighteenth] century, free coloured women were four times more likely than white women to be heads of rural households." Garrigus, "Redrawing the Colour Line," 38. See also Socolow, "Economic Roles of Free Women of Color."

62. In a study of marriage contracts and testaments drawn up by notaries in Le Cap and Port-au-Prince in the late eighteenth century, Dominique Rogers found that while Port-au-Prince notaries usually demanded from free nonwhite clients proof of free status, such as a manumission act or birth certificate, notaries in Le Cap often "ascertained that a person was free simply by reference to his or her reputation, specifically their *possession d'état de libre* (the fact that a person was considered by others to be free)." Rogers, "On the Road to Citizenship," 72. Emphasis in original. On regional distinctions in racial labeling by notaries in the late prerevolutionary era, see also Garrigus, "Vincent Ogé Jeune," 39–42.

63. Davis, *Fiction in the Archives*, 4. For an examination of legal testimonies concerning a series of riots in Paris in 1750 that employs a somewhat similar perspective, see Farge and Revel, *Vanishing Children of Paris*, esp. chap. 4.

64. Freedom act of Chonne Martin, 26 February 1806, ANOM DPPC NOT SDOM 704. See also an act concerning a woman named Marie-Claire, whose late ex-master's widow testified that she was free. Freedom act of Marie-Claire, 29 August 1806, ANOM DPPC NOT SDOM 705.

65. R. Burns, *Las Siete Partidas*, 4:983 (*Partida* IV, Title XXII, Law VII).

66. Ghachem, *Old Regime and the Haitian Revolution*, 87–88.

67. Act in favor of Marie Melie, 18 March 1808, ANOM DPPC NOT SDOM 1700. Roman law had established the basic principle (which subsequently became enshrined in both French and Spanish law) that slave status passed through one's mother. The

Siete Partidas specified three ways in which a person could be enslaved: birth to an enslaved mother, capture in war, and voluntary sale of oneself into slavery. R. Burns, *Las Siete Partidas*, 4:977 (*Partida* IV, Title XXI, Law I). The *Code Noir* also stipulated that a child's legal status followed that of his or her mother. See Sala-Molins, *Le Code Noir*, 116–17 (Article XIII of the *Code*).

68. Ferrand to M. Fortier, 4 March 1808, CARAN Colonies CC/9a/45.

69. See Garrigus, *Before Haiti*, esp. chaps. 1–2; and Dubois, *Avengers of the New World*, chap. 1.

70. Malick Ghachem has argued that many masters and slaves in colonial Saint-Domingue had used baptism as another way to circumvent official restrictions on manumission. The apparent prevalence of this strategy derived in part from the "emancipative connotations of Christian status and identity" in that colony. Ghachem, *Old Regime and the Haitian Revolution*, 87. These realities were not lost on Dominguan migrants, such as the *"nègre libre"* Jean d'Enblot. According to a 22 June 1806 notarial act created in Santo Domingo city, Jean deposited with the notary an *"attestation"* certifying that he and the *"négresse libre"* Marie had married in Artibonite (Saint-Domingue) in 1787. This act also affirmed that Jean and Marie had three children (Jean-François, Jean-Baptiste, and Jean-Simon) in "Legitimate marriage." These details suggest that Jean and Marie intended this notarial act to serve as an assurance of the freedom of their entire family, as well as evidence of the legitimacy of their children, since the children's birth to a free mother in "Legitimate marriage" implies that they were both legally free and legitimate. Jean-François and Jean-Baptiste were listed as "N.L." (*Nègre Libre*) in the act. *Dépôt* of Jean d'Enblot, 22 June 1806, ANOM DPPC NOT SDOM 1698. Per the *Siete Partidas*, marriage to a free person (including one's master) automatically freed an enslaved spouse. R. Burns, *Las Siete Partidas*, 4:982 (*Partida* IV, Title XXII, Law V).

71. For discussions of these decisions and their consequences, see Girard, "Napoleon Bonaparte"; and Dubois, *Avengers of the New World*, 251–61.

72. Scott and Hébrard, "Servitude, liberté et citoyenneté," 4.

Epilogue

1. While historians of Latin America have generally viewed Napoleon's invasion of Spain in 1808 as a watershed in Spanish-American political history, some newer scholarship has emphasized the continuities between the imperial order before 1808 and the nations that emerged in the following decades. See, for instance, Adelman, *Sovereignty and Revolution in the Iberian Atlantic*; and Hamnett, "Process and Pattern." For a discussion of French reactions to the political crisis in Spanish America after 1808, see Blaufarb, "Western Question."

2. For details on these migrations, see R. Scott, "'She . . . Refuses to Deliver Up Herself,'" 126; Vázquez Cienfuegos, *Tan difíciles tiempos para Cuba*, 295; Scott and Hébrard, *Freedom Papers*, 58–82; and Brasseaux and Conrad, *Road to Louisiana*.

3. Gilbert Guillermin, "[Illegible] Journal of the Revolution of the Eastern part of St Domingue beginning 10 August 1808," 1810, note of 10 August 1808, ANOM CMSM F3 121.

4. Guillermin, "Journal of the Revolution," "Details on the revolt of 26 September to 12 October 1808, and on the principal leaders," ANOM CMSM F3 121; Picó, *One Frenchman, Four Revolutions*, 74.

5. Montes to Ferrand, 2 August 1808, in Guillermin, "Journal of the Revolution," ANOM CMSM F3 121.

6. Pétion and Christophe both vied to succeed Jean-Jacques Dessalines, who was assassinated in 1806, as ruler of Haiti.

7. Guillermin, "Journal of the Revolution," Fifth Note, ANOM CMSM F3 121.

8. Guillermin, "Journal of the Revolution," ANOM CMSM F3 121.

9. Guillermin, "Journal of the Revolution," "Details on the revolt of 26 September to 12 October 1808, and on the principal leaders," ANOM CMSM F3 121. On the anti-French rebels' efforts to seek aid from Pétion and Christophe, see Eller, "'All would be equal,'" 113.

10. Guillermin, "Journal of the Revolution," Forty-Fourth Note, ANOM CMSM F3 121.

11. Listing of troop numbers under Ferrand, 23 September 1804, ANOM TPC D2C 371.

12. Listing of troop numbers under General Joseph Barquier, 1 January 1809, ANOM TPC D2C 371; listing of troop numbers under Barquier, 11 July 1809, ANOM TPC D2C 371.

13. Carreaux to Christóbal Huber and [Illegible], October 1808, in Guillermin, "Journal of the Revolution," ANOM CMSM F3 121.

14. Guillermin, "Journal of the Revolution," ANOM CMSM F3 121.

15. E. Paillier, report to Napoleon, 29 November 1809, CARAN AF/IV/968. According to Fernando Picó, 300 of the men who fought under Ferrand in this battle did not live to recount the humiliating defeat, while all but six of the Spanish-allied soldiers survived. Picó, *One Frenchman, Four Revolutions*, 80.

16. Guillermin, "Journal of the Revolution," details on the formation of the junta, 27 November–18 December 1808, ANOM CMSM F3 121. I thank Francisco Moscoso (personal communication, 25 November 2014) for clarifying some of the details of these events.

17. Guillermin, "Journal of the Revolution," Forty-Sixth Note, ANOM CMSM F3 121.

18. By early 1809, the French were sorely outnumbered. As noted earlier in this chapter, they fielded only 1,361 troops as of 1 January 1809, while according to one report, as of 22 February 1809 the Spanish had 2,320 men. *Bulletin Officiel de Santo Domingo*, 22 February 1809, in Guillermin, "Journal of the Revolution," ANOM CMSM F3 121.

19. Girard, *Slaves Who Defeated Napoléon*, 337–38.

20. Guillermin, "Journal of the Revolution," ANOM CMSM F3 121.

21. Guillermin, "Journal of the Revolution," Seventy-Eighth Note, ANOM CMSM F3 121.

22. Accord of capitulation of the French in Santo Domingo, 6 July 1809, ANOM CMSM F3 284.

23. On the tumultuous 1809–22 period and Santo Domingo's importance in the Spanish American independence struggles, see Eller, "'All would be equal'"; and Lora, "El sonido de la libertad."

24. Turits, *Foundations of Despotism*, 44–45.

25. For a discussion on the effects of the Haitian Revolution on slavery and race relations in Latin America, see Geggus, "Sounds and Echoes of Freedom."

26. The best known of these figures was the Venezuelan independence hero, Simón Bolívar. For a discussion of this leader's views on slavery, see Lynch, *Simón Bolívar*, chaps. 5 and 7.

27. Picó, *One Frenchman, Four Revolutions*, 98–100.

28. The Dominican Republic first became known by this name in 1844, when it gained independence from Haiti. On the Haitian occupation of 1822–44, see Turits, *Foundations of Despotism*, 44–46. On Haiti's nineteenth-century history, see Trouillot, *Haiti, State against Nation*, chaps. 1–2.

29. On these early debates on Native Americans, see Seed, "'Are They not Also Men?'" On Haitian migrants in the Dominican Republic, see Martínez, "From Hidden Hand to Heavy Hand"; and Martínez, "Onion of Oppression."

Bibliography

Archival Sources

Aix-en-Provence, France
  Archives Nationales d'Outre-mer
    8 Supplément Saint-Domingue, number 390
    Atlas Moreau de St-Méry (F3 289, F3 296)
    Collection Moreau de St Méry (Série F3), numbers 91, 121, 197, 198, 199, 200,
      201, 202, 266, 267, 273, 283, 284, and 286
    Correspondance au départ (Série B), numbers 267 and 277
    Dépôt des Papiers Publics des Colonies, Notariat de Saint-Domingue
    Direction de Fortification des Colonies, cartons 4 and 5
    État Civil, Saint-Domingue (Santo Domingo) (85 Miom 95)
    Troupes et Personnel Civil (D2C 371)
Gainesville, Fla.
  Special Collections, Latin American Collection, George A. Smathers Libraries,
    University of Florida
    Microfilmed newspaper: Les Affiches Américaines, no. 62, 3 August 1791
    Rochambeau Papers, document numbers 75, 77, 1265, 1567, 1640, 1682, and 2269
Paris, France
  Centre d'Accueil et de Recherche des Archives Nationales
    135 Archives Privées 1–2
    Les Archives du Directoire Exécutif (AF/III/61, AF/III/62, AF/III/63, AF/
      III/209, AF/III/210)
    Assemblées du Directoire (C 518, C 521)
    Collection "Colonies, Saint-Domingue," CC/9a–CC/9c
    Comité des Colonies, section D/XXV
    Comité de la Marine, section D/XVI
    Comité de Salut Public, Relations Extérieures (AF/II/64)
    Microfilm Archives (208 Mi 1, 208 Mi 2)
    Secrétairerie d'État Impériale (AF/IV/941, AF/IV/968)
    Tribunal Révolutionnaire (W 13)
Seville, Spain
  Archivo General de Indias
    Audiencia de Santo Domingo, legajos 1019, 1027, 1029, 1032, 1033, 1037, 1038,
      1042, 1101, 1102, and 1110
    Papeles de Cuba, legajos 1705, 1709, and 1742

Simancas, Spain
Archivo General de Simancas
Section "Guerra Moderna," legajos 7149, 7151, 7157, 7159, and 7160

Printed Primary Sources

Ayala, Juan de. *A Letter to Ferdinand and Isabella, 1503.* Translated by Charles E. Nowell. Minneapolis: University of Minnesota Press, 1965.

Collection générale des lois, décrets, arrêtés, sénatus-consultes, avis du conseil d'état et règlements d'administration, publiés depuis 1789 jusqu'au 1er avril 1814. Paris: Imprimerie Royale, 1818.

Correspondance de Napoléon Ier, publiée par ordre de l'Empereur Napoléon III. Vol. 6. Paris: Henri Plon and J. Dumaine, 1861.

Lacroix, Pamphile de. *La Révolution d'Haïti.* 1819. Reprint, Paris: Karthala, 1995.

Louverture, Toussaint. *The Memoir of General Toussaint Louverture.* Translated by Philippe Girard. New York: Oxford University Press, 2014 [1803].

Marat, Jean-Paul. *Chains of Slavery. A Work wherein the Clandestine and Villainous Attempts of Princes to Ruin Liberty are Pointed Out . . .* London, 1774.

McIntosh, M. E., and B. C. Weber, eds. *Une correspondance familiale au temps des troubles de Saint-Domingue.* Paris: Société de l'Histoire des Colonies Françaises et Librairie Larose, 1959.

Monte y Tejada, Antonio del. *Historia de Santo Domingo.* 4 vols. 1890–92. Reprint, Ciudad Trujillo [Santo Domingo], 1953.

Moreau de St Méry, Médéric-Louis-Élie. *Description topographique et politique de la partie espagnole de l'isle Saint-Domingue.* 2 vols. Philadelphia: Self-published by author, 1796.

———. *La description topographique, physique, civile, politique et historique de la partie française de Saint-Domingue.* 3 vols. 1797. Reprint, Saint-Denis: Société Française d'Histoire d'Outre-mer, 2004.

Nouët, Jean-Claude, Claude Nicollier, and Yves Nicollier. *La vie aventureuse de Norbert Thoret dit l'Américain, 1767–1850.* Paris: Éditions du Port-au-Prince, 2007, "*édition hors commerce*" (noncommercial edition).

Raynal, Abbé Guillaume-Thomas-François. *Histoire philosophique et politique des établissements et du commerce des Européens dans les deux Indes.* Vol. 3. Geneva, 1780.

Rodríguez Demorizi, Emilio, ed. *Cesión de Santo Domingo a Francia (correspondencia de Godoy, García, Roume, Hedouville, Louverture, Rigaud y otros, 1795–1802).* Ciudad Trujillo [Santo Domingo]: Impresora Dominicana, 1958.

———. *Las invasiones haitianas de 1801, 1805 y 1822.* Ciudad Trujillo [Santo Domingo]: Editora del Caribe, 1955.

Roussier, Paul, ed. *Lettres du général Leclerc, Commandant en Chef de l'armée de Saint-Domingue.* Paris: Société d'Histoire des Colonies Françaises et Librairie Ernest Leroux, 1937.

Saint-Venant, Jean Barré de. *Des colonies modernes sous la zone torride, et particulièrement celle de Saint-Domingue.* Paris: Brochot, 1802.

Sánchez Valverde, Antonio. *Idea del valor de la isla española.* 1785. Reprint, Ciudad Trujillo [Santo Domingo]: Editora Montalvo, 1947.

Secondary Sources

Adderly, Roseanne Marion. "'New Negroes from Africa': Culture and Community among Liberated Africans in the Bahamas and Trinidad, 1810 to 1900." Ph.D. diss., University of Pennsylvania, 1996.

Adelman, Jeremy. *Sovereignty and Revolution in the Iberian Atlantic.* Princeton, N.J.: Princeton University Press, 2006.

Alchon, Suzanne Austin. *A Pest in the Land: New World Epidemics in a Global Perspective.* Albuquerque: University of New Mexico Press, 2003.

Allen, Richard B. "The Constant Demand of the French: The Mascarene Slave Trade and the Worlds of the Indian Ocean and Atlantic during the Eighteenth and Nineteenth Centuries." *Journal of African History* 49, no. 1 (2008): 43–72.

Appelbaum, Nancy, Anne Macpherson, and Karin Alejandra Rosemblatt, eds. *Race and Nation in Modern Latin America.* Chapel Hill: University of North Carolina Press, 2003.

Ardouin, Beaubrun. *Études sur l'histoire d'Haïti.* 11 vols. Reprint, Port-au-Prince: Chéraquit, 1924 [1853–60].

Auguste, Claude B., and Marcel B. Auguste. *L'expédition Leclerc, 1801–1803.* Port-au-Prince: Deschamps, 1988.

Ayers, Edward. *In the Presence of Mine Enemies: War in the Heart of America, 1859–1863.* New York: W. W. Norton, 2003.

Ayers, Edward, William G. Thomas III, and Anne Sarah Rubin. "Black and on the Border." In *Slavery, Resistance, Freedom,* edited by Gabor Boritt and Scott Hancock, 70–95. Oxford: Oxford University Press, 2009.

Barceló, Javier Malagón. *Código Negro Carolino (1784).* Santo Domingo: Editora Taller, 1974.

Barnabé, Jean. "Les proclamations en créole de Sonthonax et Bonaparte: Graphie, histoire, et glottopolitique." In *De la Révolution française aux révolutions créoles et nègres,* edited by Michel Martin and Alain Yacou, 130–50. Paris: Éditions Caribéennes, 1989.

Baud, Michiel. "Una frontera-refugio: Dominicanos y haitianos contra el estado." *Estudios Sociales* 26, no. 92 (1993): 39–64.

Bell, Madison Smartt. *Toussaint Louverture: A Biography.* New York: Vintage, 2007.

Benítez Rojo, Antonio. *La isla que se repite.* Barcelona: Editorial Casiopea, 1998.

Bénot, Yves. *La démence coloniale sous Napoléon.* 2nd ed. Paris: Découverte, 2006.

———. "The Insurgents of 1791, Their Leaders, and the Concept of Independence." In Geggus and Fiering, *The World of the Haitian Revolution,* 99–110.

——. *La Révolution Française et la fin des colonies*. Paris: Découverte, 1988.

Benton, Lauren. "Abolition and Imperial Law, 1790–1820." *Journal of Imperial and Commonwealth History* 39, no. 3 (2011): 355–74.

Berlin, Ira, and Leslie M. Harris, eds. *Slavery in New York*. New York: New Press, 2005.

Berlin, Ira, Joseph P. Reidy, and Leslie S. Rowland, eds. *Freedom's Soldiers: The Black Military Experience in the Civil War*. Cambridge: Cambridge University Press, 1998.

Blackmon, Douglas A. *Slavery by Another Name: The Re-Enslavement of Black People in America from the Civil War to World War II*. New York: Doubleday, 2008.

Blaufarb, Rafe. "The Western Question: The Geopolitics of Latin American Independence." *American Historical Review* 112, no. 3 (June 2007): 742–63.

Bongie, Chris. *Friends and Enemies: The Scribal Politics of Post/Colonial Literature*. Liverpool: Liverpool University Press, 2008.

Boucher, Philip. *Cannibal Encounters: Europeans and Island Caribs, 1492–1763*. Baltimore, Md.: Johns Hopkins University Press, 1992.

Branda, Pierre, and Thierry Lentz. *Napoléon, l'esclavage et les colonies*. Paris: Fayard, 2006.

Brasseaux, Carl A., and Glenn R. Conrad, eds. *The Road to Louisiana: The Saint-Domingue Refugees, 1792–1809*. Lafayette: Center for Louisiana Studies, University of Southwestern Louisiana, 1992.

Brooks, James F. *Captives and Cousins: Slavery, Kinship, and Community in the Southwest Borderlands*. Chapel Hill: University of North Carolina Press, 2002.

Brown, Christopher Leslie. *Moral Capital: Foundations of British Abolitionism*. Chapel Hill: University of North Carolina Press, 2006.

Brown, Christopher Leslie, and Philip D. Morgan, eds. *Arming Slaves: From Classical Times to the Modern Age*. New Haven, Conn.: Yale University Press, 2006.

Brown, Gordon S. *Toussaint's Clause: The Founding Fathers and the Haitian Revolution*. Oxford: University of Mississippi Press, 2005.

Burnard, Trevor. "Empire Matters? The Historiography of Imperialism in Early America, 1492–1830." *History of European Ideas* 33, no. 1 (March 2007): 87–107.

Burns, Kathryn. *Into the Archive: Writing and Power in Colonial Peru*. Durham, N.C.: Duke University Press, 2010.

——. "Notaries, Truth, and Consequences." *American Historical Review* 110, no. 2 (April 2005): 350–79.

Burns, Robert J., ed. *Las Siete Partidas*. Translated by Samuel Parsons Scott. 5 vols. Philadelphia: University of Pennsylvania Press, 2001.

Cabon, Adolphe. *Histoire d'Haïti: Cours professé au Petit-Séminaire-Collège Saint-Martial*. Vol. 4. Port-au-Prince: Édition de la Petite Revue, 192?–1940.

Candelario, Ginetta E. B. *Black behind the Ears: Dominican Racial Identity from Museums to Beauty Shops*. Durham, N.C.: Duke University Press, 2007.

Cañizares-Esguerra, Jorge, and Erik R. Seeman, eds. *The Atlantic in Global History, 1500–2000*. Upper Saddle River, N.J.: Pearson Prentice Hall, 2007.

Carney, Judith. *Black Rice: The African Origins of Rice Cultivation in the Americas*. Cambridge, Mass.: Harvard University Press, 2001.

———. "Landscapes of Technology Transfer: Rice Cultivation and African Continuities." *Technology and Culture* 37, no. 1 (January 1996): 5–35.

Cassá, Roberto. "Les effets du Traité du Bâle." In Yacou, *Saint-Domingue espagnol*, 203–10.

———. *Historia social y económica de la República Dominicana*. Santo Domingo: Alfa y Omega, 2013.

Cassá, Roberto, and Genaro Rodríguez. "Consideraciones alternativas acerca de las rebeliones de esclavos en Santo Domingo." *Ecos* 2, no. 3 (1994): 155–91.

Cauna, Jacques de. "Autour de la thèse du complot: Franc-maçonnerie, révolution et contre-révolution à Saint-Domingue, 1789–1791." *Lumières* 7 (2006): 289–310.

———, ed. *Toussaint Louverture et l'indépendance d'Haïti*. Paris: Karthala, 2004.

Champion, Jean-Marcel. "30 Floréal Year X: The Restoration of Slavery by Bonaparte." In *The Abolitions of Slavery: From Léger Félicité Sonthonax to Victor Schoelcher, 1793, 1794, 1848*, edited by Marcel Dorigny, 229–36. New York: Berghahn Books, 2003. First published in 1995 by Éditions UNESCO/Presses Universitaires de Vincennes (Paris).

Chapman, Herrick, and Laura L. Frader, eds. *Race in France: Interdisciplinary Perspectives on the Politics of Difference*. New York: Berghahn Books, 2004.

Childs, Matt. *The 1812 Aponte Rebellion in Cuba and the Struggle against Atlantic Slavery*. Chapel Hill: University of North Carolina Press, 2006.

Chinea, Jorge. "Fissures in El Primer Piso: Racial Politics in Spanish Colonial Puerto Rico during Its Pre-Plantation Era, c. 1700–1800." *Caribbean Studies* 30, no. 1 (2002): 169–204.

Colwill, Elizabeth. "'Fêtes de l'Hymen, Fêtes de la Liberté:' Marriage, Manhood, and Emancipation in Revolutionary Saint-Domingue." In Geggus and Fiering, *World of the Haitian Revolution*, 125–55.

Cooper, Frederick, Rebecca Scott, and Thomas Holt. *Beyond Slavery: Explorations of Race, Labor, and Citizenship in Postemancipation Societies*. Chapel Hill: University of North Carolina Press, 2000.

Cordero Michel, Emilio. *La Revolución haitiana y Santo Domingo*. Santo Domingo: Editora Nacional, 1968.

———. "Toussaint en Saint-Domingue espagnol." In Yacou, *Saint-Domingue espagnol*, 251–58.

Coronil, Fernando. "After Empire: Reflections on Imperialism from the Américas." In *Imperial Formations*, edited by Ann Laura Stoler, Carole McGranahan, and Peter Perdue, 241–71. Santa Fe, N.Mex.: School for Advanced Research Press, 2007.

Curtin, Philip. *The Rise and Fall of the Plantation Complex: Essays in Atlantic History.* 2nd ed. New York: Cambridge University Press, 1998.

Davis, Natalie Zemon. *Fiction in the Archives: Pardon Tales and Their Tellers in Sixteenth-Century France.* Stanford, Calif.: Stanford University Press, 1987.

Debien, Gabriel. *Les esclaves aux Antilles françaises, XVIIe–XVIIIe siècles.* Basse-Terre: Société d'Histoire de la Guadeloupe, 1974.

———. *Le peuplement des Antilles françaises au XVIIe siècle: Les engagés partis de la Rochelle (1683–1715).* Cairo: Les Presses de l'Institut Français d'Archéologie Orientale du Caire, 1942.

Deive, Carlos Esteban. *Los cimarrones del Maniel de Neiba: Historia y etnografía.* Santo Domingo: Banco Central de la República Dominicana, 1985.

———. *Las emigraciones dominicanas a Cuba, 1795–1808.* Santo Domingo: Fundación Cultural Dominicana, 1989.

———. *La esclavitud del negro en Santo Domingo (1492–1844).* Santo Domingo: Museo del Hombre Dominicano, 1980.

———. *Los guerrilleros negros: Esclavos fugitivos y cimarrones en Santo Domingo.* Santo Domingo: Fundación Cultural Dominicana, 1989.

———. "Les réfugiés français dans la partie espagnole de l'île Saint-Domingue au temps de la fronde des Grands Blancs et de la révolte des Mulâtres." In Yacou, *Saint-Domingue espagnol,* 123–33.

Derby, Lauren. "Haitians, Magic and Money: Raza and Society in the Haitian-Dominican Borderlands, 1900 to 1937." *Comparative Studies in Society and History* 36, no. 3 (July 1994): 488–526.

Desan, Suzanne. *The Family on Trial in Revolutionary France.* Berkeley: University of California Press, 2004.

Dorigny, Marcel. *Anti-esclavagisme, abolitionnisme et abolitions: Débats et controverses en France de la fin du XVIIIe siècle aux années 1840.* Québec: Les Presses de l'Université Laval, 2008.

Dorsey, Joseph. *Slave Traffic in the Age of Abolition: Puerto Rico, West Africa, and the Non-Hispanic Caribbean, 1815–1859.* Gainesville: University Press of Florida, 2003.

Dubois, Laurent. *Avengers of the New World: The Story of the Haitian Revolution.* Cambridge, Mass.: Belknap Press of Harvard University Press, 2004.

———. "Citizen Soldiers: Emancipation and Military Service in the Revolutionary French Caribbean." In Brown and Morgan, *Arming Slaves,* 233–54.

———. *A Colony of Citizens: Revolution and Slave Emancipation in the French Caribbean, 1787–1804.* Chapel Hill: University of North Carolina Press, 2004.

———. "An Enslaved Enlightenment: Rethinking the Intellectual History of the French Atlantic." *Social History* 31, no. 1 (February 2006): 1–14.

———. *Haiti: The Aftershocks of History.* New York: Metropolitan Books, 2012.

Dubois, Laurent, and John Garrigus. *Slave Revolution in the Caribbean, 1789–1804: A Brief History with Documents.* New York: Palgrave, 2006.

Eller, Anne. "'All would be equal in the effort': Santo Domingo's 'Italian Revolution,' Independence, and Haiti, 1809–1822." *Journal of Early American History* 1, no. 2 (2011): 105–41.

———. "Awful Pirates and Hordes of Jackals: Santo Domingo/The Dominican Republic in Nineteenth-Century Historiography." *Small Axe* 18:2 44 (July 2014): 80–94.

Englund, Steven. *Napoleon: A Political Life*. New York: Scribner, 2004.

Farge, Arlette, and Jacques Revel. *The Vanishing Children of Paris: Rumor and Politics before the French Revolution*. Translated by Claudia Miéville. Cambridge, Mass.: Harvard University Press, 1991. First published as *Logiques de la foule: L'affaire des enlèvements d'enfants, Paris 1750* (Paris: Hachette, 1988).

Fatton, Robert. *Haiti's Predatory Republic: The Unending Transition to Democracy*. Boulder, Colo.: Lynne Rienner Publishers, 2002.

Fernández-Armesto, Felipe. *Before Columbus: Exploration and Colonization from the Mediterranean to the Atlantic, 1229–1492*. Philadelphia: University of Pennsylvania Press, 1987.

Ferrer, Ada. "Cuba en la sombra de Haití: Noticias, sociedad, y esclavitud." In González-Ripoll et al., *El rumor de Haití en Cuba*, 179–231.

———. *Freedom's Mirror: Cuba and Haiti in the Age of Revolution*. Cambridge: Cambridge University Press, 2014.

———. "Haiti, Free Soil, and Antislavery in the Revolutionary Atlantic." *American Historical Review* 117, no. 1 (February 2012): 40–66.

———. *Insurgent Cuba: Race, Nation and Revolution, 1868–1898*. Chapel Hill: University of North Carolina Press, 1999.

———. "La société esclavagiste cubaine et la révolution haïtienne." *Annales* 58, no. 2 (2003): 333–56.

———. "Speaking of Haiti: Slavery, Revolution, and Freedom in Cuban Slave Testimony." In Geggus and Fiering, *World of the Haitian Revolution*, 223–47.

Fick, Carolyn. "Emancipation in Haiti: From Plantation Labour to Peasant Proprietorship." *Slavery and Abolition* 21, no. 2 (August 2000): 11–39.

———. *The Making of Haiti: The Saint Domingue Revolution from Below*. Knoxville: University of Tennessee Press, 1990.

Fouchard, Jean. *Les marrons de la liberté*. Paris: L'École, 1972.

Franco, José Luciano. *Historia de la Revolución de Haití*. 3rd ed. Santo Domingo: Sociedad Dominicana de Bibliófilos, 2008.

Frostin, Charles. *Les révoltes blanches à Saint-Domingue aux XVIIe et XVIIIe siècles*. Paris: L'École, 1975.

Fuente, Alejandro de la. *A Nation for All: Race, Inequality, and Politics in Twentieth-Century Cuba*. Chapel Hill: University of North Carolina Press, 2001.

———. "Slave Law and Claims-Making in Cuba: The Tannenbaum Debate Revisited." *Law and History Review* 22, no. 2 (Summer 2004): 339–69.

———. "Slaves and the Creation of Legal Rights in Cuba: *Coartación* and *Papel.*" *Hispanic American Historical Review* 87, no. 4 (2007): 659–92.

Gaffield, Julia. "Haiti and Jamaica in the Remaking of the Early Nineteenth-Century Atlantic World." *William and Mary Quarterly* 69, no. 3 (July 2012): 583–614.

———. "'So Many Schemes in Agitation': The Haitian State and the Atlantic World." Ph.D. diss., Duke University, 2012.

García, Marcela. "Haitians without a Nation: A Ruling in the Dominican Republic Divides Immigrants in Boston." *Boston Globe,* 30 December 2013. http://www .bostonglobe.com/opinion/2013/12/30/haitians-dominican-republic-immigration -ruling-leaves-community-stateless/7XLAA20GHC4RV5No9fw26M/story.html. Last accessed 26 September 2015.

Garrigus, John. *Before Haiti: Race and Citizenship in French Saint-Domingue.* New York: Palgrave Macmillan, 2006.

———. "Blue and Brown: Contraband Indigo and the Rise of a Free Colored Planter Class in French Saint-Domingue." *The Americas* 50, no. 2 (October 1993): 233–63.

———. "Opportunist or Patriot? Julien Raimond (1744–1801) and the Haitian Revolution." *Slavery and Abolition* 28, no. 1 (2007): 1–21.

———. "Redrawing the Colour Line: Gender and the Social Construction of Race in Pre-Revolutionary Haiti." *Journal of Caribbean History* 30, no. 1–2 (1996): 28–50.

———. "'Thy coming fame, Ogé! Is sure': New Evidence on Ogé's 1790 Revolt and the Beginnings of the Haitian Revolution." In *Assumed Identities: The Meanings of Race in the Atlantic World,* edited by John Garrigus and Christopher Morris, 19–45. College Station: Texas A&M University Press, 2010.

———. "Vincent Ogé Jeune (1757–91): Social Class and Free Colored Mobilization on the Eve of the Haitian Revolution." *The Americas* 68, no. 1 (July 2011): 33–62.

Gaspar, David. *Bondmen and Rebels: A Study of Master-Slave Relations in Antigua.* Durham, N.C.: Duke University Press, 1985.

———. "La Guerre des Bois: Revolution, War and Slavery in Saint Lucia, 1793– 1838." In Geggus and Gaspar, *Turbulent Time,* 102–30.

Gaspar, David, and Darlene Clark Hine, eds. *More than Chattel: Black Women and Slavery in the Americas.* Bloomington: Indiana University Press, 1996.

Geggus, David. "The Arming of Slaves in the Haitian Revolution." In Brown and Morgan, *Arming Slaves,* 209–32.

———. "The Caribbean in the Age of Revolution." In *The Age of Revolutions in Global Context, c. 1760–1840,* edited by David Armitage and Sanjay Subrahmanyam, 83–100. New York: Palgrave Macmillan, 2010.

———. "The French Slave Trade: An Overview." *William and Mary Quarterly* 58, no. 1 (January 2001): 119–38.

———. *Haitian Revolutionary Studies.* Bloomington: Indiana University Press, 2002.

————, ed. *The Impact of the Haitian Revolution in the Atlantic World*. Columbia: University of South Carolina Press, 2001.

————. "Sex Ratio, Age and Ethnicity in the Atlantic Slave Trade: Data from French Shipping and Plantation Records." *Journal of African History* 30, no. 1 (1989): 23–44.

————. "Slave and Free Colored Women in Saint Domingue." In Gaspar and Hine, *More than Chattel*, 259–78.

————. "Slave Resistance in the Spanish Caribbean in the mid-1790s." In Geggus and Gaspar, *Turbulent Time*, 131–55.

————. *Slavery, War, and Revolution: The British Occupation of Saint Domingue 1793–1798*. Oxford: Oxford University Press, 1982.

————. "The Slaves and Free Coloreds of Martinique during the Age of the French and Haitian Revolutions: Three Moments of Resistance." In Paquette and Engerman, *Lesser Antilles in the Age of European Expansion*, 280–301.

————. "The Sounds and Echoes of Freedom: The Impact of the Haitian Revolution on Latin America." In *Beyond Slavery: The Multilayered Legacy of Africans in Latin America and the Caribbean*, edited by Darién J. Davis, 19–36. Lanham, Md.: Rowman and Littlefield, 2007.

Geggus, David, and Norman Fiering, eds. *The World of the Haitian Revolution*. Bloomington: Indiana University Press, 2008.

Geggus, David, and David Gaspar, eds. *A Turbulent Time: The French Revolution and the Greater Caribbean*. Bloomington: Indiana University Press, 1997.

Ghachem, Malick. *The Old Regime and the Haitian Revolution*. Cambridge: Cambridge University Press, 2012.

————. "Sovereignty and Slavery in the Age of Revolution: Haitian Variations on a Metropolitan Theme." Ph.D. diss., Stanford University, 2002.

Girard, Philippe. "Black Talleyrand: Toussaint Louverture's Diplomacy, 1798–1802." *William and Mary Quarterly* 66, no. 1 (January 2009): 87–124.

————. "Napoleon Bonaparte and the Emancipation Issue in Saint-Domingue, 1799–1803." *French Historical Studies* 32, no. 4 (Fall 2009): 587–618.

————. *The Slaves Who Defeated Napoléon: Toussaint Louverture and the Haitian War of Independence, 1801–1804*. Tuscaloosa: University of Alabama Press, 2011.

Giusti-Cordero, Juan. "Beyond Sugar Revolutions: Rethinking the Spanish Caribbean in the Seventeenth and Eighteenth Centuries." In *Empirical Futures: Anthropologists and Historians Engage the Work of Sidney W. Mintz*, edited by George Baca, Aisha Khan, and Stephan Palmié, 58–83. Chapel Hill: University of North Carolina Press, 2009.

Gonzalez, Johnhenry. "The War on Sugar: Forced Labor, Commodity Production and the Origins of the Haitian Peasantry, 1791–1843." Ph.D. diss., University of Chicago, 2012.

González, Raymundo. *De esclavos a campesinos: Vida rural en Santo Domingo colonial*. Santo Domingo: Archivo General de la Nación, 2011.

González, Raymundo, Michiel Baud, Pedro San Miguel, and Roberto Cassá, eds. *Política, identidad y pensamiento social en la República Dominicana: Siglos XIX y XX*. Madrid: Doce Calles, 1999.

González-Ripoll, María Dolores, Consuelo Naranjo, Ada Ferrer, Gloria García, and Josef Opatrny. *El rumor de Haití en Cuba: Temor, raza y rebeldía, 1789–1844*. Madrid: Consejo Superior de Investigaciones Científicas, 2004.

Graham, Sandra Lauderdale. *House and Street: The Domestic World of Servants and Masters in Nineteenth-Century Rio de Janeiro*. New York: Cambridge University Press, 1988.

Gray, Richard. "The Papacy and the Atlantic Slave Trade: Lourenço da Silva, the Capuchins and the Decisions of the Holy Office." *Past and Present* no. 115 (May 1987): 52–68.

Grinberg, Keila. "Slavery, Liberalism, and Civil Law: Definitions of Status and Citizenship in the Elaboration of the Brazilian Civil Code (1855–1916)." In *Honor, Status, and Law in Modern Latin America*, edited by Sueann Caulfield, Sarah Chambers, and Lara Putnam, 109–27. Durham, N.C.: Duke University Press, 2005.

Gross, Ariela, and Alejandro de la Fuente. "Slaves, Free Blacks, and Race in the Legal Regimes of Cuba, Louisiana, and Virginia: A Comparison." *North Carolina Law Review* 91 (2013): 1699–1756.

Guitar, Lynne. "No More Negotiation: Slavery and the Destabilization of Colonial Hispaniola's Encomienda System." *Revista Interamericana* 29, no. 1–4 (1999), http://cai.sg.inter.edu/revista-ciscla/volume29/guitar.pdf. Last accessed 26 September 2015.

Hammersley, Rachel. "Jean-Paul Marat's 'The Chains of Slavery' in Britain and France, 1774–1833." *Historical Journal* 48, no. 3 (September 2005): 641–60.

Hamnett, Brian. "Process and Pattern: A Re-Examination of the Ibero-American Independence Movements, 1808–1826." *Journal of Latin American Studies* 29, no. 2 (May 1997): 279–328.

Hardwick, Julie. *The Practice of Patriarchy: Gender and the Politics of Household Authority in Early Modern France*. University Park: Pennsylvania State University Press, 1998.

Harvard Law School. Tribute to U.S. Supreme Court Justice Harry Blackmun. http://today.law.harvard.edu/eloquent-voice-for-the-oppressed/. Last accessed 26 September 2015.

Hébrard, Jean. "Esclavage et dénomination: Imposition et appropriation d'un nom chez les esclaves de la Bahia au XIXe siècle." *Cahiers du Brésil contemporain* 53/54 (2003): 31–92.

Heuer, Jennifer. *The Family and the Nation: Gender and Citizenship in Revolutionary France, 1789–1830*. Ithaca, N.Y.: Cornell University Press, 2005.

———. "The One-Drop Rule in Reverse? Interracial Marriages in Napoleonic and Restoration France." *Law and History Review* 27, no. 3 (Fall 2009): 515–48.

Hoetink, Harry. *Santo Domingo y el Caribe: Ensayos sobre cultura y sociedad*. Santo Domingo: Fundación Cultural Dominicana, 1994.

Hoffman, Léon-François. "Un mythe national: La cérémonie du Bois-Caïman." In *La République haïtienne: Etat des lieux et perspectives*, edited by Gérard Barthélemy and Christian A. Girault, 434–48. Paris: Karthala, 1993.

Holt, Thomas. *The Problem of Freedom: Race, Labor and Politics in Jamaica and Britain, 1832–1938*. Baltimore, Md.: Johns Hopkins University Press, 1992.

James, C. L. R. *The Black Jacobins: Toussaint L'Ouverture and the San Domingo Revolution*. 2nd ed. 1938. Reprint, New York: Vintage, 1963.

James, Erica Caple. *Democratic Insecurities: Violence, Trauma, and Intervention in Haiti*. Berkeley: University of California Press, 2010.

Jenson, Deborah. *Beyond the Slave Narrative: Politics, Sex, and Manuscripts in the Haitian Revolution*. Liverpool: Liverpool University Press, 2011.

Johnson, Walter. *Soul by Soul: Life inside the Antebellum Slave Market*. Cambridge, Mass.: Harvard University Press, 1999.

Joseph, Celucien L. " 'The Haitian Turn': An Appraisal of Recent Literary and Historiographical Works on the Haitian Revolution." *Journal of Pan African Studies* 5, no. 6 (2012): 37–55.

Joseph-Gabriel, Annette K. "Creolizing Freedom: French-Creole Translations of Liberty and Equality in the Haitian Revolution." *Slavery and Abolition* 36, no. 1 (2015): 111–23.

Kafka, Judith. "Action, Reaction, and Interaction: Slave Women in Resistance in the South of Saint Domingue, 1793–94." *Slavery and Abolition* 18, no. 2 (1997): 48–72.

King, Stewart R. *Blue Coat or Powdered Wig: Free People of Color in Pre-Revolutionary Saint-Domingue*. Athens: University of Georgia Press, 2001.

Knight, Franklin W. "The Haitian Revolution and the Notion of Human Rights." *Journal of the Historical Society* 5, no. 3 (2005): 391–416.

Korngold, Ralph. *Citizen Toussaint*. Boston: Little, Brown and company, 1944.

Landers, Jane. *Atlantic Creoles in the Age of Revolutions*. Cambridge, Mass.: Harvard University Press, 2010.

———. "Maroon Women in Spanish America." In *Beyond Bondage: Free Women of Color in the Slave Societies of the Americas*, edited by David Gaspar and Darlene Hine, 3–18. Bloomington: Indiana University Press, 2004.

———. "Rebellion and Royalism in Spanish Florida: The French Revolution on Spain's Northern Colonial Frontier." In Geggus and Gaspar, *Turbulent Time*, 156–77.

———. "Transforming Bondsmen into Vassals: Arming Slaves in Colonial Spanish America." In Brown and Morgan, *Arming Slaves*, 120–37.

Lora, Quisqueya. "El sonido de la libertad: 30 años de agitaciones y conspiraciones en Santo Domingo (1791–1821)." *Clío* 182 (2011): 109–40.

Lundahl, Mats. "Toussaint L'Ouverture and the War Economy of Saint-Domingue, 1796–1802." *Slavery and Abolition* 6, no. 2 (1985): 122–38.

Lynch, John. *Simón Bolívar: A Life*. New Haven, Conn.: Yale University Press, 2006.

Madiou, Thomas. *Histoire d'Haïti*. 1847–48. Rev. ed. 8 vols. Port-au-Prince: Deschamps, 1989–91.

Mamigonian, Beatriz. "In the Name of Freedom: Slave Trade Abolition, the Law and the Brazilian Branch of the African Emigration Scheme (Brazil-British West Indies, 1830s–1850s)." *Slavery and Abolition* 30, no. 1 (March 2009): 41–66.

Martínez, Samuel. "From Hidden Hand to Heavy Hand: Sugar, the State, and Migrant Labor in Haiti and the Dominican Republic." *Latin American Research Review* 34, no. 1 (1999): 57–84.

———. "The Onion of Oppression: Haitians in the Dominican Republic." In *Geographies of the Haitian Diaspora*, edited by Regine O. Jackson, 51–70. New York: Routledge, 2011.

Matibag, Eugenio. *Haitian-Dominican Counterpoint*. New York: Palgrave Macmillan, 2003.

Métral, Antoine Marie Thérèse. *Histoire de l'expédition des français à Saint-Domingue, sous le consulat de Napoléon Bonaparte*. Paris: Fanjat Ainé, 1825.

Mills, Kenneth, William Taylor, and Sandra Lauderdale Graham, eds. *Colonial Latin America: A Documentary History*. Lanham, Md.: SR Books, 2004.

Mintz, Sidney. "Slavery and the Rise of Peasantries." *Historical Reflections/Reflexions Historiques* 6, no. 1 (1979): 213–42.

———. *Sweetness and Power: The Place of Sugar in World History*. New York: Viking, 1985.

———. *Three Ancient Colonies: Caribbean Themes and Variations*. Cambridge, Mass.: Harvard University Press, 2010.

Mintz, Sidney, and Richard Price. *The Birth of African-American Culture: An Anthropological Perspective*. Boston: Beacon, 1992.

Mintz, Sidney, and Sally Price, eds. *Caribbean Contours*. Baltimore, Md.: Johns Hopkins University Press, 1985.

Mobley, Christina. " 'Kongo, ede m kriye': Les 'Kongos' dans la Révolution Haïtienne." *Revue d'histoire de l'Amérique française*, forthcoming.

Moïse, Claude. *Le projet national de Toussaint Louverture et la constitution de 1801*. Montréal: Editions du CIDIHCA, 2001.

Monti, Laura V. *A Calendar of Rochambeau Papers at the University of Florida Libraries*. Gainesville: University of Florida Libraries, 1972.

Moya Pons, Frank. "The Land Question in Haiti and Santo Domingo: The Sociopolitical Context of the Transition from Slavery to Free Labor, 1801–1843." In *Between Slavery and Free Labor: The Spanish-Speaking Caribbean in the Nineteenth Century*, edited by Manuel Moreno Fraginals, Frank Moya Pons, and Stanley L. Engerman, 181–214. Baltimore, Md.: Johns Hopkins University Press, 1985.

———. *Manual de historia dominicana*. 9th ed. Santo Domingo: Caribbean Publishers, 1992.

Murray, Gerald F. "The Evolution of Haitian Peasant Land Tenure: A Case Study in Agrarian Adaptation to Population Growth." Ph.D. diss., Columbia University, 1977.

Nabajoth, Eric. "Toussaint-Louverture et la Constitution de 1801: Une perspective indépendantiste dans le cadre d'un régime autoritaire?" In Yacou, *Saint-Domingue espagnol*, 259–80.

Nasiali, Minayo. "Native to the Republic: Negotiating Citizenship and Social Welfare in Marseille 'Immigrant' Neighborhoods since 1945." Ph.D. diss., University of Michigan, 2010.

Neely, Sylvia. *A Concise History of the French Revolution.* Lanham, Md.: Rowman and Littlefield, 2008.

Nessler, Graham. "Arrancar el árbol de la libertad: Una interpretación de la era de Toussaint Louverture en Santo Domingo, 1801–1802." *Estudios Sociales* 40, no. 151 (2012): 11–31.

———. " 'The Shame of the Nation:' The Force of Re-Enslavement and the Law of 'Slavery' under the Regime of Jean-Louis Ferrand in Santo Domingo, 1804–1809." *New West Indian Guide* 86, no. 1–2 (2012): 5–28.

———. " 'They Always Knew Her to Be Free': Emancipation and Re-Enslavement in French Santo Domingo, 1804–1809." *Slavery and Abolition* 33, no. 1 (2012): 87–103.

Niort, Jean-François, and Jérémy Richard. "À propos de la découverte de l'arrêté consulaire du 16 juillet 1802 et du rétablissement de l'ancien ordre colonial (spécialement de l'esclavage) à la Guadeloupe." *Bulletin de la Société d'Histoire de la Guadeloupe* no. 152 (January–April 2009): 31–59.

Northrup, David. *Indentured Labor in the Age of Imperialism, 1834–1922.* Cambridge: Cambridge University Press, 1995.

Ogle, Gene. "The Trans-Atlantic King and Imperial Public Spheres: Everyday Politics in Pre-Revolutionary Saint-Domingue." In Geggus and Fiering, *World of the Haitian Revolution*, 79–96.

Ojeda, Jorge Victoria. *Tendencias monárquicas en la revolución haitiana: El negro Francisco Petecou bajo las banderas francesa y española.* Mexico City: Siglo XXI Editores, 2005.

Ortiz, Fernando. *Los negros esclavos.* Havana: Editorial de Ciencias Sociales, 1975.

Palmer, Vernon. "The Strange Science of Codifying Slavery—Moreau Lislet and the Louisiana Digest of 1808." *Tulane European and Civil Law Forum* no. 24 (2009): 83–113.

Paquette, Robert. "Revolutionary Saint Domingue in the Making of Territorial Louisiana." In Geggus and Gaspar, *Turbulent Time*, 204–25.

Paquette, Robert, and Stanley Engerman, eds. *The Lesser Antilles in the Age of European Expansion.* Gainesville: University Press of Florida, 1996.

Peabody, Sue. " 'Free upon Higher Ground': Saint-Domingue Slaves' Suits for Freedom in U.S. Courts, 1792–1830." In Geggus and Fiering, *World of the Haitian Revolution*, 261–83.

———. "*Négresse, Mulâtresse, Citoyenne*: Gender and Emancipation in the French Caribbean, 1650–1848." In *Gender and Slave Emancipation in the Atlantic World*, edited by Pamela Scully and Diana Paton, 56–78. Durham, N.C.: Duke University Press, 2005.

———. "*There Are No Slaves in France*": *The Political Culture of Race and Slavery in the Ancien Régime*. New York: Oxford University Press, 1996.

Pérotin-Dumon, Anne. *Être patriote sous les tropiques: La Guadeloupe, la colonisation et la Révolution (1789–1794)*. Basse-Terre: Société d'Histoire de la Guadeloupe, 1985.

Picó, Fernando. *One Frenchman, Four Revolutions: General Ferrand and the Peoples of the Caribbean*. Princeton, N.J.: Markus Weiner, 2011.

Piquionne, Nathalie. "Lettre de Jean-François, Biassou et Belair, juillet 1792." *Chemins critiques* 3, no. 3 (1997): 206–20.

Pluchon, Pierre, ed. *Toussaint Louverture d'après le général de Kerverseau*. Port-au-Prince: Éditions le Natal, 1999.

———. "Toussaint Louverture d'après le général de Kerverseau." In Cauna, *Toussaint Louverture et l'indépendance d'Haïti*, 157–61.

———. "Toussaint Louverture défie Bonaparte: L'adresse inédite du 20 décembre 1801." In Cauna, *Toussaint Louverture et l'indépendance d'Haïti*, 171–79.

———. *Toussaint Louverture: De l'esclavage au pouvoir*. Paris: L'École, 1979.

———. *Toussaint Louverture: Un révolutionnaire noir d'ancien régime*. Paris: Fayard, 1989.

Popkin, Jeremy. *Facing Racial Revolution: Eyewitness Accounts of the Haitian Insurrection*. Chicago: University of Chicago Press, 2007.

———. *You Are All Free: The Haitian Revolution and the Abolition of Slavery*. New York: Cambridge University Press, 2010.

Portes, Alejandro, and Alex Stepick. *City on the Edge: The Transformation of Miami*. Berkeley: University of California Press, 1994.

Price, Richard, ed. *Maroon Societies: Rebel Slave Communities in the Americas*. Baltimore, Md.: Johns Hopkins University Press, 1996. First published in 1973 by Anchor Press (Garden City, N.Y.).

Putnam, Lara. "To Study the Fragments/Whole: Microhistory and the Atlantic World." *Journal of Social History* 39, no. 3 (Spring 2006): 615–30.

Racine, Karen. *Francisco de Miranda: A Transatlantic Life in the Age of Revolution*. Wilmington, Del.: Scholarly Resources, 2003.

Régent, Frédéric. *Esclavage, métissage, liberté: La Révolution française en Guadeloupe 1789–1802*. Paris: Grasset, 2004.

Reis, João José. *Slave Rebellion in Brazil: The Muslim Uprising of 1835 in Bahia*. Translated by Arthur Brakel. Baltimore, Md.: Johns Hopkins University Press, 1993.

Renault, Agnès. "Les conditions d'affranchissements des esclaves appartenant aux immigrés français résidant à Santiago de Cuba entre 1791 et 1825." Paper presented at conference entitled *Affranchis et descendants d'affranchis dans le monde atlantique (Europe, Afrique et Amériques) du XVe au XIXe siècle: Statuts juridiques, insertions sociales et identités culturelles.* Musée d'Aquitaine, Bordeaux, France, 13–16 May 2009. Publication forthcoming; paper cited with the author's written permission.

Restall, Matthew, ed. *Beyond Black and Red: African-Native Relations in Colonial Latin America.* Albuquerque: University of New Mexico Press, 2005.

Riding, Alan. *Distant Neighbors: A Portrait of the Mexicans.* New York: Knopf, 1985.

Rivas, Christine. "The Spanish Colonial Military: Santo Domingo 1701–1779." *The Americas* 60, no. 2 (2003): 249–72.

Rivers Rodríguez, Melania. "Los colonos americanos en la sociedad prerrevolucionaria de Saint Domingue: La rebelión de Vicente Ogé y su apresamiento en Santo Domingo (1789–1791)." *Memorias: Revista digital de historia y arqueología desde el Caribe* 2:2 (2005), http://www.redalyc.org/articulo.oa?id=85502204. Last accessed 26 September 2015.

Roederer, P.-L. *Journal du Comte P.-L. Roederer.* Paris: H. Daragon, 1909.

Rogers, Dominique. "On the Road to Citizenship: The Complex Route to Integration of the Free People of Color in the Two Capitals of Saint-Domingue." In Geggus and Fiering, *World of the Haitian Revolution,* 65–78.

Sahlins, Peter. *Boundaries: The Making of France and Spain in the Pyrenees.* Berkeley: University of California Press, 1989.

Sala-Molins, Louis. *Le Code Noir, ou le calvaire de Canaan.* Paris: Presses Universitaires de France, 1987.

San Miguel, Pedro. *La isla imaginada: Historia, identidad y utopía en La Española.* San Juan: Isla Negra, 1997.

Schaeffer, Wendell. "The Delayed Cession of Spanish Santo Domingo to France, 1795–1801." *Hispanic American Historical Review* 29, no. 1 (1949): 46–68.

Schloss, Rebecca. *Sweet Liberty: The Final Days of Slavery in Martinique.* Philadelphia: University of Pennsylvania Press, 2009.

Schneider, Christian. "Le colonel Vincent, officier du génie à Saint-Domingue." *Annales historiques de la Révolution française* no. 329 (July 2002): 101–22.

Schoelcher, Victor. *Vie de Toussaint Louverture.* 1889. Reprint, Paris: Karthala, 1982.

Schroeder, Paul W. *The Transformation of European Politics 1763–1848.* Oxford: Oxford University Press, 1994.

Scott, Julius. "The Common Wind: Currents of Afro-American Communication in the Era of the Haitian Revolution." Ph.D. diss., Duke University, 1986.

———. "Crisscrossing Empires: Ships, Sailors, and Resistance in the Lesser Antilles in the Eighteenth Century." In Paquette and Engerman, *Lesser Antilles in the Age of European Expansion,* 128–43.

Scott, Rebecca. *Degrees of Freedom: Louisiana and Cuba after Slavery.* Cambridge, Mass.: Belknap Press of Harvard University Press, 2005.

———. "Paper Thin: Freedom and Re-enslavement in the Diaspora of the Haitian Revolution." *Law and History Review* 29, no. 4 (2011): 1061–87.

———. "Public Rights and Private Commerce: A Nineteenth-Century Atlantic Creole Itinerary." *Current Anthropology* 48, no. 2 (April 2007): 237–56.

———. "'She ... Refuses to Deliver Up Herself as the Slave of Your Petitioner': Émigrés, Enslavement, and the 1808 Louisiana Digest of the Civil Laws." *Tulane European and Civil Law Forum* no. 24 (2009): 115–36.

———. *Slave Emancipation in Cuba: The Transition to Free Labor, 1860–1899.* Princeton, N.J.: Princeton University Press, 1985.

Scott, Rebecca, and Jean Hébrard. *Freedom Papers: An Atlantic Odyssey in the Age of Emancipation.* Cambridge, Mass.: Harvard University Press, 2012.

———. "Les papiers de la liberté: Une mère africaine et ses enfants à l'époque de la Révolution Haïtienne." *Genèses* 66 (March 2007): 4–29.

———. "Servitude, liberté et citoyenneté dans le monde atlantique des XVIIIe et XIXe siècles: Rosalie de nation Poulard ..." *Revue de la Société Haïtienne d'Histoire et de Géographie* no. 83 (July–September 2008): 1–52.

Seed, Patricia. "'Are They not Also Men?': The Indians' Humanity and Capacity for Spanish Civilization." *Journal of Latin American Studies* 25, no. 3 (October 1993): 629–52.

Sheller, Mimi. *Democracy after Slavery: Black Publics and Peasant Radicalism in Haiti and Jamaica.* Gainesville: University Press of Florida, 2000.

Sidbury, James. "Saint-Domingue in Virginia: Ideology, Local Meanings, and Resistance to Slavery, 1790–1800." *Journal of Southern History* 63, no. 3 (August 1997): 531–52.

Silié, Rubén. *Economía, esclavitud y población: Ensayos de interpretación histórica del Santo Domingo español en el siglo dieciocho.* Santo Domingo: Editora de la Universidad Autónoma de Santo Domingo, 1976.

———. "The *Hato* and the *Conuco*: The Emergence of a Creole Culture." In *Dominican Cultures: The Making of a Caribbean Society,* edited by Bernardo Vega and translated by Christine Ayorinde, 131–60. Princeton, N.J.: Markus Weiner, 2007.

Silverblatt, Irene. *Modern Inquisitions: Peru and the Colonial Origins of the Civilized World.* Durham, N.C.: Duke University Press, 2004.

Smith, Adam. *An Inquiry into the Nature and Causes of the Wealth of Nations.* Chicago: Encyclopedia Britannica, 1952 [1776].

Smith, Jay M. "No More Language Games: Words, Beliefs, and the Political Culture of Early Modern France." *American Historical Review* 102, no. 5 (December 1997): 1413–40.

Socolow, Susan. "Economic Roles of the Free Women of Color of Cap Français." In Gaspar and Hine, *More than Chattel,* 279–97.

Stein, Barbara, and Stanley Stein. *Edge of Crisis: War and Trade in the Spanish Atlantic, 1789–1808.* Baltimore, Md.: Johns Hopkins University Press, 2009.

Stevens-Arroyo, Anthony. "The Inter-Atlantic Paradigm: The Failure of Spanish Medieval Colonization of the Canary and Caribbean Islands." *Comparative Studies in Society and History* 35, no. 3 (July 1993): 515–43.

Temin, Peter. "The Economy of the Early Roman Empire." *Journal of Economic Perspectives* 20, no. 1 (Winter 2006): 133–51.

Thornton, John. "African Soldiers in the Haitian Revolution." *Journal of Caribbean History* 25 (1993): 59–80.

———. " 'I Am the Subject of the King of Kongo': African Political Ideology and the Haitian Revolution." *Journal of World History* 4, no. 2 (Fall 1993): 181–214.

Tomich, Dale. *Through the Prism of Slavery: Labor, Capital, and the World Economy.* Lanham, Md.: Rowman and Littlefield, 2004.

Torres-Saillant, Silvio. "The Tribulations of Blackness: Stages in Dominican Racial Identity." *Latin American Perspectives* 25, no. 3 (May 1998): 126–46.

"Tratado de límites en la isla de Santo Domingo entre los reyes de España y Francia, firmado en Aranjuez el 3 de junio de 1777." In *Tratados, convenios y declaraciones de paz y comercio*, 526–34. Madrid: Imprenta de Alegría y Charlain, 1843.

Trouillot, Michel-Rolph. "Culture, Color, and Politics in Haiti." In *Race*, edited by Steven Gregory and Roger Sanjek, 146–74. New Brunswick, N.J.: Rutgers University Press, 1994.

———. *Haiti, State against Nation: The Origins and Legacy of Duvalierism*. New York: Monthly Review Press, 1990.

———. *Silencing the Past: Power and the Production of History*. Boston: Beacon Press, 1995.

Turits, Richard. *Foundations of Despotism: Peasants, the Trujillo Regime, and Modernity in Dominican History.* Stanford, Calif.: Stanford University Press, 2003.

———. "New World of Color: Slavery, Freedom and the Making of Race in Dominican History." Paper presented at CUNY Graduate Center, 23 November 2010. Cited with author's written permission.

———. "Par-delà les plantations: Question raciale et identités collectives à Santo Domingo." *Genèses* 66 (March 2007): 51–68.

———. "A World Destroyed, A Nation Imposed: The 1937 Haitian Massacre in the Dominican Republic." *Hispanic American Historical Review* 82, no. 3 (August 2002): 589–635.

Turits, Richard, and Lauren Derby. "Historias de terror y los terrores de la historia: La matanza haitiana de 1937 en la República Dominicana." *Estudios Sociales* 26, no. 92 (April–June 1993): 65–76.

Twinam, Ann. *Public Lives, Private Secrets: Gender, Honor, Sexuality, and Illegitimacy in Colonial Spanish America.* Stanford, Calif.: Stanford University Press, 1999.

Vázquez Cienfuegos, Sigfrido. *Tan difíciles tiempos para Cuba: El gobierno del Marqués de Someruelos (1799–1812).* Seville: Universidad de Sevilla, 2008.

Vega B., Wenceslao. *Los documentos básicos para la historia dominicana.* Santo Domingo: Taller, 1994.

Waters, Mary. *Black Identities: West Indian Immigrant Dreams and American Realities.* Cambridge, Mass.: Harvard University Press, 2001.

Watson, Alan. *Slave Law in the Americas.* Athens: University of Georgia Press, 1989.

White, Ashli. *Encountering Revolution: Haiti and the Making of the Early Republic.* Baltimore, Md.: Johns Hopkins University Press, 2010.

Wilder, Gary. *The French Imperial Nation-State: Negritude and Colonial Humanism between the Two World Wars.* Chicago: University of Chicago Press, 2005.

Wucker, Michele. *Why the Cocks Fight: Dominicans, Haitians, and the Struggle for Hispaniola.* New York: Hill and Wang, 1999.

Yacou, Alain, ed. *Saint-Domingue espagnol et la révolution nègre d'Haïti (1790–1822).* Paris: Karthala, 2007.

Zeuske, Michael. *Francisco de Miranda y la modernidad en América.* Madrid: Fundación Mapfre Tavera, 2004.

Index

Abolition. *See* Emancipation

Les Affiches Américaines, 39

Africans, death rate of, 9

Agé, Pierre, 108, 115, 133, 227 (n. 73)

Agriculture: small-scale, 115, 119, 122–23, 124. *See also* Plantation economy

Albert, Étienne, 84

American Civil War, 79

American Revolution, arming of slaves in, 43

Americans, in Santo Domingo, 249 (n. 137), 249 (n. 138)

Anciens libres, 97, 156, 224 (n. 33)

Antiracism, 153

Apprenticeship, 255 (n. 29)

Archive of liberty, 5

Army, French: Dominicans in, 93; and forcible recruitment, 145–46; segregation in, 107. *See also* France; Soldiers, black

Atlantic World, political climate in, 66

Ayers, Edward, 79

Bánica, capitulation of, 92–93

Baptism, 259 (n. 70)

Barbé-Marbois, François, 110

Barquier, Joseph, 188, 192

Belair, Charles, 207 (n. 52)

Belair, Gabriel, 55–56, 59, 207 (n. 52), 209 (n. 83)

Bell, Madison Smartt, 104

Belley, Jean-Baptiste, 51

Bénot, Yves, 141

Le Berceau incident, 136–38

Biassou, Georges, 23, 36, 37, 42, 192; after revolt, 61; alliance of with Spain, 42; conflict of with other leaders, 38; on liberty, 49; loyalty of to Spain, 24; manumissions offered by, 159; refusal of to switch sides, 60; rejection of French Republic by, 24; slaving by, 59, 213 (n. 151)

Black soldiers. *See* Soldiers, black

Blanchelande, Philibert François Rouxel de, 30, 33, 35

Bobadilla, Juan, 86

Boca Nigua plantation: seizure of, 150; slave revolt at, 62–63, 71, 72, 213–14 (n. 1), 214 (nn. 2, 6), 218 (n. 42); Toussaint's takeover of, 125

Bonaparte, Napoleon, 102; attempt of to oust Toussaint, 102; attempt of to reimpose slavery in Santo Domingo, 1 (*see also* Ferrand, Jean-Louis; Slavery, reestablishment of); coexistence of with Toussaint, 102; coup d'état by, 101; desire of to limit Toussaint's power, 89, 109; desire of to maintain partition of Hispaniola, 89, 109; dismantling of "integral part" doctrine by, 191; fall of, 189; and invasion of Hispaniola, 20, 110, 131, 132–35; invasion of Spain by, 185–86, 192; Italian campaign of, 90; and labor regime, 71; opposition to in Spanish-American colonies, 185–86; rise of, 89; rivalry of with Toussaint, 19–20; Toussaint as ally of, 101–2; vision of for Santo Domingo's governance, 111–12. *See also* France